T0328810

Exchange Rate Parity for Trade Development: Theory, Tests, and Case Studies
extends recent theories of incomplete markets to investigate empirically the
appropriate balance between market and state in trade relations between developed and developing countries. Yotopoulos concludes that government intervention in foreign exchange and trade is necessary in developing countries in
the early stages of development and inevitably decreases as development
progresses. More specifically, free currency markets are shown to have an
inherent distortion that leads underdeveloped countries to systematically misallocate resources. Rationing of foreign exchange prevents a "soft-currency
distortion" that commonly afflicts developing countries and can turn comparative-advantage trade into competitive-devaluation trade, with severe losses of
income and welfare. It is found that the level of underdevelopment narrowly
circumscribes and conditions the extent to which free-market, free-trade,
laissez-faire policies can be beneficial to developing countries, which is contrary to the mainstream policy paradigm as currently applied.

The analysis and tests draw on empirical research in 70 countries to confirm
the usefulness and validity of the theoretical framework. The book concludes
with extended case studies of Japan, Taiwan, the Philippines, and Uruguay and
with relevant policy recommendations.

Exchange rate parity for trade and development

Exchange rate parity for trade and development

Theory, tests, and case studies

PAN A. YOTOPOULOS

Stanford University

CAMBRIDGE
UNIVERSITY PRESS

CAMBRIDGE UNIVERSITY PRESS
Cambridge, New York, Melbourne, Madrid, Cape Town, Singapore, São Paulo

Cambridge University Press
The Edinburgh Building, Cambridge CB2 2RU, UK

Published in the United States of America by Cambridge University Press, New York

www.cambridge.org
Information on this title: www.cambridge.org/9780521482165

First published 1996
This digitally printed first paperback version 2005

A catalogue record for this publication is available from the British Library

Library of Congress Cataloguing in Publication data

Yotopoulos, Pan A.
    Exchange rate parity for trade and development : theory, tests,
and case studies / Pan A. Yotopoulos.
        p.   cm.
    Includes bibliographical references (p.   )
    ISBN 0-521-48216-X
    1. Foreign exchange rates—Developing countries.   2. Developing
countries—Commercial policy.   3. Economic development.   I. Title.
HG3877.Y68   1996
332.4'56'091724—dc20   95-24131
                                                                        CIP

ISBN-13 978-0-521-48216-5 hardback
ISBN-10 0-521-48216-X hardback

ISBN-13 978-0-521-02262-0 paperback
ISBN-10 0-521-02262-2 paperback

To the memory of Theoni who nurtured me,
and for Mary who sustained me

Contents

vii

List of Tables and Figures

Figures

Preface

I learned my economics when economic development was an active, and an activist field. It was also a popular field of economics that provided excitement – and fun – for its practitioners. Part of the excitement came from an agenda that was big. After World War II, economic development became a universal nostrum, an overriding objective of poor and rich nations alike. The new nations, in particular, came to see development as a continuation of the political struggle that brought their independence. In the all-consuming fire for development, new policy tools were forged and governments wielded them, as the case might be, with care or abandon. Import substitution industrialization, to mention just one, was at the heart of development strategy. It was backed by fixed exchange rates, foreign exchange restrictions, and controls on trade. The fun part came because things were happening. For at least 25 years, to the middle of the 1970s, the world experienced an unprecedented spurt of economic growth that was spread to most corners of the earth.

There was a profound development-paradigm shift in the early 1980s. The mainstream view on development became free markets and sound money. In an economic development setting, the ultimate test of sound money is placing the domestic currency in direct competition with other contries' currencies, especially the world's reserve currencies, by liberalization of the foreign exchange market. Again in a development setting, floating exchange rates are a prerequisite for extending the free-market idea to its logical conclusion – across national borders. Free-market, free-trade, laissez-faire is thus relied upon for the optimal allocation of resources. "Setting the prices right" weeds out inefficiency and yields an efficiency dividend for a growing economy.

The enthusiasm about the new development paradigm has not been matched by meritorious development outcomes. The "lost decade of the 1980s" is being followed by the "slipping" development decade of the 1990s. This state of the world has met with two reactions by those who think about economic development. The keep-the-course approach emphasizes that free markets and sound money have not gone far enough yet – which is another way of saying that the messiness of the real world does not measure up to the purity of the model. The other approach has been building steam for a while in the form of the "new development economics." The message is that setting the prices right might not do when there are immutable defects inherent in some markets. My own intellectual pangs about how far a market can be pushed gave shape to this book.

The real exchange rate, the relative prices of tradables and nontradables, is one pivotal set of prices that free markets and strong currency are expected to set right. But the intuition behind this proposition is not obvious. The international price of a currency, the nominal exchange rate, is formed in the world of tradables, while the real exchange rate is formed in the universe of the gross domestic product, which includes both tradables and nontradables. Intuition therefore suggests that it would be a nice surprise if setting the nominal exchange rate at equilibrium resulted in an equilibrium real exchange rate also. Expressing this in another way, there is no reason to believe that the allocation of resources that results from setting the nominal exchange rate at equilibrium in a developing country is identical with the one emanating from an equilibrium real exchange rate.

The proposition that free currency markets have an inherent distortion that makes developing countries systematically misallocate resources is subjected to analytical and emprical verification. The former was the easy part. The empirical tests that started with the published micro-ICP (International Comparisons Project) data would not have been totally conclusive without the generosity of Alan Heston, who made available to me the still unpublished data of phases IV and V (1980 and 1985) of the ICP. If the ideas in this book stand the test of time, Alan is owed an enormous debt of gratitude.

A sabbatical year in Japan came at a crucial juncture for this book in 1988–89. As research professor at the Institute of Economic Research, University of Kyoto, I found a supportive and nurturing environment to conduct the first fledgling tests of the empirical hypothesis and to sort out the antithetical views on the role of government in economic development. Whereas the analytics of the imperative for government intervention in economic development can be clear, experience shows that there is no presumption that intervention will be successful. Government failure is as frequent as market failure. Inductive observation of the environment around me suggested that the particularistic view of Japan, in vogue in current literature, is as much a caricature as is the *homo oeconomicus* view of the West. There lay the origins of the nonrevisionist interpretation of the Japanese Miracle. The view of how government contributes to or hinders economic development also inspired the other case studies in the book.

The seminal grant for this research was provided by the Center for Economic Policy Research, Stanford University. Its (then) Director and Associate Director, John Shoven and Edward Steinmueller, had either blind faith or serendipitous intuition in backing this book when it was still a glint of ideas based on a hunch. They also provided subtle guidance to keep it on course, as did Kimio Morimune, who likewise displayed blind trust in managing my stay in Kyoto.

Some complementary funding came from the Center for East Asian Studies, the North American Forum, and a Mellon Foundation grant, all at Stanford University. I am indebted to all above for providing for some travel, and for secretarial and research assistance services. I am also grateful to the good and dedicated people who held these positions, Shandon Lloyd and Sarah Brehm, in the former category, and among my competent research assistants, Robert Teh, Jorge Muñoz, Hilario Ramos, Mauricio Ramirez, Yasuyuki Sawada, and notably Eva Polbring, who kept an adept hand on reams of unruly data and also kept her good humor between the ecstasy of the discovery and the agony of the seemingly insurmountable.

This book, which started as a flickering intuition, would have been quenched if it were not for encouragement received on the way by the bemused understanding of some friends and colleagues and by the befuddled tolerance of others. Among the people who read (nearly) the entire manuscript, I am indebted to David Felix, Maxwell Fry, Scott Pearson, Jean-Philippe Platteau, and Alan Winters. Their detailed comments and their refashioning of some of the ideas helped in improving and extending the argument. Among those who applied an intially blunt concept, or a dull portion of a manuscript, on the sharpening stone of their expertise and delivered them with a cutting edge, I would like to single out: Irma Adelman, Takeshi Amemiya, Gregor Binkert, Marcel Fafchamps, Sagrario Floro, Yoshihiro Iwasaki, Alain de Janvry, Takashi Kurosaki, Bih-Jane Liu, Jeffrey Nugent, Gustav Ranis, Donato Romano, Scott Rozelle, Yasuyuki Sawada, Jia-Dong Shea, Nicholas Stern, Joseph Stiglitz, Yiannis Venieris, Rob Vos, Tadashi Yagi, Ya-Hwei Yang, Yasukichi Yasuba, and Fred Zimmerman. Finally, I have applied a good portion of these ideas on the anvil of my classroom, and I am grateful for the hammer of good students, such as Eleni Gabre-Madhin, Mandar Jayawant, Guo Li, Jim Minifie, Eduard Niesten, Susan Lund, and David Widawsky, among others.

Stanford, California
July 4, 1995

Pan A. Yotopoulos

PART I

A review of the terrain

CHAPTER 1

Introduction

For all the efforts that have gone into the economic development of less-developed countries (LDCs) in the last half-century, there have been but a half-dozen unqualified successes, almost all in East Asia. It is no wonder, therefore, that the paternity of these scarce development miracles has been vehemently contested. Free marketeers point to the reliance on private enterprise and free markets, and they emphasize the openness to trade. Statists, on the other hand, focus on the nonmarket allocation of resources and on highly distorted trade regimes. The intelligent layman, who has been caught between conflicting claims, has long suspected that the truth lies somewhere in between, and perceptive economists often have articulated that case well.

This book brings to the debate a systematic rule that helps determine the optimal mix between market and state in the process of development. The philosophical starting point is that the state need not (indeed must not) venture where the market works fairly well. In these cases, free-market, free-trade, laissez-faire capitalism will lead to Pareto-optimal outcomes. Yet, the dynamic formulation of the fundamental theorem of welfare economics just stated introduces the important exception of market incompleteness. If markets are incomplete – in space, time, or uncertainty – the free-market equilibrium generally will not be Pareto optimal. Government intervention is required, and there is no presumption that it will be successful.

The thesis of this book is that market incompleteness is systematically related to the level of underdevelopment. Therefrom derives the need for intervention in LDCs. The corollary of this argument is that as development progresses, the role of government in the development business withers away. Successful economic development should have aided the markets to evolve to the point that their equilibrium leads to Pareto optimality.

Incomplete markets in trade and foreign exchange are at the heart of the argument. One reason for this is the importance that trade has assumed in the economies of developed countries as well as in the economic miracles of the newly industrializing dragons of East Asia. Another reason for the prominence of trade in the discussion is that it appears to be the weak link in the virtuous cycle of efficiency. Efficiency requires the optimal allocation of resources based on their opportunity cost. Thus "setting the prices right" becomes an important precept of the political economy of development. The theory of comparative advantage in the open economy extends the allocative-efficiency argument by demolishing borders. Resources will be allocated efficiently provided that international market forces determine the prices of (internationally) tradable goods in the economy. And an exchange rate that is in equilibrium is considered prime among the instruments that guard free markets and free trade against price distortions.

The thesis of this book, on the contrary, is that an equilibrium nominal exchange rate is at best the outcome of successful development, not the cause of growth. As in the case of incomplete markets in general, market incompleteness in foreign exchange, which is a generic condition of underdevelopment, requires nonmarket allocation of resources. This means overriding the market and rationing foreign exchange. This, in turn, makes inevitable a regime of import controls and export management, the success of which is predicated on "good governance."

The issue, therefore, is not whether governments should intervene in development. It is, rather, how they might intervene successfully. Although state intervention in development has been common, development success has been rare. It is all too facile to make the case that governments often fail worse than markets do at times. The surprise in development is not that countries with able governments may succeed and those with inept and corrupt governments will fail. Most often development fails because of the wrong policies, instead of the wrong governments. This web of ideas is briefly previewed in what follows.

Part I of this book reviews the salient ideas that have formed the traditional foundation of theory and policy on issues of trade and development. The neoclassical edifice is grand in design and tightly built. The structuralist critique is insightful but ad hoc and episodic. The "new development economics" that focuses on incomplete markets can be described as "systematic structuralism," and it can resolve the dilemma that arises with free-marketeers on the one side and statists on the other.

Part II presents the analysis and empirical work that relate to the existence of incomplete markets in foreign exchange and trade for developing countries. The conceptual construct is an adaptation of the Australian model that distinguishes tradables and nontradables. In a non-Hicksian world where the two are not perfect substitutes, the production of nontradables can become a binding constraint for economic development. This situation arises when the prices of tradables are "high" relative to those of nontradables, with resources moving "excessively" from the latter to the former. Devaluation of the nominal exchange rate (NER) is the policy instrument of choice for shifting resources from the nontradable to the tradable sector: it immediately affects the price of tradables and, with a lag, the price of nontradables. This is another way of saying that devaluation, to be effective, requires that the prices of tradables increase faster than the prices of nontradables. The ratio of the prices of tradables to the prices of nontradables is the definition of the real exchange rate (RER). Although the NER and the RER are clearly covariant, they need not be perfectly correlated. Can one then say that setting the NER at equilibrium implies an "equilibrium" RER also? And if not, does that matter? The dynamics of the NER and the RER are at the heart of Part II of the book. A preview of some of the empirical results can best illustrate this issue, while also providing the motivation for what will follow.

The equilibrium NER is defined as the rate that balances a country's current account (tradables), appropriately also considering capital movements.[1] The equilibrium RER is more difficult to define, although it is easy to conceptualize. In an economy that produces tradables (whether they are *traded* or not) and nontradables, Pareto optimality requires that the opportunity cost of a unit of resources in the production of the former is equal to that in the latter. But what a unit of resources is and how to value a unit of output of tradables or one of nontradables can become intractable issues.

Micro-ICP (International Comparisons Project) data provide price information for a complete set of outputs of an economy, appropriately normalized by the international prices of the same commodities. Data from international trade statistics are used to define tradables ("tradeds") and nontradables on a country-by-country basis. The ratio of the prices of the two is an index of the RER. Although it cannot be used to measure the deviation of the RER from its equilibrium value, it can clearly indicate whether one country has higher prices of tradables relative to nontradables than another – i.e., it has a more under-valued RER, always in relative terms. As an example, Table 1.1 shows the countries that participated in Phase V of the ICP Surveys in 1985, ranked by the value of the RER index.

Regression analysis reveals that the value of the RER index is negatively related to the rate of growth of real GDP per capita (Table 1.2). The result remains valid when the research is extended within the endogenous growth framework to include other explanatory variables that have featured in the literature, such as the ratio of investment and of government consumption in GDP, school enrolment ratios, and so on. The other variables are dominated by the RER variable (see Chapter 7).

How are such empirical results to be explained? This is the primordial question for economists: If it works in practice, does it also work in theory? The purpose of this book is not to formulate a complete theory that links the RER with the growth process. It will, however, review the snippets of theory that corroborate the empirical evidence (see Chapters 2 and 3); it will present a

---

1 The equilibrium NER should also satisfy the intertemporal budget constraint. It is the rate that sets the discounted sum of a country's current account equal to zero (see Chapters 3, 6, and 8).

Table 1.1. *Countries ranked by the value of the RER index, 1985*

Country	RER	Country	RER
Ethiopia	1.967	Kenya	1.070
Rwanda	1.962	Morocco	1.069
Pakistan	1.747	Norway	1.013
Malawi	1.713	Netherlands	1.009
Sri Lanka	1.546	Turkey	0.998
Yugoslavia	1.542	Denmark	0.980
Greece	1.417	Australia	0.969
Ivory Coast	1.329	Belgium	0.963
Portugal	1.230	Jamaica	0.949
New Zealand	1.208	Sweden	0.933
Nigeria	1.196	Canada	0.928
Thailand	1.193	Japan	0.923
Hungary	1.192	Ireland	0.918
Egypt	1.186	Finland	0.879
India	1.178	Italy	0.831
Germany	1.155	Poland	0.829
France	1.095		

Source: Chapter 6, Table 6.2.

model of RER devaluation (Chapter 4) and one of NER devaluation (Chapter 8) that focus on the distinction between tradables and nontradables and thus help illuminate the empirical results; and it will offer an intuitive example of a special kind of market incompleteness that may exist in foreign exchange and trade and that can generate these results.

Within the RER framework, observations of relatively high prices of tradables (RER *under*valuation) can be generated through aggressive devaluation of the NER that increases the price of exports and import substitutes relative to the price of nontradables, both expressed in units of national currency per international dollar. Such NER policies can lead to overshooting the comparative advantage of a country by extending the range of tradability to commodities that are produced at "high" resource cost relative to nontrables. For instance, some countries without a climatic or resource advantage in producing grapes are known to export wine. Other countries graduate from being exporters of sugar and copra to exporting their teak forests, and on to systematically exporting nurses and doctors, while they remain underdeveloped all the same (see Chapter 11). If this happens, it may represent noncomparative-advantage trade. This in turn could imply a misallocation of resources against nontradables, which may explain the negative relationship between the RER and the real rate of growth in GDP.

Table 1.2. *A preview of the relationship between growth and real exchange rate*

	RER 1	RER 2
Test 1. All countries – 1970, 1975, 1980, 1985		
Coefficient	-0.021	-0.024
T-statistic	-2.708	-2.947
Constant	0.040	0.068
Standard error of Y estimate	0.025	0.024
Number of observations	123	123
Adjusted R^2	0.049	0.139
Test 2. All countries – 1980, 1985		
Coefficient	-0.025	-0.021
T-statistic	-2.720	-2.051
Constant	0.040	0.042
Standard error of Y estimate	0.024	0.024
Number of observations	86	86
Adjusted R^2	0.070	0.064
Test 3. All countries – 1985		
Coefficient	-0.031	-0.022
T-statistic	-3.290	-1.963
Constant	0.051	0.033
Standard error of Y estimate	0.019	0.017
Number of observations	37	37
Adjusted R^2	0.214	0.322
Test 4. All countries – 1980		
Coefficient	-0.021	-0.021
T-statistic	-1.270	-1.165
Constant	0.032	0.045
Standard error of Y estimate	0.027	0.028
Number of observations	49	49
Adjusted R^2	0.013	0.000
Test 5. All countries – 1970, 1975		
Coefficient	-0.023	-0.034
T-statistic	-1.995	-2.533
Constant	0.056	0.096
Standard error of Y estimate	0.023	0.022
Number of observations	37	37
Adjusted R^2	0.076	0.123
Test 6. Low and middle income countries – 1970, 1975, 1980, 1985		
Coefficient	-0.019	-0.025
T-statistic	-1.851	-2.416
Constant	0.035	0.073
Standard error of Y estimate	0.030	0.029
Number of observations	74	74
Adjusted R^2	0.032	0.112

Source: Chapter 7, Tables 7.1–7.6.
Notes:
The dependent variable is annual rate of growth of real per capita GDP for a 5-year period, centered on the year of observation. RER is defined as the ratio of relative prices of tradables to nontradables appropriately normalized by international prices and aggregated using expenditure weights. RER 1 reports the coefficient of the simple regression. RER 2 reports the coefficient of the RER after controlling for time (the slowdown of growth in the 1980s), DC–LDC status, and trade regime.

The intuitive explanation offered above will be fleshed out in subsequent chapters. Its two analytical components need be highlighted at this point. First, it implies that there is an inherent distortion in currency markets that makes LDCs have high RER. Second, this distortion leads LDCs to a systematic misallocation of resources. If so, this line of reasoning leads to another paradox. It implies that it is *under*valuation of the NER – or wanton depreciation of the home currency – that causally relates to low rates of growth. Conventional wisdom, on the contrary, sees the problem as NER *over*valuation, which is considered both endemic among LDCs and responsible for inferior development outcomes. The two views can be reconciled if the NER and RER, while covariant, do not possess the property of separation:[2] setting the one at an equilibrium value does not necessarily imply equilibrium for the other. In fact, one would not expect a priori this to be the case, since the NER is formed in the market of tradables alone, while the RER involves the prices of both tradables and nontradables. Then the issue is reduced to nonseparation in the market of tradables and nontradables. One can hypothesize that nonseparation, and thus an *incomplete market*, may be systematically related to the level of underdevelopment. The argument for market incompleteness in foreign exchange is symmetrical to the economics-of-information approach to credit markets; only that the origins in this case lie with issues of *reputation* (see Chapter 3).

One way of understanding nonseparation that leads to market incompleteness is to compare a developed country (DC) and an LDC along the continuum of possibilities for transforming nontradable output (or the resources that produced it) into tradables. To enhance the intuition suppose both countries are overindebted, e.g., the United States and Mexico. The former, with hard currency, can service its foreign debt by producing either tradables or nontradables, whereas the latter, with soft currency, is required to withdraw resources from nontradables to produce exports, and thus hard currency to meet its obligations. The operational implication of the distinction between hard and soft currency is that the former is treated as a store of value internationally. This quality of a hard currency is based on reputation, which in this case means that there is a credible commitment to stability of relative dollar prices (towards other hard currencies, or, say, gold). Reputation is often treated as a binary

---

2 The strict condition of nonseparation is the existence of nonzero cross-partial derivatives. As an illustration from the equilibrium model of the household, under the condition of separation in production and consumption, maximization in the former also implies maximization in the process of consumption. The value of the maximized profit enters the household utility function, which in turn is solved to give, e.g., the income–leisure equilibrium. If, on the other hand, a unit of leisure cannot be turned at will into a unit of work (if there is a failure in the labor market) there is nonseparation and the two equilibria do not obtain jointly (Lau, Lin, and Yotopoulos, 1978).

commodity, and a currency being soft is accepted as probative evidence that there is no credible commitment against devaluation. The empirical implication of this difference between Mexico and the U.S. is an asymmetric relationship between Americans who do not wish to hold pesos as a store of value as compared to Mexicans who hold dollars. The shift in the demand curve for dollars by Mexican peso-holders makes the prospect of devaluation a self-fulfilling prophecy. The difference between hard and soft currency, therefore, lies in issues of reputation and asset-value dynamics. Free convertibility of the peso does not automatically enshrine it as an international store of value, unless convertibility is built on a solid foundation of reputation that would allow the peso to be treated as an international store of value.

With the peso, then, being a soft currency and the Mexican debt being denominated in dollars (*because* the peso is soft currency), Mexico cannot service its foreign debt from the proceeds of producing nontradables. These are traded in pesos. Nonseparation between tradables and nontradables implies that maximization in the latter sector is constrained by the foreign exchange requirement that has to be achieved in the tradable sector. But in the U.S. separation obtains, and maximizing in one sector implies maximization also in the other. Unlike in the U.S., resources in Mexico have to be shifted away from the nontradable sector to produce tradable output in order to procure the dollars for servicing the debt. Devaluation is the policy control instrument for such resource shifts; and it, in turn, entails further loss of reputation. How far can this process go? Returning to the intuition about "equilibrium" real exchange rates, the previewed empirical results might just indicate that in certain cases the production of tradables has been pushed to the point that they become too expensive in terms of domestic resource cost, and relative to nontradables. When this happens, the point is reached when not all trade is necessarily comparative-advantage trade. It becomes competitive-devaluation trade.

Ricardo analyzed this case in terms of relative productivity differentials. It has been extended by others to also cover relative factor endowments. To the extent that nontradables are more labor-intensive than tradables, developing countries may be better endowed for producing the former than the latter. The case can be made even stronger, since the production of tradables is not only capital- and technology-intensive, but it also requires managerial inputs that are scarce, and some essential markets that are missing in LDCs. Forward markets in foreign exchange are crucial for trade, since they afford opportunities for hedging by buying insurance against foreign exchange fluctuations. They exist for hard currencies, but not for soft. As a result, dealing in tradables in LDCs involves higher risk, which is accompanied by more pronounced fluctuations (usually devaluation) of the NER. The same argument can be made about insurance markets that are relatively scarce in LDCs (see Chapter 3).

Having started from an intuition on asset-value dynamics in the foreign exchange market, we have interpreted the empirical relationship between high prices of tradables and low development outcomes as originating from non-separation in tradables and nontradables and systematic incompleteness in the foreign exchange and trade markets. The market ailment is systematic with underdevelopment. As development occurs, tradable-specific resources accumulate, learning effects accrue, and markets develop, with tradables becoming less expensive to produce. In the same process, reputation effects combine to make the currency less soft. The distinction between tradables and nontradables becomes less and less important as development progresses, until it becomes immaterial because separation in the two sectors has been achieved. In the interim, however, when the market is incomplete, rationing is required in the foreign exchange market. There is no presumption in this case that setting the NER at its market-clearing level will lead to Pareto-optimal outcomes. It is likely to lead, instead, to a depreciating currency, and ultimately through an "undervalued" RER, to "trade bias"; i.e., it leads to pushing the production of tradables too far, thus creating Pareto losses. On the obverse side of the issue, an appreciating NER, through decreasing the prices of tradables relative to those of nontradables, decreases the value of the RER index, and, in face of the empirical evidence, leads to higher rates of growth. The stylized empirical finding, therefore, is of development success with a low RER and failure with high values of the index. Undervaluation, not overvaluation, of the NER may be the problem. This finding is certainly unorthodox and controversial.

Nonprice closure and overvaluation in the foreign exchange market calls for the control of the trade market also. An overvalued NER can stifle exports by making them expensive in terms of foreign currency, thus restricting demand, and by making tradables cheap in terms of domestic currency, thus restricting supply. The obverse side of the same proposition is that an overvalued NER can precipitate a flood of imports and import-substituting activities, which may be of the "wrong kind." Imports, therefore, need to be controlled, and exports need to be subsidized. But those interventions that are the logical consequences of market incompleteness raise the issue of economic rents and rent-seeking activities.

Within the incomplete market framework, government control and regulation are not viewed as the only origins of economic rents. Rents are also the result of incomplete markets, and as such they precede regulation. The issue of rent-seeking activities, therefore, reduces to who captures the economic rents and how are they utilized. They can be captured by the elites and be used to the detriment of economic development. Or they can be captured by a competent and honest government and be ploughed back into economic development. Good governance is a very important variable that could not be entered in the endogenous growth analysis of Chapter 7. This omission makes it even more surprising that the relationship between RER and the rate of growth is so strong. Good governance is commonly referenced to the process of development teleologically – by the outcomes. One way to approach the issue operationally is to examine how the process has worked in practice by identifying specific policy instruments that are mapped into certain development outcomes.

Part III, therefore, fills this gap. It analyzes cases of success in development that combined selective overriding of incomplete markets with ploughing the rents back into the process of development. It also presents cases of failure, where the wrong posture on economic rents offset the right economic policy or compounded the results of adopting policies that failed to override incomplete markets. By linking the analytical scaffold with the empirical content of the case studies, the approach highlights systematic components of development policy that can account for success or failure. More specifically, the case studies treat as policy instruments the systematic interventions in certain incomplete markets that assume strategic importance in the process of development, most notably, foreign exchange, trade, labor, and capital. They specify as successful policy outcomes the broadly based increase in incomes among the population – pluralistic economic development. The juxtaposition of instruments and outcomes in cases of success and failure illustrates that "appropriate" is an important qualifier to intervention. The precondition for appropriate intervention is competence in government, with policy makers knowing when intervention is warranted and when it should be avoided at all cost. Moreover, since market intervention opens up opportunities for rent-seeking activities, integrity in government becomes another precondition that delimits who captures the economic rents and for whom. The juxtaposition of success and failure cases of economic development helps illustrate the importance of good governance – with its two components, competence and integrity – for self-sustained economic development.

CHAPTER 2

Trade and development:
The contours of the landscape

Economic development has at times been punctuated by an intense ideological debate that is raging between free-marketeers and interventionists. The free-marketeers seem to have won the day, at least as far as international trade is concerned. On both sides the argument is grounded on good theoretical premises and is buttressed by eclectically assorted empirical evidence.

Neoclassical orthodoxy has emphasized (but to a lesser or greater degree) the importance of undistorted markets and market-clearing prices as instruments that lead not only to macroeconomic stability, but also to high levels of investment, efficiency, growth, and, ultimately, improved living conditions. Structuralists, on the other hand, have focused on various features of developing countries that constitute a special case and therefore call for intervention (Chenery, 1979, Table 2-1). The structuralist position, being greatly diffused, has rightly drawn the charge that it is "an eclectic collection of ideas, not a systematic challenge" to the neoclassical orthodoxy (Dornbusch and Fischer, 1984, p. 571).

This chapter reviews the neoclassical foundations of economic development that support the ideas of laissez faire and free trade. It proceeds with a characterization of the structuralist position, based on the introduction of the demand side in the neoclassical edifice. The next chapter introduces concepts of the "new development economics" that extend the exceptions to the neoclassical paradigm to cover incomplete markets. Finally, a special market incompleteness is introduced in international trade and foreign exchange that forms the foundation for "systematic structuralism."

The classical foundations: The neoclassical tradition of development economics

The classical beginnings

Development economics started with the Parable of the Invisible Hand of Adam Smith. His *Inquiry into the Nature and Causes of the Wealth of Nations* (1776) could be titled in modern jargon "The Study of the Growth of Nations' GDP." The implicit Smithian model of three factors of production treats land as quasi fixed, labor as endogenously determined in what later became a

Malthusian process towards subsistence wages, and capital stock as partly exogenous. The lever for growth in this system is capital accumulation. Moreover, efficiency becomes an important factor in the combination of the inputs of production – in fact so important that the vignette of the pin-maker and the division of labor occupies the very first chapter of the *Wealth of Nations*. Adam Smith, a shrewd observer of the world that had then embarked on the early stages of the Industrial Revolution, described the outcome of efficiency in terms of returns to scale. The same was true of his justification for free trade: the removal of tariffs and trade restrictions would increase the size of the market, thus inducing finer division of labor and increased efficiency. Smith's classical system thus focused on capital accumulation and on efficiency as the operational handles for increased productivity and economic development.

Malthus and Ricardo, jointly, are responsible for having refined Smithian ideas and having advanced the classical theory of development. Malthus fully specified Smith's implicit endogeneity of labor. In the *Essay on the Principle of Population* (1798), he advanced the geometric/arithmetic growth relationship between population and resources. Human populations grow in a geometric progression to the greatest size that their food supplies, which grow only in an arithmetic progression, can support at a tolerable level of misery. Should living standards increase beyond the bare minimum, the pressure of population on limited land resources results in lower labor productivity, forcing consumption below the subsistence point. Thus, the main checks to population are "positive," including war, disease, hunger, and

> ... [T]he vices of mankind [which] are active and able ministers of depopulation. They are the precursors in the great army of destruction; and often finish the dreadful work themselves. But should they fail in this war of extermination, sickly seasons, epidemics, pestilence and plague advance in terrific array, and sweep off their thousands and ten thousands. Should success be still incomplete, gigantic inevitable famine stalks in the rear, and with one mighty blow, levels the population with the food of the world (Malthus, 1798, pp. 139–140).

The whole panoply of the positive checks, therefore, includes "unwholesome occupations," "severe labor," malnutrition, especially of children, wars, poverty, hunger, famine, disease, epidemics, and plague; in one word – misery. They are all associated with population pressure on land, which was formalized later in terms of the law of diminishing returns.

In the first edition of the *Essay* (1798), two temporary relief valves to population pressure forestall the inevitable positive check. First, increases in land area due to colonization, or land improvements through the accumulation of capital, can temporarily prevent the erosion of the levels of living. This is a preview of the Ricardian principle of diminishing returns and of Malthus' later (1815) foray into rent, complete with the afterthoughts of Ricardo on technological change and capital deepening. The second relief mechanism is the "preventive check," which is abstinence from sexual relations, accomplished either by delay of marriage or by continence within marriage. The positive check operated through food supplies based not on the bounty, but on the meanness of nature. The preventive check rested also on human deprivation by the strong assumption that the delay of marriage was mostly activated through the threat of misery. Therein lie the origins of the dilemma as seen by the early Malthus: better living conditions lead to early marriages and to rapid population increases, which outstrip the food supplies until either the positive or the preventive check comes into operation and an equilibrium population is restored. Thus Malthus earned his sobriquet as a prophet of doom.

Under a good deal of pressure from friends, Malthus expressed less somber thoughts in the second edition of the *Essay* (1803) and in his later works (1824). The emphasis is shifted from the positive to the preventive check, more specifically to the "moral restraint" that determines the "prolificness of marriages" and the "earliness of marriages." A careful reading of Malthus' later works establishes him as an accomplished early socioeconomic modeler who anticipated the demographic transition. He launched the literature on the determinants of population growth, complete with the importance of education, the status of women, and the "social capillarity thesis," and replete with policy measures for curbing the reproductive tendency (Yotopoulos, 1980). Yet his notoriety as the prophet of doom still endures.

Malthus' ideas on the pressure of population on land were further developed in close association with Ricardo and are known as the Ricardian theory of rent. The Ricardian rent on land is determined at the margin of cultivation – the least productive land, which, according to Malthusian ideas, barely yields the subsistence wage. Moreover, diminishing returns prevail in agriculture.

> Thus we have seen that from the necessity of having recourse successively to land of a worse quality, in order to feed an increasing population, corn must rise in relative value, corn will exchange for more of such money, that is to say, it will rise in price. . . . But when the rises in price of corn is [sic] the effect of the difficulty of production, profits will fall; for the manufacturer will be obliged to pay more wages, and will not be enabled to remunerate himself by raising the price of his manufactured commodity (Ricardo, 1817, p. 78).

We can write for the subsistence annual wage $w = qp(1 + k)$, where q is the quantity of corn (grain) that enters the subsistence diet per year, p is its price, and k is the proportion of the subsistence budget that is spent on commodities other than corn (which, being the mainstay of the English workingman's diet, may be considered as equivalent to "food"). Denote by m the marginal product of land, i.e., the amount of corn a worker can grow per year on one unit of marginal-quality land. Assuming that no rent is paid for using the marginal

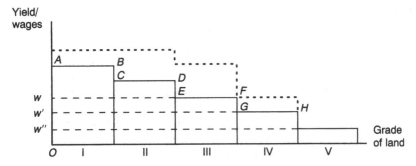

Figure 2.1. *Ricardian rents*

land, the gross value of corn produced on that piece of land, *mp*, is related to
the wage by $mp = w(1 + v)$, where v is the gross markup covering nonwage
costs and normal profits. By eliminating the w between the two relationships
we can write:

$$1 + v = m/q(1 + k) \qquad (2.1)$$

where k and q can be considered as constant technical parameters. The equation
shows that the rate of normal profit on the marginal land, and therefore the
normal profit throughout the economy, is directly related to m, the productivity
of labor on the marginal land (Dorfman, 1991). It is a combination of return on
entrepreneurship and return on capital invested in cultivating that land. Moreover, pure economic rents accrue to the landlords of inframarginal land. However, the landed gentry in Ricardo's social structure is parasitical, and rents,
therefore, do not contribute to capital accumulation.

In Figure 2.1, consider three grades of land under cultivation, with yields
respectively shown at the level of *AB* for grade I, *CD* for grade II, and *EF* for
grade III. The wages (including profits of the managers of land) would be equal
to the yield in the marginal grade of land, and are represented by *w*. The price
of agricultural output is also determined by the yield of land. The rent accruing
to the landlords is indicated by *wABCDE*. As a result of population growth,
cultivation is expanded to the next inferior grade of land, IV. Wage (and profit)
will decline to *w′*, which we define as the level of subsistence,[1] price of
agricultural output will increase, and rents will increase in all the inframarginal
grades of land. Should population pressure depress the wages farther, to *w″* for
example, the Malthusian positive check takes over to restore the balance
between population and resources. Meanwhile, the ratio of profits to wages

---

1 Ricardo referred to the diminishing returns to labor and the necessity of decreasing wages in
order to bring new lands into cultivation as the "iron law of wages."

increases in response to the inexorable increase in agricultural prices due to the expansion of cultivation to inferior grades of land.

Subsequent Ricardian ideas on technological change and capital deepening provided yet another mechanism for the relative increase in agricultural prices: increase in wages and general improvement in the standards of living. The increase in profits provides the wherewithal for financing technological change and capital deepening in countries where "manufactures flourish" (DCs). This is shown in Figure 2.1 by the dotted line showing increased yields due, e.g., to irrigation. The result is that wage *w* again becomes sustainable, and may even become operational, depending on the dent in the labor force that the Malthusian positive check imposed. Meanwhile profits increase, and so may the rents accruing to the landlords.[2] A parallel process of capital accumulation and increasing productivity is taking place in the manufacturing sector, only at a more rapid pace in comparison to agriculture, and even faster as development occurs. Thus the trend in relative prices and in the sectoral terms of trade favors agriculture. In the formulation of the Ricardo Principle (see Chapter 3) this becomes equivalent with the relative decrease in prices of tradables as development occurs.

This basic classical edifice of the process of growth saw small stylistic changes in the next 150 years: John Stuart Mill shone his classicist's light on the importance of education; Marx, with his "industrial reserve army," introduced the idea of unlimited supplies of labor; Alexander Hamilton in the United States advocated industrial development fostered by protective tariffs and governmental investment in infrastructure, which Friedrich List elevated to the infant industry argument.

The neoclassical edifice

Development again became a mainstream field with Joseph Schumpeter. In his *Theory of Economic Development* (1934), he shifted attention entirely away from increases in the quantity of capital and spotlighted innovation as the engine of growth. Moreover, since innovation is discontinuous and often requires massive investment, the peaks and troughs of the business cycle were connected with the life cycle of innovation-related booms. The dynamic of the individual entrepreneur provided the homeostatic mechanism that created and competed profits away, thus fuelling economic development.

Harrod's (1939) contribution to the aggregate growth theory became the

2 Ricardo later advocated the repeal of the corn laws that discouraged the importation of cheap food. His political-economy argument was founded on the classical primacy of capital accumulation as the lever of growth. Restriction of corn imports resulted in extending cultivation to poorer lands in order to feed the population. This reduces *m* and, therefore, normal profits that were available for investment. See also Chapter 3, note 3.

cornerstone of the post-World War II empirical literature on economic development. The model refers to a closed economy, where equilibrium in the output market requires that investment is equal to savings,

$$I = sY, \tag{2.2}$$

where I is planned investment, Y is income and s is the savings rate. Since I is equal to dK/dt, with K being the capital stock, dividing by K we get the Harrod–Domar equation

$$g = s/k, \tag{2.3}$$

where $g = (dK/dt)/K$, the growth rate of the capital stock, and $k = K/Y$, the capital–output ratio. Equation (2.2) can be considered as an identity ex post; then (2.3) describes the equilibrium or "warranted" growth of capital. Moreover, if the capital–output ratio is constant, then the growth of capital is equal to the growth in output.

The Harrod–Domar equation is the Keynesian addition to the classical edifice of growth: savings rates and capital–output ratios are the determinants of growth, as opposed to capital accumulation and efficiency. This formulation became the cornerstone of the majority of development plans that were spawned in the first quarter-century of the modern development era.

The basic growth model has been extended with a series of contributions. Solow's (1957) article – building on the work of Denison (1967) and Abramovitz (1956) – established the procedure for decomposing the increase in output into the contributions of the growth of factors of production and the growth of "total factor productivity." Starting from a general production function such as

$$Y = F(K, L, t) \tag{2.4}$$

and differentiating with respect to time, we have

$$\left(\frac{\partial Y}{\partial t}\right)/Y = \alpha\left(\frac{\partial K}{\partial t}\right)/K + \beta\left(\frac{\partial L}{\partial t}\right)/L + \frac{F_t}{Y} \tag{2.5}$$

where $\alpha = KF_K/Y$, and $\beta = LF_L/Y$, the competitive shares of capital and labor, and subscripts denote partial derivatives. The growth of output is accounted for (on the right-hand side of the equation) by the contribution of greater quantities of factors of production (the first two terms) and by the residual (the last term), which measures "total factor productivity." By applying the decomposition equation, Solow found that the increases in capital and labor fell far short of explaining the vast increase in the nonfarm output in the United States from 1909–1949. The residual "total factor productivity," which is plausibly identified with technological progress, accounted for more than one-half the growth of output.

This framework has been refined to incorporate embodied technological progress (Solow, 1962), learning by doing (in a seminal article by Arrow, 1962), and has been generalized to also capture factor-specific quality augmentation (Lau and Yotopoulos, 1989). The empirical applications with data from international cross-sections and time series all lead to the conclusion that after accounting for the growth in the traditional factors of production, the residual contribution claims the spoils in explaining the growth of output. This has been a humbling finding for the classical–neoclassical approach to economic development. Even worse, a model that assigns a predominant role to an exogenously determined technology as an engine of growth has empirical implications that are not consonant with the modern experience of development. Given the nonrival nature of exogenous technological innovations and the opportunities for their dissemination in open economies, the expectation is that growth rates would tend to converge, with the variance attributed to transitory differences in capital accumulation across countries. This is patently not the case when real incomes (whether in constant prices or in purchasing power parity terms) are compared across countries. We will return to this issue in the next chapter.

The one outstanding characteristic of the classical edifice of development economics, as founded by Adam Smith and remodeled by a series of classical and neoclassical economists, is the preeminence of the traditional factors of production, especially capital accumulation and efficiency. The latter can take the form of allocative efficiency, the one-time gains from restoring optimal allocation of resources, and of "total factor productivity," or "technological change," which are probably "names for our ignorance." The emphasis of the classical–neoclassical approach is exclusively on the role that supply factors play in economic development.

The salient ideas of the orthodox development paradigm and the theoretical grounding of the neoclassical system

We use the term "orthodox development paradigm" to identify a few salient ideas shared by both neoclassical economists and orthodox Marxists. Three main themes are interwoven in this literature and have been very influential in formulating development policy.

First, the "monoeconomic claim" means that development becomes a system on a world-wide scale with all the component parts organically related. The development process is "stylized" in "normal patterns of growth" from which countries temporarily deviate. For Marx the developed countries reflect to the less developed world "an image of its future" (Marx, 1867). Hirschman (1982, p. 388) remarks that "the underdeveloped countries were expected to perform like wind-up toys and to lumber through the various stages of development singlemindedly."

Not only is development a world-wide system; development economics also has world-wide applicability. Individuals are "agents" whose nonergodic behavior implies that individual traits are self-canceling according to the law of big numbers. And both orthodox Marxists and neoclassical economists reject the view that underdeveloped countries, as a group, possess special economic and social characteristics that make them stand apart from the developed countries; as a result, they reject the view that traditional economic analysis, developed in the latter, must be recast in significant respects when dealing with LDCs.

The opposite extreme to the monoeconomic claim is imminent empiricism as practiced by old-fashioned institutional economists and neo-Marxists. This approach assigns an infinite weight to the "special case." Instead of looking for a theory, the imminent empiricist looks at special characteristics hard enough and long enough until some "general principles" become clear, less by formal logic than by insight.

Second, orthodox development economics is profoundly optimistic (Yotopoulos and Nugent, 1976, p. 10; Streeten, 1979; Nugent and Yotopoulos, 1979; Hirschman, 1982). Optimism is reflected in the view that secular progress characterizes the past, the present, and the future. More specifically for our theme, there is abounding optimism in the prospects of economic development, which can be transmitted and spread in several ways: through trade, aid, private investment, the productive utilization of surplus value, public enterprises, and so on. The impact that world expansion of industrialization can have for accelerated growth in the periphery has been emphasized by both orthodox Marxists (Marx, Rosa Luxemburg, Lenin, Bukharin) and by a host of neoclassical and mainline development economists (W. A. Lewis, Chenery, Prebisch, Mahalanobis). The optimism of the orthodox paradigm is based on the "mutual benefit claim," which views development as a positive sum game, a process that has only gainers. The implication of the optimistic outlook of orthodox development economics is that "all good things go together," from growth in GDP, to employment, to income distribution, and so on (Hirschman, 1982).

Third, the orthodox paradigm describes the progress as ordered, harmonious, and evolutionary. It is irrelevant whether the mechanism is the Invisible Hand, which is on the whole and in the long run benevolent, or the dialectic process that is subject to a logical inevitability leading eventually to utopia and the dictatorship of the proletariat. Moreover, progress is in general gradual, continuous, and cumulative and rests on automatic mechanisms. Both the Invisible Hand and the dialectic process can be viewed as homeostatic mechanisms which are tripped by the operation of incentives in the former, and by the class struggle in the latter, in order to achieve progress. The outcome of the homeo-static process is an equilibrium position, a stable pattern of interactions that occurs when everybody is maximizing simultaneously.

In a monoeconomic world system the characteristics of development, opti-mism, and ordered harmony, along with the implication of the applicability of automatic mechanisms, are viewed to transcend the national boundaries in both versions of orthodox development economics. The neoclassical theory of in-ternational trade (more precisely Samuelson's proof of factor–price equaliza-tion) is a definite statement of the proposition that free exchange will spread the benefits of development across the world through specialization and the divi-sion of labor. In the process, uniform world prices become applicable (Streeten, 1979; Hirschman, 1982). Similarly, the solidarity of the proletariat is interna-tional and any deviation along national or ethnic lines is revisionism and a result of "false consciousness."

The orthodox paradigm delivers development broadly, among classes and across the world, in a trickling-down process that is akin to the system of the communicating vessels of elementary hydraulics: the pressure in the vessel with higher initial endowments leads to raising the water level in the other vessel. The mechanism that trips off change and restores equilibrium is the pressure created by nonidentical endowments. Its impulse is transmitted through the pipeline that connects the vessels. Analogously, development is initiated by incentives arising from inequality and is promoted by the market mechanisms that connect the rich and the poor. According to this paradigm, therefore, what is required for development is to create the proper incentives through the appropriate price signals and to correct for market imperfections so that the signals can be properly transmitted. Development then becomes a self-propelled process that leads to the homogenization of the rich and poor until they become indistinguishable, at least up to exogenous factors like the quantity of talents they possess or their tastes for risk taking. Where inequalities persist in the development outcomes, it is the role of the government to intervene through tax and redistribution policies.

The efficiency and optimality of the unfettered market that inspires the orthodox development paradigm can be rigorously restated in terms of the two fundamental theorems of welfare economics (Srinivasan, 1988). The first wel-fare theorem states that every competitive equilibrium is Pareto optimal. Pareto optimality obtains if no departure from a state can make someone better off without making somebody else worse off, i.e., if benefits to some can only come at a loss to others, or, under a weaker formulation, the gainers cannot fully compensate the losers. The second welfare theorem holds that every Pareto-optimal allocation can be supported as the equilibrium of the laissez faire, market economy provided that income can be redistributed through nondistortionary means, such as lump taxes and subsidies. In combination, the two theorems imply that both efficiency of resource allocation and distributional equity (Pareto-type, or "improved" after policy interventions) can be achieved in competitive equilibrium.

Both theorems entail a set of restrictive assumptions, among others that competition exists, consumers' preferences are concave, firms' technologies are convex, and all goods are homogeneous. The violation of any of these assumptions causes the welfare theorems to fail, which implies that the market equilibrium will not be Pareto efficient and may not even exist. The traditionally identified causes of market failure include the existence of externalities, public goods, monopolies, lack of property rights, missing markets, and nonconvex technologies that yield increasing returns to scale. However, the fundamental theorems imply that market mechanisms alone can yield Pareto-optimal outcomes, unless the stated conditions do not hold. The general presumption, in other words, is in favor of the market and against government intervention. The role of the government is limited to its Smithian core duties: to provide order, justice, basic infrastructure, and so on. And it extends to compensate for the exceptions to the restrictive assumptions of the theorems. For example, the empirical evidence about the importance of economies of scale in LDCs led to theories of balanced and unbalanced growth in different sectors of the economy for the purpose of offsetting the lumpiness of capital investment. The policy interventions of identifying (through measuring linkages) and promoting key sectors, and of subsidizing large-scale capital investments followed. Similarly, the preoccupation with aid in the 1960s was founded on the assumption that trade was important for growth since it released the supply limitations of individual commodities. Trade, in turn, was constrained by a single limit on the supply of foreign exchange, which aid helped to remove. The two-gap literature provided the theoretical foundation for such interventions.

The structuralist critique

In the classical theory of international trade, equalization of factor prices is implicitly assumed. Under the assumption of international immobility of factors of production, with the exception of capital, international trade activates forces that will eventually eliminate the international disparity in factor prices. In this free-market, free-trade world, unequal exchange is ruled out by definition and the equilibrium will occur at mutual benefit. In the structuralist critique, on the other hand, world prices are not determined in the long run by supply and demand considerations. They are determined, instead, by growth-equilibrium conditions, whereas supply and demand affect the variable quantities in the system, such as employment or the volume of trade. In this sense the structuralist models are fixed-price models.

The examples of structuralist approaches that follow will set the stage for the innovations that the "new development economics" has brought into the subject.[3]

Unequal exchange

Prebisch, in the early 1950s, was among the first to be concerned with the stubborn inequality in international prices and to challenge the conventional wisdom. He argued that the secular terms of trade tended to turn against the agricultural products of the South and in favor of Northern industrial trade (Prebisch, 1959). In his model, both North and South specialized in a single commodity.

In a rudimentary presentation of the model we may assume a two-country (North = n and South = s) two-commodity world, with trade specializations in wine for n and ale for s. The gross product of each country, Y_i, is given by

$$Y_i = q_i L_i \qquad i = n, s \tag{2.6}$$

where q_i is the average productivity of labor and L_i employment for wine in the North and ale in the South. We normalize by the price of the Southern commodity and we define $P = Q^s/Q^n$ as the price of wine in terms of ale, where the fraction represents the respective quantities that are exchanged in trade. We can write the respective import demand functions, M, as

$$M^n = M^n\left(Y^n, \frac{1}{P}\right) \tag{2.7}$$

$$M^s = M^s(Y^s, P) \tag{2.8}$$

and the trade balance equation as

$$\frac{1}{P} M^n - M^s = 0,$$

or

$$M^n = PM^s \tag{2.9}$$

By totally differentiating (2.7) to (2.9) we derive the expressions for the income and price elasticities of demand for North and South, respectively,

$$dM^n = \frac{\partial M^n}{\partial Y^n} dY^n + \frac{\partial M^n}{\partial \left(\frac{1}{P}\right)} \left(-\frac{dP}{P^2}\right) \tag{2.7a}$$

---

3 Following the tradition of this literature, and for economy of presentation, the models presented are one-factor (labor) models. In the two-country development statics of DCs and LDCs the omission of capital, if anything, leads to underplaying the adverse effects on the latter that are labor-abundant and capital-scarce.

$$dM^s = \frac{\partial M^s}{\partial Y^s} \, dY^s + \frac{\partial M^s}{\partial P} \, dP \tag{2.8a}$$

$$dM^n = P \, dM^s + M^s \, dP \tag{2.9a}$$

Writing e_i and η_i, $i = n, s$, respectively, for income and price elasticities (of demand for the Southern good in the North) and substituting from (2.7a) and (2.8a) into (2.9a), we have

$$e^s \frac{dY^n}{Y^n} M^n - \eta^s \frac{dP}{P} M^n = P\left(e^n \frac{dY^s}{Y_s} M^s + \eta^n \frac{dP}{P} M^s\right) + M^s \, dP \tag{2.10}$$

Writing g_i, $i = n, s$, for the rate of growth of gross product in the two countries (and remembering that $M^n = PM^s$), we have

$$\left(e^s g^n - \eta^s \frac{dP}{P}\right) PM^s = \left(e^n g^s + \eta^n \frac{dP}{P}\right) PM^s + M^s \, dP$$

$$e^s g^n - e^n g^s = (\eta^s + \eta^n + 1) \frac{dP}{P}$$

$$\frac{dP}{P} = \frac{e^n g^s - e^s g^n}{|\eta^s| + |\eta^n| - 1} \tag{2.11}$$

If the Marshall–Lerner conditions hold (the sum of the absolute value of the price elasticities for exports and imports is greater than unity), the denominator of (2.11) is positive. Furthermore, assume that the North's income elasticity for the Southern good is small, $e^n > e^s$. Then the South must face in the long run either slower economic growth ($g^s < g^n$), or a deterioration in the terms of trade ($dP/P > 0$). In other words, the terms of trade depend on the interrelationship between the growth rates and the income elasticities of demands for exports.

In this formulation of unequal exchange, international prices, or the terms of trade, are not determined by supply and demand considerations but by a comparison of trading equilibria. By observing that the income elasticity of demand for raw materials from the South is lower than the demand for manufactured exports from the North, Prebisch reached the conclusion of the inevitability of industrialization as a remedy to unequal exchange. This is the theoretical background of Latin America's import-substitution industrialization drive.

Factoral terms of trade and the pivotal position of agriculture

Lewis made two important contributions to the argument of unequal exchange. In his early writings (Lewis, 1954, 1958), he explicitly brought into the argument food production and the importance that agricultural development assumes as a precondition of self-sustained growth. Later (Lewis, 1978a,b) he released the dubious assumption of fixed labor productivities by introducing explicitly the unlimited supplies of labor.

The unequal-exchange argument above can be extended into three commodities, where one is common for North and South (food) and two are products of international division of labor and specialization (steel for the North and coffee for the South). All three commodities are tradable and they are produced with one factor of production, labor. Suppose that the North can produce with one unit of labor either two units of food or five units of steel, and that labor productivities are nonvariable as the scale of either output changes. Under the same assumption of constant productivities, suppose the South produces either one unit of food or 10 units of coffee. With all three commodities tradable, arbitrage will equalize the world price of food (say at two units of food per unit of labor, which is the minimum-cost Northern price). With food as the numeraire, the prices of steel and coffee must settle around one steel to four coffee (five-to-twenty being the respective productivities in terms of food labor value). Changes in the terms of trade depend on the relative changes of the respective Northern and Southern labor productivities. If technical progress is faster in Northern food production than in steel, the Southern terms of trade will deteriorate even with unchanged relative productivity between food and coffee. The only way the South can improve its terms of trade is by raising its productivity in food production relative to coffee.

In his later work Lewis deals with the broad sweeps of history and introduces the unlimited supplies of labor into the model of unequal exchange. In the second half of the 19th century two different migration streams, each about 50 million people strong, headed for the then agricultural countries. From China and India the migrants settled in the tropical countries to work in mines and plantations. From Europe the migrants settled in the new countries in the temperate zones, United States, Canada, Argentina, Chile, Australia, New Zealand, and South Africa. Both temperate and tropical settlements initially traded in primary commodities: minerals, tea, rubber, or peanuts for the tropics, wool, frozen meat, and wheat for the temperate climates. Two questions arise: How were the terms of trade initially set for the exports of the tropical and temperate settlements? And what explains the different roads to development that the respective countries followed?

The opportunity cost of the labor of the new migrants set the respective wage rates. For the temperate migration stream the opportunity cost was determined in the farms of Europe, which had already undergone their agricultural revolution and by 1900 yielded 1600 pounds of wheat per acre. The corresponding marginal productivity of labor became the reservation wage rate for the European migrants. The yield of grains in China's and India's backward agriculture, on the other hand, was only 700 pounds per acre. Its equivalent labor productivity set a low reservation wage rate.

Given the floor wage rate in agriculture, the specialization of the two migrant streams of labor and the terms in which they were exchanging their products with the center were both determined endogenously. The products of the temperate countries fetched prices in international trade that could support the relatively high standard of living set by European opportunity cost wages. Prices of tropical products settled correspondingly at lower levels in accordance with the modest opportunity cost of labor in Chinese and Indian agriculture. Furthermore, should productivity in tropical commodities increase, unlimited supplies of Asian migrants were ready to depress wages to subsistence levels again. According to Lewis

> This analysis clearly turns on the long-run infinite elasticity of the supply of labor to any one activity at prices determined by farm productivity in Europe and Asia, respectively. This is applied to a Ricardian-type comparative cost model with two countries and three goods. The fact that one of these goods, food, is produced by both countries determines the factorial terms of trade, in terms of food. . . . One important conclusion is that the tropical countries cannot escape from these unfavorable terms of trade by increasing productivity in the commodities they export, since this will simply reduce the prices of such commodities. . . . The factorial terms of trade can be improved only by raising tropical productivity in the common commodity, domestic foodstuffs (Lewis, 1978a, p. 16).

The belief that the division of the world into the rich North (DCs) and poor South (LDCs) was due to unfavorable terms of trade is thus, according to Lewis, a fallacy. Poverty is intrinsically related to endogenous structural economic and social characteristics; it is not the outcome of the trade specialization of a specific country:

> If 60% of the tropical labor force is in low-productivity food, the rest will get low prices whether it exports agricultural or industrial products. . . . The terms of trade are bad only for tropical products, whether agricultural or industrial, and are bad because the market pays tropical unskilled labor, whatever it may be producing, a wage that is based on an unlimited reservoir of low-productivity food producers (Lewis 1978a, pp. 36–37).

As an example, the industrial exports of developing countries, such as textiles, suffer from bad terms of trade that serve as a vehicle for transferring surplus from the South to the North, while both Denmark and Australia who are agricultural exporters have good enough terms of trade to support high living standards. The solution, therefore, does not lie in reforming the international economic order by reshuffling the patterns of trade specialization around the globe; it rather lies in eliminating the low-productivity pool of workers that keeps the opportunity cost of developing countries' products very low.

> The way to create a new international economic order is to eliminate the 50 to 60 percent of low-productivity workers in food by transforming their

productivity. This would change the factorial terms of tropical trade and raise the prices of the traditional agricultural exports. It would also create an agricultural surplus that would support industrial production for the home market (Lewis, 1978a, p. 37).

We will formulate an extended Lewis-type model[4] to study the impact of sectoral policies on the terms of trade in this chapter and the effect of devaluation on real exchange rates in Chapter 3.[5]

In a two-country, three-product Lewis-type model both North and South produce a staple commodity (agricultural) for domestic consumption, and one export commodity each. The production functions for the two countries and the equilibrium price equations are given in equations (2.12) and (2.13), where superscripts n and s denote North and South, respectively, subscripts T and N denote tradables and nontradables, and the nontradable sector in the North has been suppressed:

$$Y^n = q^n L^n \tag{2.12a}$$

$$Y^s_T = q^s_T L^s_T \tag{2.12b}$$

$$Y^s_N = q^s_N L^s_N \tag{2.12c}$$

$$P^n = (1 + v)w^n/q^n \tag{2.13a}$$

$$P^s_T = (1 + v)w^s_T/q^s_T \tag{2.13b}$$

$$P^s_N = w^s_N/q^s_N \tag{2.13c}$$

where Y is gross product, P price of output, L the quantity of labor and q its average productivity, w the wage rate, and v is the rate of return to capital (which is uniform as the result of the assumption of the international mobility of capital). In keeping with the Lewis tradition, there is sectoral labor mobility in the South, and the wage is defined by the average productivity in the nontradable sector:

$$w^s_T = w^s_N = q^s_N \tag{2.14}$$

Equations (2.12) and (2.13) contain the information necessary to study the terms of trade. The (net) *barter* terms of trade, h, are expressed as the ratio of prices of exports to prices of imports. Given the equality of v for North and South the barter terms of trade, the ratio of the two prices above, can be expressed as in equation (2.15):

$$h = \frac{P^n}{P^s_T} = \frac{w^n}{w^s_N} \frac{q^s_T}{q^n} \tag{2.15}$$

4 Similar models have been presented by Ocampo (1986) and Bardhan (1982).
5 The models of real and nominal exchange rates in Chapters 4 and 8 complement the discussion of the external terms of trade.

$$P^n = P_T^s \left(\frac{w^n}{w_N^s} \frac{q_T^s}{q^n} \right) \tag{2.16}$$

From the production function define the *factoral terms of trade, f,* as the ratio of Northern to Southern wages. This expresses the amount of Southern labor that can be purchased with one unit of Northern labor, given the price of the Northern commodity. By substitution from (2.15) the factoral terms of trade can then be written

$$f = \left(\frac{w^n}{w_T^s} \right) = \frac{P^n q^n}{P_T^s q_T^s} \tag{2.17}$$

Given Lewis' assumption that the wage rate in the South is equal to the marginal productivity of labor in agriculture, by substitution from (2.16) we can explicitly introduce wages and productivities in the nontradable sector:

$$f = \left(\frac{w^n/q^n}{w_N^s/q_T^s} \right) \frac{q^n}{q_T^s} = \frac{w^n}{w_N^s} \tag{2.18}$$

Thus the factoral terms of trade are determined by both the wage in the North and the wage in the nontradable sector in the South. Then using equation (2.14)

$$w_N^s = q_N^s$$
$$w^n = \lambda q^n \tag{2.19}$$

$$f = \frac{\lambda q^n}{q_N^s} \tag{2.20}$$

The term $\lambda \geq 1$ can be interpreted with reference to Lewis' discussion of the historical migration movements and other institutional factors that determined the wage differentials between North and South. The effect of unionization of labor in the North is one interpretation (as per Bardhan, 1982). It can also be interpreted as capturing the historical accident of the agricultural productivity differential in mid-19th century between the regions of origin of the two migration streams – Europe and Asia. This differential determined the reservation price of the migrants and thus the wage rates.

In this model, productivity in the nontradable sector plays a key role in determining the factoral terms of trade. Writing for percent changes

$$\frac{df}{f} = \frac{d\lambda}{\lambda} + \frac{dq^n}{q^n} - \frac{dq_N^s}{q_N^s} \tag{2.21}$$

four conclusions follow.

(1) Improvement in productivity in the nontradable sector in the South ($dq_N^s > 0$) implies $df/f < 0$, i.e., *improves* factoral terms of trade in the South.

(2) Improvement in productivity in the tradable sector in the South ($dq_T^s > 0$) implies $df/f = 0$, i.e., factoral terms of trade *don't change*.

(3) Improvement in productivity in the North ($dq^n > 0$) implies $df/f > 0$, i.e., factoral terms of trade *deteriorate* for the South.

(4) Increase in the power of unions in the North ($d\lambda > 0$) implies $df/f > 0$, i.e., factoral terms of trade *deteriorate* for the South.

Lewis has formulated the above argument to emphasize that the unequal-exchange interpretation of the terms of trade between North and South is not so much the result of insidious acts of commission by the North as it is a feature of the structure of the South and especially of its neglect of the agricultural sector.

By introducing the demand side into the traditional argument of unequal exchange, Lewis made agricultural development a precondition for the improvement in the terms of trade of the South and for overall economic development.

Class structure and economic development

In Lewis' analysis of the historical experience, export agriculture became the growth sector both in temperate and tropical countries. Some of the former – Australia, New Zealand, and Canada – took advantage of trade to industrialize and now belong in the First World. Argentina, Chile, and South Africa, along with the tropical countries, still belong in the Third World. Why did development abort despite thriving export trade and, in the case of Argentina, Chile, and South Africa, advantageous terms of trade also? The introduction of the concepts of articulation/disarticulation brings into focus the role that socio-economic class structure plays in the process of development, and it helps answer Lewis' question.

The concept of articulation/disarticulation is based on the "contradiction in the generation and the distribution of surplus value" (profits versus wages) and first surfaced in the neo-Marxist literature (Terray, 1972; Rey, 1973; Bettelheim, 1972; Leclau, 1979; Althusser and Balibar, 1979). It has more recently been emphasized by de Janvry (1981) and it finds its parallels in orthodox development literature in concepts such as dualistic development, development participation, and pluralistic economic development that refer to the interface between development and income distribution.[6] In the development literature such concerns started with Rosenstein-Rodan's (1943) "big push" theory, and they have attracted considerable attention recently with the work of Murphy, Shleifer, and Vishny (1989a,b) and Eswaren and Kotwal (1993). The latter show the importance of income distribution and of population size in gener-

6 de Janvry's model has been challenged by Baland (1989).

ating the effective demand that can nurture domestic industry past its infant stage. Still, disarticulation has broader connotations than the early development agenda for state intervention. The contribution of the model of disarticulation is the emphasis on the heterogeneity of social and economic structures and, especially, the shift in the search for proximate causes of underdevelopment from colonial exploitation and terms of trade to internal factors, most notably the role of social classes.

Disarticulation can best be understood by starting from its opposite – articulation. Development is articulated when the different economic sectors are closely linked, so that growth originating in one is transmitted throughout the economy. Similarly, the social classes that correspond to different economic sectors are mutually supportive in the sense that increases in income in one class trickle down to the others. In short, articulated development closely replicates the conditions of the orthodox development paradigm, the monoeconomic claim, the mutual benefit claim, and the ordered, harmonious, and evolutionary nature of the process.

In Figure 2.2 we have an agricultural sector that produces the subsistence good and an industrial sector that produces consumer durable goods and capital goods. On the supply side, the upper portion of the graph for both sectors, there exist interindustry linkages, backward and forward, both within each sector and between the two sectors. They are indicated by the broken-line arrows connecting the two sectors which describe the degree of sectoral articulation or interindustry linkages. Linkages imply that the production of the subsistence good draws for intermediate products on the capital goods sector and vice versa with food processing and light manufactures activities.

On the demand side the incomes of the corresponding social classes are determined by the return to capital for capitalists and the return to labor for workers. Capitalists have derived demand for capital goods, which is met either by the domestic capital goods sector or through imports. They also contribute to the final demand for agricultural goods and for light manufactures, such as consumer durable goods; so do the workers. Thus, the derived demand for capital goods and the final demand for wage goods are again closely linked so that an exogenous increase in either leads to an increase in the other, which makes the wage and income determination in the system endogenous. The demand linkages are indicated by the broken-line arrows at the bottom of the diagram that describe the degree of social articulation, or demand linkages.

Disarticulated development is characterized by the existence of sectoral and social dualism. In the extreme case, the dualistic cleavage between sectors and classes is watertight. On the production side, there may exist a modern growth sector ("key sector") but its growth fails to be transmitted to the rest of the economy. On the consumption side, similar social dualism exists. The market for the modern sector is geographically and socially distinct from the market

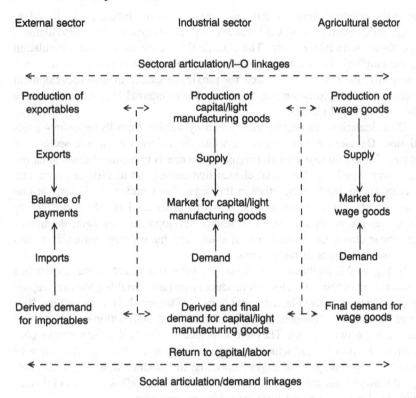

Figure 2.2. *Structure of articulated economy*
Source: Adapted from de Janvry (1981), p. 33; by permission of the publisher, Johns Hopkins University Press, for the World Bank.

for the traditional sector. The former expands from the exogenous increase in demand of the goods of the modern sector that originate abroad or from increased demand that comes from growth in profits and in rents that accrue to a privileged middle income class and the wealthy. Growth in demand of the modern sector is not transmitted (in the extreme case and only weakly transmitted in intermediate cases) to the traditional sector. Furthermore, the absence of a link between capitalists and wage earners (i.e., between profits and wages) on the demand side implies that an increase in wages and in the income of labor would not lead to the expansion of production and to higher profits in the modern sector. Wages are therefore viewed "only as a loss" that leads to the decrease in the incomes of capitalists, not in their growth. Under these con-

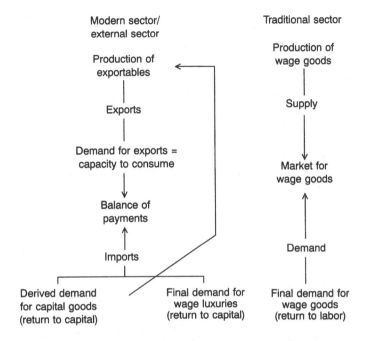

Figure 2.3. *Structure of disarticulated export-enclave economy*
Source: Adapted from de Janvry (1981), p. 32.

ditions, wages are delinked from the productivity of labor in the modern sector and stagnate. Wages stagnate in the traditional sector also. The outcome is deficiency of demand in both sectors and failure to increase capital accumulation. Even where technological advance in the production of the wage good takes place, increases in the productivity of labor are not reflected in wage increases. In both sectors, therefore, the modern and the traditional, wages are exogenously determined rather than set through considerations of marginal productivity.

A stylized example of extreme disarticulation and dualism, say of an export enclave economy, is shown in Figure 2.3. The exporting enclave may be a plantation, a mine, or an export-oriented industry. The traditional sector is the wage good sector. In comparison to Figure 2.2, the absence of the broken-line arrows indicates that on the production side there exists sectoral disarticulation without any forward or backward interindustry linkages between the production of raw materials and the output of the plantation or the mine. On the consumption side, also, social disarticulation exists. The return to capital is partly used to increase the capacity to produce by importing foreign capital goods and equipment. It is for the most part channeled to final demand, which also is satisfied through the import of luxuries for the elites and consumption goods for the middle class. The geographical and social location of the modern sector is abroad – the economies of the center – and as a result entirely distinct from the geographical and social location of the traditional sector. A similar model of disarticulation can be elaborated for a three-sector economy where the modern sectors are one export enclave and one luxury-import-substituting sector with the third, the traditional sector, again being entirely distinct and with no linkages to the rest of the economy (de Janvry, 1981, pp. 32 ff.).

The articulation/disarticulation model has testable implications that refer to the economic, social, and political class structure. Classical economists, from Malthus to Ricardo and Marx, considered the tendency for reducing the wage bill and for holding down labor costs as one way of increasing profits ("surplus value"). The exogenous determination of wages in the case of disarticulation and the tendency to suppress the wage bill towards the subsistence level become important testable characteristics of the model. Since employers see labor only as a "cost," they favor cheap food policies for the urban sector as helping to keep wages low. Such food policies include imports of "cheap" food from abroad and agricultural price policies that tax producers in order to subsidize the food-cost of urban wage laborers.[7] In an articulated economy, on the other hand, wages are tied to the productivity of labor and wage increases lead to increasing effective demand that benefits the entire economy and the particular sector in question. Depending on social priorities and the structure of production, such wage increases in an articulated economy can be given through minimum wage legislation, worker retraining, targeted tax cuts and subsidies, and so on. In the articulated case employers view wage increases not only as a "cost," but also as a "gain" in stimulating demand. The impact of increased demand on profits offsets the adverse effect of the increase in the wage bill.

Other testable features of the economic articulation model, besides wage policies, are available. The "growth sector" (key sector) on the final demand side is likely to represent consumption goods for the masses (domestic agriculture, small appliances) at the early stage of development of an articulated economy; it is likely to represent luxury consumption or import substitution industries that cater to the middle classes in the case of disarticulated development. Labor intensive technology, with the wage bill an important component of value added, is a characteristic of articulation; capital intensive technology is the prevalent mode of production in the growth sector under disarticulation. Both the demand and the production side are geographically and socially

---

7 Under conditions of massive urban unemployment, industrial wages can even be below the subsistence needs of the worker as long as the worker's family in the traditional sector makes up the difference between wages and subsistence needs. This is what de Janvry (1981, pp. 36–37) calls semiproletarianization of labor.

spread under articulation; they are geographically concentrated, usually in the capital city, and they are socially located either in a middle class enclave or abroad through export demand in the disarticulated model.

An economic model can test jointly several characteristics of articulation. The component of sectoral articulation can be tested through input–output approaches by measuring interindustry linkages. The component of social articulation can be tested by measuring demand linkages. Finally, both together can be tested by developing the appropriate system of linkages from a social accounting matrix.

Under disarticulation, the class structure rather than imperialism becomes the crucial actor in underdevelopment. Social classes, besides their importance for the functional distribution of income, also become pivotal in creating and perpetuating disarticulation through political alliances. In a disarticulated economy, for example, where the production of exportables and of luxuries are the growth sectors, political power is likely to reside with international capital and the metropolitan bourgeoisie (the class connected with international capital), with the dependent ("comprador") bourgeoisie (which trades in the production of exportables and luxuries), and with the landed elites (which rely on cheap imports of capital goods to produce agricultural exports and industrial raw materials and rely on imports of middle class consumption goods and consumer durables to maintain their consumption standards). The logic of social disarticulation implies cheap labor, cheap capital imports, and cheap food. In an articulated economy, on the other hand, where wage goods are the growth sector, the dominant political alliance is likely to consist of the agrarian bourgeoisie and the national bourgeoisie (which are involved, respectively, in the production and trade of wage goods) and of the peasantry, the artisans, and the urban and rural proletariat. These broad social groups have an interest in pluralistic development strategies that result in a broad spread of development and in popular participation in the process of growth. de Janvry (1981, pp. 106–140, especially pp. 123 ff.) presents a number of historical examples of the structuralist specification of Latin American economic development along social and economic class lines.

Returning to Lewis, the countries that became successful cases of development, Australia, New Zealand, and Canada, had an articulated economy. High incomes per capita fostered demand for manufactures and opportunities for import substitution, which was, at times, promoted by erecting barriers to British exports. Domestic savings and capital accumulation increased the productivity of labor, further increasing wages and the demand for manufactures and for primary inputs. Strong interindustry sectoral linkages and strong final-demand linkages ensured that growth spread from the export sector to the wage-good sector and to the manufacturing sector (in terms of the stylized structure of Figure 2.2).

The problem with aborted development in the tropical countries was that wages were not endogenously determined, and thus were not rising with productivity to create demand linkages and social articulation. The growth sector involuted and grew unto itself, until its growth was dissipated. The diagnosis of aborted development was somehow different in some temperate new countries – Argentina, Chile, and South Africa. Trade was more profitable than in the tropical countries and surplus existed that could have financed industrialization. Three factors compromised the articulation of development and led to an abortive take-off. First, profits from trade and especially from plantations and mines were captured by foreigners as economic rents and were leaked back to the home country. International capital and the metropolitan bourgeoisie were the dominant social classes in these countries. Second, the indigenous dependent bourgeoisie, which made its profits from trade, relied on imported or import substituted luxuries for its consumption, in the process destroying the local industry that could have created demand linkages with the wage-goods sector. Finally, primary production was dominated by the landed elites (precapitalist and junker latifundistas) who opposed measures for broad industrialization behind protective tariff walls, because such measures might deflect resources from agriculture and raise factor prices, or because they might result in raising the prices of manufactured goods, which influenced importantly their standard of living (Lewis, 1978a, p. 24).

The outcome of the development process depended on the relative political strength of the ruling classes and the class alliances. The strength of the metropolitan bourgeoisie, the dependent bourgeoisie and the landed elites led to disarticulated development in Chile, Argentina, and South Africa. In Canada, Australia, and New Zealand, on the other hand, politics was not dominated by an old, landed aristocracy. The national bourgeoisie, agrarian bourgeoisie, peasantry, merchants, artisans, and proletariat captured the state and used their power to protect wages and to expand industrialization around the wage-good production. A model of articulated development ensued.

Conclusion

The discussion in this chapter has focused on the spread of development among countries. The neoclassical paradigm sets international trade at the center of the automatic, equilibrating mechanisms that diffuse growth across the world. Nevertheless, as Arrow (1974) observed, inequality in economic development among countries presents a challenge for neoclassical theory to explain. The neoclassical approach outlined above would explain differences in per capita income by differences in physical and human assets per capita. This explanation poses two problems: How did these differences in assets come to be in the first place? And, in any case, the differences in income seem much too vast to be explained by differences in factor endowments. Especially for the latter question, international trade, and more specifically capital mobility across borders, would be expected to reduce differences in wages, thus restoring equality in rates of growth.

The structuralist critique that emphasizes the "barriers" and the "bottlenecks" to development provides one answer to the Arrow puzzle. In much of the less-developed world the legal system is unable to assign property rights clearly or to enforce them once assigned. Religious, ethnic, and political divisions, not to mention a poorly built physical infrastructure, create substantial barriers to development and impede the dissemination of information about prices, costs, and available technology. The absence of a long tradition of entrepreneurship and of a managerial class substantially increase the risk attached to any given undertaking. The general climate of uncertainty and the high cost of collecting information make for the absence of well-functioning capital markets. Chenery (1979, Table 2-1) provides a comprehensive list of the barriers that account for underdevelopment in structuralist models and the interventions that become appropriate.

The barriers and bottlenecks argument of the structuralists has attracted most of the attention. Still, in contrast to the neoclassical paradigm that focuses largely on the supply side – the contribution of the conventional factors of production and especially of capital accumulation and efficiency gains – the most lasting insight of the structuralists is the emphasis placed on the demand side. The unequal-exchange models incorporate demand and postulate specific elasticity values that constrain the growth in the South. So does the analysis of the factoral terms of trade that links productivity and unlimited supplies of labor in the residual sector, agriculture, with underdevelopment in the South.

It will come as no surprise that both the supply and the demand side have to be treated concurrently, and thus the neoclassical and structuralist approaches should be viewed as nonrival and complementary. Lewis' parable of the International Economic Order draws the distinction between North and South on a historical accident – the difference in agricultural productivities in the countries of origin of the two migration streams in the 18th century. This is a refreshingly different view from the standard Marxist approach of colonial exploitation. In combination with the discussion on the class structure it can also provide a systematic rule for distinguishing between success and failure in economic development: the extent to which the economic rents that are created in the process of development are broadly spread among the population. Pluralistic economic development makes domestic demand a powerful locomotive of growth to be matched with the supply side that was appropriately emphasized in the neoclassical paradigm.

The "new development economics" approach in the next chapter provides a more complete, and especially systematic, view of unequal development. The class structure specified by Lewis will enter the analysis in the form of good governance or, in its absence, in the form of directly unproductive profit-seeking activities and the wasteful competition for appropriating economic rents.

Appendix: North–South convergence in a Lewis-type model

The Lewis model on the factoral terms of trade can be modified slightly to address the issue of convergence in per capita incomes between North and South. We retain the same basic assumptions with the exception that we compare the average product of labor in n and s, instead of comparing wages (the marginal product of labor in n with the average product of labor in s).

As previously, the production functions and the equilibrium price equations are given in equations (A2.1) to (A2.6). Superscripts n and s denote North and South, respectively, subscripts T and N denote tradables and nontradables, and the nontradable sector in the North has been suppressed.

$$Y^n = q^n L^n \tag{A2.1}$$

$$Y^s_T = q^s_T L^s_T \tag{A2.2}$$

$$Y^s_N = q^s_N L^s_N \tag{A2.3}$$

$$P^n = (1 + v)w^n/q^n \tag{A2.4}$$

$$P^s_T = (1 + v)w^s_T/q^s_T \tag{A2.5}$$

$$P^s_N = w^s_N/q^s_N \tag{A2.6}$$

where Y is gross product, P price of output, L the quantity of labor and q its average productivity, w the wage rate, and v the rate of return to capital (which is uniform as the result of the assumption of the international mobility of capital). In keeping with the Lewis tradition, there is sectoral labor mobility in the South, and the wage is defined by the average productivity in the non-tradable sector:

$$w^s_T = w^s_N = q^s_N \tag{A2.7}$$

By taking the ratio of (A2.4) to (A2.5), the expression for the barter terms of trade between n and s, the P^n, can be expressed in terms of P^s_T:

$$P^n = P^s_T \left(\frac{w^n}{w^s_N} \frac{q^s_T}{q^n} \right) \tag{A2.8}$$

The ratio of average productivities of labor, C, is taken as proxy of per capita incomes. Convergence in per capita incomes occurs as the ratio C tends to one.

$$C = \frac{P^n Y^n/L^n}{P^s Y^s/L^s} = \frac{P^n q^n}{(P^s_N Y^s_N + P^s_T Y^s_T)/L^s} \tag{A2.9}$$

$$C = \frac{P^n q^n}{\dfrac{L^s_N}{L^s} P^s_N \dfrac{Y^s_N}{L^s_N} + \dfrac{L^s_T}{L^s} P^s_T \dfrac{Y^s_T}{L^s_T}} = \frac{P^n q^n}{\alpha P^s_N q^s_N + \beta P^s_T q^s_T} \tag{A2.10}$$

where $\alpha = L_N^s/L^s$, $\beta = L_T^s/L^s$, $\alpha + \beta = 1$.

Substituting from (A2.3) to (A2.6)

$$C = \frac{P^n q^n}{\alpha q_N^s \dfrac{q_T^s}{(1 + v)q_N^s} + \beta q_T^s}$$

$$= P^n \frac{q^n}{q_T^s}\left(1 / \frac{\alpha + \beta + v\beta}{1 + v}\right) \tag{A2.11}$$

By substituting for P^n in (A2.11) from (A2.8), and introducing w_N^s from (A2.7) and the Bardhan assumption of the relationship between productivity and wages in the North, $w^n = \lambda q^n$, we have:

$$C = \frac{\lambda q^n}{q_T^s}\left(\frac{(1 + v)^2}{\alpha + \beta + v\beta}\right) \tag{A2.12}$$

In equation (A2.12) the term in parentheses is constant. Differentiating and expressing in percent form the changes in the convergence factor we have:

$$\frac{dC}{C} = \frac{d\lambda}{\lambda} + \frac{dq^n}{q^n} - \frac{dq_T^s}{q_T^s} \tag{A2.13}$$

This expression is different from equation (2.21) in the text by the last factor. It is the productivity of the tradable sector in the South that matters for overall convergence of incomes. The increase in the productivity of the nontradable sector in the South does not affect the income differential. This result is a pure form of Ricardian productivity differentials.

CHAPTER 3

Incomplete markets and the "new development economics"

The Arrow–Debreu (1954) extension of the fundamental theorems of welfare economics has cast new light on the role of governments as economic agents, especially in developing countries. In a pure Walrasian economy, or Arrow–Debreu economy, competitive equilibrium will lead to Pareto optimality as long as there is a sufficient number of markets to span the commodity space. This is an exacting condition and goes beyond the exceptions to the static version of the fundamental theorems of welfare economics that were discussed in Chapter 2. In effect, the dynamic version of the theorems requires that a *complete* set of futures markets exists in time, space, and uncertainty.

In an Arrow–Debreu world, combinations of other goods or contingent claims can span missing or incomplete markets and thus achieve a Pareto-efficient, competitive equilibrium. Competitive equilibrium can obtain, for example, in the wool–spinning–yarn sector, despite the fact that historically only two out of the three markets have been observed, those for wool and yarn. Processing margins implicit in the price of yarn have often made the spinning market redundant. Similarly, there are four possible markets that link the present with the future in the foreign exchange market of dollars in terms of yen: the spot foreign exchange market, the forward foreign exchange market, the spot lending market, and the spot borrowing market. Of the four, three markets are sufficient to span the commodity space: a Japanese exporter can convert yen into dollars in the spot market and lend dollars to a future date, thus hedging the dollar risk of his exports to the U.S. This makes redundant the forward market for dollars. In the Arrow–Debreu world, where a complete set of markets for inputs and outputs is assumed to exist in time, space, and uncertainty, competitive equilibrium will lead to Pareto optimality.

In a real world, which is not strictly Arrow–Debreu, certain markets that are necessary to bridge the commodity space may be missing, and notably so in LDCs. Markets for insurance and futures markets are ready examples. More frequently, there exist certain markets that systematically do not clear in most LDCs: there is rationing of credit, unemployment of labor, and control of foreign exchange. A special condition, particularly relevant in LDCs, is non-separation in production and consumption, which is the outcome of either missing markets or poverty. The technical condition for nonseparation is the existence of nonzero cross-partial derivatives.[1] With nonseparation, some markets systematically do not clear.

The obverse side of the Arrow–Debreu world is that laissez-faire, free-market capitalism in general will not lead to Pareto-efficient outcomes if some markets are incomplete in the sense that they fail to "get the prices right." Equilibrium in markets that do not clear is not characterized by "demand equals supply" or by "unique" ("monoeconomic") prices. In an open economy, the law of one price does not hold. In such cases, tax-subsidy interventions can generate Pareto improvements. If no simple tax-subsidy scheme is feasible, other forms of intervention become applicable. In that event the best solution consists of intervention in which the principal can directly observe and enforce the actions of the agent; the second-best entails designing incentives to promote the desired action. An incomplete market in foreign exchange, e.g., may call for intervention by quotas cum "growth policy packages" (see Chapters 9–11).

The dynamic version of the second fundamental theorem of welfare economics does not say that the government ought to do anything in specific, nor does it specify how the potential for intervention can be realized. After all, government failure is as frequent as market failure (Stern, 1989, p. 616). However, the theorem strongly implies that there is no presumption any more that the Invisible Hand will lead to competitive equilibrium and achieve Pareto-efficient outcomes.

This approach of the "new development economics" goes beyond the stated exceptions to the fundamental theorem that were featured in the previous chapter. It also transcends the "barriers" and the "bottlenecks" to development that were addressed by the structuralists. In an non-Arrow–Debreu world the ailment of the market is more general. It typically relates to imperfect information that entails market incompleteness. This book will also add reputation as a specific source of market incompleteness in foreign exchange and trade regimes. While problems of information and reputation arise in various environments, they seem to be correlates of poverty and thus more prevalent in LDCs. The important insight of the new development economics is that the systematic relationship between market incompleteness and the state of underdevelopment may limit the applicability of orthodox, neoclassical economics to LDCs.

Cases of incomplete markets

A complete market will provide all goods and services that can be produced at a cost lower than what individuals are willing to pay. Having an incomplete market in a final good impacts on welfare. But the study of market incom-

---

1 See Chapter 1, note 2, for a more elaborate definition of separation.

pleteness focuses specifically on factor markets. In the orthodox development framework inputs are the sources of growth and therefore incomplete factor markets impact welfare more broadly. Some typical examples of incomplete markets will be discussed in this section. They all reduce to information failures and most commonly to information asymmetries. Next, this section introduces, and the balance of this book develops, a novel type of market incompleteness that is systematically related to the level of underdevelopment: incompleteness in the foreign exchange market, which has important implications for the foreign trade market and distinct connotations for industrial policies. This specific form of market incompleteness will be related to issues of reputation.

Capital goods markets

Economic development involves in a significant way decisions about the future. So do, quintessentially, the capital markets, whether we refer to the market for capital goods or the market for credit. By examining the incompleteness of capital markets, we gain an important insight into the "special case" of economic development.

Linking the present and the future through timed bundles of goods related one with another through the rate of interest is a truncated way of dealing with uncertainty. The pertinent information about commodities in the future includes both their quantities and prices. This requires the existence of forward markets, which may or may not become redundant by the existence of another market. In general, forward contracts are rare. They exist only for some hard currencies, some commodities, real estate, and little else. Why are futures markets missing in most cases?

The link between the present and the future can be seen in the simplest case of a forward market, that for pork bellies. The quantity and price that refer to a June contract can be easily referenced to quantities bought in the January spot market and carried at their spot price plus storage cost into the future. The uncertainty in the case of pork bellies is of small order, as compared to the uncertainty associated e.g., with future capital goods. Arrow has made the case as follows:

> [T]he demand for capital goods at any point of time is dependent on the prices and sales of the product at future points of time. Therefore the demand for future capital goods will depend on expectations about the product at some still more removed time. If we assume only that we will not have markets for products at some distant point of time, then the resulting uncertainty will reflect itself in a failure of the market for capital goods in the nearer future, which will create in turn still further uncertainties (Arrow, 1974, p. 9).

This uncertainty due to some missing future markets is compounded by the uncertainty that resides in future changes in technology and tastes. Both affect transactions in capital goods more vitally than transactions in other commodities. Unless the missing markets can be spanned by some other "contingent" markets, the Walrasian equilibrium reached in capital goods markets may not be Pareto optimal.

Credit markets[2]

As in the case of markets for capital goods, issues of information are germane to the incompleteness of the credit markets. The credit transaction involves a promise to repay in the future, which may or may not be totally credible. Such a promise can be broken. The borrower may default on his loan.

The case of credit can be described as an instance of asymmetric information between creditor and lender that generates incentive problems. Can such problems be addressed by free markets in a competitive price setting? In credit markets characterized by excess demand, an increase in the rate of interest for the purpose of equating supply and demand is likely to exacerbate the incentive problem and the probability of default with it. This may happen in two ways. First, past some critical rate of interest, high-quality borrowers either will seek credit elsewhere or will leave the market altogether. This leaves the lenders who charge high interest rates with a preponderance of borrowers who have high probability of default. Second, the higher the interest rate, the greater is the attraction of the more risky projects for the borrowers, and thus the greater is the probability of default. Both effects imply a nonmonotonic relationship between the expected return of the loan and the interest rate, with the former increasing less rapidly than the latter and beyond a certain point declining. This leads to the conclusion reached by Stiglitz and Weiss (1981) that there exists an optimum rate of interest that the lender charges, which is below the market-clearing rate of interest. The implication is that the lender will engage in credit rationing – sorting among seemingly indistinguishable borrowers. Quantity rationing, in turn, implies that, given the supply of credit, there exist potential borrowers who are unable to obtain loans, irrespective of the interest rate they are willing to pay.

The availability of collateral is normally used as an instrument of credit rationing. But noncollateralized credit still exists, and it is the rule rather than the exception in LDCs. Moreover, Stiglitz and Weiss extend their analysis to also cover collateral, in the sense that increasing the collateral requirement beyond an optimum point again leads to adverse selection of risk. This happens under three specific circumstances. The first case is when borrowers have the same amount of equity and there are increasing returns to scale in

2 This section draws on Floro and Yotopoulos (1991, Chapter 2).

production, so that the smaller projects have a higher probability of failure. Since collateral increases the debt–equity ratio of a given project, the probability that the smaller, and default-prone, projects are undertaken increases. The second situation is when potential borrowers have different equity and all projects require the same investment. Controlling for the amount of collateral required, the presumption is that wealthy borrowers may be those who in the past have succeeded in risky endeavors and thus are less risk-averse. Conversely, the more conservative investors who have invested in safe projects are less able to furnish a given amount of collateral. Finally, the adverse-selection-of-risk effect of the collateral may offset its direct positive effect in another general case, even if there are no increasing returns to scale in production and all individuals have the same utility function. Assuming that the wealthier individuals are also less risk-averse, one would expect that those who can put up the most capital in collateral are also willing to take the greatest amount of risk. Under some plausible conditions, the risk effect can be so strong as to lower the lender's expected return. The above cases illustrate clearly that interest rate cum collateral is still not sufficient for the full sorting of borrowers.

The problems arising with interest rate and collateral are due to the existence of moral hazard and adverse selection of risk (Jaffe and Russell, 1976; Stiglitz and Weiss, 1981). They belong in the general category of situations where the "price–quality theorem" holds, i.e., when the expected quality of a commodity is a function of its price (Akerlof, 1970). Equilibrium in such cases is no longer synonymous with price closure – the automatic process of equating supply and demand if prices do their job. Overriding price closure and imposing rationing, i.e., quantity closure, still achieves equilibrium as long as the problems that are solved automatically in a free market process by laissez-faire capitalism are handled so that a system of stable interactions arises. In the case of credit, two such problems are most important. The sorting of the borrowers who are more likely to pay from those who are less likely to deliver becomes a central issue. Another problem is how to structure incentives and control mechanisms that make the repayment of the loan more likely by providing reinforcement for borrowers to act prudently. How are these problems solved under quantity closure? The discussion above suggests that the interest rate and the collateral are not the only covenants in the credit contract. Interlinkage of the credit transaction with another market, such as the delivery of output or the sale of inputs, becomes another common feature in credit transactions. So does a preexisting personalistic relationship between the two transacting parties that allows for efficient gathering of information and for close monitoring of the contract. Floro and Yotopoulos (1991; Yotopoulos and Floro, 1992) provide a theoretical and empirical analysis of the equilibrium under quantity closure in informal credit markets in agriculture. Platteau, Murickan, and Delbar (1985) study credit within the same framework in fishing villages in South Kerala.

Insurance markets

One of the markets frequently missing in LDCs is that for insurance. An explicit insurance market consists of the aggregation of claims that are contingent upon broad events that are subsets of states, such as weather failure or automobile accidents. Information problems account for incomplete markets in insurance. In modeling agricultural production in LDCs we usually consider output, for example, as a function of labor input, expressed in efficiency units (effort), and a disturbance term reflecting the randomness of the weather and other missing variables. Since both arguments are not observable to the contracting party, a case of moral hazard and adverse selection arises, which is well developed in the literature (Kreps, 1990; Rasmussen, 1989; Greenwald and Stiglitz, 1986). The provision of insurance under these circumstances may attenuate the incentives for expending maximum effort.

Greenwald and Stiglitz (1986) have shown that the information failure inherent in an insurance transaction afflicts the competitive market outcome. The competitive equilibrium is not the one that will produce the contract that will maximize consumers' expected utility, subject to the insurance company at least breaking even. Pareto improvements can be generated by fine-tuning, on the one hand, the welfare loss from risk-bearing that insurance does not cover, and on the other, the deadweight loss from failing to take adequate accident precautions in the face of insurance. In the case of fire insurance and accident protection, the instruments for Pareto improvements consist of tax-subsidy interventions, such as subsidizing fire extinguishers and taxing the consumption of alcohol that could inhibit drunk driving. In the case of health insurance, where the true state of one's health is not observable, the strict limitations of coverage aimed at preexisting conditions can be removed by universal coverage that increases the insurance pool.

To the extent that the outcome of insurance is smoothing consumption, a properly designed credit contract could have made the insurance market redundant. The credit market, however, also suffers from incompleteness, as the previous analysis indicated. The same outcome of smoothing consumption is variously achieved by certain implicit insurance schemes that exist, especially in LDCs. To the extent that they lie outside the market, they do not make the explicit insurance market redundant, and thus they do not remedy the market incompleteness (Platteau, 1991). Land fragmentation, crop diversification, and intercropping serve to decrease the microenvironmental risk in farming. Migration and remittances smooth the income of the household (Rosenzweig, 1988).

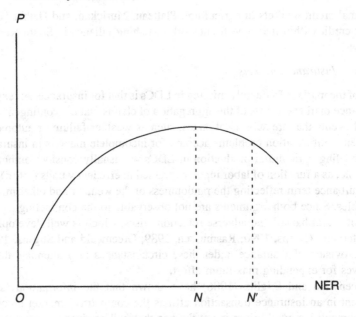

Figure 3.1. *Combinations of profit levels and nominal exchange rates in an incomplete market*

High fertility serves as an insurance mechanism, especially in rural areas (Cain, 1981), as does the extended family system (Nugent, 1985).

Incomplete markets in foreign exchange

The existence of an incomplete market in foreign exchange is critical to the theme of this book. The basic intuition that will be developed further in succeeding chapters is as follows.

The relationship between the nominal exchange rate (NER) and profitability is not monotonic. Furthermore, and especially for LDCs, the free-market competitive-equilibrium price of the nominal exchange rate lies in the declining part of the profitability curve. In Figure 3.1, where P stands for profit (or Pareto-optimal outcomes) a NER at N' is non-optimal. It will be called "undervalued" in the subsequent chapters. The optimal value of the NER, N, obtains only as a result of rationing. This property of the nominal exchange rate parallels the relationship between the rate of interest and profitability.

What accounts for the inherent tendency of the competitive-equilibrium price of the NER to be undervalued? This section will develop the antecedents of an incomplete market in foreign exchange and will formulate the incompleteness hypothesis fully.

The systematic underpinning of market incompleteness in foreign exchange and trade: Ricardian productivity differentials

The structuralist analysis in the previous chapter cast doubts on the causality going from prices of tradables to productivity in the tradable sector. The Ricardo Principle, on the other hand, reverses the causality and makes prices of tradables and nontradables, and their deviations, the systematic outcome of productivity differentials in the two sectors.

The Ricardo Principle relates to the general observation that prices of non-tradables (relative to tradables) tend to be cheap in LDCs and increase as incomes grow. The converse is true for prices of tradables. This observation, which has intuitive appeal, was founded by Ricardo on productivity differentials in the production of tradables and nontradables, which change systematically in the process of development.

Ricardo distinguished between the "home sector," characterized by diminishing returns, and the manufacturing sector with its increasing efficiency. The characteristics of the production function in the two sectors account for productivity differentials. These, in turn, are reflected in the prices of the respective commodities, which grow faster in the "home sector" as compared to the manufacturing sector. In comparisons among countries, Ricardo observed that agricultural (nontradable) prices would be higher "where manufactures flourish" (developed countries):

> [Productivity differences] will in some measure account for the different value of money in different countries; it [sic] will explain to us why the prices of home commodities, and those of great bulk, though of small value, are, independently of other causes, higher in those countries where manufactures flourish (Ricardo, 1817, p. 76).

In Ricardo's specification the "home sector" accounts for the bulk of the commodities that constitute the basic subsistence of the population, and they are not traded internationally. The manufacturing sector can be identified with tradables – commodities of "small bulk though of great value." In general, productivity improvements are higher in the tradable sector than in the non-tradable sector, and they are higher in countries with a higher rate of growth, thus causing relative prices of tradables to nontradables to decrease with development.[3]

Ricardo's Principle has been fully developed subsequently by authors such as Taussig (1928, Chapter 5), Harrod (1939, Chapter 4), Usher (1963), Balassa (1964), Samuelson (1964), Bhagwati (1984), and others.[4] In the process, it has been expanded to include not only productivity differentials, on which Ricardo focused, but also relative factor endowments: labor is relatively cheap at the early stages of development, and so are nontradables, which are labor intensive. The productivity differential gap between rich and poor countries is smaller in the nontradable sector (e.g., haircuts) than in the tradable sector (e.g., automobiles). In the tradable sector, the "law of one price" holds, which tends to equalize prices of tradable goods among countries (allowing, perhaps, for a constant c.i.f.–f.o.b. band representing transportation costs, tariffs, and subsidies). Given equal prices of tradables in DCs and LDCs, wages will be high in countries that have high productivity in tradables – the DCs; they will be low in countries that have low productivity in tradables – the LDCs. More precisely, and as a result of the operation of the "law of one price," the ratio of wages in the tradable sector between DCs and LDCs tends to be proportional to the ratio of their respective average productivities.

In a two-country, four-commodity case, with superscripts D and L denoting DC and LDC, and subscripts T and N denoting tradables and nontradables, respectively, the wage determination is based on the marginal productivity condition. Writing $\bar{P}$ for the world price, Y for the average productivity of labor, and α and β for the share of labor in output in tradables and nontradables, respectively ($\alpha < \beta < 1$), we have the wage (w) equation:[5]

$$\bar{P}\alpha^D Y_T^D = w^D \tag{3.1}$$

$$\bar{P}\alpha^L Y_T^L = w^L \tag{3.2}$$

where $\alpha^D Y_T^D$ is the share of labor times the average productivity, which is the marginal product of labor for the DC; a similar interpretation holds for $\alpha^L Y_T^L$ for the LDC.

As a result of the operation of the law of one price ($\bar{P}$), the ratio of wages

---

3 World prices of agricultural commodities have been secularly declining. This might seem inconsistent with the Ricardo Principle. As the ensuing discussion will illustrate, the definition of tradability is relative and has to be made on a case-by-case basis. The story of English agriculture in the early 19th century provides a stylized example. Ricardo was campaigning for the abolition of the corn laws, precisely for the purpose of turning maize into a tradable and so decreasing its (import) price. By the same reasoning, a good part of agricultural commodities in LDCs are now tradables. Among the nontradables are certainly the subsistence staple commodities, which no country that faces a foreign exchange constraint can afford to import in large quantities.

4 The Ricardo Principle is also known as the Balassa–Samuelson differential productivity model (Heston, Nuxoll, and Summers, 1994).

5 The underlying production function in this example is Cobb-Douglas in labor and capital.

in the two countries can be written as the product of their average productivity of labor and a multiplicative constant:

$$\frac{\alpha^D}{\alpha^L} \frac{Y_T^D}{Y_T^L} = \frac{w^D}{w^L} \tag{3.3}$$

Wages are determined endogenously in equation (3.3), and the greater Y_T^D or the greater α^D is, the higher w^D relative to w^L. In other words, in the DC tradable sector the general level of wages is pulled up by the higher productivity of labor (in presumably more capital- and technology-intensive production). On the other hand, given low productivity, wages are low in the LDC tradable sector. Moreover, given the price $\bar{P}$, the ratio of wages in the tradable sector between DCs and LDCs is equal to the ratio of their respective average productivities (times a constant).

The law of one price does not operate in the nontradable sector where, as a result, we have country-specific prices of nontradables. We rewrite equation (3.3) as

$$\frac{P_N^D}{P_N^L} \frac{\beta^D}{\beta^L} \frac{Y_N^D}{Y_N^L} = \frac{w^D}{w^L} \tag{3.4}$$

where the notation is as previously and β denotes the share of labor in the nontradable sector. Does P_N^D/P_N^L systematically change in the process of development?

Relative wages in the nontradable sector are still influenced by labor productivity in tradables. The high wage in the tradable sector in the DC carries over to the nontradable sector also, despite the low DC productivity in nontradables, which is close to the LDC productivity. Correspondingly, the low tradable-sector wages in the LDC carry over to the nontradable sector, despite the fact that the LDC productivity there is not so low. Not only then is $w^D/w^L > 1$, but it also follows from Ricardo's Principle that the higher wages in the nontradable sector in the high-tradable-productivity country (DC) cannot be fully offset by greater nontradable-productivity advantage, since productivity differentials in the nontradable sector are rather small. Then the higher wages in the DC must lead to higher prices of nontradables there as compared to the LDC, i.e., $P_N^D/P_N^L > 1$.[6] This is precisely the result that Ricardo developed intuitively in the quote that opened this section.

Figure 3.2 provides an illustration of the Ricardo Principle that covers both the original productivity-differential case and the more recent factor-proportions version (Heston et al., 1994). The capital–labor ratio, k, for the DC and the LDC is on the horizontal axis. The vertical axis has, respectively, the marginal physical product of labor (M) for the tradable on the left scale (αY_T)

---

6 For a complete formulation of the Ricardo Principle see Appendix to this chapter.

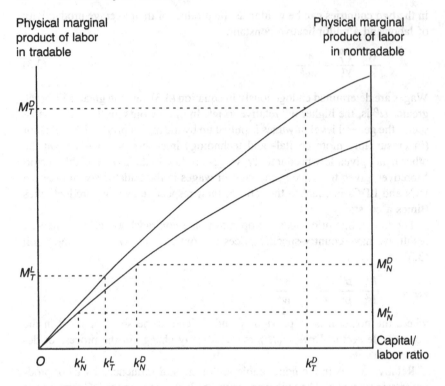

Figure 3.2. *A schematic illustration of the Ricardo Principle for a rich and a poor country*
Source: Heston et al. (1994).

and for the nontradable on the right scale (βY_N) for DC (D) and LDC (L). Given the factor proportions on the horizontal axis, the LDC is operating with marginal physical products of labor M_T^L and M_N^L in tradables and nontradables, respectively, and the DC is operating with M_T^D and M_N^D. Under the assumptions in equation (3.3) that the law of one price holds in the tradable sector and the price of tradable $P_T^D = P_T^L = 1$ (and the exchange rate between DC and LDC is 1) the left scale of the diagram is also the wage scale, and $w^D = M_T^D$ and $w^L = M_T^L$. Competitive labor markets would equalize wages in the T and N sectors in both countries. The marginal cost (C) of nontradables from equation (3.4) will be the wage divided by the marginal physical product of labor, $P_N^D = C_N^D = M_T^D/M_N^D$ in the DC and $P_N^L = C_N^L = M_T^L/M_N^L$ in the LDC. By the productivity differential assumption, the figure is drawn so that $(M_T^D/M_N^D) > (M_T^L/M_N^L)$. It follows that $P_N^D > P_N^L$. So the figure confirms Ricardo's intuition that the ratio of prices of tradables to nontradables declines as development occurs.

Given the systematic relationship between prices of tradables and non-tradables at different levels of income, the share of tradables and nontradables in the budget (and GDP) as incomes grow is determined by the Gerschenkron effect. It states that demand tends to adjust to a country's factor proportions: nontradables being relatively cheap in LDCs tend to assume high weight in the budget and the converse for the DCs, where tradables tend to be consumed in greater proportions.

The Ricardo Principle leads to an intuition that systematically relates the "equilibrium" nominal and the "equilibrium" real exchange rate (RER). The former is determined in the market for tradables alone, and it is defined as the rate that satisfies the intertemporal budget constraint, which states that the discounted sum of a country's current account is equal to zero. In other words, it is the rate that, in the long run, balances the trade account (tradables), appropriately considering also capital movements. The RER, on the other hand, is determined by both tradables and nontradables, and expresses the opportunity cost of nontradables foregone to produce at the margin a unit of tradables. Clearly, the NER and the RER, although different variables, are correlates. But how likely is it that the allocation of resources that results form setting the NER at its equilibrium value is identical with the one that obtains with an equilibrium RER? If there are systematic factors driving the RER that become irrelevant for the determination of the NER, or vice versa, the two equilibria need not correspond. In fact they systematically diverge as will be argued in the following section.

It is, of course, difficult to determine the equilibrium RER and it is also difficult to determine the equilibrium NER. For our purposes, mercifully, neither equilibrium value is needed. An index of the RER will be estimated with international panel data in Chapter 6 and it will be used to test the hypothesis of resource misallocation.

Incomplete exchange and trade in a quasi-Australian model

The important intuition in Lewis' argument, which was developed in Chapter 2, is that he introduces not only the factoral terms of trade, but also the distinction in marginal productivities between tradables (T), commodities that enter international trade, and nontradables (N), which do not.[7] The Ricardo

---

7 A more rigorous and operational definition of tradables and nontradables will be given in Chapter 6. For present purposes, one can think of N in LDCs as domestic transport, construction, electricity, certain services, e.g., of nurses, soldiers, and civil servants, and the basic subsistence commodity of the population, e.g., broken rice, feed-wheat, potatoes, cow peas, and fava beans.

Principle is also based on the same distinction between T and N. A model that builds on this distinction will be developed further in the next chapter and will be termed "quasi-Australian."

The premise in this book is that the distinction is immaterial for DCs but it is crucial for LDCs. In the former N output, or the resources that produce it, can be readily transformed to T output in production or in exchange, and vice-versa for T output being transformed into N output. Separation in the market of T and N makes equilibrium in the two markets coincide, and therefore makes the distinction redundant.[8] In LDCs nonseparation in the two markets makes the distinction relevant. By extension, we will argue, there is no presumption in LDCs that if equilibrium obtains in the real world, with resources allocated efficiently at the margin between T and N, the NER will also assume its equilibrium value. Conversely, a market-clearing NER does not also imply an RER equilibrium.

The distinction between separation and nonseparation (and the relevance of distinguishing T and N) corresponds to the distinction between hard and soft currency.[9] In a DC, all output is traded in local currency, which is likely to be hard. In an LDC, N is traded in soft currency, e.g., pesos, while T is traded in dollars. The dollar is a hard currency because it is accepted as a store of value internationally. This quality is based on "reputation," which in the specific case means that there is a credible commitment to stability of relative dollar prices (towards other hard currencies, or, say, gold). If the peso, on the other hand, is expected to devalue, there is no credible commitment for stability of relative peso prices. The empirical implications of this difference become especially important in a regime of financial liberalization that frees the foreign exchange. There is an asymmetric demand from Mexicans to hold dollars as a store of value – a demand that is not offset by Americans holding peso-denominated assets. The ensuing shift in the demand curve for dollars by Mexican peso-holders leads to devaluation of the peso and to further loss of reputation. It is a basic time-inconsistency proposition that can trigger currency substitution and a spiral for further depreciation of the domestic currency.[10] Asymmetric currency substitution represents a reverse Gresham's law, in which the good currency drives out the bad.[11] The difference between hard and soft currency, therefore, lies in issues of reputation and asset–value dynamics. Free convert-

---

8 For a rigorous definition of separation see Chapter 1, note 2.
9 While there is a continuum between hard and soft currency, for the purpose of this discussion the distinction will be treated as binary.
10 For the dynamics of a simple model of currency substitution where the expected rate of depreciation enters, see Calvo and Rodríguez (1977) and Agènor (1994).
11 For the case of asymmetrical currency substitution – where there is no demand for domestic money from nonresidents – see Ramírez-Rojas (1985), Cuddington (1983), Wallace (1979), and Miles (1978). For more detailed treatment see Chapter 11.

ibility of the peso does not automatically enshrine it as an international store of value, unless convertibility is built on a solid foundation of reputation that would allow the peso to be treated as an international store of value.

This working hypothesis raises an important issue: How is currency substitution, which relates to financial flows, transmitted to the real economy?[12] Consider an equilibrium situation in which a bundle of resources produces T or N, measured such that one unit of each is worth \$1. Entrepreneurs should be indifferent between producing one unit of T or one of N. But since the soft currency may be devalued, it becomes risky for the Mexican entrepreneur to produce (or hold) one unit of N that could not be converted for later spending into \$1. Expressed in another way, entrepreneurs are attracted to producing T because that is the only way they can acquire \$1 they wish to hold for asset purposes. With the relative productivities of the bundle of resources (measured at "normal" prices) remaining unchanged, N becomes undervalued and resources are biased towards T. This is manifest in a relative price of N that is too low compared with productivities – or too high an RER.

This dilemma does not exist for the DC producer. In hard currency, \$1 of T will always be worth \$1 of N, as opposed to the soft currency, where the expectation of devaluation becomes a self-fulfilling prophecy. Controlling for the other determinants of devaluation in LDCs, the process alone of converting soft currency into hard for asset-holding purposes tends to make the market-clearing NER too high. This is manifest in a relative price of tradables that is too high compared with productivities – again too high an RER.

The essence of the hypothesis is that distortions inherent in free currency markets lead LDCs systematically to misallocate resources. Under these circumstances, policies that would reduce the RER would lead to a better allocation of resources.

A high RER is the manifestation of such resource misallocation. The misallocation is not triggered by differentials in marginal productivities, which, ex hypothesi, have remained constant. It is triggered by the expectation of devaluation of the soft currency, which depresses the price of N. Imposing contraction on the economy may contain expectations but it is likely to further decrease the price of N and thus fail to restore equilibrium. Supply-side policies that tend to decrease the price of T by increasing efficiency in production are more promising for restoring equilibrium. At the least, they may contribute to redressing the competitive-devaluation trade and to restoring comparative-advantage trade. The trigger for the resource misallocation is in the financial sector. One set of policies in that sector that would reduce the RER is intervention in the foreign exchange market to reduce the NER by rationing or protection. Appreciation of the foreign exchange rate will be reflected in lower prices of T.

12 I am indebted to Alan Winters for this formulation of the hypothesis.

The policy implications of the asset–value dynamics hypothesis are far-reaching for issues of intervention and for the sequence of liberalization in LDCs. The prevalent opinion on the latter is that liberalization in the foreign account has to wait until the financial sector has been stabilized (McKinnon, 1991). Domestic inflation causes flight to foreign currencies and thus creates pressures on the foreign exchange market that can best be handled by rationing. The present argument, however, extends this reasoning to apply beyond domestic stable and unstable currencies to international hard and soft currencies. As long as an LDC has a soft currency, the same motive of portfolio diversification will lead to capital flight and pressures on the foreign exchange whether inflation in the domestic sector has been tamed or not. Moreover, it is not simply the instability in the financial sector that makes government intervention in the foreign exchange market warranted, nor is it gratuitous meddling by the government that makes the currencies of LDCs nonconvertible. Both are symptoms, whereas the underlying cause of market incompleteness is the existence of reputation effects that create an asymmetry between hard and soft currencies for store-of-value considerations. The policy implication of this diagnosis is that the foreign exchange and trade markets should be the very last in the sequence of liberalization. Liberalization there may have to wait until a country's currency has become "hard" in the international arena. This is not achieved through premature convertibility. It is, rather, a matter of economic fundamentals and the outcome of self-sustained development.

This hypothesis will be further advanced in the subsequent chapters and it will be empirically tested in Chapter 7. It is revisited in Chapter 11, which juxtaposes the mechanisms and the outcomes of financial integration in Taiwan and Uruguay.

Pitfalls and pay-offs of intervention in incomplete markets

Government intervention provides opportunities for government failure. Consider the "tragedy of the commons" that Hardin (1968) described. In a communal pasture a utility-maximizing herdsman is driven to add as many cattle to his herd as the commons will bear. Overgrazing in this case is the result of a missing market – lack of property rights. Defining property rights will eliminate the problems of free-riders and moral hazard. Distributing these rights, however, becomes another problem, since the poorest among the shepherds will be unable to buy the land rights and land will be concentrated in the hands of the wealthy. On the other hand, if the government gives the land away or sells it below its market value to a targeted population, it encourages rent-seeking behavior with several adverse effects. To begin with, incentives are created for nonbeneficiaries to lobby or to bribe government officials to obtain the land. The size of these incentives (and of the rents captured by government officials) will be related to the amount by which the land is undervalued. In addition, as population grows or more people become landless, the government will be pressured to continue giving land away. Temporary and one-time solutions to problems have a tendency of becoming permanent if they convey rents to a powerful and vocal group. Finally, land rights alone will not solve the problem in the absence of enforcement of both private and public rights on land (Nabli and Nugent, 1989).

The issue of incentive compatibility has been formalized in the public-choice theory that deals with the interaction of various interest groups (Buchanan, 1986). Its focus has been sharpened for the case of trade and development in the literature on directly unproductive profit-seeking activities (Bhagwati, 1982; Rowley, Tollison, and Tullock, 1988) and of rent-seeking activities (Krueger, 1974). Markets, as well as political coalitions, are moved by self-interest and place constraints on what can be achieved by governments. Such constraints disrupt the neat quantity-closure schemes of government intervention. Commodities are resold in the black market, interest-group action affects the structure of protection through tariffs and quotas, and government officials in charge of rationing can curry favor (Stern, 1989, p. 618).

A truncated discussion of the rent-seeking consequences of intervention – as the present discussion must by necessity be – runs the risk of totally missing some salutary effects that can be associated with overriding certain markets. Figure 3.3 shows quantity closure in the foreign exchange market at the overvalued rate P_Q. The issue of rent-seeking relates to the decision of who gets the rationed quantity of foreign exchange, OQ, and at what price in the range between P_Q and P_R. It may help appreciate the qualitative aspects of government intervention if one considers the two extreme ways to approach the issue.

Quantity rationing can be represented as overriding the supply curve. With supply SS' there are three possibilities, or combinations thereof, for allocating quantity OQ: foreign exchange can become available at price P_Q and up to quantity OQ to any demanders, however chosen; the government auctions the rationed foreign exchange at price P_R; the price is still P_Q but venal bureaucrats impose transaction costs (in terms of bribes or reciprocation) of $P_Q P_R$. In either case, the issue becomes who captures the economic rents of rationing. Rent-seeking is commonly viewed as a zero- or negative-sum game. As a result, the game is formulated as trying to increase an interest group's share in a fixed stock of wealth at the expense of another group.

Quantity rationing can also be represented as overriding the demand curve. It amounts to a shift in the demand, $D'D'$, by imposing a consistent criterion that disqualifies certain claimants of foreign exchange. This makes sense if economic rents are viewed within a positive-sum-game framework, with the benefits in the long run accruing both to the interest group that obtained the foreign exchange at price P_Q and to the economy at large. Consider the case that the

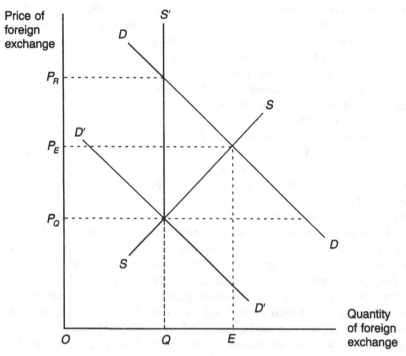

Figure 3.3. *Alternative quantity-closure outcomes*

foreign exchange is made available at the overvalued rate to an infant industry on the condition that it is used to import (cheap) raw materials and intermediate products. The economic rent of the foreign exchange subsidy could even make up for the price subsidy that the infant industry normally requires. This amounts to shifting the cost of protection from the public at large to the other claimants of foreign exchange, say the importers of consumption goods, and to the classes that demand such imports. For success, this requires that the infant industry takes advantage of the subsidy to reach its threshold level of economies of scale and becomes self-supporting. If this happens, the final outcome of overriding the foreign exchange market is to achieve *dynamic* economies of scale for the specific industry and positive-sum games for the economy in the long run.

The difference between the two cases described, overriding the supply curve and shifting the demand curve, turns on who captures the economic rents of intervention and for what purpose. One extreme solution is that a ruling elite captures the rents and they end up in bank accounts in Miami or Zurich or in financing imposing schemes of import-substitution-industrialization that cater to the needs of the middle-income classes and of the wealthy. The other extreme alternative is that an honest and benevolent government collects the economic rents and reinvests them in economic development (Wade, 1990). The real world, of course, is somewhere in between the two extremes: not all economic rents captured by individuals are wasted and not all governments are competent and honest. This is where the attributes of competence and integrity in government become important qualifiers for the success or failure of economic development.

The need for integrity in government is obvious. Integrity provides the guarantee that the economic rents of intervention are not subverted into private gains, whether directly or indirectly, as was described in the case of overriding the supply curve. Competence is necessary because intervention should not be wanton. It should only apply in cases of market failure or when markets are incomplete. It should also be focused on achieving dynamic comparative advantage down the road and on devolving positive-sum games. Moreover, a competent bureaucracy is necessary because intervention breeds intervention and eventually becomes very hard to manage. In the example just cited, intervention in the foreign exchange market was coupled with intervention in the import market by targeting foreign exchange exclusively to imports of raw materials and intermediate products. An overvalued foreign exchange makes exports expensive, thus requiring subsidies, which were delivered in the case discussed through the import subsidy to raw materials and intermediate inputs. Appropriate intervention, therefore, implies that growth-policy packages are put into place.

Both components together, competence and integrity, constitute good governance, which is a necessary condition for successful intervention. In fact Reynolds (1985) goes as far as reducing the grand themes of development to the role that governments have played. This may be ambiguous and a trifle tautological. At the conceptual level, however, and ex post, the existence of good governance is evidenced in economic development outcomes that spread the benefits of growth broadly among the population. The operational discriminant of good governance becomes pluralistic economic development, or the shared-benefits approach, that results in economic empowerment of broad social and economic classes among the population (World Bank, 1993a). Why should the quality of development outcomes be judged on development participation grounds? One standard approach is the humanitarian concern of development that requires a minimum safety net in support of the poorest of the poor. This is not the motivation for pluralistic economic development as used in the context of this book. More important is that the broad spread of economic development among the population creates effective domestic demand, which in turn becomes the engine of growth (Murphy et al., 1989a,b; Eswaren and Kotwal 1993). This is a Keynesian proposition that was predated by Henry

Ford's insight: it is smart to pay employees enough to enable them to purchase the products they produce.

This interpretation of the economic rents of intervention is not at great variance with the rent-seeking version of collective-action theory. If the government lacks competence and integrity, the second-best approach is to allow price closure to destroy the economic rents. However, in a world where not all political systems are corrupt and not all governments are incompetent, successful intervention in incomplete markets can lead to improved development outcomes.

Conclusion

The conclusion to the previous chapter highlighted Arrow's (1974) observation that the persistence of inequality among countries in the era of modern economic development provides a challenge for the neoclassical paradigm to explain. The partial, and ad hoc, explanation of the structuralist economists was sketched in Chapter 2.

Arrow provides his own explanation for the observed nonconvergence in per capita incomes around the world: there exist differences in the production possibility sets of different countries. This reduces the issue to imperfect information, since differences in production possibility sets say something about the transmission of knowledge across countries. Thus a thriving literature was launched in the field of the new development economics that goes under the name of endogenous growth. As the review in Chapter 7 indicates, the theoretical and empirical focus of endogenous growth has so far been the violation of the restrictions imposed in the static version of the fundamental theorems of welfare economics, most notably increasing returns and the economies of agglomeration.

This chapter sets the stage for developing a second branch of the endogenous growth approach. It starts from the dynamic version of the fundamental theorems of welfare economics that requires a complete set of markets – markets that span time, space, and uncertainty. Market incompleteness, rather than economies of scale, provides the rationale for intervention in the credit market for example. Moral hazard and adverse selection of risk arise in credit markets because of specific information constraints. Information, therefore, has been generally treated as the cause of market incompleteness in the new development economics. This chapter extends the specification by admitting reputation as an additional cause of market incompleteness. The theoretical and empirical work in the next section builds on this foundation to focus on one market that is especially incomplete and has so far eluded the attention of development economists and of trade specialists: the foreign exchange market.

Two of the factors that account for this incompleteness were introduced in this chapter. The nonseparation between tradables and nontradables is a special characteristic of LDCs. Moreover, as the discussion of the Ricardo Principle suggested, and as the empirical analysis in Chapter 6 will confirm, there is a systematic relationship between the prices of tradables and nontradables in the process of development. This introduces a systematic component in the devolution of the real exchange rate as development occurs: it tends to appreciate. In the interim, and in the stage of underdevelopment, the low productivity in tradables tends to be compensated by high NER that makes inefficient production profitable and draws resources away from the nontradable sector. This introduces a trade bias that accounts for misallocation of resources.

The second factor that enters exchange rate incompleteness is related to the distinction between hard and soft currencies, and the tendency of the latter to be chronically undervalued in a regime of free exchange rates with an open capital account. The origins of this tendency lie in basic asset–value dynamics considerations. They suggest that there is an asymmetry between a hard and a soft (LDC) currency, since the former will be used broadly as a store of value in an open economy while the latter most likely will not. Reputation failure in this case – as opposed to information failure in the more familiar cases in the literature – becomes the antecedent of market incompleteness. Reputation can also be considered as systematically related to the level of development. As development occurs, reputation accrues and the soft currency of an LDC ratchets up the continuum towards hard currency.

The thesis is that in an open economy LDC, there is a *systematic incompleteness* in the foreign exchange market. It is manifested in a resource allocation under an equilibrium NER that differs from that under an equilibrium RER; the former allocation is systematically biased toward tradables. Moreover, the divergence in the two outcomes, and the degree of resource misallocation, decreases as development proceeds.

The succeeding chapters supply the theoretical scaffolding for this hypothesis, which is tested specifically in Chapter 7 within the endogenous growth framework. The policy implication of the hypothesis is that quantity, as opposed to price closure, applies in the foreign exchange market in LDCs. Rationing of foreign exchange, in turn, necessitates intervention in the trade market as well. The proactive role that systematic market incompleteness prescribes in LDCs makes good governance, with its two components of competence and integrity, an important precondition for successful economic development. As development progresses, on the other hand, and the market infrastructure is being put into place, the proper role of government gradually withers away, and the paradigm of free-market, free-trade, laissez-faire capitalism again becomes appropriate.

Appendix: The Ricardo Principle[13]

In considering the implications of Ricardo's productivity differentials we should show that: (a) the relative price of nontradables in terms of tradables is higher in DCs (static); (b) the relative price of tradables in terms of nontradables decreases with development (dynamic, first order). Moreover, from the empirical investigation (Chapter 5), we should show that (c) the relative price of tradables in terms of nontradables decreases faster in LDCs than in DCs (dynamic, second order).

We rewrite equations (3.1) and ff., derived from Cobb-Douglas functions, as:

Tradables	Nontradables	
$\bar{P}_T \alpha^D Y_T^D = w^D$	$P_N^D \beta^D Y_N^D = w^D$	Developed country
$\bar{P}_T \alpha^L Y_T^L = w^L$	$P_N^L \beta^L Y_N^D = w^L$	Less-developed country

where,

α^D, α^L = share of labor force in T sector in DC and LDC, respectively;
β^D, β^L = share of labor force in N sector in DC and LDC, respectively;
Y_T^D, Y_T^L = productivity of labor in T sector in DC and LDC, respectively;
Y_N^D, Y_N^L = productivity of labor in N sector in DC and LDC, respectively;

We assume the following relations:

$P_T^D = P_T^L = \bar{P}$, because of the law of one price;
$P_N^D \neq P_N^L$, because in N sector the law of one price does not operate;
$\alpha^D + \beta^D = 1$, $\alpha^L + \beta^L = 1$ and $\alpha^D > \alpha^L$, $\beta^D > \beta^L$;
$Y_T^D > Y_T^L$, $Y_N^D > Y_N^L$, $(Y_T^D - Y_T^L) > (Y_N^D - Y_N^L)$.

(a) *Ricardo static*

$$\frac{P_N^D}{\bar{P}} > \frac{P_N^L}{\bar{P}} \tag{A3.1}$$

From equations (3.1) and ff., we know that the price level in a given sector of a given country is $P = w/kY$, where k is the labor share of the sector in the economy of the country. Then, substituting this latter relation into (A3.1), we obtain:

$$\frac{w^D/\beta^D Y_N^D}{w^D/\alpha^D Y_T^D} > \frac{w^L/\beta^L Y_N^L}{w^L/\alpha^L Y_T^L}$$

13 I am indebted to Donato Romano for the prooofs in this appendix.

and thus

$$\frac{\alpha^D Y_T^D}{\beta^D Y_N^D} > \frac{\alpha^L Y_T^L}{\beta^L Y_N^L}$$

which is always satisfied, provided the assumptions we made earlier about the relative magnitude of the shares of labor and the productivity of labor in each sector in each country hold. Note that we implicitly assumed the same wage rate for both sectors within each country; of course, $w^D \neq w^L$.

(b) *Ricardo dynamic, first order*

We can rewrite equation (A3.1) as

$$\frac{\bar{P}}{P_N^D} < \frac{\bar{P}}{P_N^L} \tag{A3.2}$$

(c) *Ricardo dynamic, second order*

We will show that

$$\ln\left(\frac{\bar{P}}{P_N^L}\right) \geq \ln\left(\frac{\bar{P}}{P_N^D}\right) \tag{A3.3}$$

This implies

$$\ln\left(\frac{\beta^L Y_N^L}{\alpha^L Y_T^L}\right) \geq \ln\left(\frac{\beta^D Y_N^D}{\alpha^D Y_T^D}\right)$$

Considering $\alpha^L = 1 - \beta^L$, $\alpha^D = 1 - \beta^D$ we have

$$\ln\left(\frac{\beta^L Y_N^L}{(1 - \beta^L)Y_T^L}\right) \geq \ln\left(\frac{\beta^D Y_N^D}{(1 - \beta^D)Y_T^D}\right)$$

Rearranging terms,

$$\ln\left(\frac{Y_T^D}{Y_T^L}\right) - \ln\left(\frac{Y_N^D}{Y_N^L}\right) \geq \ln\left(\frac{\beta^D}{1 - \beta^D}\right) - \ln\left(\frac{\beta^L}{1 - \beta^L}\right)$$

or

$$\ln\left(\frac{Y_T^D}{Y_T^L}\right) - \ln\left(\frac{Y_N^D}{Y_N^L}\right) \geq \ln\left(\frac{\beta^D(1 - \beta^L)}{\beta^L(1 - \beta^D)}\right) \tag{A3.4}$$

For the left-hand side, and from the assumption $(Y_T^D - Y_T^L) > (Y_N^D - Y_N^L)$ we have

$$\ln\left(\frac{Y_T^D}{Y_T^L}\right) - \ln\left(\frac{Y_N^D}{Y_N^L}\right) = \ln\left(\frac{Y_T^D Y_N^L}{Y_T^L Y_N^D}\right) > 0$$

For the right-hand side, and from the assumption $\beta^D < \beta^L$, $\alpha^D < \alpha^L \leftrightarrow 1 - \beta^D > 1 - \beta^L$ we have

$$\ln\left(\frac{\beta^D(1 - \beta^L)}{\beta^L(1 - \beta^D)}\right) < 0$$

Therefore, (A3.4) is always satisfied under these assumptions and (A3.3) is verified.

PART II

Theory and empirical analysis

CHAPTER 4

Market incompleteness in
an open-economy LDC

Conventional trade theory has generally credited free-market, free-trade, lais-sez-faire capitalism with producing equilibrium, market-clearing prices and leading to Pareto optimality. An economy is considered efficient in production if the supply of any good (or service) cannot be increased without reducing the supply of another good. The last qualification about decreasing the supply of another good has to be interpreted broadly in an open economy, since trade is considered an indirect form of production: a certain good whose supply was decreased for producing another can now become available by exchanging exports for it. The point of operation in this trade-extended production possi-bility frontier is determined by the relative border prices of exports and imports. Border prices, therefore, determine the opportunity cost of a good and of the resources used to produce it, if the alternative of using a good were to export it. Similarly, scarcity values measure what the good is worth to the economy, which can be calculated from the production possibility frontier (PPF) by the value of the additional exports a good could be turned into. Opportunity costs are equated with scarcity values for production efficiency. Border prices, there-fore, represent efficiency prices, and no need for shadow-pricing of inputs or outputs arises.

The above describes fully the conventional textbook approach to interna-tional trade where the commodity produced, and exports and imports, are considered a Hicksian composite good of all commodities that enter consump-tion and trade in the economy. Such a situation is shown in Figure 4.1a (on page 70), where the axes of the PPF represent goods N and T. The economy produces at B and consumes at A^1, which represents a definite Pareto improvement.

We can improve on the real-world relevance of this model by distinguishing two sectors, one producing commodities that are tradable, in the sense that they could be imported and exported, and the other nontradable. The reasoning above that considers border prices as efficiency prices still holds for the trad-ables (Little and Mirrlees, 1974, Chapter 12). For nontradable goods (such as domestic transport, construction, or electricity) the case in the shadow-pricing, benefit–cost literature is less clear-cut. Their social marginal cost of production can be evaluated at shadow prices, which are not always fully transparent, or it can again be referenced indirectly to border prices through the substitutability of inputs in the process of production of tradables and nontradables, and the substitutability of tradable and nontradable outputs in the consumption basket. Frenkel and Johnson (1976, pp. 27–28), for instance, observe that first, factors used in producing nontradables are still potentially tradable ("in the sense that in the relevant run of time a barber has the alternative of being a machine tool operator producing machinery or consumers' durables for import substitution") and their opportunity cost in producing tradables is reflected in the factor prices and through these in the prices of nontradables. Second, even if there is no factor–price link, the prices of tradables still adjust to those of nontradables ". . . through tastes, supply conditions and the overall budget restraint." On these grounds, the authors feel they are justified in considering the deviation of prices of tradables from nontradables "a transient feature of the adjustment process," and therefore ". . . the abstraction of the main core of the analysis from the existence of nontradable goods is of secondary matter." This is the standard argument of separation in the process of production and consumption. Still, Frenkel and Johnson carefully modify it in their conclusions:

> The existence of nontraded goods does, however, become relevant in the empirical application of the theory, in both the static case when price indexes may differ from the prediction of simple purchasing power parity theory, . . . and the dynamic case of growth of productivity at different rates in the traded and nontraded sectors, which implies different price trends in the two sectors when factor mobility equalizes factor prices between them (Frenkel and Johnson, 1976, p. 28).

This chapter presents a formal welfare maximization model that incorporates the distinction between tradables and nontradables. It is a standard model, known in the literature as Australian.[1] The only modification that will be introduced refers to the determination of the real exchange rate which in the parent model is endogenous. It will be, instead, a parametric exogenous variable in this analysis to reflect the considerations of market incompleteness that were introduced in the previous chapter. When this distinction is drawn, the analysis that follows will be termed "quasi-Australian."

A welfare model with tradables and nontradables

The closed economy

The simplest diagrammatic representation of an Australian model can build on a standard production function where labor, L, is the only factor of production and produces either tradables, T, or nontradables, N, at constant returns to scale and with fixed coefficients. Capital, K, is the sector-specific fixed input in the production function. We write the production function

---

1 The model is an adaptation of the Dornbusch (1980, pp. 100–108) dependent-economy model that applies to a small LDC that is a price-taker in international trade. For a nondiagrammatic treatment of the Australian model see Corden (1977).

$$Q_i = Q_i(L_i; K), \ i = T, N \tag{4.1}$$

where Q_i is the sector-specific output.

We assume that the economy is at its potential output level, i.e., wages are flexible to clear the labor market. We write the demand of labor in each sector in terms of product–wage and the sector-specific capital, and in equilibrium they sum to full employment,

$$L_T(W/P_T; K) + L_N(W/P_N; K) = L \tag{4.2}$$

where W is the annual wage rate, P_T and P_N are the prices of tradables and nontradables, respectively, and L the full-employment sum of labor demands.

Under full employment, we can solve for the equilibrium wage rate $\bar{W}$, as a function of output prices and capital,

$$\bar{W} = W(P_N, P_T; K) \tag{4.3}$$

Similarly, output can be expressed in value terms, Y, using the price of N as the numeraire,

$$Q_N(L_N; K) + vQ_T(L_T; K) = Y \tag{4.4}$$

where $v = P_T/P_N$, and Y is in real terms (i.e., Y/P_N).

We have thus expressed full-employment output in each sector in terms of relative prices. The relative price of tradables in terms of nontradables, v, is defined as the real exchange rate; and a rise in v, the relative price of tradables, is defined as devaluation. Such a rise in v, from equation (4.2), lowers the equilibrium relative wage in terms of tradables and raises the real wage in terms of nontradables. Similarly, from equation (4.4), output of tradables is an increasing function of v, while output of nontradables is decreasing in v. The PPF is well-behaved and is expressed in terms of nontradables as

$$vQ_T = F(Y - Q_N) \tag{4.5}$$

The consumption decisions are made by price-taking consumers in a utility-maximization framework. Therefore, the demand functions for output, D_i, depend on the real exchange rate and real expenditure, E:

$$D_T = D_T(v, E); \qquad D_N = D_N(v, E) \tag{4.6}$$

By analogy to income in equation (4.4), real expenditure is measured in terms of P_N,

$$E = D_N + vD_T \tag{4.7}$$

Given real expenditure, a rise in v reduces the demand for tradables in (4.6), due to the operation of both the income and the substitution effect. By the same token, an increase in the relative price of tradables increases the demand for nontradables as a result of the substitution effect, while the income effect is probably negative. In any event, the usual assumption is that the substitution effect dominates the income effect. Thus we write for nontradables, as in equation (4.7a):

$$\left.\frac{dD_T}{dv}\right|_{(dE/E)=0} < 0; \qquad \left.\frac{dD_N}{dv}\right|_{(dE/E)=0} > 0; \tag{4.7a}$$

Equations (4.1)–(4.7) are sufficient to describe the equilibrium in the closed economy. Equilibrium implies that the sectoral markets for output clear:

$$D_N = Y_N; \qquad D_T = Y_T \tag{4.8}$$

The open economy

The conventional approach to international trade is shown in Figure 4.1a, with commodities N and T along the axes representing Hicksian composite goods that are aggregates of goods produced, both importables and exportables. The implicit assumption is that the terms of trade between imports and exports remain constant. Structuralist approaches to international trade, which assume different elasticities between exports and imports, are cast in terms of two commodities. They have played an important role in the "elasticity approach" to exchange rate determination.[2]

This chapter introduces yet another approach to the open economy. An Australian model distinguishes two commodities, tradables and nontradables, with constrained possibilities of substitution in the process of production and consumption. In the conventional model, equilibrium prices arise independently in the process of producers' maximizing profits and consumers' maximizing welfare. This is the condition of separation in production and consumption. Nonseparation characterizes the Australian model. While excess demand for tradables can be satisfied if international borrowing is allowed, excess demand for nontradables is not feasible. Consumers, therefore, cannot maximize their welfare by simply considering their budget constraints and the relative prices. They need to take into account the producers' decisions also. There is no separation between production and consumption decisions if: (1) there is no possibility of international borrowing (i.e., if there is a foreign exchange constraint); or (2) the supply of nontradables becomes binding. As a result, an Australian model admits two causes of imbalance in the trade account: imbalance between income and expenditure, or a disequilibrium in the nontradable goods market.

From the basic national income accounting equations (4.4) and (4.7), consider a disequilibrium in income and expenditure:

2 See Chapter 2.

$$Y - E = v(Q_T - D_T) + (Q_N - D_N) \tag{4.9}$$

An excess of income over expenditure is equal to excess supply (or shortage in demand) of either tradables and/or nontradables. Tradables alone, however, enter the foreign balance:

$$v(Q_T - D_T) = (D_N - Q_N) + (Y - E) \tag{4.10}$$

Equation (4.10) indicates that an unbalanced trade account is the result of either an imbalance in income and expenditure, or alternatively, a disequilibrium in the nontradable goods market. We analyze the two components separately.

Suppose equation (4.10) shows a balance-of-payments disequilibrium in the sense that there is an excess demand for tradables in the left-hand side. It is the outcome of imports exceeding exports and it results in a current-account deficit.[3] Assuming for the moment that there is equilibrium in the market for nontradables, i.e., demand equals supply, then there must be aggregate excess demand in the economy when one considers tradables and nontradables together. Demand is generated by expenditure, which therefore must be greater than income in the right-hand side of equation (4.10). Another way to express the same inequality is that *absorption* of resources in producing consumption and investment goods, or total expenditure, is greater than income.

At first blush, the obvious remedy for external disequilibrium is found in its inception. Reducing absorption (*disabsorption*), by employing monetary or fiscal policies, will reduce the demand for imports, decrease the excess demand for tradables, and help restore the current-account balance. The unfortunate aspect is that it will also reduce the demand for nontradables, thus creating unemployment in the resources producing them and an internal imbalance. The message is simple: If it is necessary to achieve two targets, external and internal balance, disabsorption is not sufficient; two instruments are required.

The *switching* instrument is based on the real exchange rate, v. By raising the price of tradables relative to nontradables, patterns of production and absorption are switched. On the production side, resources will move out of nontradables and into tradables. This will relieve the foreign-account imbalance by making more tradables available for export or import substitution; it will also improve the imbalance in notradables by shedding the excess supply that would have led to unemployment. These effects are further reinforced by the operation of the demand side. The decrease in demand for tradables works along with the increased supply to restore foreign balance. The substitution effect increases the demand for nontradables thus offsetting, by assumption, the income effect that initially led to a decrease in demand.

---

3 Movements of capital and liquidation of foreign exchange reserves will be ignored in this presentation.

The discussion of equation (4.10) so far has implicitly incorporated the assumption that v is strictly an endogenous variable. If this assumption is dropped, then the market for nontradable goods could clear at a level that imposes undue contraction in the economy. This will reflect both on the long-run external equilibrium in which the trade account balance is equal to zero, and on the short-run external equilibrium in which the trade surplus/deficit is equal to the difference between income and expenditure. This modification makes the standard model quasi-Australian.

In which sense is v a parametric exogenous variable in the system? In the equilibrium of the closed economy, v is indeed determined endogenously in the markets of tradables and nontradables. In the open economy, however, an LDC is assumed to be a price-taker in tradables, the price of which is given in foreign exchange. The foreign exchange rate, which translates tradable prices into domestic currency, is certainly not determined endogenously in the market of tradables and nontradables. It is more often a policy control instrument. When it is determined in a general equilibrium system, it reflects long-run balance-of-payments considerations, as opposed to strictly long-run trade account balance considerations. As the discussion of asset–value dynamics in the previous chapter indicated, even in the short-run, external equilibrium requirements reflect not only the trade account balance but also portfolio investment and especially the precautionary demand for foreign exchange by savers in LDCs who wish to diversify their portfolia by including hard currency. This latter demand is not matched by savers in the hard currency trading partner countries who do not hold the soft currency as a store of value.

The determination of v is the crucial assumption that distinguishes this model from the standard Australian model where v is endogenously determined and, as a result, any disequilibrium in the three accounts above is only transitory. In a quasi-Australian model, on the other hand, v is neither a strictly endogenous variable, nor a policy control instrument assigned exogenously. The policy control instrument is the nominal exchange rate, which is transmitted to v through its immediate impact on the price of tradables. If the nominal exchange rate, for whatever reason, tends to become too high, then the real exchange rate can overshoot its equilibrium value and become undervalued (Chapter 3). In this event, market clearing in the tradable sector will induce excessive contraction in the economy.

Diagrammatics

The model presented in the basic equations of the previous sections can be expressed in terms of the familiar Salter–Swan diagrams of international trade.[4]

4 The origins of the reference are in Salter (1959).

The conditions for nonseparation become clear in the diagrams. In the process it is also demonstrated that a devaluation that proposes to create a surplus in the balance of payments – and thus to restore external balance under certain circumstances familiar in the case of overindebted LDCs – involves a real cost in terms of lower levels of welfare. The implication of the model is that certain alternatives to devaluation, such as nonprice closure in the foreign account with control of imports and subsidy to exports, can achieve the same purpose of surplus in the trade account at a lower GDP cost.

The PPF of equation (4.5) is shown in Figure 4.1a, with the axes indicating tradables T and nontradables N (as opposed to commodities Y and X in the classical interpretation). The relative price of T in terms of N, v, is given by the inverse of the slope of the frontier and clearly depends on the composition of output between T and N.[5] An increase in P_T shifts the tangency to the left showing the substitution effect in the production of N. The situation is shown in Figure 4.1a by going from point A^0 to B as a result of a price shift from v^0 to v^1. The shift represents a devaluation, defined as an increase in P_T/P_N, and shown by the increase in the slope of the tangent, N/T.

Point A^0 in Figure 4.1a lies on the tangency between the PPF and the utility curve[6] and is an equilibrium point in the sense that the production and consumption of T are equal and the same stands true for N, i.e., the markets for tradables and nontradables clear. We thus have two concepts of equilibrium. Once this commodity equilibrium holds, an equilibrium in the external account is also implied (net balance of trade is equal to zero). This is a third equilibrium concept. Finally, a fourth concept of equilibrium is that income, Y, is equal to expenditure, E. This also is satisfied at point A^0, as well as at any other point that lies on the price line that goes through A^0, and thus produces a combination of T and N that is equivalent to expenditure at A^0. The latter two equilibrium concepts are described by equation (4.10).

In Figure 4.1b the price of tradables relative to nontradables, v_0, corresponds to that of Figure 4.1a. Following Dornbusch (1975, 1980), the horizontal axis of Figure 4.1b presents real expenditure and income in terms of nontradables.[7] All equilibrium concepts already mentioned – namely, the markets for N and T clear and income is equal to expenditure, $Y = E$, along with equilibrium in the balance of payments, i.e., zero trade surplus or deficit – can be shown in Figure 4.1b by point a^0. The income curve, YY, goes through a^0 and is upward sloping. Figure 4.1a suggests that an increase in the relative price of tradables

5 In Figure 4.1a, v is drawn by solving equation (4.5) for Q_T, i.e., $Q_T = (1/v)(Y - Q_N)$
6 For simplicity, we have drawn a homothetic utility function and as a result all points of tangency between the indifference curves and the given price line must lie on a linear expansion path through the origin.
7 For a detailed exposition of the diagrammatic argument see Binkert (1992).

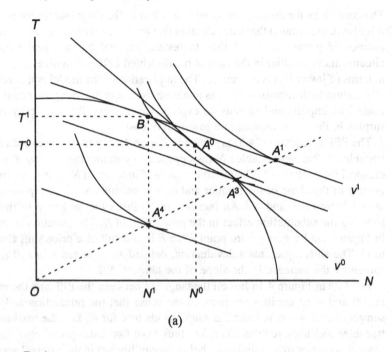

(a)

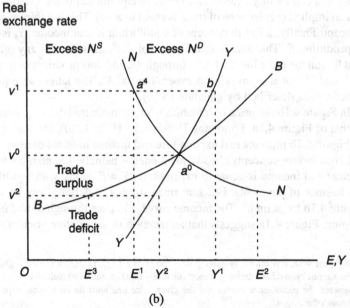

(b)

Figure 4.1. *Internal and external balance in the dependent-economy model*

(a tangency to the left of A^0 in Figure 4.1a) will yield an increase in output measured in terms of N, as shown by the extension of v^1 intersecting the N axis to the right of the extension of v^0. The relationship is described by equation (4.5). The line YY, therefore, in Figure 4.1b has an upward slope. An increase in the price of tradables, v, also reduces demand and increases supply for T and causes therefore a trade surplus, as shown in equation (4.10). Restoring external balance, i.e., elimination of the trade surplus, requires increased spending on T, which is shown in greater levels of E and Y on the horizontal axis of Figure 4.1b. Thus, the external balance curve BB also is positively sloped. Points that lie above the line BB represent a trade surplus, whereas those below represent a trade deficit. A decrease in the price of tradables, v, implies that the market of N clears at higher expenditure levels, as shown in equations (4.5) and (4.6). The schedule of NN is, therefore, downward sloping. Points to the left of NN represent excess supply of nontradables, while those to the right represent excess demand.

Figures 4.1a and 4.1b can be used to study the meaning of disequilibrium. Figure 4.1a is familiar from the classical model of international trade, in which the axes correspond to Hicksian composite goods, say Y and X, instead of T and N. In that model, autarky at A^0 with the real exchange rate at v^0 is compared with devaluation to v^1 that increases trade and leads to a new tangency at a higher indifference curve, A^1. The welfare gains of trade are shown by comparing the two indifference curves through A^0 and A^1.

Point A^1 is not feasible in a tradable–nontradable model since it violates the N-constraint, as shown in Figure 4.1b. At real exchange rate v^1 point b shows income at Y^1 but point a^4 corresponds to equilibrium expenditure on non-tradables at E^1. At that level of spending there is excess demand for non-tradables and a trade surplus, the latter being equal to $Y^1 - E^1$ (or a^4b).

Expenditure at E^1 plus the trade surplus could have still constituted income–expenditure equilibrium in the conventional analysis, since the proceeds from tradables could have been used to fund increased expenditure on N. This is the meaning of separation. Given the PPF and prices, producers maximize profits by setting income at point B, while consumers maximize utility independently by setting expenditure at point A^1 (Figure 4.1a). In an Australian model, nonseparation renders excess demand for nontradables meaningless within a general equilibrium framework. One way the nontradable constraint can be satisfied is through disabsorption: an austerity policy could shift the YY schedule to the left so that income equals expenditure at E^1, thus safeguarding the trade surplus. Failing that, the price of nontradables will tend to increase to restore equilibrium at v^0.

The reverse situation can be illustrated at real exchange rate v^2. Assume that a country cannot borrow abroad anymore and thus cannot run a trade deficit. The maximum expenditure consistent with a trade balance is E^3, although potential output on the *YY* schedule is Y^2. At E^3 (and at Y^2) there is excess supply of nontradables. If the trade deficit could have been funded with nontradables, the situation would have been more tenable. This is the crucial assumption that underlies the argument of the "expansionary devaluations." An increase in the real exchange rate from v^2 to v^0 sets off the switching effect by drawing idle resources into tradables, thus decreasing the supply of nontradables. At v^0 income and expenditure are at equilibrium at a higher level – the well-known implication of the conventional model with separation.

The poor countries' Dutch disease

The Australian model has been used extensively to illustrate the Dutch disease of deindustrialization.[8] An exogenous shock leads to a surplus in the trade account and the real exchange rate, which is determined endogenously, appreciates. The result of the combination of the absorption and the switching effect is deindustrialization. The application of the Australian model in this chapter reverses this process. The shock is a persistent deficit in the balance of payments that leaves no room for further borrowing. Servicing the debt requires an exogenously determined surplus in the trade account. How is the real exchange rate set as a parametric exogenous variable, and what are the contractionary implications of this poor-man's version of the Dutch disease?

In Figure 4.2 we construct the constrained expenditure frontier. A price line v determines the output of nontradables on the PPF and this output must equal consumption. Since, with the price given, the ratio of tradable to nontradable consumption is fixed, we therefore know consumption of tradables also. Servicing the foreign debt requires that a particular gap is generated between production and consumption of tradables. For any point on the PPF, the size of the gap determines the feasible combinations of expenditure on tradables and nontradables. In Figure 4.2 the locus of such points lies below the income frontier (the PPF) by a constant vertical distance, $DC = FG = k$, which represents the quantity of tradables expressed in prices of nontradables.[9] By constructing such successive constrained-expenditure frontiers, we derive curve *OHCE* which describes the points at which the market for nontradables clears, given expenditure which is lower than the level of income (output). Each point as one moves from *E*, to *H*, and *O* relates to a progressively higher v (more-undervalued real exchange rate), a greater export surplus of tradables, and a market of nontradables that clears with greater contraction in the economy.

The constrained expenditure frontier has been drawn so that k represents the surplus in the balance of payments that is diverted away from domestic ex-

---

8 See Corden and Neary (1982) and Neary and van Wijnbergen (1986).
9 See also Appendix to this chapter.

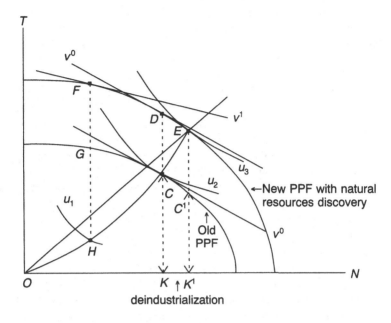

Figure 4.2. *A Dutch disease interpretation*

penditure, say for the purpose of servicing foreign debts. One can show that once the level of the desirable surplus, *CD*, has been exogenously determined, the appropriate real exchange rate is v^0, and any greater devaluation results in a lower level of welfare.[10] In the Australian model v^0 is the equilibrium real exchange rate, and it is endogenously determined. In a quasi-Australian model, however, a nominal exchange rate that is set exogenously too high (undervalued) can lead to overshooting of the real exchange rate, e.g., at v^1. In Chapter 3 the mechanism that yields too high a nominal exchange rate in LDCs was specified in terms of asset–value dynamics. As a result of the overshooting of

10 Curve *OHCE* is the locus of points at which the market for nontradables clears, given expenditure lower than the level of income by a multiple of a constant factor *k*. By construction, *FG* = *DC*, therefore, the amount of tradable surplus is the same. But point *C* lies on a higher indifference curve than point *G*, as can be proven graphically. By the preceding assumption, the vertical distance between *G* and *F* is equal to the vertical distance between points *C* and *D*. Now, the slope of the line v^0 is steeper than the slope of a line drawn between points *F* and *D* (or points *G* and *C*). Hence point *G* would always be below line v^0 going through point *C*. Now, pick a point on v^0 northeast of point *G*. Such a point must lie on a lower indifference curve than point *C* but at a higher welfare level than that generated by *G*. Hence *C* lies on a higher indifference curve than point *G*.

the nominal exchange rate, there is excess contraction of the economy as seen by comparing points F and H to D and C. There is also an excess surplus in the balance of payments, GH, which can be spent on tradables. The contraction, however, is not remedied, since the constraint is in the nontradable sector. A "growth policy package" that promotes the output of the nontradable sector can improve welfare, as the following section will discuss.

The Dutch disease interpretation can be shown in Figure 4.2 by considering point C on the constrained expenditure frontier as representing the equilibrium before the discovery of natural resources. The two sectors in the economy are the industrial, T, and the services, N. The third sector of the natural resources is not shown in the diagram. The discovery of oil has led to an inflow of foreign exchange that results in an outward shift of the frontier, and expenditure at point E.[11] Although point E is definitely welfare-improving, the level of manufacturing production (T-output in the figure) has declined from KC to K^1C^1. The appreciation of the real exchange rate at point E is associated with the deindustrialization. The antidote for the Dutch disease is imposing a lump-sum tax of an amount equal to the rent of the discovered natural resource. As long as the tax is not used to increase demand for N, the equilibrium is clearly characterized by C and D. Hence, both appreciation and deindustrialization can be avoided. Moreover, the proceeds of the tax and the surplus in the balance of payments can be used to further stimulate production of N by shifting the PPF outward.

The poor-man's version of the Dutch disease is clearly not symmetrical with its predecessor, since devaluation is inevitable, equilibrium is reached at a lower level of welfare, and no trade or budget surplus exists to finance expansion of the PPF. Stagnation sets in, instead of the avoidable deindustrialization.

Dynamics

So far we have examined only real exchange rate adjustment policies, more precisely the adjustment from v^0 to v^1 in Figures 4.1a and 4.1b, which leads to the increase in production of T and to a greater or lesser shortage of N. The shortage of N is introduced in the quasi-Australian model by dropping the assumption that v is identically both the real and the nominal exchange rate. This implies that internal equilibrium (on the Y schedule) is not simultaneously achieved with external equilibrium (on the B schedule) as a result of an adjustment in v that also clears the nontradable market (N schedule). The reason is that v is only one policy instrument, while two are needed to achieve three goals.

---

11 The implicit assumption in the diagram is that the discovery of oil does not cause the withdrawal of labor from the other two sectors.

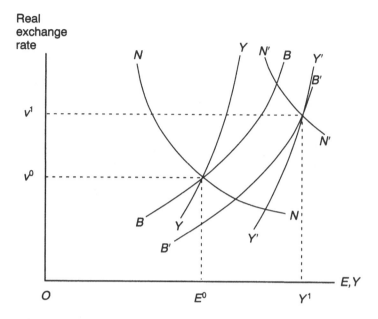

Figure 4.3. *Dynamics of internal and external balance*

Consider a two-instrument adjustment – devaluation with an industrial policy that promotes nontradable production. As a result of devaluation, income
(measured in terms of P_N) increases, since prices of nontradables decrease. It is
shown by the shift to $Y'Y'$ in Figure 4.3. Similarly, the $B'B'$ curve has shifted
as a result of the increase in the prices of tradables. Without an industrial policy
in the nontradable sector, and with the previous NN schedule, expenditure
remains at E_0 with the familiar shortage of N. The purpose of the industrial
policy is precisely to remedy this shortage by a shift to $N'N'$. The new equilibrium is at Y^1, where income is equal to expenditure.[12]

The intuition of the Ricardo Principle gives rise to other dynamic considerations that are introduced by modifying Figure 4.1. Suppose that LDCs are better
at producing nontradables than at producing tradables because of resource
endowments or productivity considerations. This can be shown by a flatter PPF
to the left of A^0 than the one shown in Figure 4.1a. The undervaluation of the
nominal exchange rate, the resulting overshooting of the real exchange rate, and

---

12 The purpose of the figure is to highlight the two equilibrium points, E_0 and Y_1. Since the
individual schedules show market-clearing situations, this shift does not occur sequentially, as
it was presented above for simplification.

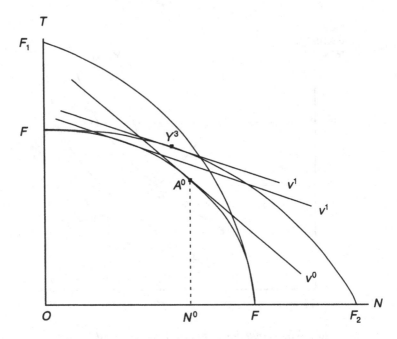

Figure 4.4. *Growth-policy packages in the dependent economy model*

the contraction imposed on the economy could then be more severe. Conversely, if productivity in the tradable sector increased, the effects of the incomplete market in foreign exchange that leads to the overshooting of the real exchange rate would be contained.

The dynamics of economic development imply that more T and/or N will be produced as the PPF shifts outward, say on account of spending foreign exchange on improving production capacity. Can "growth-package" interventions that involve the appropriate industrial policies lead to higher levels of welfare through nonhomothetic displacement in the PPF, such as T-biased extensions or N-biased extensions?[13] The counterpart of this proposition is that more growth could result from channeling foreign exchange receipts into production activities, as opposed to consumption.

Industrial policy can be neutral with respect to T and N, leading to a parallel displacement of the PPF, or else it can be oriented towards T, FF_1, or towards

13 This clearly implies an imperfection in the market with myopic consumers as opposed to a development-oriented government. Whatever the conceptual merits of this case, the fact that most countries engage in certain types of industrial policies makes it empirically attractive.

N, FF_2, as shown in Figure 4.4.[14] We can revert to Figure 4.3 to show the impact of an N-biased industrial policy, together with the real exchange rate devaluation to v^1. For any level of T chosen on the FF frontier, more N are now available on the FF_2 frontier. This means that income, expressed in terms of N, has now shifted to the right in Figure 4.3, to $Y'Y'$. The same industrial policy has affected the amount of T produced through its relationship with income, i.e., by lowering the import coefficient of T. $B'B'$, also shifts to the right, since for a given level of income $Y'Y'$, fewer T are needed to keep the trade account in balance. This is equivalent to a shift in domestic demand for T. The expansion of N on the FF_2 frontier also leads to higher income (and expenditure), expressed in terms of N. As the curves are drawn in Figure 4.3, at real exchange rate v^1 and income–expenditure at Y^1, a long-run sustainable equilibrium exists, since income equals expenditure, the trade account is in balance, and the N market clears. Moreover, this level of equilibrium is higher than the level that would have obtained if industrial policies had not contained the undue contraction that resulted from exchange rate overshooting.

The same analysis can be graphed to show how a long-run equilibrium can obtain that supports a real exchange rate lower than either v^0 or v^1. The combination of exchange rate policy and industrial policy opens up a new set of possibilities for the economy.

From nominal to real exchange rate: Is there an incomplete market?

We may now return to Figure 4.2 and the definition of v^0 as the real exchange rate, in the sense that it yields the targeted surplus of tradables $CD(= FG)$ with the least contraction of the economy and the greatest possible expenditure on nontradables, OK (as compared, say, to real exchange rate v^1). What are the chances that this equilibrium real exchange rate is overshot and a disequilibrium one obtains? It turns out this is the canonical situation in LDCs, as Chapter 7 will conclude.

The basic assumption of the Australian model is that the equilibrium of the real exchange rate is endogenously determined, or at least it can be set by policy interventions. In reality, however, the policy control variable is the nominal exchange rate. The modification, therefore, that the quasi-Australian model introduced makes the real exchange rate a parametric exogenous variable. Three scenaria can explain how a nominal exchange rate that is set at equilibrium is likely to result in an undervalued real exchange rate and a more severe contraction in the economy than is necessary.

---

14 A variety of industrial policies that can lead to such results are discussed in Chapters 9–11. For fixing ideas at this point it is sufficient to consider the simple device of limiting imports to raw materials and intermediate products that are targeted to the T or N production sectors, respectively.

First, setting the nominal exchange rate at its competitive equilibrium price does not guarantee that the real exchange rate will be at equilibrium also. The nominal exchange rate relates to the prices of tradables. At best, a nominal exchange rate devaluation is transmitted instantly to P_T and thus it is fully reflected in the real exchange rate devaluation. But simultaneously, the excess demand for nontradables would set in motion forces for increasing P_N and reversing the effects of devaluation. The rate at which devaluations decay becomes an empirical issue that arises in linking the real exchange rate with the nominal exchange rate.[15] In general, the sooner the N-constraint leads to a rise in P_N, the shorter the half-life of devaluation is. Knowing the value of the elasticity of the real exchange rate with respect to the nominal exchange rate is important in targeting the magnitude of the nominal exchange rate devaluation that would achieve a certain surplus in the trade account. The lower this elasticity is, the greater the incentive for the policy maker to overshoot the real exchange rate towards undervaluation.

Second, the capital account balance that has been assumed away throughout this chapter can now be revisited. Deficits in the balance of payments represent more than excess demand for tradables in LDCs. They also reflect excess demand for foreign exchange, especially in hard currency, by governments and individuals who fear devaluation and attempt to diversify their portfolio.[16] This is the issue of asset–value dynamics raised in Chapter 3. Since this precautionary demand is not matched by savers in the hard currency trading partner countries, the excess demand for foreign exchange (as opposed to excess demand for tradables) accounts at least partly for the persistent deficits in the balance of payments of LDCs. If the equilibrium nominal exchange rate were set to balance in the long-run the trade and capital account (i.e., if the market in foreign exchange were freed) the ensuing real exchange rate, which considers only the prices of tradables and nontradables and thus the trade account alone, would end up being undervalued.

Third, in the stylized open-economy LDC the real exchange rate is the switching instrument that, by devaluation, is expected to coax more resources into tradables and away from nontradables. Should tradables be systematically more expensive in LDCs than nontradables, in terms of domestic resource cost (the Ricardo Principle), the nominal exchange rate has to be high enough to offset that comparative disadvantage. Competitive devaluations are triggered for conferring foreign exchange advantage where comparative advantage based

15 To be addressed in Chapter 8.
16 By symmetry, once the economy has accumulated sufficient hard currency for asset purposes, the balance-of-trade surplus need only be large enough to generate incremental demand for hard currency. Unless wealth is accumulating rapidly, this would be a rather small amount. Thus, the particular argument has relevance to the disequilibrium in the transition from a closed economy LDC to an open economy DC.

on initial endowments does not exist. This problem, on the other hand, can be addressed by supply-side measures that improve efficiency and increase the productivity of the economy in producing tradables. This restores comparative-advantage trade as opposed to competitive-devaluation trade.

The argument on market incompleteness between the nominal and the real exchange rate implies that equilibrium in the one market does not also entail equilibrium in the other. Moreover, if the target is equilibrium in the real exchange rate – and failing supply-side interventions for increasing the productivity of the tradable sector – the foreign exchange market has to be overridden. Quantity closure of the nominal exchange rate means overvaluation. Furthermore, by overriding the nominal exchange rate interventions in trade also become necessary.

Conclusion

A respectable body of literature on economic development has focused on bottlenecks that exist in LDCs and on the supply limitations of individual commodities. This has led to a policy preoccupation with trade (and aid), since it replaces diverse supply limitations by a single limit on the supply of foreign exchange. This reasoning sanctioned the drive for exports and for the long-run improvement in the balance of trade as one of the principal strategies for economic development. The "two-gap" literature is just one example of this mainstream view.

Australian-type models challenged the preoccupation with foreign exchange by making explicit the trade-off between exports and N-production. But even then, the possibility that shortage in N-supply may become a binding constraint in economic development has been largely overlooked. To that effect, this chapter introduced a slight modification into the Australian model of welfare maximization with tradables and nontradables. The real exchange rate is not a strictly endogenous variable that fully adjusts to clear the market of nontradables once maximization in the internal (income) and external (balance of payments) account has been achieved. Instead, the real exchange rate is a parametric exogenous variable, and it is determined via the nominal exchange rate, which is the policy control instrument. The determination of the nominal exchange rate in turn allows for factors that featured in Chapter 3, notably the asset–value dynamics that in LDCs shift the demand for foreign exchange to the right. Under this realistic assumption it turns out that an overshooting of the equilibrium real exchange rate is likely if the nominal exchange rate is allowed to find its equilibrium level. This one assumption of the quasi-Australian model is sufficient to make the shortage of nontradables the real constraint in the economy.

Once the nominal and the real exchange rates are not identically the same, setting the former at equilibrium is not sufficient to produce equilibrium in the three accounts – internal, external, and nontradables. Two instruments are necessary to operate in three variables. The dynamics section illustrates the principle by introducing an industrial policy that shifts the nontradable (expenditure) schedule to the right. Equilibrium in all three schedules can then be achieved at higher levels for all variables. The operation of such industrial policies in the real world is illustrated in Part III of the book.

This chapter dealt with the real exchange rate. The nominal exchange rate, which is the policy control instrument, was discussed only tangentially to illustrate a likely market incompleteness that may exist in LDCs where there is nonseparation between tradables and nontradables. The intuition is that, whether the nominal exchange rate is set at equilibrium or it is undervalued, it is most likely to lead to an undervalued real exchange rate and a severe contraction in the economy. Chapter 8 will introduce the nominal exchange rate explicitly in a formal model. The conclusion in that chapter that nominal exchange rate devaluations can be contractionary reinforces the parallel conclusion in this chapter about real exchange rate devaluations.

Appendix: Constrained-equilibrium expenditure curve

This section provides proof that for any given target of trade surplus (i.e., for a given constrained expenditure frontier) there is a unique real exchange rate that will generate this trade surplus at the lowest welfare cost possible. This unique real exchange rate will also satisfy market clearing in the nontradable sector. The proof is based on the assumption of homothetic indifference curves and endogenously determined real exchange rates.

> *Definition.* The constrained-equilibrium expenditure curve is the locus of points in the tradable–nontradable goods space such that each point satisfies: (1) supply of nontradables is determined by the real exchange rate, v; (2) at that same real exchange rate v, the level of expenditure is such that the demand for nontradables equals the supply of nontradables.

The way to think about this is as follows. Suppose we are given some value of the real exchange rate exogenously, v. Then producers pick a mix of tradable and nontradable output based on this given price. Now the demand for nontradables depends on relative prices, v, and on expenditure, E. So we ask the question: given v, and given the output mix chosen by producers, is there a level of E that would clear the nontradables market? The term constrained refers to the necessity of setting expenditure below income so that the market for nontradables clears. The term equilibrium refers to the market-clearing requirement in the nontradable market. In Figure A4.1 we show how this curve is constructed.

At the real exchange rate v^1, production is at point B. Market clearing requires that consumption be at point B also. Thus the bliss point B, where $Y = E$, is on the constrained-equilibrium expenditure curve.

At the real exchange rate v^z, production is at point z (no production of nontradables). Hence the market-clearing condition must be zero demand for nontradables. So the origin where $E = 0$, also belongs on the constrained-equilibrium expenditure curve.

Pick an arbitrary real exchange rate, v^2, between v^1 and v^z. Production is now at point A_p. Extend the slope of the real exchange rate v^2 to the right until it becomes tangent to some indifference curve u_1 at point A. Consider the ray OA. All indifference curves passing through ray OA must have a slope at that point equal to v^1 (by assumption of homotheticity of indifference curves). Hence the point A_c, which is below point A_p (hence consumption equals production) and along ray OA (hence the indifference curve at A_c must have the same slope as v^1), must belong to the constrained-equilibrium expenditure curve.

The curve OA_cB is the constrained-equilibrium expenditure curve.

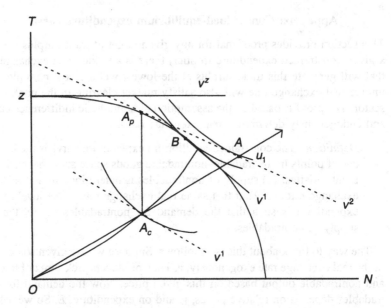

Figure A4.1. *Construction of the constrained-equilibrium expenditure curve*

Remark 1. To insure that the constrained-equilibrium expenditure curve is defined along all points on the curve OA_cB, we have to make some assumptions about the indifference curves. Let $-U'_T(N, T)/U'_N(N, T)$ be the marginal rate of substitution between N and T. Then we shall assume that: (1) $\lim_{N\to\infty} -U'_T(N, T)/U'_N(N, T) = 0$ and (2) $\lim_{N\to 0} -U'_T(N, T)/U'_N(N, T) = \infty$. This guarantees that for any v we pick such that $0 \leq v \leq \infty$, the corresponding point on the constrained-equilibrium consumption curve exists.

Remark 2. If a point A_c is on the constrained-equilibrium consumption curve, then the slope at that point is equal to the slope of the production possibility frontier above that point. This follows from the way the constrained-equilibrium expenditure curve is constructed.

Proposition. Suppose a trade surplus of size k is to be generated. Then there exists a unique real exchange rate, v^1, and a corresponding point on the constrained-equilibrium expenditure curve U_c that will generate this surplus. Furthermore, any other production cum consumption point that generates a trade surplus of size k will have lower welfare.

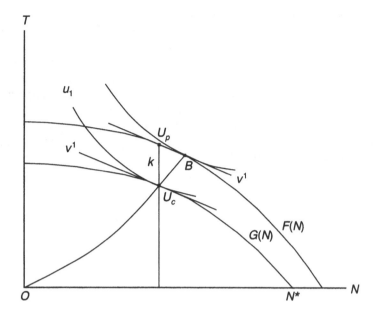

Figure A4.2. *The constrained-equilibrium expenditure curve*

Proof. There are two parts to this proposition. The first part is an existence and uniqueness argument. The second part is an optimality argument.

Consider Figure A4.2. The curve *OB* is the constrainedexpenditure consumption curve. Let k be the size of the trade surplus to be generated. Now $F(N)$ is the production possibility frontier. Let $G(N) = F(N) - k$. Hence the lower transformation curve $G(N)$ is always k units lower than the original transformation curve. The point where the constrained-equilibrium curve, *OB*, and $G(N)$ cross is the point U_c. The corresponding real exchange rate v^1 is the slope of the point U_p. Since U_c is on the constrained-equilibrium expenditure curve, there must be market clearing at U_c. Since it is also along the $G(N)$ curve, a trade surplus of amount k is being generated. Hence there exists a unique real exchange rate v^1 with consumption at point U_c that generates a trade surplus of size k and satisfies market clearing in the nontradable market. This proves the first part of the proposition about existence and uniqueness.

To prove the second part about optimality we argue thusly. The point U_c lies on the constrained-equilibrium expenditure curve. Hence the slope of the indifference curve passing through that point must have a slope equal to the slope of the production possibility frontier at U_p (see remark 2 above). So the slope of the indifference curve at U_c is equal to v^1. But since $G(N) = F(N) - k$, if we take the derivative of $G(N)$ with respect to N we find that $G'(N) = F'(N)$.

That is, for any given N such that $0 \le N \le N^*$, the slope of $G(N)$ is equal to the slope of $F(N)$. (Here N^* is the value of N such that $G(N^*) = 0$.) So at the point U_c the slope of $G(N)$ is also equal to v^1.

So we find that at point U_c we have the following properties: (1) slope of $G(N)$ at that point is v^1; (2) slope of the indifference curve u_1 at that same point is also equal to v^1. The real exchange rate v^1 is the separating hyperplane between $G(N)$ and the community-indifference curve. In other words, indifference curve u_1 is the highest indifference curve that is tangent to the production possibility frontier $G(N)$. Hence there is no other point on $G(N)$ that will have greater welfare than U_c.

CHAPTER 5

The relationship between real
and nominal exchange rates

The previous chapter demonstrated that the distinction between tradables and nontradables becomes important in a variety of circumstances that often prevail in LDCs. The empirical investigation of purchasing power parities in this chapter will reveal the regularities that exist between relative prices of tradables and nontradables in the process of development. The empirical links between the real and nominal exchange rates will also be investigated.

Purchasing power parity and exchange rates

The measurement of purchasing power parity (PPP) was designed to lead to comparisons of real incomes across countries. Such comparisons, however, are based on price level comparisons. Prices have multiple uses, among others as guides for the allocation of resources and as markers of efficiency. Should inappropriate prices arise, Pareto losses can be related to the violation of the restrictions of the fundamental theorems of welfare economics.

Suppose that certain price index calculations revealed that the price level at region X is 50% higher than at region Y. A new price emerges, the "bridge price," which is the ratio of price in Y to price in X, or 0.66. This is the number by which one multiplies a given national income in X to give it the same purchasing power as a corresponding income in Y. Such "bridge prices" are often fairly uninteresting when they are used merely as income-ranking devices. In certain cases, however, they cease being simply "bridges" and assume a role in allocating resources. Any bias that exists in defining and constructing such prices would carry over to the allocation process as well. If the "bridge" does not simply join two regions of a country but two countries in an open-economy world, its definition becomes more complicated and may be subject to systematic biases.

Consider first a simple two-country, one-commodity world. The GNP comparison for the two countries is given by the ratio of the sum of the homogeneous output produced, Q^I/Q^W, where Q is output (in real terms) and superscripts indicate countries – I for India and W ("world") for the comparator country. The output of the two countries can be normalized on a per-unit basis, by using, for example, the cost of production as numeraire. The ratio of the output produced per unit of labor cost in the two countries, q^I/q^W, is a price. In this example it can serve as the exchange rate, i.e., the translation of the cost of production (price) of the commodity in country I in terms of its cost in country W. The aggregation problem is trivial in this example. The multicommodity world becomes more complicated since commodities are non-homogeneous and as a result nonaggregable, and because costs of production need proper weighting to be expressed as a ratio. The ideal commodity index is impossible to obtain in a multicommodity world. The next best solution is to evaluate the quantities of output at their prices, P, and work with notional expenditure, E,

$$\frac{\sum_{i=1}^{n} E_i^I}{\sum_{i=1}^{n} E_i^W} = \frac{\sum_{i=1}^{n} P_i^I Q_i^I}{\sum_{i=1}^{n} P_i^W Q_i^W} \tag{5.1}$$

From notional expenditure one can derive the quantity ratio of commodities and the ratio of prices,

$$\frac{\sum_{i=1}^{n} Q_i^I}{\sum_{i=1}^{n} Q_i^W} = \frac{\sum_{i=1}^{n} (E_i^I/P_i^I)}{\sum_{i=1}^{n} (E_i^W/P_i^W)} \tag{5.2}$$

$$\frac{\sum_{i=1}^{n} P_i^I}{\sum_{i=1}^{n} P_i^W} = \frac{\sum_{i=1}^{n} (E_i^I/Q_i^I)}{\sum_{i=1}^{n} (E_i^W/Q_i^W)} \tag{5.3}$$

As in the previous case of the one-commodity world, equation (5.2) expresses the ratio of the real GDP of the two countries.[1] The ratio of their respective prices in equation (5.3) gives the conversion factor, which translates expenditure into real GDPs.

Equations (5.1) to (5.3) can be normalized appropriately to form the basis of comparisons in a multicountry, multicommodity world. The foundation of such normalization is the construction of a bridge index based on equation (5.3) that translates each country's GDP into common units, such as "international prices." It is a bridge index because it stands as a simple translator between own prices, expressed in this case in rupees, and international prices, expressed, e.g., in dollars. This is the way we tend to look at exchange rates.

An alternative way of looking at the bridge index is based on the duality between prices and costs of production. Prices express, at the margin, the transformation in production of real resources into output. Domestic prices express the opportunity cost of domestic resources in producing a "representa-

---

1 While algebraically correct, the derivation of the left-hand side hand side of equation (5.2) implies that P^I and P^W on the right-hand side are price indexes.

tive" basket of GDP. International prices, on the other hand, express the opportunity cost of domestic resources in producing a basket of GDP indirectly, through exchange in international trade. If that were the end of the story, the bridge index based on equation (5.3) would be fairly uninteresting: it expresses the exchange rate, which is a translation of domestic currency into international currency (rupees into dollars).

Exchange rates that convey the information equation (5.3) does, far from being uninteresting bridge indexes, are in fact "super prices" that have real implications for the economy. It makes a difference whether the policy maker follows the signals on opportunity cost of resources coming from the numerator of equation (5.3) or those emitted from the denominator of the fraction. The numerator expresses opportunity cost in producing a basket of GDP, which includes both tradables and nontradables. The denominator, on the other hand, refers to an open economy, where the opportunity cost of resources is judged in terms of producing only tradables, which is a subset of GDP. The systematic deviation between these two types of prices in the process of development becomes important in this respect. It turns out that the less developed an economy is relative to its trading partners, the more conflicting the signals that emanate from the numerator and the denominator of equation (5.3). In other words, the deviation of the opportunity cost of resources in producing GDP from that in producing internationally tradable commodities varies inversely with a country's level of development, as the following discussion will illustrate.

Measurement of real exchange rates

The discussion above has distinguished two issues: purchasing power parity comparisons of income in two countries; and the price comparisons that form the basis for purchasing power parity calculations. The measurement of real exchange rates focuses on price comparisons. Although the intention is to calculate the bridge index of equation (5.3), which is a mere translator of real incomes from one currency to another, what is actually derived is a hybrid that has significant policy implications for the allocation of resources.

A substantial amount of confusion exists about the empirical definition and measurement of real exchange rates. It will help clarify the issues if one keeps in mind a two-by-two matrix of external versus internal terms-of-trade definitions and of absolute versus relative price definitions. The terms of trade are external when they concentrate on prices of exports and imports, P_X and P_M; they are internal when they refer to prices of tradables and nontradables, P_T and P_N. Whether real exchange rates try to capture the external or the internal terms of trade, they can be expressed in terms of absolute prices, or more often in terms of price indexes.

Absolute versus relative purchasing power parity

For a given income, purchasing power depends on (the reciprocal of) prices. The most obvious bilateral comparison of purchasing power between, say, India and the U.S., would involve an identical basket of commodities, with components prescribed in appropriate physical quantities, priced both in Indian and U.S. prices, P and P^*, respectively. The purchasing power of rupees in India is then $C^1 = (1/P^1)$ and that of dollars in the U.S. is $C^* = (1/P^*)$. The ratio $c = C^*/C^1$ is the ratio of prices of the Indian basket divided by the prices of the U.S. basket and is expressed in rupees per dollar.

Most often, comparisons across countries involve nonhomogeneous baskets (that we call GDP). Then the weights for the n commodities that enter the comparison between India and the U.S. matter. The ratio of purchasing power in the U.S. and India is

$$C_t^{PPP} = \frac{C_t^*}{C_t^1} = \frac{\sum_{i=1}^{n} a_i P_{it}}{\sum_{i=1}^{n} b_i P_{it}^*} \tag{5.4}$$

where

$$C_t^1 = (1/\sum_{i=1}^{n} a_i P_{it}^1), \qquad C_t^* = (1/\sum_{i=1}^{n} b_i P_{it}^*)$$

and they are commodity purchasing power parity indexes; a_i and b_i are the weights. The expression for the parity ratio, $c = C_t^*/C_t^1$ is the commodity purchasing power parity (PPP). It is expressed above in absolute terms, rupees per dollar.

Under certain conditions the parity ratio c becomes the "PPP exchange rate" and it is equivalent to the nominal exchange rate e. The requirement is that the law of one price holds for all n commodities. This means that (McKinnon, 1979, p. 119):

(1) All goods are perfectly tradable with zero transport cost;
(2) there exist no tariffs or other artificial barriers to foreign trade, such as exchange controls;
(3) foreign and domestic goods are perfectly homogeneous within each commodity category;
(4) the weights used in computing the purchasing powers of foreign and domestic commodities are the same.

With these conditions satisfied absolute PPP holds and $c = e$. Should the price index in India increase, it is reflected in a proportional devaluation of the nominal exchange rate of the rupee toward the dollar. The equilibria in the real and nominal exchange rates correspond in the sense that the allocation of resources under either is identical.

When comparable absolute data do not exist, one relies on changes in prices between time 0 and t to calculate price indexes ($\tilde{P}$):

$$\tilde{P}^1_t = \frac{\sum\limits_{i=1}^{n} a_i P^1_{it}}{\sum\limits_{i=1}^{n} a_i P^1_{i0}} \tag{5.5}$$

$$\tilde{P}^*_t = \frac{\sum\limits_{i=1}^{n} b_i P^*_{it}}{\sum\limits_{i=1}^{n} b_i P^*_{i0}} \tag{5.6}$$

The ratio of the inverse of equation (5.6) to the inverse of equation (5.5) is the relative PPP index:

$$C^{PPI}_t = v = \frac{\tilde{P}^1_t}{\tilde{P}^*_t} \tag{5.7}$$

The v in equation (5.7), however, is different from $c = C^*_t/C^1_t$ in equation (5.4) and the C^{PPP}_t and C^{PPI}_t are comparable only in very special circumstances. The reason is that $\tilde{P}$ is a pure number, and so is C^{PPI}_t in equation (5.7), whereas equation (5.4) is expressed in rupees per dollar. Moreover, by knowing the direction of change from equation (5.7), we do not also know the destination, unless we are told where we started from, which equation (5.4) does.

If we are willing to accept the value of C^1_0 and C^*_0 from equation (5.4) we can multiply by equation (5.7) and have rupees per dollar again. Moreover, suppose we knew that absolute PPP held at time 0, and the nominal and the real exchange rates were in equilibrium. Then equation (5.8) serves to measure the real exchange rate in period t and to indicate deviations from equilibrium as in equation (5.4) under the stated conditions:

$$E^{PPP}_t = v_t = c_0 \frac{\tilde{P}^1_t}{\tilde{P}^*_t} \tag{5.8}$$

This is the relative version of PPP that states that changes in prices serve to indicate changes in the real exchange rate.

Cassel (1921) and Keynes (1923) were the first to use the short-cut method of the relative version of PPP to track the impact that price movements had on real exchange rates. They substituted for c_0 in equation (5.8) the nominal exchange rate e_0 for the year 1913 and for the countries they studied, pairwise. The P's that entered equation (5.8) were the prices of the commodities that entered trade among the countries, again pairwise and with base year 1913. It may seem that in this application equation (5.8) captures, at best, the external terms of trade. And in any event, the "exchange rate PPP" that they measured is distant from the commodity PPP, C^{PPP} of equation (5.4) we started with.

The two concepts of commodity PPP and exchange rate PPP are not exactly equivalent. The former refers to the entire basket of commodities that enter GDP; the latter concentrates on a subset of commodities that enter international trade (tradables). Cassel and Keynes, however, anchored in year 1913, the end of the gold standard era, in order to analyze the post-World War I period. During the reign of the gold standard, in the early 20th century, there were both unrestricted international trade and unparalleled exchange rate stability. Moreover, the monetary authority could increase the money supply only in a fixed proportion to the gold reserves. Domestic currency, therefore, could be used interchangeably for the purchase of the home commodity, nontradables, or for imports. For this specific case, the prices of tradables and of their complement into the GDP, nontradables, were determined roughly in the same way. Export proceeds and inflows of capital expanded both reserves and the monetary base, and either could be turned into tradables or nontradables interchangeably. In this sense there existed full substitutability between the two – separation in production and consumption, as was noted in Chapter 3. With separation between tradables and nontradables the exchange rate, e_0, represented, in effect, both the shadow price of converting tradables into nontradables and that of converting the domestic currency into foreign.[2] Under the circumstances the assumption Cassel and Keynes made was valid: purchasing power parity held in 1913 and the equilibrium nominal and real exchange rates coincided.

The collapse of the gold standard has in effect reimposed "bimetallism" on the world in a very important sense: the tradables trade in foreign exchange, while the nontradables trade in domestic currency. This is what compelled Cassel and Keynes to exercise extreme caution in selecting the base year. The problem has been accentuated in the years of restricted trade and artificially fixed exchange rates that followed World War I and World War II, and in the post-1973 period of fluctuating exchange rates. There can be no presumption anymore that any single base year represented equilibrium real exchange rates. Tracking, therefore, the deviations from equilibrium through price changes becomes pointless.

External-terms-of-trade real exchange rates

The most common practice of estimating real exchange rates is still based on the Cassel–Keynes method. An improvement was introduced to account for some of the concerns noted above by extending the price coverage in principle to include nontradables, i.e., to capture the internal terms of trade. Equation (5.9) is a simplified form of equation (5.8):

2 In what follows the two processes will be called the determination of the internal and external terms of trade, and they are related with the real and the nominal exchange rate for the former and the latter, respectively.

$$R_E = \frac{e\tilde{P}^*}{\tilde{P}} \tag{5.9}$$

where R_E is the external-terms-of-trade exchange rate, e is the nominal exchange rate, and the prices of the home country and the foreign country have been expressed in relative terms (indicated by tilde) through the use of a general price index. The GDP deflator is a common approximation of the general price index, and equation (5.9) is rewritten as:

$$R_E = \frac{e\tilde{P}^*_{GDP}}{\tilde{P}_{GDP}}$$

In the process, the twin issues of the base period and of evaluating the direction of change without knowledge of where one started from, as pointed out in equation (5.8), have been obscured.

For reasons mostly of convenience, the consumer price index, CPI, is used as an alternative proxy of GDP deflators:

$$R_E = e\frac{\tilde{P}^*_{CPI}}{\tilde{P}_{CPI}} \tag{5.10}$$

The CPI in equation (5.10) is considered sufficiently broad-based to approximate the GDP deflator. In an alternative interpretation, the CPI is considered as capturing the change in the price of tradables, especially when contrasted with the real exchange rate based on the wholesale price index, WPI:

$$R_E = e\frac{\tilde{P}^*_{WPI}}{\tilde{P}_{WPI}} \tag{5.11}$$

Equations (5.11) and (5.12) are often interpreted as linking the real exchange rate with the prices of tradables and nontradables, respectively. The WPI, by concentrating on intermediate inputs, includes a higher proportion of nontradables (and thus greater nontradable weights) than either the implicit deflator or the CPI, which include final goods and services (but exclude publicly financed services). The arbitrariness and other disadvantages of these proxies have been discussed extensively in the literature.[3]

The real exchange rate concepts discussed so far emphasize the demand side. A change in the external terms of trade induces consumers to change the composition of their demand: to reduce expenditure, to the extent that they have become poorer, and to switch expenditure between home and foreign goods. But changes in prices induce producers also to change the composition of their supply. The internal-terms-of-trade real exchange rates capture this distinction.

3 For example see a broad review in Officer (1976).

Internal-terms-of-trade real exchange rates

The internal-terms-of-trade definition of the real exchange rate measures the opportunity cost of domestic resources in producing tradables and nontradables. In this formulation we define it as *the* real exchange rate, RER:[4]

$$RER = P_T/P_N \qquad (5.12)$$

where P_T and P_N are sums of appropriately normalized and weighted prices of $i = 1, \ldots, N$ tradables and $i = N + 1, \ldots, T$ nontradables for a country. As Edwards (1989, p. 5) notes, equation (5.12) summarizes the "incentives that guide resource allocation across the tradable and nontradable sectors." As such, it describes a country's competitiveness, in the sense that optimal resource allocation equalizes at the margin the cost of production (and thus the prices) of tradables and nontradables. In this sense, competitiveness is different from the notion of comparing prices of home and foreign goods to reveal comparative advantage; and competitiveness differs from the notion of comparing the domestic resource cost of producing two tradables to determine which one a country should export under free trade.

This "dependent-economy" definition of RER captures the supply side in the sense that it provides information on changes in incentives guiding the allocation of resources in producing a basket of GDP that consists of tradables and nontradables. Moreover, this definition of the RER in absolute terms sidetracks many of the problems mentioned in the previous section, especially the use of price indexes as proxies for prices of tradables and nontradables, and it also gets around the massive evidence rejecting the PPP theory of real exchange behavior. As a result, this variant of the real exchange rates has become quite popular in recent years (Edwards, 1989; Khan and Lizondo, 1987; Khan and Montiel, 1987; Frenkel and Moussa, 1984; Harberger, 1986).

The problem that arises, however, is that ratios of opportunity costs of tradables and nontradables, in absolute terms, make no sense unless they are properly normalized. Such normalization can rely on the productivity of factors of production (e.g., the marginal product of labor in producing tradables or nontradables), on reference to wage rates, and so on. But such normalization is hard to obtain empirically. In the following section where the methodology of the International Comparisons Project (ICP) is introduced, the normalization relies on international prices. In the meanwhile, the practice in the empirical literature is to rely on shortcuts that have the unhappy implication of reintroducing some of the problems that the definition of the RER had solved.

---

4 Our definition of the real exchange rate, RER, has prices of tradables in the numerator and of nontradables in the denominator in order to make devaluation of the nominal and the real exchange rate equivalent: an increase in the number of rupees per dollar, or an increase in the price of Indian tradables relative to nontradables.

Edwards (1988, p. 48) distinguishes four dependent-economy definitions of RER involving prices of tradables, nontradables, or some proxy or subaggregate thereof. They are all expressed as changes in indexes from a base period, and $\tilde{R}$ stands for the change in internal-terms-of-trade real exchange rate, which is not computed as in equation (5.12):

(1) $\tilde{R}_1 = \tilde{P}_T^* / \tilde{P}_N$, where the world price of tradables, P_T^*, and the (domestic) price of nontradables, P_N, express changes in price indexes, as indicated by the tilde. The implicit assumption in this formulation is that the law of one price holds, and thus the numerator represents the change in the price of home tradables.

(2) $\tilde{R}_2 = \tilde{P}_T / \tilde{P}_N$, where domestic prices of tradables and nontradables are also expressed as changes in indexes.

(3) $\tilde{R}_3 = \tilde{P}_M / \tilde{P}_N$, and

(4) $\tilde{R}_4 = \tilde{P}_X / \tilde{P}_N$, where prices of imports, P_M, prices of exports, P_X, as well as prices of nontradables, are all expressed as changes in indexes.

The shortcut measurement of the internal terms of trade, R_2, represents an improvement in the measurement of the real exchange rate as compared to the external-terms-of-trade approximations in the previous section. Yet, the major problem still remains: the direction of movement says nothing about one's destination unless the origin is also known. Price indexes are of no help in gauging the real exchange rate as long as there is no information about the prices of tradables and nontradables that obtained at real-exchange-rate equilibrium. The ideal still remains the RER definition in equation (5.12), where prices of tradables and nontradables are expressed in absolute values, as long as they are properly normalized. Such normalization is provided by the ICP, where home commodity prices are appropriately weighted and expressed per unit of international currency. From these absolute PPPs one can proceed to construct RERs, as will be presented in Chapter 6.

Measurement of absolute purchasing power parity

The ICP was launched to develop comparability in the GDP of various countries by making possible real (quantity) comparisons based on equation (5.2) above (Kravis, Kenessey, Heston and Summers, 1975; Kravis, Heston and Summers, 1978a,b, 1982; Kravis, 1984). Since direct comparison of sums of nonhomogeneous quantities is not possible, the approach is based on estimating the right-hand side of equation (5.2), which involves the respective expenditures and prices. While the purpose of the ICP was to concentrate on Q's, we will use the microdata of the project to spotlight the P's.

The raw data for the ICP are national prices for a list of about 2000 commodities, with uniform technical specification so that they can be rendered internationally comparable. The PPPs are first computed for 151 commodity categories as averages (simple or weighted) of the prices for individual subcategories in each commodity. Second, these commodity-category PPPs are weight-averaged (with expenditure weights) to obtain the "international prices." Third, the PPPs for commodity aggregates (e.g., GDP, consumption, capital formation, government, tradables, nontradables, etc.) are obtained as ratios of the value of the aggregate based on the national prices and its value based on the international prices. The basic information has been collected from a number of "benchmark" countries in five-year intervals starting in 1970. It has been extrapolated to a large number of countries (see Appendix, this chapter) by constructing various national GDP indexes and their subaggregates, all expressed in PPP, and by linking them for all countries involved.

In outlining the methodology in more detail we will concentrate on the bilateral comparison of GNP per capita between country I (India) and W (U.S.).[5]

The lowest level of disaggregation is the 2000 commodity subcategory. It is aggregated into i commodity categories ($i = 151$). Starting, e.g., with commodity category rice, the aggregation in equation (5.2) involves the various subcategories of rice (k), which are added up in expenditure terms and in domestic currency:

$$E_i^1 = \sum_{j=1}^{k} P_{ij}^1 Q_{ij}^1 \tag{5.13}$$

where i is commodity and j is commodity subcategory. Monetary variables are expressed in Indian rupees, and all quantities are in per-capita terms.

To establish international comparability for India we need an expression of purchasing power parity, PPP_i, that relates Indian prices to U.S. (world) prices. The PPP_i is derived from the domestic prices of the k commodity subcategories, P_{ij}^1, and their world prices, P_{ij}^W:

5 In an attempt to simplify the presentation we have overlooked the most important attribute of the ICP: it also provides multilateral comparisons with the index numbers possessing transitivity, additivity, and base-country invariance. The Geary–Khamis method for multilateral aggregation is used. The method solves a system of ($m + n + 1$) simultaneous equations for m basic categories (about 151 commodities) and n countries, one of which is the base country. The solutions produce m international prices and ($n - 1$) PPPs. In the multilateral comparisons system PPPs express the ratio of expenditure in national currency and expenditure in international prices (as opposed to expenditure in nominal exchange rates that emerges from the bilateral comparisons). International prices of basic commodity categories are the quantity-weighted average prices of the n countries, with their currencies having been converted to the base-country currency by using the PPP. The PPP and the international prices are determined simultaneously. For details on the Geary–Khamis method see Kravis et al. (1975, Chapter 5).

$$PPP_i = \prod_{j=1}^{k}\left(\frac{P_{ij}^1}{P_{ij}^W}\right)^{Q_{ij}^1/\Sigma_{j=1}^k Q_{ij}^1} \tag{5.14}$$

where PPP_i is the geometric mean of the ratio of domestic price to world price for commodity i.

Notional quantity, Q_i^1, can now be calculated from equations (5.13) and (5.14) as expenditure in domestic currency, E_i^1, divided by the purchasing power parity, PPP_i,

$$Q_i^1 = \frac{E_i^1}{PPP_i} \tag{5.15}$$

Multiplying notional quantities by world prices gives the real expenditure in India of commodity i, R_i^1:

$$R_i^1 = Q_i^1 P_i^W \tag{5.16}$$

Such calculations of real expenditure expressed in world prices form the basis for a flexible aggregation of the ICP data base. For example,

$$GDP^1 = \sum_{i=1}^{n} R_i^1 \tag{5.17}$$

and in the same way one can define any subaggregate of GDP, such as the subsets of tradables and nontradables.

Once notional expenditure has been expressed in world prices, linking one country's PPP with a numeraire country becomes important for multicounty comparisons. From equation (5.15) one can express expenditure in per-capita terms and normalize Indian expenditure in world prices by U.S. expenditure in world prices.

Equation (5.18) expresses Indian PPP per capita income as percent of U.S. PPP income:

$$\frac{\sum_{i=1}^{n} R_i^1}{\sum_{i=1}^{n} R_i^{US}} = \frac{\sum_{i=1}^{n} Q_i^1 P_i^W}{\sum_{i=1}^{n} Q_i^{US} P_i^W} \tag{5.18}$$

An alternative way of normalizing the Indian per capita income is to use the nominal exchange rate, rupees per dollar, in order to express it in international (i.e., U.S.) prices:

$$\frac{\sum_{i=1}^{n} N_i^1}{\sum_{i=1}^{n} N_i^{US}} = \frac{\sum_{i=1}^{n} Q_i^1 P_i^W / e}{\sum_{i=1}^{n} Q_i^{US} P_i^W} \tag{5.19}$$

where e is the foreign exchange rate, rupees per U.S. dollar, and N_i is the GDP converted from local to international currency by the use of the exchange rate.

The ratio of equation (5.19) to equation (5.18) is written

$$\frac{\sum_{i=1}^{n} N_i^I / \sum_{i=1}^{n} N_i^{US}}{\sum_{i=1}^{n} R_i^I / \sum_{i=1}^{n} R_i^{US}} = \frac{(\sum_{i=1}^{n} Q_i^I P_i^W / e) / \sum_{i=1}^{n} Q_i^{US} P_i^W}{\sum_{i=1}^{n} Q_i^I P_i^W / \sum_{i=1}^{n} Q_i^{US} P_i^W} \tag{5.20}$$

It expresses the value of India's GNP per capita at own prices, normalized by the U.S. nominal GDP per capita, divided by the per capita GDP of India in world prices, normalized by the U.S. per capita GDP in world prices (which is identical to the nominal U.S. GDP per capita). The ratio in equation (5.20) defines P^*, which is the price level of GDP (i.e., the PPP of GDP), over the nominal exchange rate, both expressed with respect to the U.S. The inverse of this ratio is defined as the "exchange rate deviation index" (ERD).

Purchasing power parity prices and real exchange rates

The most common applications of the ICP have emphasized PPP and expenditure comparisons among countries. We focus instead on price comparisons, with emphasis on the level of aggregation that distinguishes between the tradable and nontradable subsets of GDP.

Solving equation (5.15) for PPP_i, instead of notional quantities, aggregating, and normalizing by the numeraire country, we can form any appropriate index of PPP, indicated as PPP_I. Writing for nontradables in India $i = 1, \ldots, N$, and for tradables $i = N + 1, \ldots, T$, we can form the PPP index for nontradables and tradables, P_N and P_T, respectively:

$$P_N = \prod_{i=1}^{N} \left(\frac{P_i^I}{P_i^{US}} \right)^{Q_i^I / \Sigma_{i=1}^{N} Q_i^I} \tag{5.21}$$

$$P_T = \prod_{i=N+1}^{T} \left(\frac{P_i^I}{P_i^{US}} \right)^{Q_i^I / \Sigma_{i=N+1}^{T} Q_i^I} \tag{5.22}$$

The $i = 1, \ldots, N$ is defined for commodities that are nontradable in India, and the $i = N + 1, \ldots, T$ for commodities that are tradable in India; Q_i^I is defined in equation (5.15). The PPP indexes in equations (5.21) and (5.22) are expressed in rupees per U.S. dollar.

What can we tell about P_T and P_N as development occurs? More generally, considering equations (5.20), (5.21), and (5.22) together, what can we tell about the relationship between the nominal exchange rate and the ratio of any country's prices to world prices? Consider India's price vector, P_I^I, and the U.S. price vector, P_I^{US}. Should they be proportional to world prices, P_I^W, we have $P_I^I = \alpha P_I^W$, $P_I^{US} = \beta P_I^W$ and therefore

$$PPP_I(I, US) = \frac{\alpha}{\beta} = v \tag{5.23}$$

Should all prices be proportional to world prices, the PPP_I is constant at any level of aggregation. In the definition of absolute PPP, it is assumed that v is constant at a certain (meaningful) level of aggregation, such as for tradables or for GDP. However, it is rather unlikely for that to occur. Even if all tradables were traded freely, transportation cost is proportional to weight rather than price. Therefore, proportionality cannot hold even within tradables at a certain level of aggregation. On the other hand, if no systematic distortion exists, one would expect PPP_I to be distributed around a mean value of v. This is the relative version of PPP. This does not seem to hold under empirical examination either. The Ricardo Principle, on the other hand, suggests (and empirical evidence confirms) that there is a *systematic* relationship between the PPP_I, especially in the form of P_T and P_N, and the level of development.

Table 5.1 shows GDP per capita and some subaggregates, in "home prices" and in "international prices," for six groups of countries, all expressed relative to the U.S. as in equation (5.18). The index of price levels (rows 9–14) represents the appropriate aggregation of PPPs of a country, again expressed as a percent of the U.S. PPPs (multiplied by 100). Row 15 shows the exchange rate deviation index, the inverse of equation (5.20). A major finding of the ICP research is that the ERD tends to 1 as the per capita income in row 4 converges to that of the numeraire country, which is also the richest (Kravis et al., 1982, Chapter 3). This is shown more clearly in the next table.

Table 5.2 shows the 34 countries included in the ICP for 1975, grouped by income level averages and arranged in ascending order. The columns in the table show indexes, expressed relative to the U.S. and multiplied by 100. The nominal (exchange-rate-converted) and real (PPP-converted) GDP per capita for each country group is given in columns 2 and 3. The exchange rate deviation index (ERD, column 4, also last row in Table 5.1) summarizes the findings from comparing the nominal to real GDP per capita. The ERD for the lowest income countries is over 2½ times greater than the one for the high income countries. Moreover, the ERD declines monotonically, asymptotically approaching one, with increasing levels of income.

The last three columns of Table 5.2 refer to price levels and are the link between the columns on nominal and real GDP per capita. The deviation between the latter two measured by their ratio, the ERD, is due to the fact that the purchasing power of the currency (the price level) in low income countries is higher (lower) than the exchange rate would suggest. In the last column of the table the ratio of the purchasing power to the exchange rate (the reciprocal of ERD) is the price level in a country relative to that of the numeraire country.

The figures in Table 5.2 reveal that the behavior of price levels for tradables and nontradables is systematic and largely consistent with the Ricardo Principle. Prices of nontradables are low as a percent of U.S. prices at early levels of development and increase with per capita incomes. Prices of tradables are in

Table 5.1. *Per capita GDP and price levels, 1975, for six groups of countries by income class*

Per-capita quantity converted by	Income class[a]					
	1	2	3	4	5	6
Exchange rates (U.S. $)						
1. Consumption	132	665	1026	1946	3484	5183
2. Capital formation	29	177	402	809	1296	1185
3. Government	16	97	159	230	596	808
4. GDP	177	939	1587	2985	5376	7176
PPPs (international $)						
5. Consumption	467	1171	1893	2526	3552	4984
6. Capital formation	90	319	583	956	1442	1457
7. Government	89	170	291	275	460	735
8. GDP	646	1660	2677	3757	5454	7176
Index of price level (U.S. = 100)						
9. Consumption	40.1	50.1	59.2	69.1	102.8	100.0
10. Capital formation	60.4	63.7	91.5	93.2	121.4	100.0
11. Government	25.4	45.9	56.8	74.8	132.0	100.0.
12. GDP	40.7	51.7	64.5	73.6	107.4	100.0
13. Tradables	60.7	70.7	86.6	97.9	118.5	100.0
14. Nontradables	24.9	37.2	46.5	53.4	96.7	100.0
15. Exchange rate deviation index[b]	2.64	2.11	1.61	1.39	0.97	1.00

Source: Kravis (1984), p. 27.
Notes:
[a]The class intervals (with U.S. per-capita GDP of $7176 equal to 100) and the countries in each real-income class are:
1)   0–14.9   Malawi, Kenya, India, Pakistan, Sri Lanka, Zambia, Thailand, Philippines
2) 15.0–29.9   Korea, Malaysia, Colombia, Jamaica, Syria, Brazil
3) 30.0–44.9   Romania, Mexico, Yugoslavia, Iran, Uruguay, Ireland
4) 45.0–59.9   Hungary, Poland, Italy, Spain
5) 60.0–89.9   U.K., Japan, Austria, Netherlands, Belgium, France, Luxembourg, Denmark, Germany
6) 90.0–100.0   U.S.
Entries are unweighted averages.
[b]Per capita GDP in international dollars (line 8) divided by per capita GDP converted by the exchange rate (line 4). The ERD is derived as the average for the countries in each income class and therefore does not correspond to the result of the division above.

general significantly higher than prices of nontradables, with no clear trend as development occurs.[6] Correspondingly, the ratio of prices of tradables to nontradables tends to be high at early stages of development and decreases for the higher income countries, asymptotically tending to 1.0, the value of the numeraire country. The Gerschenkron effect is reflected in the shares of tradables

6 Heston et al. (1994) extend the analysis of the regularities in prices of tradables and nontradables for the years 1980 and 1985.

Table 5.2. *Indexes of GDP per capita and of price levels, 1975 (U.S. = 100)*

Country	Indexes of GDP per capita			Indexes of price levels[d]		
	Nominal[a]	Real[b]	ERD[c]	Tradables	Nontradables	GDP
Group I[e]	3.70	9.01	2.64	60.0	24.9	40.6
Malawi	1.93	4.90	2.55	56.5	23.5	39.3
Kenya	3.36	6.56	1.95	72.6	35.0	51.2
India	2.03	6.56	3.23	51.4	14.1	31.0
Pakistan	2.64	8.23	3.12	46.4	19.3	32.1
Sri Lanka	2.55	9.30	3.65	47.5	12.2	27.4
Zambia	6.89	10.30	1.49	95.5	47.3	67.0
Thailand	5.00	13.00	2.61	48.9	26.4	37.4
Philippines	5.24	13.20	2.51	61.5	21.2	39.7
Group II[e]	12.09	23.13	2.11	70.7	37.2	51.7
Korea	8.12	20.70	2.54	53.1	26.9	39.3
Malaysia	10.90	21.50	1.98	76.6	32.5	50.6
Colombia	7.92	22.40	2.83	52.0	23.2	35.3
Jamaica	19.60	24.00	1.23	111.5	58.6	81.6
Syria	10.00	25.00	2.50	45.7	36.7	40.0
Brazil	16.00	25.20	1.58	84.9	45.1	63.4
Group III[e]	24.23	37.32	1.61	86.6	46.5	64.7
Romania	24.30	33.30	1.37	113.2	42.2	73.0
Mexico	20.40	34.70	1.70	82.2	39.7	58.9
Yugoslavia	23.20	36.10	1.56	82.8	48.0	64.2
Iran	22.10	37.70	1.70	76.1	43.3	58.7
Uruguay	18.20	39.60	2.17	60.5	34.0	46.0
Ireland	37.20	42.50	1.14	104.9	71.9	87.7
Group IV[e]	38.63	52.35	1.39	97.9	53.4	73.5
Hungary	29.60	49.60	1.68	84.0	40.0	59.7
Poland	36.00	50.10	1.39	103.8	46.4	71.9
Italy	47.90	53.80	1.12	111.3	69.8	89.1
Spain	41.00	55.90	1.36	92.1	57.2	73.4
Group V[e]	81.22	76.01	0.97	118.5	96.7	107.5
U.K.	57.60	63.90	1.11	106.0	74.9	90.1
Japan	62.30	68.40	1.10	95.1	84.9	91.2
Austria	69.80	69.60	1.00	111.2	90.7	100.3
Netherlands	84.50	75.20	0.89	118.6	109.3	112.3
Belgium	87.80	77.70	0.88	120.7	106.2	113.0
France	89.60	81.90	0.91	123.9	95.5	109.4
Luxembourg	90.20	82.00	0.91	120.5	97.9	110.0
Denmark	104.50	82.40	0.79	144.5	107.6	126.8
Germany	94.70	83.00	0.88	126.0	103.0	114.2
Group VI[e]	100.00	100.00	1.00	100.0	100.0	100.0
U.S.	100.00	100.00	1.00	100.0	100.0	100.0

Source: Kravis et al. (1982), Tables 1.2 and 6.12; by permission of the publisher, Johns Hopkins University Press, for the World Bank.
Notes:
[a]Nominal GDP per capita = GDP per capita converted to dollars at nominal exchange rate. Base value (for U.S.) = \$7,176.
[b]Real GDP per capita = GDP per capita converted to dollars at purchasing power parity. Base value (for U.S.) = \$7,176.
[c]ERD = exchange rate deviation index. It is the per capita GDP in international dollars (col. 3) divided by per capita GDP converted by the exchange rate (col. 2).
[d]Indexes of price levels = purchasing power parity (home currency per dollar) divided by exchange rate (home currency per dollar) times 100.
[e]Group figures are simple averages.

and nontradables in GDP, which determine the implicit weights used to produce the GDP price index. The inverse of the latter gives the exchange rate deviation index, ERD, which was discussed in the previous section.

The classification between tradables and nontradables that underlies Table 5.2 is arbitrary: it defines nontradables as consisting of services and construction and tradables as the rest of the sectors.[7] Despite that, it has been used extensively in the literature.[8] In Chapter 6, the distinction between tradables and nontradables will be drawn in an operational way that can support the definition of the RER in equation (5.12).

Conclusion

This chapter reviewed the empirical literature on the measurement of purchasing power parity and the real exchange rate. The absolute PPP that compares the prices of an identical basket of commodities in two countries has been elusive. It has been approximated by price indexes in two countries that are commonly linked by the nominal exchange rate. To the extent that nominal exchange rates are formed in the world of tradables alone, such indexes are closer to the external terms of trade of a country. The internal terms of trade, on the other hand, can be expressed by the ratio of prices of tradables to nontradables, which is the definition of the real exchange rate. It reflects the opportunity cost of converting resources in producing GDP, as opposed to the opportunity cost of producing only tradables, which are a subset of GDP. The real exchange rate has also commonly been approximated by using various relative indexes in combination with the nominal exchange rate.

The methodology of the International Comparisons Project provides ratios of expenditures, but also ratios of quantities and prices, that are comparable across countries. In principle, such prices, appropriately normalized, can be aggregated over tradables and nontradables, as will be more precisely defined in Chapter 6. In principle, therefore, the derivation of absolute real exchange rates is feasible. Moreover, the sample of empirical results from the ICP that was presented suggests that the relative prices of tradables to nontradables vary systematically in the process of development. This systematic relationship, in principle again, can become the foundation for linking nominal exchange rates, which relate to tradables, to real exchange rates, which also include nontradables and are thus more closely referenced to GDP.

---

7 Services are defined to include "categories in which expenditures are entirely on personnel (for example domestic services, teachers, and government employees), repairs of various kinds (footwear, auto), rents, public transport and communication, public entertainment, and household services" (Kravis et al., 1978a, p. 123).
8 See, for example, Kravis and Lipsey (1977), among others.

Appendix: Extensions of purchasing power parity measurement

The raw data on which Tables 5.1 and 5.2 are based came from a set of "benchmark" countries and refer to year 1975 (Kravis et al., 1982). Published data are also available for a smaller number of countries for the years 1970 and 1973 (Kravis et al., 1975). Subsequently, the benchmark years 1980 and 1985 have also been collected for a number of benchmark countries and they are being processed for publication (and have been made available for this study by Alan Heston). Based on the most recent benchmark years available, Summers and Heston (1984, 1988, 1991) have extended the coverage to a total of 115 countries (to 1980), 130 (to 1985), and 138 (to 1988) for the three sources, respectively. For our purposes, the shortcut method of extrapolation from the set of benchmark countries to the world sample is of interest. In this exercise the role of equation (5.20), as the ratio of the (per capita) GDP valued at "own prices" to that valued at "international prices," becomes crucial. It yields the exchange rate deviation index, ERD, of Tables 5.1 and 5.2. The extrapolation problem consists of estimating ERD for the world set of countries from the relationships revealed in the study of the benchmark countries (and years). More specifically, this relationship relates the "own prices" to the "international prices" and certain other variables. ERD is a fraction, with the numerator expressing a country's per capita income adjusted for purchasing power parity and the denominator the per capita income in nominal terms, or exchange-rate converted, both referenced relative to the numeraire country. The empirical extrapolation of the ratio n/r, the inverse of ERD, is based on the equation:

$$n/r = aP_T + (1 - a)P_N \qquad (A5.1)$$

where n is the nominal, or exchange-rate converted GDP per capita and r is the real, or PPP-converted GDP per capita, both expressed as indexes with the U.S. equal to one. The coefficients a and $(1 - a)$ are the country's proportions of expenditures on traded and nontraded goods, the respective prices of which are again expressed relative to the numeraire country.

According to the law of one price, P_T, the relative price of tradables, tends to one. All that is needed then is P_N and the value of a in order to calculate r. P_N, however, is not known except for the benchmark countries. Since P_N is a function of per capita income, n, then r is also a function of per capita income, plus other variables. Finally, the empirical extrapolation of the ratio n/r uses not only per capita income (and its square) as explanatory variables but also variables to account for the "openness of a country" (*OP*, expected to have a negative sign) and its "price isolation" (*PI*, expected to have a positive sign), all expressed relative to the numeraire country:

$$\ln r = b + c_1 \ln n + c_2 (\ln n^2) + d_1 \ln OP + d_2 \ln PI + u \qquad (A5.2)$$

Whereas, conceptually, the index of the nominal per capita income (in "international prices") is the appropriate dependent variable and the index of the real GDP per capita (at "own" prices) is the independent variable, the causality has been reversed in the estimating equation (A5.2) above. Thus r for the nonbenchmark countries is estimated from their nominal per capita income and the other variables. The estimation of the exchange rate deviation index in this application is equivalent to estimating the deviation between the purchasing power parity exchange rate and the nominal exchange rate from information on the level of the nominal income plus the other variables.

Two issues are brought to the surface from the discussion of the extensions of the measurement procedures. First, whether it is admissible to approximate purchasing power parities (or real incomes) by using nominal exchange rates (or nominal incomes) for the nonbenchmark countries. This issue has been adequately discussed in the literature (e.g., Marris, 1984). The short answer is that failing more detailed information collected at the country level, judicious shortcut extrapolations will have to do. The estimates, however, should be employed with caution. For example, the replication by the author of the ICP methodology for the collection of data and the derivation of PPP in Taiwan, for 1985, revealed that sizeable differences exist with the extrapolations of Penn World Tables 5 (Yotopoulos and Lin, 1993). Indicatively, the national price level of GDP (PPP of GDP divided by the nominal exchange rate) is 0.57 as compared to 0.71 in Penn World Tables 5. This difference is responsible for an underestimation in the latter of the real per capita GDP for 1985 by about 20% (from U.S. \$5681 to U.S. \$4524).

The second issue relates to the potential use of extrapolated ERDs, which are broadly available, for inferring the real exchange rate where micro-ICP data are not available. This will remain in the agenda for future research.

CHAPTER 6

Empirical investigation of real exchange rates: Tradability and relative prices

The discussion in the previous chapters was predicated on the distinction between tradables and nontradables. Moreover, it postulated the existence of a systematic relationship between the level of development and the relative prices of tradables and nontradables. The analysis in effect implies that whereas the distinction may not matter greatly for DCs, not only is it valid for LDCs but, if ignored, it introduces a systematic element of resource misallocation in the economy. For LDCs in specific the signals emitted by border prices (of tradables) do not always correspond to the opportunity cost of resources of producing tradables in terms of nontradables.

The empirical question of tradability and the observed patterns in the price deviations between tradables and nontradables are especially important for our argument. The empirical evidence in Tables 5.1 and 5.2 related directly to the law of one price and only indirectly to tradability. The systematic deviations between the aggregate price indexes and the levels of development captured by the ICP are consonant with the predictions of the tradable–nontradable differential productivity model, as Chapter 5 indicated. Unless, however, tradables and nontradables are specifically identified, and their price movements analyzed, the link between the ICP price indexes and the Ricardo Principle is incomplete. The purpose of this chapter is to provide such a link.

The elements of tradability

As noted in Chapter 3, the foundation of Ricardo's distinction between tradables and nontradables lies in the specification of the production function, particularly with respect to factor proportions and technology. Agriculture, with traditionally high labor intensity, is the stylized Ricardian nontradable.[1] Manufactures, on the other hand, which are capital- and technology-intensive, are tradables. The factor endowment/technology mix is reflected in productiv-

---

1 The notion that agriculture is the archetypical nontradable may be troubling to some, not the least because its productivity is extremely low in some LDCs. The point here is that productivity in the other tradable commodities is likely to be even lower. Tradedness that is adopted below as the empirical rule of tradability is consistent with this classification. LDCs have low ratios of exports plus imports for most agricultural commodities to total expenditure in GDP for the same commodities.

ity and ultimately in relative prices. Both ample labor supplies at the early stages of development and small productivity differentials with more developed countries make nontradables relatively cheap in LDCs. As development occurs, labor productivity grows slowly in nontradables (output of the traditional sector – agriculture) and their prices increase relative to those of tradables (output of the modern sector – manufacturing), where productivity grows faster. The tradable–nontradable relative price behavior, viewed at the international level, becomes intensified because of the presence and absence, respectively, of possibilities for commodity arbitrage. International trade in tradables is responsible for trade (export/import) discipline and for the operation of the law of one price.

Of the many underlying attributes of a commodity that determine Ricardian tradability, emphasis has shifted to price behavior and specifically to the extent to which (international) commodity arbitrage is reflected in uniform prices. Thus the distinction corresponds to the specification of the market structure for a commodity, from perfect markets to extremely fragmented markets. In relating commodity characteristics with price behavior, it will help if one considers a continuum that ranges from (pure) goods in the tradable extreme, to (pure) services in the nontradable end of the range. These are mapped on the continuum from the perfect to the extremely fragmented markets, respectively. Where exactly a commodity lies in this continuum depends largely on its inherent physical characteristics, which determine whether an "arm's-length" transaction is possible (pure goods) or face-to-face interaction between the transacting parties is also required (services).[2]

Transactions in goods establish rights over objects and the appropriability of these rights is possible with relatively small transaction cost. Transactions in services, on the other hand, involve substantial costs associated with face-to-face interactions. Services require direct application of human labor by the supplier to the final consumer. In the extreme case, therefore, international tradability of services involves the movement of producers. In this case it is transport cost which may render a good nontradable.

---

2 This distinction between goods and services draws on the definition of Hill (1977, pp. 317–318): "A good may be defined as a physical object which is appropriable and therefore transferable between economic units. . . . A service – on the contrary – may be defined as a change in the condition of a person, or of a good belonging to some economic unit, which is brought about as the result of the activity of some other economic unit, with the agreement of the former person or economic unit." In the context of Hill, service involves the *change in a condition* and therefore can only be the object of an obligation, as opposed to the object of an appropriable right.

This definition largely overlaps with the one by Fuchs (1968), who considers services commodities that are intangible, instantaneous (in that they "perish in the very instant of production"), produced next to the consumer and with his own participation; they cannot be stored, transported, or accumulated. Hill's definition sets out more clearly the issues of appropriability and transactions costs.

Since services are produced at the point of consumption, a service transaction involves the obligation by a party to deliver according to certain specifications. This means that services are ordinarily more "customized" than goods, i.e., their markets are more imperfect. And since normally it is impossible to establish with certainty the intentions of a party to deliver, it also means that services ordinarily involve some amount of trust (reputation). Trust goes beyond a simple personalistic relationship. It can be viewed as the qualitative factor-augmenting, face-to-face interaction that is needed for the production of services. Trust becomes an important element of cost in transactions involving uncertainty.[3] The requirements of a personalistic relationship and of trust, taken together, determine the labor intensity of the output. "Services," therefore, not only have higher transaction costs; they are also more labor intensive than "goods." Both transaction costs and labor intensity hamper the tradability of services. And the farther a commodity lies toward the "pure service" end of the continuum, the less it would be expected to enter international trade, especially in the case of LDCs.

We have so far identified some inherent characteristics in commodities that specify their location in the continuum between "pure goods" markets and "pure services" markets. The same continuum corresponds to the range between perfect markets and (extremely) fragmented markets. It can thus be described in terms of market imperfections. The classical market imperfections of special importance for international trade are due to economies of scale, learning curves, and the dynamics of innovation. Market imperfections also arise because of market failure and market incompleteness. The existence of market imperfections gives rise to economic rents.

Government intervention may also result in increasing market imperfections and thus give rise to economic rents. Traditional literature emphasizes barriers to entry as the cause of economic rents. Market fragmentation creates economic rents, which special interests seek to appropriate and are able to perpetuate under certain conditions. The role of government in this process is singled out in the stylized paradigm of the "rent-seeking economy": market fragmentation and economic rents derive from government regulation that imposes barriers of entry and couples them with price controls (Krueger, 1974).

---

3 Trust, or reputation, while it increases the "quality-weighted" amount of labor entering services, may be produced under economies of scale and can result in decreasing the ultimate cost per unit of labor ("shadow wage rate"). While LDCs may be better suited from the point of view of factor proportions for the production of services, such as banking, air travel, or restaurants, they are unlikely to be net exporters if international trade in those services is liberalized because of the high cost of producing "trust" in comparison to the DCs. The success of McDonalds and other international fast-food chains is evidence of this proposition.

International tradability and transaction costs

We can generalize the formulation of commodity-related characteristics, market-related characteristics, and government-related characteristics that limit tradability and thus give rise to economic rents in terms of transaction costs. Within the context of the new institutional economics, fragmented markets and the economic rents they create are the natural outcome of the existence of nonzero transaction costs. These represent costs that are not normally included in the conventional costs of production of neoclassical theory: costs of information, negotiation, coordination, monitoring, enforcement, and so on. Transaction costs are only in part due to the existence of incomplete property rights; they are also the result of the prevalence of alternative norms of economic behavior, alternative types of contracts, and differences in the "architecture" of socioeconomic systems.[4] Within this context, the approach of the new institutional economics tries to isolate the transaction costs that, when taken into account, explain why an apparent economic rent is not in fact an economic rent, and thus not a profit opportunity for a new potential entrant.

We have defined tradability in terms of "tradability transaction costs," which originate in the characteristics of the commodity (including transport costs), in the type of market in which it is traded (such as perfect or imperfect), or in government fiat. By doing so we have in fact produced an empirical rule for judging the degree to which a good is tradable: the extent of its price correlation with international prices. Prices of tradable goods need not be identical to international (border) prices as converted by the foreign exchange rate. In fact, transport costs and other transaction costs will ensure that they are not, and tariffs and subsidies might become additional wedges. Nor is it necessary that any trade actually occur for a commodity to be considered tradable. High correlation indicates that international prices matter for these goods; that they should be considered tradable is thus compelling. Such an approach would also allow for a graduated spectrum of tradability to be established: the correlation coefficient could be used directly as an index of relative tradability.

Figure 6.1 can help illustrate the relationship between tradability transaction costs and the categorization of a commodity as tradable or nontradable. Consider a commodity that is produced and consumed at home. It can become tradable, and thus comparable to an identical commodity abroad, by incurring a fixed "tradablity transaction cost" (Dornbusch, 1980, Chapter 6). The most convenient characterization of such a case is the iceberg transport cost, where

---

4 Sah and Stiglitz (1986, p. 716), who coined the term, define architecture as describing ". . . how the constituent decision-making units are arranged together in a system, how the decision-making authority and ability is distributed within a system, who gathers what information and who communicates what with whom."

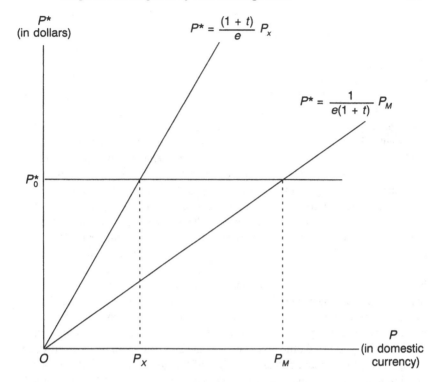

Figure 6.1. *Transaction costs and tradability*

the iceberg sheds a fixed percentage per unit of its volume as it travels. Writing P for the domestic price in local currency and P^* for the world price in dollars, and by comparing the two prices, we can determine whether the commodity is traded or not. Noting t for the tradability transaction cost and e for the nominal exchange rate, the commodity is exported if the domestic price is less than the export price, $P < P_X$, where $P_X = eP^*/(1 + t)$; it is imported if the domestic price is greater than the import price, $P > P_M$, where $P_M = eP^*(1 + t)$. The cone formed by P_M and P_X in Figure 6.1 defines, respectively, the highest domestic price that brings the commodity to the margin of becoming exportable, and the lowest domestic price that brings it to the margin of becoming importable. The region in between, described by the cone in the figure, represents the region of nontradability, given the world price. At price P_0^*, the nontradability region is $P_X P_M$.

In the discussion above, the exchange rate, e, links P_X and P_M to P^*. A devaluation – an increase in the exchange rate – increases both P_X and P_M and thus tilts both lines defining the margin of tradability downwards. The converse is the case for an appreciation of the domestic currency. An increase in transport cost has the same effect as devaluation on P_M – it increases it, but it decreases P_X, thus unambiguously increasing the cone of nontradables. Devaluation, therefore, acts as an increase in import cost (tariff) on importables. But the same increase in transport cost can offset the impact of devaluation on exportables unless it is countered by a subsidy. There is an asymmetry between the devaluation that displaces horizontally both lines in Figure 6.1 and the transport cost (tariff/subsidy) that impacts on the two lines differentially. Moreover, subsidies (and tariffs) are more flexible since they can be targeted on a specific commodity. Devaluation is generic. It increases the whole range of exportables and decreases that of importables, thus affecting all tradable commodities.

The definition of tradability so far has been positivist: it is based on the wedge that transaction costs drive between the domestic and international price of a good. Part of this wedge, however, is due to government action. This can be entirely arbitrary, since a government can, at its discretion (and as long as it is not plagued by an excessively porous border), make any good nontradable by fiat. (Making it tradable may prove more difficult, or at least more expensive.) On the other hand, manipulating the interface between domestic and foreign markets gives a government a powerful policy control variable, which if skillfully used can promote economic development – as opposed to serving more narrowly focused objectives, such as the short-run welfare of a particular group. The development-enhancing effect of the government fiat that makes a good nontradable becomes the normative part of the definition.[5] Its operational aspect is found in the Ricardo Principle, and depends on the actual (or potential) productivity differential. The normative aspects of tradability will be discussed in the comparative-development part of this book (Chapters 9–11).

The empirical content of tradability

The iceberg approach to tradability with fixed per-unit costs helps clarify issues. It does not address the multiple sources of tradability transaction costs. These relate to commodity characteristics, market characteristics, and government action, and as a result account for commodity-specific t_i's. This issue has been addressed in studies that involve significant disaggregation.[6]

One study that merits special mention is Richardson (1978). Although quite

5 The same normative element enters an alternative definition of tradability that distinguishes tradables (nontradables) by reference to "efficiency prices" and traded (nontraded) commodities with reference to market prices.
6 For example, Kravis and Lipsey (1977) examine price behavior in 4-digit SITC (standard industrial trade classification) detail for certain manufacturing sectors. Richardson (1978) covers a score of select commodities in the U.S. and Canada.

restricted in terms of commodity coverage, it adopts the most appropriate econometric approach for the operational definition of tradability in terms of the extent (and success) of commodity arbitrage. In studying the price behavior of certain commodities in the U.S. and Canada, the commodity's national price is regressed on the nominal exchange rate, the foreign price, the transfer cost (transport plus tariff) and a residual. The expected value of the coefficient for "pure goods" (tradables) is one and for "pure services" (nontradables) it is zero. The test of significance of the deviation of the estimates from the expected values becomes the test of tradability – and of the operation of the law of one price. In the "weak version" of the hypothesis, Richardson first correlates differences of the variables; the criterion of tradability becomes the extent to which acceleration/deceleration of foreign prices appears related to acceleration/deceleration of domestic prices and exchange rates.

The shortcoming of disaggregate studies is that they do not extend the commodity coverage to be exhaustive of GDP. Marris (1984) links the definition of tradability to empirical concepts forged by the International Comparisons Project, more specifically to the exchange rate deviation index (ERD).

Consider a continuum of tradability – corresponding to the continuum between "pure goods" and "pure services" – with the commodity-specific transfer cost (transport plus tariff) determining the degree of tradability. Although all commodities are conceivably tradable, whether they are actually traded or nontraded depends on the transfer cost, relative to the price of the commodity. Let P_i be the domestic price of commodity i, and P_i^* its international price converted to domestic currency at the nominal exchange rate. The ratio of domestic to international price for a commodity, P_i and P_i^*, respectively, indicates the extent to which that commodity enters international trade. If

$$P_i/P_i^* < 1 \tag{6.1}$$

commodity i is "cost-advantaged" and it will be produced domestically both for consumption and export, but will not be imported. Cost-disadvantaged commodities, on the other hand, will be produced domestically for consumption and as import substitutes, but will not be exported. This is shown in Figure 6.1. Since two commodities are comparable only if they are both accessible at the same place at one time, the unit cost of transfer, in domestic currency, between the foreign and the home market enters the picture. It has been defined in the previous discussion as "tradability transaction cost."

Assume for the moment that all goods are tradable, and even stronger, there are no goods that are not traded to some degree. Writing t for the tradability transaction cost of making a commodity accessible to the domestic market, we have:

$$P_i = P_i^* + t_i \tag{6.2}$$

The index of domestic to international prices is

$$P_i/P_i^* = 1 + t_i/P_i^* \tag{6.3}$$

By appropriately weighting the sum of i for such commodities we can form an index of domestic to foreign prices. We can write for the weights $w_i = P_i^* x_i$, where x_i is the per-capita consumption of the commodity at international prices. By multiplying in equation (6.3) we write:

$$
\begin{aligned}
w_i P_i/P_i^* &= w_i + w_i t_i/P_i^* \\
&= w_i + P_i^* x_i t_i/P_i^* \\
&= w_i + x_i t_i
\end{aligned}
\tag{6.4}
$$

Summing for equation (6.4) we have:

$$\sum P_i x_i / \sum P_i^* x_i = 1 + \sum x_i t_i / \sum w_i \tag{6.5}$$

The left-hand side of equation (6.5) consists of the GDP at domestic price levels in the numerator and the GDP at international price levels in the denominator. It is, by definition, the country's inverse of ERD, as shown in Chapter 5 by (the inverse of) equation (5.19), and as it appears in the data of Table 5.2, as the ratio of the nominal and the real columns.

In further specifying the value of t, suppose we apply equation (6.5) to an array of commodities ordered by increasing value of t, where t is defined negatively for cost-advantaged commodities and positively for cost-disadvantaged ones. The deviation of the value of ERD from unity in the equation is thus determined by the sign of $\sum x_i t_i$: negative signs (and ERD less than one) indicate that cost-advantaged commodities (tradables) predominate, whereas the GDP is more heavily weighted towards nontradables if the sign is positive (and ERD is greater than one). Notice that by changing transaction cost t_i for the ith commodity, the comparative-advantage ordering of the components of GDP changes. Tradability, in other words, becomes policy-induced. A subsidy on exports amounts to increasing the range of negative t's in the array by increasing the number of cost-advantaged commodities and thus tradability. So does a tax on imports, which decreases the number of cost-disadvantaged commodities in the array.

A given ordering of the array of transaction costs is independent of the exchange rate, whereas the signs and the values of t are not. Devaluation of the exchange rate is in some aspects equivalent to across-the-board protection as described above: it uniformly increases the domestic price of all foreign commodities and it moves the entire array of domestic commodities towards more tradability. As a result, the relatively more tradable domestic commodities (those closer to negative t's) become traded and the least tradable foreign commodities become nontraded. There lies precisely the difference between devaluation and protection. Tariffs and subsidies do not shift the array indiscriminately but can be targeted with an eye to commodities that in the future will have (without protection) lower t's than the mean (dynamic comparative advantage).

International macroequilibrium is defined as a free-trade world where ERD = 1; i.e., the nominal and the PPP exchange rate fully correspond. In this situation, the mean of the t-arrays of the two trading partners is zero, with the cost-advantaged and the cost-disadvantaged commodities symmetrically distributed around the mean. The equilibrium nominal and real exchange rates would lead to an identical distribution of resources only in a real world composed of countries that have identical t-determinant factors. What precisely these factors are becomes contingent on the choice of paradigm. In the studies by Krueger (1978), for example, the equilibrium real exchange rate is defined as the one that would prevail in the absence of "government distortions," which are taxes, subsidies, tariffs, and quantitative restrictions. Edwards (1989, Chapter 2) incorporates structuralist elements into an otherwise monetarist analysis. The equilibrium real exchange rate is a function of "exchange rate fundamentals." These are specified as world prices, technology, tariffs, interest rates, capital and exchange restrictions, and the composition of capital expenditures. Based on Ricardian considerations, one could add to the list factors such as per capita incomes, along with resource endowments and factor-price ratios, which are correlates of per capita incomes, and also perhaps tastes.

Our approach to estimating the real exchange rate is positivist and empirical. With data from the International Comparisons Project (ICP), we compute the ratio of a country's prices of tradables to nontradables, normalized by the international prices of the same commodities, whether these are in the tradable or nontradable international set.

The criterion of tradability plus tradedness

In equation (6.5) ERD is defined for the entire array of commodities, from the most cost-advantaged to the extreme of nontradables. By forming two subsets of GDP, for tradables and nontradables, we can formulate operationally the real exchange rate, RER, that was defined in Chapter 5.

Let us index nontradables as $i = 1, \ldots, N$ and tradables as $i = N + 1, \ldots, T$ and write:

$$P_T = \left(\sum_{i=N+1}^{T} P_i x_i \right) \Big/ \left(\sum_{i=N+1}^{T} P_i^* x_i \right) = 1 + \frac{\sum\limits_{i=N+1}^{T} x_i t_i}{\sum\limits_{i=N+1}^{T} w_i} \tag{6.6}$$

$$P_N = \left(\sum_{i=1}^{N} P_i x_i \right) \Big/ \left(\sum_{i=1}^{N} P_i^* x_i \right) = 1 + \frac{\sum\limits_{i=1}^{N} x_i t_i}{\sum\limits_{i=1}^{N} w_i} \tag{6.7}$$

The real exchange rate, defined as the ratio of equations (6.6) and (6.7), has many analogies to the previous interpretation of the ERD. A value greater than one indicates that tradability has been pushed to the point that a country has a cost disadvantage in the production of tradables, in terms of the opportunity cost of domestic resources in producing nontradables. The converse is true for a value less than one. Moreover, the deviation of the ratio of the relative prices of tradables to nontradables from one measures the degree of overvaluation (less than one) or undervaluation (greater than one) of the real exchange rate.

Operationally, the price of tradables and nontradables is derived from equations (5.21) and (5.22) of Chapter 5,[7]

$$RER = \frac{P_T}{P_N} = \frac{\prod_{i=N+1}^{T} \left(\frac{P_i^1}{P_i^{US}} \right)^{Q_i^1 / \Sigma_{i=N+1}^{T} Q_i^1}}{\prod_{i=1}^{N} \left(\frac{P_i^1}{P_i^{US}} \right)^{Q_i^1 / \Sigma_{i=1}^{N} Q_i^1}} \qquad (6.8)$$

The operational definition of the RER is equivalent to the theoretical definition. It can be proven that equations (6.6) and (6.7) correspond to the numerator and the denominator of equation (6.8), respectively.

It still remains to determine how to delineate the two subsets of commodities, $i = 1, \ldots, N$ and $i = N + 1, \ldots, T$, i.e., the range of nontradables and tradables. Tradability is certainly related to tradedness. It could therefore be defined based on the empirical–positivist rule of whether a good enters (international) trade or not. One could then define two mutually exclusive categories of traded and nontraded goods. This heuristic approach, however, fails to address some important issues. Is any participation in international trade sufficient to make a good traded? In such a case, few nontraded goods would probably remain. Even the proverbial haircuts would turn into traded goods, since it is only transport cost that would prevent a hairdresser to commute from London to New York – and it has certainly not prevented Mr. Vidal Sassoon from doing so. Should one measure the degree of tradedness by assigning a weight according to the share of a good's output that is actually traded?

Empirically, we have addressed the issue by resorting to the standard definition of openness in an economy that involves the ratio of imports and exports to GDP. The binary classification into tradables and nontradables was made by adopting an arbitrary cut-off point of trade value (the sum of exports and imports) for a commodity group of 20% of the total commodity expenditure in GDP. By distinguishing a large number of commodity groups (starting with the 152 basic commodity classification of the ICP) and by weighting both prices

---

7 It will be recalled that PPP prices are derived by the division of the respective nominal into the real expenditure, on a per-capita basis, and are expressed relative to the nominal (equals the real) expenditure in the U.S. See Chapter 5, equation (5.20).

and the participation of each individual commodity into tradability by actual expenditure weights, we have effectively blunted the arbitrariness of the criterion.

While the standard definition of openness is conceptually simple, the asymmetry with which exports and imports enter GDP can pose problems in its implementation. The former are included in GDP, while the latter are not. As a result, an increase in tradables that originates in an increase in exports is treated differently in calculating the degree of openness than the same increase in imports. The same problem arises if one takes the ratio of tradables to domestic disappearance, which includes imports but excludes exports. The problem is solved by an alternative symmetric definition of openness,[8] with the cut-off point for tradables again at 0.2:

$$\frac{M_i + X_i}{D_i + (M_i + X_i)/2} \geq 0.2 \tag{6.9}$$

where for commodity i, M are imports, X are exports, and D is production for domestic consumption (i.e., total domestic disappearance). The denominator in the index becomes the average of total production and total domestic disappearance.[9]

Data for implementing the definition of the RER in equation (6.8) are derived from the basic commodity classification of the ICP. Nominal and real per capita expenditures are available at the level of the basic commodity classification (152 commodities), along with their prices. They are expressed in domestic currency per U.S. dollar. Quantities can be derived from this basic information. These data were processed to derive prices of tradables and nontradables in a flexible aggregation form.

8 The measure of openness of an economy that is closest to ours is by Carvalho and Haddad (1980), who take the ratio of imports *minus* exports to domestic production plus imports minus exports. The index is conceptually deficient, since within a certain domain, where imports are greater than exports, an increase in exports leads to a decrease in the value of the index. The World Bank (1987, p. 82) has developed a classification system for openness that uses four criteria: effective rate of protection (which biases domestic production towards import substitution); use of quantitative controls such as quotas and import licensing; use of export incentives; and degree of exchange rate overvaluation. Such a system was used to classify countries as inward/outward oriented, and it is not appropriate for the purposes of our analysis. For further discussion see Chapter 7.

9 The variables in the formula are defined as follows within the national income utilization accounting:

D = production for domestic consumption
$D + X$ = total production
$D + M = A$ = total domestic disappearance (expenditure)

The average of total production and total expenditure is $[(D + X) + (D + M)]/2$, which is the denominator in equation (6.9). As an index of openness it has the property that it behaves symmetrically whether increased tradability comes from higher exports or imports. This particular symmetric index is due to Binkert (1992).

Table 6.1. *Index of RER, benchmark countries, 1970, 1975, 1980, 1985*

Country	1985	1980	1975	1970
Africa				
Cameroon		1.199		
Egypt	1.186			
Ethiopia	1.967	1.701		
Israel		1.138		
Ivory Coast	1.329			
Kenya	1.070	0.891	2.067	1.037
Madagascar		1.403		
Malawi	1.713	1.588	1.138	
Morocco	1.069	1.029		
Nigeria	1.196			
Rwanda	1.962			
Senegal		0.695		
Tanzania		0.790		
Tunisia		0.825		
Zimbabwe		1.186		
Asia and Oceania				
Australia	0.969			
India	1.178	1.036	1.962	1.525
Japan	0.923	1.206	1.071	1.097
Korea		1.461		0.971
Malaysia			1.580	1.083
New Zealand	1.208			
Pakistan	1.747	0.832	0.821	
Philippines	2.072	1.614	1.523	1.688
Sri Lanka	1.546	0.855	1.593	
Thailand	1.193		1.140	
Europe				
Austria	0.991	0.972	1.314	
Belgium	0.963	0.965	0.902	1.112
Denmark	0.980	0.959	0.985	
Finland	0.879			
France	1.095	1.027	1.080	1.185
Germany	1.155	0.973	1.027	1.010
Greece	1.417	1.406		
Hungary	1.192	1.255		
Ireland	0.918	1.148	1.031	
Italy	0.831	1.131	1.293	1.112
Netherlands	1.009	1.102	0.972	1.331
Norway	1.013	1.001		
Poland	0.829			
Portugal	1.230	1.226		
Spain	1.094	0.953	1.157	

(*continued on next page*)

Table 6.1 *(continued)*

Country	1985	1980	1975	1970
Sweden	0.933			
Turkey	0.998			
United Kingdom	0.990	0.883	0.936	0.896
Yugoslavia	1.542	1.274	0.939	
South America				
Argentina		0.999		
Bolivia		1.213		
Brazil		1.112	1.261	
Chile		1.249		
Colombia		1.437	1.737	
Ecuador		0.818		
Peru		0.757		
Uruguay		1.031	1.126	
Venezuela		1.005		
Central and North America				
Canada	0.928	0.936		
Costa Rica		1.069		
Dominican Republic		1.262		
El Salvador		1.384		
Guatemala		1.240		
Honduras		1.322		
Jamaica	0.949		1.279	
Mexico		1.346	2.009	
Panama		0.808		

Note:
The RER index is based on the symmetric definition of openness and adopts a cut-off point of 0.2.
See text.

The data for the definition of tradability come from the United Nations, *Yearbook of International Trade Statistics*, which provides in 5-digit SITC classification for each country the value of exports (f.o.b.) and imports (c.i.f.) in U.S. dollars. The 5-digit classification was reaggregated to establish concordance with the ICP data. Commodity groups were designated as traded or nontraded depending on whether the total value of trade was greater or less than 0.2 of the national expenditure on each commodity group. Finally, once a commodity was characterized in the binary classification of tradability, the ICP data on nominal and real expenditures were aggregated over the tradable and nontradable commodities to provide the respective prices and the RER index.

Table 6.1 gives the RER index for the benchmark countries in the various

Table 6.2. *Sensitivity of ranking by RER index to different criteria of tradability, 1975*

Country	RER at 0.2	Country	RER at 0.3
Kenya	2.067	Kenya	2.086
Mexico	2.009	Mexico	2.025
India	1.962	India	1.977
Colombia	1.737	Malaysia	1.644
Korea	1.704	Sri Lanka	1.613
Sri Lanka	1.593	Colombia	1.596
Malaysia	1.580	Philippines	1.544
Philippines	1.523	Malawi	1.502
Austria	1.314	Korea	1.488
Italy	1.293	Italy	1.351
Jamaica	1.279	Austria	1.311
Brazil	1.261	Brazil	1.292
Spain	1.157	Jamaica	1.279
Thailand	1.140	Ireland	1.263
Malawi	1.138	Spain	1.201
Uruguay	1.126	Thailand	1.158
France	1.080	Uruguay	1.155
Japan	1.071	Yugoslavia	1.148
Ireland	1.031	Pakistan	1.128
Germany	1.027	France	1.073
Denmark	0.985	Japan	1.067
Netherlands	0.972	Germany	1.026
Yugoslavia	0.939	Denmark	0.982
United Kingdom	0.936	Netherlands	0.961
Belgium	0.902	United Kingdom	0.933
Pakistan	0.821	Belgium	0.910

phases of the ICP. The index adopts 0.2 as the cut-off point of tradability. This is the RER index used in the empirical work.

By changing the cut-off point of tradability, the value of the index, of course, changes. As a result, the RER index cannot be used for cardinal measurement and the equilibrium value of the real exchange rate (that by definition would have been one) cannot be determined. However, as visual inspection of Table 6.2 indicates, the rank ordering of the countries remains largely invariant as the tradability cut-off point is changed to 0.3. The same remains true for other (reasonable) arbitrary changes of the cut-off point. The ranking of countries by the value of the RER index will be sufficient for the empirical analysis in Chapter 7.

The normalization procedure: A throwback to the law of one price?

The normalization procedure employed involves the international prices of the identical commodities in the basic 152-commodity classification of the ICP, whether we deal with the price indexes of commodities in the tradable or the nontradable group. A normalization procedure can be arbitrary. As long as it is consistent, it serves. However, two specific issues have been addressed in the literature relating to normalization by international prices. First, does it imply that the law of one price holds? Second, and beyond the law of one price, what is the precise mechanism by which prices of international goods influence national prices, especially in the case of nontradables?

The cautious approach to the law of one price states that, if it holds, it can at best hold for selected DCs only, and not for LDCs. The extreme position on the law is represented by the "monetary approach" to the balance of payments, which rests on the small-country assumption in implying that all goods have common world-market prices.[10]

Does the normalization procedure imply that the international price of a good, whether tradable or not, influences the national price of the same good that is not traded? This is not strictly the case, although an indirect relationship is bound to exist. First, goods that are classified as "nontraded" within a country are normalized by the international prices of the identical commodities, whether tradable or nontradable. The international nontradable subset is relatively small, compared to any national nontraded subset. Thus commodities in the national nontraded subset are likely to be matched with the same commodities that belong in the tradable international subset in the normalization procedure. Tradables and nontradables would be in one-to-one correspondence in countries j and k if tradability was the result of commodity characteristics alone, and commodity i was homogeneous in countries j and k. To the extent that tradability is also government-determined and market-structure induced, there is a systematic relationship between the range of tradability and the level of development (increasing). The normalization, therefore, expresses the shadow price of a commodity in an ideal, perfect-market world, where all goods become potentially tradable.

Even the commodities that are matched with international nontraded commodities (such as government services?) are expected to reflect the impact of world prices because of the existence of the complement of the nontradable subset in the universe, the tradable commodities, and especially because of the

10 For a comparison of the elasticity approach and the monetary approach to the balance of payments and for some empirical tests based on the distinction between tradables and nontradables see Kravis and Lipsey (1978). See also Chapter 5, pp. 87–93 for an elaboration of the monetarist position on the law of one price with reference to prices of tradables and nontradables.

existence of some factors of production that can produce either tradables or nontradables. The argument was first formulated by Haberler (1936, pp. 35 and 37). He pointed out that many traded goods are raw materials, semimanufactured commodities, and foodstuffs and they enter into the production of nontradable commodities, which must reflect the prices of tradable goods. He argued further that the constraint of the balance of payments may induce a general deflation in a country, which affects the price of home and export goods alike.

The argument is generalized by Srinivasan (1982) within a review of the shadow–price/project–evaluation literature. From the theory of nonoptimal taxation (Diamond and Mirrlees 1971, 1976) we have the familiar result that the relative world prices become the relative shadow prices for government production, on the assumption that all commodities can be viewed as a constant-returns industry, in using (exporting) one unit of one commodity and producing (importing) units of the other at the international price of the commodity. Similarly, it is known that under the assumption of constant-returns activities for the entire commodity set, the shadow prices for the public sector are the same as producer prices for the private sector. An interesting combination of these two special cases follows.

> Suppose that $n = 2m$ commodities fell into two mutually exclusive and collectively exhaustive categories: the first m being goods traded internationally at fixed relative prices and the remaining m being primary factors of production. Suppose further that each of the m traded commodities are produced by domestic constant returns-to-scale activities using primary factors. Then using $(m - 1)$ "production" activities consisting of, say, exporting a unit of the first commodity in exchange for importing an amount of each of the other $(m - 1)$ traded commodities equal to its relative world price along with the remaining m constant-return production activities, we can span the commodity set consisting of all the $2m$ commodities. Thus, the given world prices for traded commodities determine *all* shadow prices (Srinivasan, 1982, p. 234).

The introduction of nontradables directly into the analysis complicates matters further. Little and Mirrlees (1974, p. 167) suggest that since the shadow price of a commodity would equal its shadow cost of production, i.e., the value at shadow prices of the bundle of inputs used to produce one unit, and since there are as many equations as prices, there must exist a solution. The problem then is reduced to the special case discussed earlier. Srinivasan (1982, p. 237) shows that the conditions are actually more restrictive than implied by Little and Mirrlees. In any event, he concludes that although the assumptions are rather ad hoc and unrealistic, they are not more so than in any applied welfare analysis. Under certain conditions, nontradable prices can be linked to tradable goods prices. Therefore, even the extreme case of normalizing the national price of a nontraded commodity by its international price could be admissible.

Conclusion

Tradability has various attributes that relate not only to the characteristics of a commodity, but also to the type of market in which a commodity is traded, to transport costs, and to government action regarding the specific commodity. The tradability transaction cost reflects these attributes. As it changes, it can make a nontradable commodity into tradable and vice versa. In this sense, a change in tradability transaction cost resembles a change in the nominal exchange rate, but for the fact that the former is commodity-specific while the latter is generic, moving all commodities up or down the range of tradability.

The operational definition adopted for the empirical analysis in this book reduces tradability to tradedness. The extent to which a commodity enters international trade (imports plus exports) in each country defines the set of tradables and nontradables. The RER index is then calculated by flexible aggregation of price and expenditure data from the basic categories of the ICP.

The calculated values of the RER index are presented for all benchmark countries for the four phases of the ICP – 1970, 1975, 1980, and 1985. The data in Table 6.1 are employed for the empirical work in the next chapter.

CHAPTER 7

An endogenous growth model of
incomplete markets in foreign exchange

An empirical analysis of economic development that relies on international cross-section data is bound to grapple with the question (first featured in Chapter 2) that Arrow (1974) raised in his Nobel Prize lecture. Arrow observed that cross-country inequality in economic development is not readily amenable to the neoclassical explanation of differences in physical and human assets per capita. Two stylized facts about the experience of economic growth beg for an explanation (Kaldor, 1961; Kuznets, 1966). First, output per worker has risen secularly, and rates of productivity growth show no systematic tendency to decline. Thus growth in per capita incomes has been sustained in many instances. Second, there is great variance in growth performance across countries. This divergence does not seem to be random. But it is not autoregressive either, since there does not exist a strong correlation between the level of income at the beginning of the period and the growth outcome at the end.

Arrow's observation inspired a thriving literature that focused on issues of "convergence" (initiated by Baumol, 1986). A subset of this literature is the "endogenous growth" of the Romer–Lucas class of models (Romer, 1986, 1990; Lucas, 1988; Grossman and Helpman, 1992; Barro, 1990, 1991; Rivera-Batiz and Romer, 1991; Levine and Renelt, 1992).[1]

The empirical analysis in this chapter builds upon the tradition of this literature. The conventional reduced-form equations of endogenous growth models incorporate variables that can account for the exceptions to the static version of the fundamental theorems of welfare economics, such as the existence of economies of scale. The innovation in this chapter is that it also introduces a set of variables that reflect the existence of incomplete markets. It extends, therefore, the endogenous growth model to the dynamic version of the fundamental theorems that refers to the existence of a non-Arrow–Debreu world. A further innovation lies in the specification of the sources for market incompleteness. While the conventional analysis seeks the origins of incomplete markets in problems of asymmetric information, the ailment that accounts for the incomplete market in foreign exchange is asymmetric reputation (Chapter 3).

---

1 For the insights and historical perspective that inform the endogenous growth theory see Grossman and Helpman (1994), Pack (1994), Romer (1994), and Solow (1994).

The structural model

The endogenous growth literature attempts to associate specific differences in development performance with a set of explanatory variables that extend beyond the neoclassical set of formal inputs of production. The empirical hallmark of this chapter is that the RER is considered one of the crucial variables of interest because it incorporates information about market incompleteness in foreign exchange and, by extension, in trade. The motivation is to control for the effect of the stylized endogenous growth variables while assessing the impact of RER on measures of development performance.

The conventional endogenous growth models

The role of capital accumulation was eminent in the early attempts to explain sustained growth in per capita incomes. Solow (1957) formalized the idea that capital deepening could give rise to increasing labor productivity and could thus jumpstart a dynamic process of investment and growth. The concept of capital accumulation was extended to include also accumulation of knowledge. This form of technological progress, deepening in physical and human capital, helps "explain" the ubiquitous "Solow residual." Moreover, technological progress can account for a nondiminishing marginal product of capital and thus allows for capital formation to grow even after the stock of capital becomes "too large" relative to other resources.

But what is technological progress? The early view attributed technological progress to exogenous factors, in the sense that it was the outcome of events occurring outside the economic sphere. It was just driven by time. This approach, however, is at variance with the stylized facts of the growth experience as formulated earlier (Chapters 2 and 3).

Arrow (1962) was the first to deal with technological progress as an outgrowth of activities in the economic sphere. His "learning by doing" made knowledge a by-product of capital accumulation that created positive externalities for the rest of the economy. Arrow's ideas have led to formalizing two structural variants of the endogenous growth model.

The so-called "AK models" generate endogenous growth through linearity in capital accumulation within a production function that can be derived from some underlying framework (Rebelo, 1991). For illustrative purposes, assume a Cobb–Douglas production function

$$Y = TC^{\alpha}L^{1-\alpha} \tag{7.1}$$

where T represents the efficiency of technology, C is the capital asset, and L is labor (that also includes human capital). The household behavior embodied in this function includes arbitrage between the labor supply and the capital asset, and the arbitrage equation is

$$L = aC \tag{7.2}$$

The endogeneity of growth in this model lies in the household behavior captured in equation (7.2). By substituting (7.2) into (7.1) we have defined capital in a broad sense as $K = C + L$. Then from (7.2) we have

$$Y = Ta^{1-\alpha}C \tag{7.3}$$

$$C = K - L = K - aC \tag{7.4a}$$

$$C = \frac{K}{1 + a} \tag{7.4b}$$

By substituting (7.4a) into (7.3) we have

$$Y = Ta^{1-\alpha} \frac{K}{1 + a}$$

Finally, redefining $A \equiv T[a^{1-\alpha}/(1 + a)]$ gives the eponymous AK-type production function:

$$Y = AK \tag{7.5}$$

Next, endogeneity of the determinants of the technological coefficient T is established. The R&D version of the structural equation for endogenous growth focuses on innovation (Romer, 1990; Grossman and Helpman, 1992). Profit-maximizing entrepreneurs, in their efforts to decrease costs and raise the productivity of conventional factors of production such as capital and labor, search for innovations. Technological progress is the endogenous outcome of such a search. The basic idea behind these models is summarized by two equations:

$$Y = TC^{\alpha}L_Y^{1-\alpha} \tag{7.6a}$$

$$\frac{\dot{T}}{T} = \gamma L_A \tag{7.6b}$$

where there are two types of labor: L_Y is used in the production of output, and L_A is used in the search for innovations. The first equation is the familiar Hicks-neutral technological change equation. The case is made that increasing returns to scale enter this production function through the knowledge that is produced by the second equation. Knowledge is a nonrival and nonexcludable good. Once knowledge has been discovered, one agent using it in production does not prevent others from using it simultaneously. Moreover, the creators of technical knowledge have difficulty in preventing others from making unauthorized use of it. It is at least partially nonexcludable. A capital good, on the other hand, can be used only at one place at a time and its owner can prevent use by others. The nonrival and nonexcludable nature of technology introduces increasing returns to scale in the production function in equations (7.6). Given a stock of knowledge, by doubling capital and labor one doubles output without any further increase of knowledge being required. When the microprocessor was discovered there was a step-up in output; but further increases in output relied on increases in capital and labor applied with the microprocessor. Once the breakthrough was made to apply microprocessors on a circuit board, the blueprints for the computer could be duplicated at virtually zero cost and only capital and labor were required to produce more computers. The endogenous nature of knowledge thus yields increasing returns to scale.

The empirical implementation of either variant of the reduced-form equations proposes to identify variables that are endogenous to the economic system and can be used as proxies for technological change. The estimation procedure quantifies the impact of such variables on development. By combining the two formulations for timed output with the Harrod–Domar equations, the growth rate becomes a linear function of the rate of savings:

$$\dot{K}_t = s_t Y_t \tag{7.7a}$$

$$\dot{Y}/Y = \dot{K}/K = A_t s_t \tag{7.7b}$$

$$G_t = A_t s_t; \qquad A_t = T_t \frac{a^{1-\alpha}}{1+a} \tag{7.7c}$$

$$\frac{\dot{A}_t}{A_t} = \frac{\dot{T}_t}{T_t} = \gamma L_A \tag{7.7d}$$

where t indicates time and dots indicate change. In these equations, s represents the "effective" net savings rate, instead of the aggregate nominal savings rate. Therefore, the rate of aggregate growth in output, G, is equal to that in capital and is the product of a technology term A and the effective savings rate. The properties of this formulation of the endogenous growth model have been explored in a number of papers.[2]

An endogenous growth model with incomplete markets

The basic hypothesis in this book is about development performance and exchange rate policies, as reflected in the values of NER and RER. The development performance is an observable characteristic of the international

---

2 For examples see Barro (1990), Rebelo (1991), Roubini and Sala-i-Martin (1992), and Pagano (1993).

cross section of countries, but the outcome of exchange rate policies that pursue an equilibrium RER and NER is not, since the equilibrium value of an exchange rate as such is not immediately known. There is a presumption, however, that if the foreign exchange market is incomplete, achieving equilibrium in one exchange rate, say the nominal, does not imply equilibrium in the real rate also. Furthermore, should the NER be allowed to find its market-clearing rate in an LDC without foreign exchange restrictions, the domestic currency is likely to be subjected to further systematic depreciations. This presumption for spiral devaluations is based on asymmetric reputation, which is systematically related to the level of underdevelopment (Chapter 3). Devaluation would cause the prices of tradables to increase relative to nontradables. In this sense a "high" NER will be reflected in high RER. Should the foreign exchange market be systematically incomplete in the above sense, it cannot be relied upon to produce Pareto-optimal outcomes. The obverse side of this proposition is that overriding the foreign exchange market, by intervention in the NER, is likely to improve development outcomes.

The operational procedure for testing for market incompleteness is to use the value of the RER index as a proxy to infer the value of the NER. The test of the hypothesis consists of explaining the intercountry variance in rates of growth of real GDP per capita, *GRGDPC*, by the variance in their *RER*. An inverse relationship is expected: countries that have low *RER* – the result of controlling the level of NER – have the higher rates of growth in GRGDPC. Should such a relationship exist, three challenges arise: to infer causality going the right way (from *RER* to *GRGDPC*); to translate the relationship in terms of the *NER*, which is the policy control variable; and to relate the results to incomplete markets.

The formal introduction of the *RER* into an endogenous growth framework rests on equation (7.7c) above. One existing interpretation of the model in equation (7.7c) emphasizes the distinction between the flow of savings and the effective savings rate. A proportion of the flow of savings, $1 - \phi$, is lost in the process of financial intermediation because of the action of government (financial repression, faulty supervision) or the failure of the market (information problems, lack of financial instruments, financial inefficiencies). One can think of $1 - \phi$ as the disintermediation loss of savings. A simple equation has been used to capture the endogenous nature of the effective savings rate and the disintermediation cost (Roubini and Sala-i-Martin, 1992; Pagano, 1993):

$$G_t = A_t \phi s_t^* \tag{7.8}$$

where, $0 < \phi < 1$, s^* is the nominal savings rate, and $s = \phi s^*$.

Equation (7.8) can be used to construct an endogenous growth framework incorporating the *RER*. In an open economy, s^* is the weighted average of the domestic and foreign savings rate. An incomplete market in foreign exchange based on reputation asymmetries can affect both the foreign and the domestic component of savings. Demand for hard currency in an LDC as a substitute for the home currency is as likely to create financial hoardings as it is to induce financial savings. The depreciating value of domestic currency that follows and the expectation of inflation, *GINFL*, is bound to decrease the flow of foreign savings. Further decline in effective savings can occur as devaluation is reflected in higher prices of tradables and nonoptimal flows of resources from the nontradable sector. High propensity of unproductive government consumption, *GOVCONS*, will also crowd out total savings available to private agents.

This story can be formalized explicitly by assuming that ϕ is a function of the real exchange rate index, *RER*, and of *GOVCONS*, and s^* is a function of *GINFL*,

$$G_t = A_t \phi(RER, GOVCONS) s_t^*(GINFL), \qquad \phi_1 < 0, \ \phi_2 < 0, \ s_{t1}^* < 0 \qquad (7.9)$$

The empirical test of the endogenous growth model utilizes a cross section of countries that are at different levels of development. One has to account for differences in per capita incomes, since DCs are not afflicted by the market incompleteness which, ex hypothesi, is the mechanism that produces systematically high NER values for LDCs. This is done by including as a variable the value of the real GDP per capita, or else a dummy that distinguishes between low/middle income countries and DCs.

Next, we will incorporate the usual endogenous growth formulation of technological progress as it appears in equations (7.6b) and (7.7d) above. The single parameter A of the AK model is unbundled in this approach to highlight specifically L_A, the skilled labor that spearheads the search for innovations. The complete specification of the process of the search for innovations is not independent of the stage of technological development in a country. LDCs have the advantage of latecomers in development in relying on the process of the diffusion of technology through trade and through human capital spillovers.

Since Adam Smith first formulated the traditional trade–growth nexus, the extent of the market has been considered a determinant of efficiency. This is usually captured by the openness of an economy, *OPEN*, which is a measure of a ratio of trade to GDP. More recently a second effect, the direction of trade, *DIR*, has become a prominent variable. Controlling for the volume of trade, the direction-of-trade variable may capture the technological spillovers from trading with more-developed partners. One advantage of such trade is that the innovation-producing skilled labor of DCs is extended to LDCs through technological diffusion (Grossman and Helpman, 1991). In formalizing this interpretation one may consider the L_A of equation (7.7d) as consisting of two components. The L_{Af}, the foreign component of the skilled labor is proxied by *DIR*, while the domestic component, L_{Ad}, is a function of education, *SECENRL*. Finally, investment, *INV* (as opposed to the accumulated stock of capital) becomes an important vehicle for technological diffusion because of the vintage effect of new capital.

With the above considerations, the specification of the technology component of the endogenous growth equation becomes:

$$A_t = A(INV, OPEN, DIR, SECENRL), \quad A_1 > 0, A_2 > ?, A_3 > 0, A_4 > 0 \quad (7.10)$$

The two equations, (7.9) and (7.10), constitute a linkage between the specific hypothesis of market incompleteness and the extant theory and empirical analysis:

$$G_t = A(INV, OPEN, DIR, SECENRL)\phi(RER, GOVCONS)s_t^*(GINFL) \quad (7.11)$$

where G_t is the growth rate of real per capita GDP.

Various formulations of the linear version of this equation will be estimated in what follows.

Implementation of an endogenous growth framework

The dependent variable

Per capita income is a common proxy for development; its rate of growth is the generally accepted performance indicator. Like the endogenous growth literature, this chapter follows this tradition.[3]

By using benchmark-country data, the analysis covers the period 1970–1985 at five-year intervals. The dependent variable, therefore, was derived by fitting the logarithmic growth rate of the annual observations of real per capita GDP on time for each five years.[4]

There are the possibilities of lagging the rate of growth, or centering it on the benchmark year. The latter option was taken for conceptual reasons that refer to causality going from *RER* to the rate of growth. The real rate of growth of per-capita GDP (*GRGDPC*) was taken. The source is Penn World Tables 5 (Summers and Heston, 1991). It is commonly chosen in endogenous growth studies over the rate of growth of nominal GDP per capita. Moreover, since the latter is derived by NER conversion of national currency units, it becomes an inappropriate variable for testing a hypothesis relating to the systematic deviation between RER and NER at various levels of development.

---

3 The growth rate rather than the level of income is the appropriate variable for this empirical work because of the asset–value dynamics formulation that becomes the foundation of market incompleteness. See below.

4 The rule of regressing ln GDP per capita on time for up to four different five-year spans (depending on the number of benchmark observations for each country) was actually mixed where the fit of the regression for five years was poor ($r^2 < 0.6$). The average of the annual growth for five years was taken in such cases, which totaled to approximately one-fifth of the observations.

The explanatory variables of primary interest

The strategic variable in this formulation of the endogenous growth hypothesis is the RER index. The empirical test of the hypothesis relates *RER* to *GRGDPC*. It has to account for two factors that, if left uncontrolled, could bias the estimated relationship between the two variables. Market incompleteness is systematically (and negatively) related to the level of development. In using the *RER* as a proxy for market incompleteness one has to control for the stage of development, and specifically for the binary distinction between DCs and LDCs. Per capita income is a common proxy for that purpose and it is used in the analysis in real terms (*RGDPC*). As an alternative, a dummy variable is used with a value of 0 for DCs and 1 for LDCs, whether of low or middle income (*DumL/M*).[5] The classification of countries as low-, middle-, or high-income is from the World Bank (1992a). An interaction variable that is a composite of the RER index and real per capita income is also introduced in the analysis. It serves as an on–off variable to explore if the impact of the RER changes across income levels. The second problem relates to the general slowdown in growth since the 1980s. A dummy variable with the value of 1 for the observations of 1980 and 1985 is also used (*Dum80/85*). In both cases the pooled data have been partitioned so that the influence of these two factors has been excluded from the analysis.

A variable that appears often in endogenous growth studies is some index of the volume of trade (*OPEN*) as a proxy for the openness of the economy. In this study, however, *OPEN* is more than a stylized endogenous growth variable that is expected to be positively associated with growth. After controlling for *RER*, it becomes an open question whether more or less trade is associated with high-growth-rate regimes. The most common index of *OPEN* is a variable measuring the volume of trade. The ratio of exports to GDP, or that of exports plus imports to GDP, has been used commonly for measuring the openness of the economy. Experimentation with both the single (World Bank "Stars" and Penn World Tables 5) and double indexes for this variable showed that the results did not change greatly; the latter index was chosen. An index that includes both exports and imports, however, presents a problem of asymmetrical treatment of the two components, since an increase in exports (which are part of GDP) is also reflected in the denominator but not an increase in imports (which are not part of GDP). An appropriate measure of *OPEN* that obviates this problem was defined in Chapter 6:

$$OPEN = M + X/[D + (M + X)/2]$$

---

5 There are reasons to believe that the *DumL/M* is a better proxy for controlling for the level of development than the *RGDPC*. The intergroup variance in per capita incomes for DCs is considerable, but the expected variance in the deviation between their NER and RER is zero.

where M is imports, X exports, and D is production for domestic consumption (i.e., total domestic disappearance, minus imports).

As already mentioned, the direction of trade (DIR) is used to capture the technological spillovers from trading with more-developed partners. It also serves to further sharpen the implications of market incompleteness. Partners at relatively similar levels of development (and economic structure), have less incomplete markets relative one to another. South–South trade, for example, must be hampered less by market incompleteness than North–South trade. Moreover, the normalization procedure for domestic prices in the ICP is by numeraire country (United States) prices. It serves as a proxy for normalization by DC prices. To the extent that an LDC trades with other LDCs (South–South trade), the appropriate normalization factor would be the latter countries' prices. Both these considerations, along with the technological spillover effect, can be controlled by accounting for the share of a country's trade with LDC partners. The considerations are reflected in the DIR variable, representing a country's OECD-partner trade (as a ratio of total trade).

Other studies of this type have used variables of openness that refer to the distortion between domestic and international prices. Normally, they measure the deviation of the nominal exchange rate from the black-market exchange rate, or the deviation of extrapolated values of PPP prices from certain international prices (Dollar, 1992). Such variables, if they measure successfully what they intend to capture, would be expected to covary with the RER variable. Experimentation with them confirms this expectation, as will be discussed in a later section.

The stylized endogenous growth variables

Classical growth accounting has been limited by its use of physical endowments and technology as the main explanatory variables of growth. The endogenous growth literature, on the other hand, has been spurred by the inability of the traditional production function approach to account fully for intercountry differences in developmental outcomes as expressed by rates of growth. It has shifted emphasis, therefore, to the factors that have been traditionally neglected, most of them relating to economic structure, human capital, and the openness of the economy.

The empirical analysis in this study has experimented with most of the stylized factors that enter the endogenous growth literature, as long as data were available for the entire period covered. A choice set of factors were seriously considered and retained in the analysis.

The investment share in GDP (INV) is a supplemental variable describing the physical endowments. It is the most common variable in studies of endogenous growth, being included in 33 of the 41 studies surveyed in Levine and Renelt

(1992). It is also the only variable that exhibits a robust correlation with the rate of growth of GDP in an "extreme bounds" analysis of all the previous studies that the same authors conducted. The source for INV data is *World Bank National Accounts*.[6]

The inclusion of human capital variables in endogenous growth models is intended to capture quality differences in the labor force. They commonly relate to education and are measured by an index of educational attainment, by mean years of schooling, or by school enrollment, in that order of preference. It is difficult to construct an operational concept around educational attainment, and it is even more difficult to measure it. As a minimum, it would require that a population matrix be built by age, level of education, and skill specification, as an indicator of quality. Data on mean years of schooling are easier to obtain from decennial censuses. School enrollment data are more commonly reported by national authorities at the source. They exist for most countries on an annual basis, compiled by UNESCO. When they are used for longitudinal cross-country comparisons they suffer from the fact that data gaps have been filled with "estimates" based on interpolations, intrapolations, extrapolations, and projections from the last available observation for the country.[7] Secondary school enrollment (*SECENRL*) is the variable most commonly used in endogenous growth studies, and it is also adopted here (Isenman, 1980; Ahmad, 1995).

Demographic variables that relate to the quality of the labor force include age and sex distribution of the population, life expectancy rates, and infant mortality rates. Although widely available, these variables need to be used with caution in endogenous growth models since life expectancy and infant mortality, as reported by the World Bank, suffer the same "data gap" problem discussed with school enrollment data.[8] Health and nutrition also affect productivity. They can be measured by the number of doctors (population per doctor) and by calorie consumption. The former is not available for all the countries or for the entire period; nor are there data on the gap between availability and requirements of calories per adult equivalent. The rate of growth of population (*GPOP*) is also an appropriate variable, especially when the dependent variable is growth in per capita income. Next to *INV*, it is the

6 Data are from the World Bank "Stars" databank. The alternative of expressing *INV* in real terms (from Penn World Tables 5) was also tried, and the difference in results was negligible.

7 Behrman and Rosenzweig (1994) find that the data gaps are systematically related to a country's level of development and refer to "made-up" educational data for LDCs because of this problem. They also note that enrollment data are usually reported to the national authority on school-opening dates, and therefore they tend to be overestimates.

8 As an example, see last date of data observation for demographic variables produced by the World Bank in World Bank (1993b, pp. 377–379); for a number of LDCs it is closer to the 1970s than the 1990s.

second most common variable that has featured in endogenous growth studies (Levine and Renelt, 1992). The data for this variable are from the World Bank "Stars" data files.

Sectoral shares are the most common economic-structure variables (Chenery, 1979). Value added in agriculture as a proportion to GDP is usually inversely related to the level of development, productivity, and wages and thus features in several endogenous growth modeling attempts. Lack of data on sectoral shares for a large number of countries in the sample prevented experimentation with this variable.

Among the other frequently used structural variables are the average rate of government consumption expenditure in GDP (*GOVCONS*); the average rate of (change in) inflation (*GINFL*); and the average growth rate of domestic credit. The *GOVCONS* variable is from Penn World Tables 5, while *GINFL* is from the World Bank "Stars" files. Data for the growth of domestic credit were not available for the years of the study.

The variable *GOVCONS* intends to capture one (negative) aspect of the quality of government. It is a feeble attempt, as will be explained presently. Another variable that has been used as a qualitative proxy for governance is the number of revolutions and coups (Barro, 1991). It is a derivative of the index of socioeconomic instability that Venieris and Gupta (1983, 1986) developed and associated with savings, consumption, and investment behavior, and alternately with growth. Alesina and Perotti (1993) also deal with sociopolitical instability within the context of the negative relationship between inequality and growth. Inequality results in demands to alter the established order; political instability, in turn, reduces investment. The full set of data required for our purposes is not available for these alternative variables that measure the quality of government. Moreover, as will also be discussed below, such variables do not adequately define the disposition of the economic rents, which is the primary focus of our analysis.

Appendix Table A7.1 provides the basic statistics for all the variables used in the analysis.

The empirical analysis

Ordinary least squares results

The substantial body of endogenous growth literature has established two facts. It is not hard to devise econometric specifications in which sundry variables measuring economic policy are significantly correlated with economic growth. It is almost impossible, however, to discover explanatory variables that are robust enough so that their estimated coefficients do not depend importantly on the conditioning set of information. Levine and Renelt (1992) reviewed 41 studies and found over 50 variables that correlated significantly with growth in various papers. But only one, the ratio of investment in GDP, had a robust coefficient in an "extreme bounds" analysis (Leamer, 1983, 1985).

The presentation of the results of seven nested tests in Tables 7.1 to 7.7 is organized in five models that group variables so as to provide an immediate indicator of the robustness of the maintained hypothesis. Following Leamer's specification-search method the operational procedure is to regress *GRGDPC* on *RER*, the main variable of interest, and successively on a greater number of variables. By regressing the dependent variable on all possible combinations of independent variables, the robust ones are identified as those that have no sign switches, have small variations in coefficient values, and hold their statistical significance across all combinations. Moreover, comparing the test results across different groupings of countries and different years in the sequence of tables enables the reader to determine the spatial and time-period dimensions of the robustness of the maintained hypothesis.

In model I, *RER* appears as the single conditioning variable. Model II increases the number of explanatory variables to three, by including the two dummy conditioning variables that describe the state of the world within which the RER operates. *DumL/M* (= 1) accounts for the fact that incomplete markets in exchange rates are the characteristic of LDCs only and not of DCs; *Dum*80/85 (= 1) accounts for the slowdown of the rate of growth in the latter period of this study. Model III includes *OPEN* and *DIR*, another two variables of primary interest that describe the trade regime that complements the RER policy instrument. Model IV increases the number of explanatory variables to six, by including *INV*, the only variable that has proven robust in other endogenous growth studies. Model V increases the number of explanatory variables to 10 by adding *GINFL*, *GOVCONS*, *SECENRL*, and *GPOP*. The last four variables are among those most commonly used in endogenous growth studies, and they were chosen, as were the new variables in each group, because they do not measure the same phenomenon with the main variable of interest. By inspecting the change in the value of the coefficient of a certain variable across groups, the reader can draw conclusions about the robustness of each variable. All explanatory variables enter the regressions of the rate of growth of real GDP per capita independently and linearly.

The first group of models reported (Table 7.1) is the longitudinal analysis for the sample of 123 observations (62 countries) for the years 1970, 1975, 1980, and 1985. The coefficient of *RER* has the expected negative sign and is consistently significant. The maintained hypothesis construes the inverse relationship between *RER* and *GRGDPC* as evidence that interventions in an incomplete foreign exchange market can lead to better developmental outcomes. Moreover, the coefficient of *RER* is robust, as evidenced from the fact that it varies within a very narrow range (from −0.020 to −0.024) as other

Table 7.1. *Cross-section/time-series regressions on growth, all countries, 1970, 1975, 1980, and 1985*

Explanatory variables	I	II	III	IV	V
			Model		
Constant	0.040	0.056	0.068	0.043	0.044
RER	−0.021	−0.022	−0.024	−0.020	−0.022
	(−2.708)	(−2.774)	(−2.947)	(−2.450)	(−2.683)
Dummy low/middle		−0.003	−0.003	−0.004	0.004
($DumL/M$ = 1)		(−0.668)	(−0.601)	(−0.824)	(0.493)
Dummy 1980/1985		−0.017	−0.017	−0.016	−0.016
($Dum80/85$ = 1)		(−3.652)	(−3.474)	(−3.439)	(−3.346)
Openness ($OPEN$)			−0.010	−0.012	−0.017
			(−1.127)	(−1.352)	(−1.731)
Direction of trade (share			0.015	0.023	0.022
of OECD) (DIR)			(0.904)	(1.410)	(1.341)
Investment in GDP (INV)				0.104	0.089
				(2.812)	(2.277)
Rate of inflation (change)					−0.023
($GINFL$)					(−1.960)
Government consumption in					−0.000
GDP ($GOVCONS$)					(−0.178)
Secondary school enrollment					0.012
($SECENRL$)					(0.880)
Population growth ($GPOP$)					−0.048
					(−0.460)
Sample size	123	123	123	123	123
Adjusted R^2	0.049	0.142	0.139	0.187	0.193
Standard error	0.025	0.024	0.024	0.023	0.023
F-statistic (zero slopes)	7.333	7.754	4.944	5.682	3.923

Notes:
The dependent variable is annual rate of growth of real per capita GDP, $GRGDPC$, for the five-year period centered on the year of observation. For definition of independent variables see text. Numbers in parentheses are T-statistics.

variables are added seriatim in the regressions for all the tests reported in the table.

In model II, the two dummy variables condition for the state of the world in which the growth–RER nexus becomes relevant. The coefficient of $DumL/M$ remains invariant as the other variables are introduced, but it is insignificant.

A conceivable interpretation of the negative sign is that, given the value of RER, the rate of growth is lower the more incomplete the market is (i.e., for low and middle income LDCs). The coefficient of the *Dum*80/85, on the other hand, is robust and fully captures the slowdown of the growth in the period.

In model III, the two trade variables are added. The coefficient of *OPEN* is consistently negative, albeit significant only in the last iteration with model V. Its sign is different from the expected (and elusive) result in the literature. The canonical result in endogenous growth studies is a negative coefficient for the share of trade in GDP.[9] While this finding is puzzling for the orthodox approach to trade and development, it can be readily explained in this interpretation. Controlling for the value of the *RER*, one would expect a negative relationship between *GRGDPC* and *OPEN*. Countries that control the level of NER have low RER, grow fast, and are expected to have lower volume of trade than would have obtained in free foreign-exchange markets. The more open the economy is, as a result, the lower the rate of growth.

The *DIR*, on the other hand, has a positive but nonsignificant coefficient. The sign indicates that, controlling for *RER* and *OPEN*, the benefit of trade arises from the technological spill-over of having more-developed trading partners (proxied by OECD). The *INV* variable itself in model IV is highly significant, with values ranging from 0.089 to 0.104, which is very close to the modal values reported in other studies for the same variable. This coefficient presents a strong link with the celebrated and most significant result that other studies of endogenous growth have established (Levine and Renelt, 1992).

Among the variables added in model V, the coefficient for *GINFL* is significant and has the expected negative sign. The coefficient of *GPOP* has the correct negative sign but is insignificant. Finally, *SECENRL* and *GOVCONS* have proven as difficult to capture in this study as they have in the parallel literature.

The models reported in Table 7.2 are for the period of 1980 and 1985, with 86 observations (61 countries). This partition of the data makes the dummy for the slowdown of growth redundant. The results remain very close to those reported in the first test. The coefficients for *RER* are significant and robust, with a negative value ranging from −0.017 to −0.025. The signs and the values for *DumL/M*, *OPEN*, and *DIR* remain roughly the same and are again nonsignificant. The coefficient of *INV*, however, is significant (in one case) and has roughly the same values that it had in Table 7.1. The other variables in model V retain the sign and previous level of significance of their coefficients.

The nested models in Tables 7.3 and 7.4 report single-year results for 1985 and 1980, respectively. The story on *RER* remains consistent with respect to the sign and the size of the coefficients. But with the degrees of freedom drastically reduced (37 observations for 1985 and 49 for 1980), some of the previously

---

9 The one exception to this result is Dollar (1992), to be discussed below.

Table 7.2. *Cross-section/time-series regressions on growth, all countries, 1980 and 1985*

Explanatory variables	Model				
	I	II	III	IV	V
Constant	0.040	0.039	0.042	0.022	0.020
RER	−0.025	−0.020	−0.021	−0.017	−0.019
	(−2.720)	(−2.028)	(−2.051)	(−1.619)	(−1.798)
Dummy low/middle		−0.008	−0.010	−0.011	−0.002
(*DumL/M* = 1)		(−1.297)	(−1.525)	(−1.604)	(−0.158)
Openness (*OPEN*)			−0.007	−0.009	−0.016
			(−0.695)	(−0.912)	(−1.406)
Direction of trade (share			−0.007	0.005	0.005
of OECD) (*DIR*)			(−0.358)	(0.237)	(0.226)
Investment in GDP (*INV*)				0.091	0.078
				(2.003)	(1.551)
Rate of inflation (change)					−0.022
(*GINFL*)					(−1.741)
Government consumption in					0.000
GDP (*GOVCONS*)					(0.213)
Secondary school enrollment					0.014
(*SECENRL*)					(0.827)
Population growth (*GPOP*)					−0.073
					(−0.653)
Sample size	86	86	86	86	86
Adjusted R^2	0.070	0.077	0.064	0.098	0.099
Standard error	0.024	0.024	0.024	0.024	0.024
F-statistic (zero slopes)	7.397	4.570	2.461	2.845	2.043

Notes:
The dependent variable is annual rate of growth of real per capita GDP, GRGDPC, for the five-year period centered on the year of observation. For definition of independent variables see text. Numbers in parentheses are *T*-statistics.

strong coefficients become insignificant, including *RER* for 1980 and *INV* for both years.

The models in Table 7.5 are for the period 1970 and 1975 (37 observations, 26 countries). The compatibility of these results with the pooled regressions in Table 7.1 is remarkable: the coefficients of *RER* are consistently significant, with robust negative values of from −0.023 to −0.034; *INV* retains the same values of coefficients of about 0.09 to 0.11 but they become nonsignificant;

Table 7.3. *Cross-section regressions on growth, all countries, 1985*

Explanatory variables	Model				
	I	II	III	IV	V
Constant	0.051	0.047	0.033	0.026	0.036
RER	−0.031	−0.024	−0.022	−0.020	−0.024
	(−3.290)	(−2.089)	(−1.963)	(−1.582)	(−2.040)
Dummy low/middle		−0.008	−0.019	−0.019	−0.041
(*DumL/M* = 1)		(−1.064)	(−2.308)	(−2.257)	(−0.314)
Openness (*OPEN*)			−0.005	−0.005	−0.017
			(−0.450)	(−0.423)	(−1.405)
Direction of trade (share			−0.056	−0.048	−0.051
of OECD) (*DIR*)			(−2.319)	(−1.642)	(−1.591)
Investment in GDP (*INV*)				0.033	−0.022
				(0.490)	(−0.283)
Rate of inflation (change)					−0.005
(*GINFL*)					(−0.174)
Government consumption in					0.001
GDP (*GOVCONS*)					(1.747)
Secondary school enrollment					−0.000
(*SECENRL*)					(−0.054)
Population growth (*GPOP*)					−1.111
					(−2.869)
Sample size	37	37	37	37	37
Adjusted R^2	0.214	0.217	0.322	0.305	0.458
Standard error	0.019	0.019	0.017	0.018	0.016
F-statistic (zero slopes)	10.827	6.000	5.267	4.162	4.387

Notes:
The dependent variable is annual rate of growth of real per capita GDP, GRGDPC, for the five-year period centered on the year of observation. For definition of independent variables see text. Numbers in parentheses are *T*-statistics.

DIR emerges again as a strong variable that signals the value of trading with technologically advanced partners. The balance of the variables have the same signs and are not significant as earlier. The only surprise is the positive (but not significant) sign of the *DumL/M*. The breakdown of the sample between 1975 and 1970 was not possible due to degrees of freedom problems: there are only 12 observations for 1970.

Table 7.6 reports the models for the longitudinal analysis of the entire sample

Table 7.4. *Cross-section regressions on growth, all countries, 1980*

Explanatory variables	Model				
	I	II	III	IV	V
Constant	0.032	0.033	0.045	0.023	0.029
RER	−0.021	−0.020	−0.021	−0.019	−0.022
	(−1.270)	(−1.112)	(−1.165)	(−1.091)	(−1.172)
Dummy low/middle		−0.003	−0.002	−0.003	0.002
(*DumL/M* = 1)		(−0.390)	(−0.169)	(−0.236)	(0.098)
Openness (*OPEN*)			−0.005	−0.009	−0.014
			(−0.317)	(−0.555)	(−0.710)
Direction of trade (share			0.025	0.031	0.032
of OECD) (*DIR*)			(0.788)	(0.968)	(0.921)
Investment in GDP (*INV*)				0.102	0.085
				(1.532)	(1.057)
Rate of inflation (change)					−0.019
(*GINFL*)					(−1.060)
Government consumption in					−0.000
GDP (*GOVCONS*)					(−0.001)
Secondary school enrollment					0.008
(*SECENRL*)					(0.269)
Population growth (*GPOP*)					0.000
					(0.004)
Sample size	49	49	49	49	49
Adjusted R^2	0.013	0.006	0.000	0.006	0.000
Standard error	0.027	0.028	0.028	0.028	0.029
F-statistic (zero slopes)	1.614	0.868	0.579	0.947	0.622

Notes:
The dependent variable is annual rate of growth of real per capita GDP, GRGDPC, for the five-year period centered on the year of observation. For definition of independent variables see text. Numbers in parentheses are *T*-statistics.

(74 observations, 59 countries) omitting the DCs. The results are again comparable with those of test 1: the coefficient of the *RER* is consistently significant and robust, with negative values ranging from −0.019 to −0.026; the *INV* variable has a significant coefficient of 0.11 to 0.12; and the dummy for low-income LDCs (as opposed to low/middle-income LDCs in the previous tests) is negative but nonsignificant. *OPEN* and *DIR* have the correct signs as previously, but the latter is nonsignificant.

In the regressions reported so far, the level of development has been proxied

Table 7.5. *Cross-section/time-series regressions on growth, all countries, 1970 and 1975*

Explanatory variables	Model				
	I	II	III	IV	V
Constant	0.056	0.059	0.096	0.065	0.080
RER	−0.023	−0.029	−0.034	−0.031	−0.033
	(−1.995)	(−2.129)	(−2.533)	(−2.320)	(−2.205)
Dummy low/middle		0.007	0.008	0.007	0.008
(*DumL/M* = 1)		(0.816)	(0.927)	(0.837)	(0.585)
Openness (*OPEN*)			−0.028	−0.027	−0.023
			(−1.545)	(−1.497)	(−0.999)
Direction of trade (share			0.053	0.049	0.042
of OECD) (*DIR*)			(1.898)	(1.768)	(1.337)
Investment in GDP (*INV*)				0.109	0.086
				(1.630)	(1.048)
Rate of inflation (change)					−0.019
(*GINFL*)					(−0.473)
Government consumption in					−0.000
GDP (*GOVCONS*)					(−0.607)
Secondary school enrollment					−0.003
(*SECENRL*)					(−0.111)
Population growth (*GPOP*)					0.083
					(0.121)
Sample size	37	37	37	37	37
Adjusted R^2	0.076	0.068	0.123	0.167	0.067
Standard error	0.023	0.023	0.022	0.022	0.023
F-statistic (zero slopes)	3.981	2.305	2.268	2.439	1.287

Notes:
The dependent variable is annual rate of growth of real per capita GDP, GRGDPC, for the five-year period centered on the year of observation. For definition of independent variables see text. Numbers in parentheses are *T*-statistics.

by a binary variable, *DumL/M*. This choice is consistent with the interpretation of the origins of market incompleteness in asymmetric reputation, as reflected in the existence of a hard or soft national currency. This hypothesis is further refined by the introduction of an interaction variable, *RER∗RGDPC*, which consists of the RER and the real per capita GDP. The results for this set of models are shown in Table 7.7 for the pooled cross section and time series for all countries and years. They are consistent with the maintained hypothesis: as

Table 7.6. *Cross-section/time-series regressions on growth, low- and middle-income countries, 1970, 1975, 1980, and 1985*

Explanatory variables	Model				
	I	II	III	IV	V
Constant	0.035	0.060	0.073	0.046	0.090
RER	−0.019	−0.023	−0.025	−0.021	−0.026
	(−1.851)	(−2.286)	(−2.416)	(−2.021)	(−2.407)
Dummy low (*DumL* = 1)		−0.007	−0.008	−0.005	−0.010
		(−0.995)	(−1.038)	(−0.696)	(−1.061)
Dummy 1980/1985		−0.023	−0.023	−0.022	−0.019
(*Dum*80/85 = 1)		(−2.981)	(−2.858)	(−2.804)	(−2.459)
Openness (*OPEN*)			−0.017	−0.026	−0.049
			(−0.896)	(−1.365)	(−2.238)
Direction of trade (share			0.009	0.012	0.016
of OECD) (*DIR*)			(0.341)	(0.487)	(0.546)
Investment in GDP (*INV*)				0.108	0.121
				(1.970)	(2.057)
Rate of inflation (change)					−0.044
(*GINFL*)					(−2.398)
Government consumption in					−0.000
GDP (*GOVCONS*)					(−0.152)
Secondary school enrollment					−0.015
(*SECENRL*)					(−0.624)
Population growth (*GPOP*)					−0.664
					(−1.308)
Sample size	74	74	74	74	74
Adjusted R^2	0.032	0.126	0.112	0.148	0.191
Standard error	0.030	0.028	0.029	0.028	0.027
F-statistic (zero slopes)	3.427	4.500	2.848	3.120	2.720

Notes:
The dependent variable is annual rate of growth of real per capita GDP, GRGDPC, for the five-year period centered on the year of observation. For definition of independent variables see text. Numbers in parentheses are *T*-statistics.

the level of per capita income rises the effect of *RER* becomes inconsequential – very small but positive. This interaction variable captures the RER impact of high per capita incomes. It is thus different from *DumL/M* that relates to all other effects of the level of development on growth, except for the RER. Some of these effects have now turned positive, although nonsignificant. The rest of the coefficients in Table 7.7 remain close to those in Table 7.1.

Causality tests and alternative models

The empirical results of the five models of regressions are remarkably consistent in all the tests performed for the pooled time series/international cross-section data and for all the combinations of subsets. The grand theme that emerges has at its foundation the negative relationship between the *RER* and *GRGDPC*, the rate of growth of real GDP per capita. The first question that arises relates to the causality between the two.

The ordinary least squares (OLS) results presented so far rest on the assumption that the right-hand side variables are truly exogenous. This is a strong assumption that can be tested explicitly. If it is not warranted, the maintained hypothesis will be reformulated in functional forms that do not require the exogeneity assumption.

The variables most likely to be endogenously related to growth in the maintained hypothesis are *RER* and *INV*. The issue of endogeneity can be formulated as a testable hypothesis by specifying three separate equations and testing for the independence of their respective residuals. Should those be independent, the null hypothesis that *RER* and *INV* are exogenous is confirmed.

One basic specification of the three equations is as follows:

$$RGDPC_t = f(Constant, DumL/M, Dum80/85, RER, OPEN, DIR,$$
$$INV, GINFL, GONCONS, SECENRL, GPOP) \qquad (7.12a)$$

$$RER_t = f(Constant, RGDPC, NER) \qquad (7.12b)$$

$$INV_t = f(Constant, RGDPC) \qquad (7.12c)$$

The growth equation involves the complete set of variables reported in the OLS tests, with the exception of *RER* and *INV*. The RER equation is specified according to the theoretical precepts as a function of real per capita GDP (the Ricardo Principle) and the nominal exchange rate (the real pass-through, as will be discussed in Chapter 8). In the estimation *NER* is the percent change in the nominal exchange rate and it is calculated per U.S. dollar with the market-rate data of the IMF *International Financial Statistics*. The investment equation follows the usual specification in the literature as a function of real per capita income.

The Hausman test of exogeneity is performed following the Maddala (1988) procedure. In the test, the *RER* and *INV* variables take on the fitted values as estimated from (7.12b) and (7.12c). The results are reported in Appendix Table A7.2, columns (1) and (2). The hypothesis that the coefficients of *RER* and *INV* are zero cannot be rejected. The null hypothesis that *RER* and *INV* are exogenous variables is thus confirmed. This vindicates the use of the OLS estimation in the previous section.

An alternative specification of the RER equation is also possible:

$$RGDPC_t = f(Constant, DumL/M, Dum80/85, RER, OPEN, DIR,$$
$$INV, GINFL, GONCONS, SECENRL, GPOP) \qquad (7.13a)$$

Table 7.7. *Cross-section/time-series regressions on growth, all countries, 1970, 1975, 1980, and 1985*

Explanatory variables	Model				
	I	II	III	IV	V
Constant	0.040	0.056	0.051	0.034	0.036
RER	−0.021	−0.022	−0.026	−0.022	−0.024
	(−2.708)	(−2.774)	(−3.215)	(−2.668)	(−2.892)
Dummy low/middle		−0.003	0.009	0.005	0.010
(*DumL/M* = 1)		(−0.668)	(1.151)	(0.592)	(1.095)
Dummy 1980/1985		−0.017	−0.018	−0.017	−0.017
(*Dum*1980/85 = 1)		(−3.652)	(−3.785)	(−3.644)	(−3.484)
Interaction (*RER*RGDPC*)			0.000	0.000	0.000
			(2.000)	(1.415)	(1.231)
Openness (*OPEN*)			−0.010	−0.012	−0.016
			(−1.156)	(−1.345)	(−1.642)
Direction of trade (share			0.011	0.019	0.018
of OECD) (*DIR*)			(0.670)	(1.168)	(1.083)
Investment in GDP (*INV*)				0.091	0.086
				(2.411)	(2.179)
Rate of inflation (change)					−0.025
(*GINFL*)					(−2.081)
Government consumption in					0.000
GDP (*GOVCONS*)					(0.068)
Secondary school enrollment					0.005
(*SECENRL*)					(0.344)
Population growth (*GPOP*)					−0.013
					(−0.121)
Sample size	123	123	123	123	123
Adjusted R^2	0.049	0.142	0.161	0.194	0.197
Standard error	0.025	0.024	0.023	0.023	0.023
F-statistic (zero slopes)	7.333	7.753	4.893	5.200	3.720

Notes:
The dependent variable is annual rate of growth of real per capita GDP, GRGDPC, for the five-year period centered on the year of observation. For definition of independent variables see text. Numbers in parentheses are *T*-statistics.

$$RER_t = f(Constant, RGDPC, NER, LaggedGRGDPC) \qquad (7.13b)$$

$$INV_t = f(Constant, RGDPC) \qquad (7.13c)$$

The rationale for including both real per capita income and its lagged growth in the RER equation is the Chenerian idea that the patterns of growth determine the sectoral composition of output (Chenery, 1960). It is conceivable that rapid growth is biased towards the tradable sector and the result, with a lag, is the decline in the price of tradables. In such a case, the causality goes from past growth to current *RER* values and to present growth. The results for alternative specifications of the growth equation are reported in columns (3) to (10) in Appendix Table A7.2. This time the null hypothesis that *RER* and *INV* are exogenous variables is rejected.

Based on the results above we assume that *RER* and *INV* are endogenous explicitly. We estimate the extended specification model of equations (7.13a) to (7.13c) as a linear simultaneous equations system by three-stage least squares (3SLS). The results of the estimation are reported in Appendix Table A7.3. In columns (1) to (3) we observe that once the *DumL/M* is dropped from equation (7.13a) the coefficients of *RER* become negative and significant. The coefficient of *INV*, however, is nonsignificant. Therefore we estimate only the system of equations (7.13a) and (7.13b) and we treat *INV* as an exogenous variable. The results in columns (4) and (5) are now as expected and very close to the OLS results reported in the previous section.

In a model of two or more regression equations, the disturbances may be correlated. The multivariate regression gives a multiple equation estimator without simultaneity problems on endogenous variables on the right-hand side of the equations. The results of the generalized least squares (GLS) estimation of equations (7.13a) and (7.13b), imposing joint-estimation of cross-equation constraints, are shown in column (6) of Appendix Table A7.3. Finally, in column (7) appear the results of the full information maximum likelihood method (FILM), which also becomes appropriate for simultaneous equation models under the assumption that the disturbances are multivariate normal.

The conclusion is that enhanced econometric specification, if anything, served to buttress the stark results that the OLS estimation produced. The *RER* variable is consistently related to growth, with a negative sign under various specifications and alternative estimation techniques. The robustness of its various estimates is rather remarkable.

Causality: An interpretation of market incompleteness

Causality in economics is not a heuristic attribute that is established merely by mechanistic causality tests. It is, rather, an empirical implication of a model of mind – a hypothesis that is grounded on extant theory. The Ricardo Principle is a hypothesis potentially consistent with our results. Is it possible that we are just observing the Ricardo Principle at work: the prices of tradables relative to nontradables decline as development occurs?

The crucial distinction is between the level of development and the rate of growth. The test of the Ricardo Principle involves the level of development that is measured by per capita income. It was presented in Tables 5.1 and 5.2 (Chapter 5) where the price index for GDP[10] increases monotonically with the level of income of the country groups. This is the loose test of the Ricardo Principle. Alternatively, and more strictly, the Ricardo Principle is confirmed by the ratio of prices of tradables to nontradables that decreases for increasing levels of income in Table 5.2.[11] Table 7.8 presents the results of the test of both versions of the Ricardo Principle with the international cross-section/time series for the 123 countries in Table 6.1. The regression of the logarithm of real GDP per capita on the national price level of GDP, or alternatively on the national price level for tradables or for nontradables (price of tradables or nontradables divided by the NER) yields positive coefficients. The value of the coefficient of nontradables in comparison to that of tradables suggests that the normalized prices of the former increase faster as development occurs. This is expected, since LDCs start off with lower prices of nontradables. The same dependent variable, the logarithm of GDP per capita, regressed on the RER gives a negative and significant coefficient, which is entirely different from that in Tables 7.1 to 7.7. The interpretation of this coefficient is that the relationship between prices of tradables and nontradables is systematically related to the level of underdevelopment. As countries approach the per capita income level of the numeraire country, their normalized prices of tradables and nontradables converge and the value of the index – always relative to the U.S. – tends towards one.

This study has gone beyond the Ricardo Principle in formulating a hypothesis with causality going from *RER* to the rate of growth of real GDP. In the spirit of the endogenous growth literature, the observed variance in *RER* across countries becomes the explanatory variable of the intercountry variance in rates of growth. The link between the two is an intermediate variable, the NER. Devaluation of NER is the policy intervention that generates high RERs through its immediate impact on the prices of tradables. The value of the *RER* index implies nothing about RER over- or undervaluation, let alone about the equilibrium value of RER. Similarly, it implies nothing about the equilibrium value of NER. However, examined within an international cross section, high values of the index are more likely than low values to be associated with undervalued NER. Expressed in another way, high prices of tradables, as reflected in high RER, are likely to be associated with a depreciated domestic

10 The price index of GDP is defined as the PPP divided by the nominal exchange rate and normalized by the same index for the U.S., the numeraire country, which is 100.
11 The definition of tradables in Tables 5.1 and 5.2 includes only services, government and construction (Kravis et al., 1982). The same definition is adopted by Heston et al. (1994) in a recent study that extends the previous results to cover all four ICP benchmark studies for 1970, 1975, 1980, and 1985. That definition of tradability differs from the definition of this study which is country- and commodity-specific (Chapter 6).

Table 7.8. *Test of the Ricardo Principle: Regressions of real per capita income, all countries, 1970, 1975, 1980, and 1985*

Explanatory variables	Coefficient			
Constant	9.996	7.001	7.024	6.880
RER	−1.527			
	(−5.566)			
National price level for GDP		1.671		
		(5.870)		
National price level for tradables			1.519	
			(5.551)	
National price level for nontradables				1.867
				(7.572)
Sample size	123	123	123	123
Adjusted R^2	0.204	0.222	0.203	0.322
Standard error	0.901	0.891	0.902	0.832

Notes:
The dependent variable is the ln of real per capita income. The price variables are defined as the relevant PPPs divided by the NER.

currency, reflected in a high NER. The causality goes from undervaluation of NER to low rates of growth of GDP.[12] This is a novel and provocative position. It runs counter to the mainstream view. Overvaluation of the NER is commonly considered endemic among LDCs and NER devaluation is the orthodox policy instrument for delivering development stimuli, as for example with stabilization and structural adjustment programs (Krueger, 1980; Khan, Montiel, and Haque, 1990).

Why should some countries, specifically LDCs, tend to have "high" NERs that lead to high RERs? Two alternative and complementary explanations were introduced in Chapter 3. The Ricardo Principle holds (and Tables 5.1 and 5.2 confirm) that tradables are more expensive to produce than nontradables in a relationship that is systematically related to the level of underdevelopment in LDCs. For a country in search of scarce foreign exchange, devaluation of the NER is the free-market, free-trade outcome that makes the expensive (in domestic currency) tradables more profitable to produce. Devaluation is thus causally related to the high cost of producing tradables.

---

12 A case can also be made for reverse causality, from NER to the growth rate. In a high-growth environment there will be an increasing demand for domestic currency, both for transactions purposes and also conceivably as the result of increasing confidence in the asset properties of the currency. In this case NER will be driven down. The operative word in the text, however, is undervaluation. Given the high value of NER, causality is likely to go as indicated.

The second explanation draws on asset–value dynamics relating to hard and soft currencies (Chapter 3). Consider an equilibrium situation in the real world where a bundle of resources produces tradables or nontradables, measured such that one unit of each is worth $1. Entrepreneurs should normally be indifferent between producing tradables or nontradables because each can be converted into $1 for later spending. But in developing countries this does not necessarily hold: producing/holding nontradables is risky since they trade in local currency, which is "soft" and may be devalued. Expressed in another way, entrepreneurs are attracted to producing tradables because that is the only way they can acquire $1 they wish to hold for asset purposes. The productivity of resources in the meanwhile has remained constant. Thus, relative to productivities measured at "normal" prices, nontradables become undervalued and resources are biased away towards tradables. This is manifest in a relative price of nontradables that is too low compared with productivities – or too high a real exchange rate. This dilemma does not exist for the producer whose local currency is the dollar, which is "hard." In hard currency, $1 of tradables will always be worth $1 of nontradables, as opposed to the soft currency for which the expectation of devaluation becomes a self-fulfilling prophecy. In the process of converting soft currency into hard for asset-holding purposes the market-clearing NER becomes too high. This is manifest in a relative price of tradables that is too high, again compared with productivities.

One important conclusion can be drawn from the process just described: a specific distortion in currency markets leads LDCs systematically to misallocate resources. It is captured by the negative sign of the relationship between the rate of growth of real GDP per capita and RER. The policy implication, in turn, becomes that market-clearing NERs are not tantamount to equilibrium RERs. Policies that reduced the RER would achieve a better allocation of resources. One such set of policies is intervention in the foreign exchange market to reduce the NER by rationing or protection.

The question arises why improving Pareto efficiency is related to development performance as opposed to the level of development. Efficiency outcomes are usually one-shot improvements that affect the flow variables, such as growth rates, only once. In this particular case, however, the efficiency losses are related to asset–value dynamics. The reputation effects that give rise to devaluation do not disappear; they create the environment, instead, for consecutive devaluations. This is demonstrated empirically in Chapter 8, where NER devaluation decays in the process of pass-through form nominal to real exchange rates. Thus the stage is set for repeating the devaluation, and for further efficiency losses, unless these are stemmed by intervention that overrides market-clearing of the NER.

Two policy implications arise from the two complementary processes that lead to undervalued NER and Pareto losses in LDCs. On the supply side the high cost (in terms of domestic resources) of producing tradables can lead to competitive-devaluation gaming. The policy response is to increase efficiency in producing tradables, so that competitive-devaluation trade becomes again comparative-advantage trade. The downside of this response is the Ricardo Principle. Especially at this time and age, an LDC may have to wait to become developed before it efficiently produces a broad range of tradables that can profitably enter international trade.

The policy implication from the demand side for foreign exchange is more targetable, but equally treacherous. If inherent asset value dynamics tend to produce a systematically market-clearing NER that is "too high," then over-riding the foreign exchange market can achieve "low" NERs. Rationing is tantamount to NER overvaluation. It is also consistent with the central hypothesis of this book that there is an incomplete market in foreign exchange. Moreover, operating with an overvalued NER does not necessarily imply overvaluation of RER. It is in principle consistent with "equilibrium" RER, because of the Ricardo Principle and the systematic relationship that exists between the prices of tradables and nontradables in the process of development. With NER affecting the former more directly than the latter, a one-to-one correspondence between equilibrium NER and equilibrium RER does not hold. In LDCs, if NER is at equilibrium, RER is likely to be undervalued; and an overvalued NER is more likely to be associated with an equilibrium RER. Another way to explain the negative relationship between RER and growth is that near-Pareto-optimality obtains the closer the real economy is to equilibrium. Or, conversely, an undervalued RER (in the extreme case the RER that corresponds to the market-clearing NER) extends the range of tradability into the area where exports (or import substitutes) are produced at high domestic resource cost in relation always to the nontradables that could have been produced in their place. This is again an implication of the Ricardo Principle.

The systematic nature of the relationship is at the heart of the Ricardo Principle. The market incompleteness, and thus the need for rationing, abates as development occurs. The prices of nontradables increase relative to those of tradables, and eventually free-market, free-trade, laissez-faire policies can be allowed to determine the NER. This is another way of saying that separation in the market of tradables and nontradables has been restored and the condition of market incompleteness has been remedied.

Comparison with other studies

The theme of this book is the nexus between development and trade.[13] The main intermediate variable in this nexus is the RER. The traditional approach, in general, infers the value of the RER from a set of trade-policy variables that determine whether a trade regime is outward- or inward-oriented.[14] It is then hypothesized that an overvalued exchange rate encourages the growth of the

13 For excellent recent reviews of this literature, see Edwards (1993) and Rodrik (1995b).
14 For examples, see Balassa (1978) and Krueger (1980).

nontradable sector and leads to inward orientation; it is usually associated with the experiences of Latin America and Africa. Outward orientation is reflected in real exchange rates that foster the growth of the tradable sector and encourage exports; it is associated with the (East and Southeast) Asian experience. Since the implication of the real exchange rate for growth cannot be tested directly in the conventional approach, it is tested indirectly through the trade-regime orientation. One component of the trade-regime orientation is the volume of trade. Outward orientation (and "advantageous" or undervalued RER) induces more trade, especially exports, which are taken to be associated with more growth. The converse is the case for inward orientation (and overvalued RER). Besides this indirect relationship between growth and RER that operates through trade-regime orientation/volume of trade, the conventional approach also utilizes as independent variables other proxies for trade policy instruments and for incentives to export.

By comparison, the approach in this chapter is to regress directly the rate of growth of real GDP per capita, *GRGDPC*, on the index of *RER*. The negative and consistently strong relationship is interpreted with reference to NER as opposed to under- or overvalued RER: countries in the sample that have high RER must also have high NER. Since they grow more slowly than countries with low values of RER, the policy implication follows that overriding the NER market – rationing foreign exchange at a price below its market-clearing value – is likely to lead to higher growth rates. This implication is consistent with an incomplete market model for foreign exchange. Besides the *RER* variable, the volume of trade (*OPEN*) and the direction of trade (*DIR*) enter the regression linearly and independently to measure the impact of revealed trade strategy, as opposed to serving as proxies for trade-regime orientation. On *OPEN*, the expectation is contrary to the conventional model. If quantity closure (rather than price closure) is appropriate for the NER market (i.e., rationing), higher rates of growth must be inversely related to the trade volume. This expectation is confirmed by the empirical results. So is the one about the *DIR* variable, which captures the technological benefits accruing from trade with more advanced partners.

The conventional approach to the relationship between trade and development rests on a long and venerable tradition. It has drawn, with somewhat qualified success, on a number of recent empirical studies.

Chenery (1960; Chenery, Robinson, and Syrquin, 1986) was the first in a long list of researchers who introduced openness in the analysis of development as an explanatory variable of the economic structure. The tradition has been continued in the neoclassical analysis of the sources of growth (Feder, 1983) and has been carried on with the endogenous growth studies. It is supplemented by various measures of price distortions and of policy instruments, such as effective rates of protection.

Openness in the traditional literature is commonly measured as share of exports in GDP and occasionally as the share of both exports and imports in

GDP. The causality between openness and growth rests on three channels that go from the former to the latter. The traditional position, originating with Adam Smith, attributes to export growth the benefits of increasing the size of the market, of economies of scale, and of increased efficiency. An increase in exports also helps loosen a binding foreign exchange constraint and through an increase in imports of intermediate products and raw materials can lead to further growth in output (McKinnon, 1964; Chenery and Strout, 1966). Finally, export growth also may represent an increase in foreign effective demand for the country's output and thus may result in growth. Sound as this causality link may be, the issue of a negative relationship also has been raised (e.g., Bhagwati, 1979) and the possibility of reverse causality going from output growth to export growth cannot be dismissed.[15]

An alternative (and occasionally an additional) specification of the independent trade variable considers the relationship between various trade-policy instruments and growth. The World Bank (World Bank, 1987; Greenaway and Nam, 1988) has developed an index of trade policy orientation (ranging from strongly outward-oriented regimes to strongly inward-oriented regimes) that has been related to developmental outcomes.[16] In an alternative approach, Leamer (1988) has contributed an index of trade-policy instruments based on a cross-country factor-endowments model. The variable that he derives attributes to government intervention all the measured residuals from the fitted regression.[17]

The incentive structure for trade has been captured by the effective rate of protection or by the deviation around a set of prices. De Long and Summers (1991) use a dummy for high levels of the effective rate of protection (>40%) as well as the World Bank index of development-policy orientation. The deviation of the NER from the black-market rate of exchange is another such variable (Levine and Renelt, 1992).

A general assessment of the introduction of trade-policy measures in endogenous growth models is provided by Levine and Renelt (1992, p. 959) who performed sensitivity analysis on the results of over 40 studies: "A large variety of trade policy measures were not robustly correlated with growth when the equation included the investment share also." It appears that the relationship between trade and growth operates through the intermediate variable of investment, which is spurred by trade. The same reservations apply when a subjective measure of trade-policy orientation is used as the independent variable. Pritchett (1995), who compared various versions of this variable, concluded that alternative measures of outward orientation produce entirely different country rankings.

One index of price distortions that has received broad acceptance (Levine

---

15 It was formally tested by Jung and Marshall (1985) and was accepted in a number of cases.
16 The index has been severely criticized, e.g., by Taylor (1991, p. 107).
17 The index presents serious anomalies in ranking countries with respect to trade regimes (Rodrik, 1995b). It has been used in an endogenous-growth model by Edwards (1992a).

and Renelt, 1992; Pritchett, 1995) is due to Dollar (1992).[18] The index measures price distortions as deviations of actual price levels from a reference level that is consistent with a country's natural endowments. This sounds unexceptionable, but for the fact that the actual price level is the "national price level of consumption" (the PPP index of consumption divided by the NER) and the reference price level is the regression line of national price levels on GDP per capita for the subset of 95 LDCs in the Penn World Tables 4 data set.[19] The relationship actually estimated is a loose form of the Ricardo Principle and is related to the regression results reported in column 3 of Table 7.8.

Table 7.9 shows the results of estimating the Dollar regression of the national price level of consumption along with the national price level of GDP, of tradables and of nontradables. The data are the 80 observations for 46 LDCs in our sample for which both the Penn World Tables IV data and the prices of tradables and notradables are available. Of the four national-price-level regressions on real per capita income (RGDPC) only the one of the national price level of consumption has a negative (but not significant) coefficient, as Dollar's hypothesis requires (column 2). The regression of growth, however, on the deviations of the same variable from the fitted line has a negative and significant coefficient – a result similar to the one reported by Dollar (column 3). Dollar interprets negative deviations from this relationship (low national price levels) as a measure of outward orientation, which is conducive to growth, and positive deviations (high national price levels) as an indicator of inward orientation that deters growth. The estimated coefficients of the regression of the rate of growth (GRGDPC) on these deviations are considered as confirmation of the hypothesis that outward orientation is conducive to development.

Is there any reason why (systematic) deviations around the regression line of the national price level on per capita GDP measure trade regime orientation and predict the rate of growth of GDP? The simple explanation is that ". . . outward orientation policies reflect in a level of the real exchange rate that encourages exports"; and that ". . . misalignment of the real exchange rate is negatively associated with growth" (Dollar, 1992, pp. 523, 524). Moreover, ". . . a country maintaining a high price level over many years would clearly have to be a country with a relatively large amount of protection (inward orientation)" (Dollar, 1992, pp. 525–526). Thus positive price deviations are directly related to the national price level (of consumption), and to protectionism, and inversely related to the degree of outward orientation of a country.

There are a number of contradictory criteria in this definition, and they reveal confusion between the NER and the RER. Concerning "real exchange misalignment" that discourages exports, one should note that high values of RER

18 This index also presents anomalies in ranking various countries and has been challenged by Rodrik (1994).
19 Besides GDP per capita, its squared term and also population density and its square, total GDP and regional dummy variables were also considered in some regressions. They did not materially change the results.

Table 7.9. *Rethinking of the Dollar test*

| | Regressions | |
| | | |
Variable	Column (1) variable on RGDPC	GRGDPC on deviation from column (2) regression[a]
(1)	(2)	(3)
1. National price level of consumption	-4.8e-06	-0.062
T-statistic	(-1.391)	(-2.071)
Constant	0.645	0.072
Adjusted R^2	0.033	0.040
2. National price level of GDP	4.2e-05	-0.009
T-statistic	(2.753)	(-1.147)
Constant	0.502	0.020
Adjusted R^2	0.088	0.016
3. National price level of tradables	4.7e-05	-0.018
T-statistic	(3.743)	(-1.831)
Constant	0.544	0.028
Adjusted R^2	0.102	0.038
4. National price level of nontradables	5.2e-05	-0.007
T-statistic	(4.171)	(-0.629)
Constant	0.440	0.017
Adjusted R^2	0.163	0.006
5. Real exchange rate (RER)	-4.2e-05	-0.019
T-statistic	(-2.343)	(-1.656)
Constant	1.366	0.029
Adjusted R^2	0.043	0.012

Notes:
In conforming with Dollar's test, the table includes only LDCs (46 countries, 80 observations).
[a]The deviation ("distortion") index is derived by dividing the actual value of the variables in column (1) by the fitted value from the regression in column (2).

(i.e., high rather than low prices of tradables) encourage exports. Are they likely to be associated with low prices of the national level of consumption, which is the Dollar criterion? The intuition on the relationship is not clear, since consumption includes both tradables and nontradables. But low national prices of consumption are likely to correspond to high levels of NER, which is the denominator of the national price level. And high NERs are likely to be associated with high prices of tradables. If this is correct, outward orientation that allows for free and floating exchange rates would result in high NER (and high RER) and should be associated with high rates of growth, according to the hypothesis. This hypothesis is contrary to the empirical results in this chapter. It is tested in the specification of Dollar in the table.

The RER regression (test 5) controls for the NER bias, since the prices of tradables and nontradables, in the numerator and demoninator, respectively, are normalized per unit of international currency (Chapter 6). Thus the regression adds transparency to the finding that high national prices of consumption are related to low rates of growth. Among tradables and nontradables that enter consumption, high prices of the former are causally related to low rates of growth according to the maintained hypothesis of this chapter – and this is borne out by the results in column (3) where the coefficient of the latter, though negative, is nonsignificant. The results reported in test (5) are consistent with the tests that preceded in this chapter: the relative price of tradables (and thus the RER) declines with per capita income, and relatively high deviations from the fitted line, i.e., high prices of tradables, are negatively related to growth.

The conclusions from the discussion of the national price level of consumption and the RER are consistent. Low RER values are conducive to growth, and so are low NER values that are more likely to covary with low RER values. This is a proper characterization of inward-looking countries, and the conclusion is that they grow fast. Outward-looking contries, on the other hand, are likely to have free (floating) and high NER, which can be translated as low prices of consumption; these countries grow slowly. So the basic hypothesis of Dollar is correct if restated to account for the NER bias and for the prices of tradables: controlling for the NER, low prices of tradables are conducive to growth. The problem with the original test of the hypothesis is that a low national price level of consumption can be attained through low prices of tradables (and nontradables) or through high NER; in the latter case the hypothesis reduces to "devaluation is good for growth," which is often incorrect; and in any event, the trade-regime orientation has been mislabeled, since the inward-looking countries are more likely to have low prices of tradables, and thus grow faster than the outward-looking countries that are likely to have high NER, and thus high prices of tradables.

Why are the strong results surprising? Development policy failure and development politics failure

Empirical studies in economics are only too elliptical in allowing for the presence of government. So were the regressions reported in this chapter. By introducing *GOVCONS*, a perfunctory attempt was made to introduce a false dichotomy. Activities of government that are wasteful, funnel funds to endeavors that do not promote growth, and expend resources in distorting incentives were proxied by the government consumption variable. This leaves unaccounted for the other side of government that includes the provision of growth-promoting public goods, tax policies that are designed to close the gap between private and social costs, and interventions for the purpose of placing the economy on a higher growth path. This feeble attempt was fruitless, as it has been in general in other endogenous growth models. Whereas ignoring the role of government in other studies may be defensible, it is not here.

The policy conclusion derived within the analytical framework of incomplete markets is that government intervention can be welfare-improving; yet there is no presumption that it will succeed. Government failure is as frequent as market failure. Translated in terms of the immediate objective of this study, it means that overriding the foreign exchange market and setting the real exchange rate close to equilibrium is a necessary condition for achieving optimality and growth. But quantity rationing of foreign exchange is also not a sufficient condition for optimality. The variable that measures the RER can at best only represent the necessary condition of having an overvalued NER through intervention. That it is strongly and robustly related to growth without also accounting for the sufficient condition, which is good governance, is truly remarkable.

It is common for intervention to create incentive distortions and resource misallocations. Hence the counsel of wisdom is to entrust development to free-market, free-trade forces. When markets are incomplete, however, the incentive distortions preexist, and they will not disappear if there is no intervention. But intervention raises a host of other issues. How can policy makers distinguish between markets that require intervention and those that are best left to their own devices? What specific form of intervention should be adopted? How are various interventions to be sequenced? Competence in government cuts through the thicket of all possible forms of intervention, most of which could be wanton and many downright injurious.

Distortions create economic rents. In Krueger's (1974) formulation, rent-seeking accounts for the resources wasted in the attempt of expropriating and capturing economic rents. Quantity rationing in the foreign exchange market, for example, creates scarcity rents, and resources are wasted in an attempt to capture them. Overvaluation of the NER creates black-market activities and fosters competition to appropriate the black-market premia. By the same token, smuggling, underinvoicing, and overinvoicing are rewarded.

The existence of economic rents is inevitable, whether they are created by the incomplete market or by the government intervention that addressed it. The important issue, however, becomes who captures the economic rents and how are they used. One extreme solution is that a ruling elite captures the rents, and they end up in bank accounts in Miami and Zurich or in financing imposing schemes of import-substitution industrialization that cater to the needs of the middle-income classes and the wealthy. At the other extreme an honest and benevolent government wrests the economic rents and reinvests them in economic development. An example of this case is allocating overvalued foreign exchange to imports of raw materials and intermediate products, which, in turn, are targeted to certain strategic exporting sectors that thus receive an implicit subsidy. This result requires integrity in government, along with the competence to identify the export sectors that could have dynamic comparative advantage down the road.

The real world, of course, is somewhere in between the two extremes: not all economic rents captured by individuals are wasted, and not all governments are competent and honest. Similarly, implementing "appropriate growth packages" (in the example above, dedicating import subsidies to export promotion) is not the only way to develop. By analogy, there is no a priori reason why the solution to the primordial Kruegerian struggle for capturing economic rents ends up in putting the government out of business. And this is especially true if good governance exists and it is graced with both competence and integrity.

At the conceptual level, and ex post, the existence of good governance is evidenced in economic development outcomes that spread the benefits of growth broadly among the population. This is pluralistic economic development that results in economic empowerment of broad social and economic classes among the population. Why should the quality of development outcomes be judged on development participation grounds? One standard approach is the humanitarian concern of development that requires a minimum safety net in support of the poorest of the poor. This is not the motivation for pluralistic economic development used in this work. More important, the broad spread of economic development among the population creates effective domestic demand, which, when properly sequenced, can in turn become the engine of growth (Bourguignon, 1990; Murphy et al., 1989b; Eswaren and Kotwal, 1993).[20] This Keynesian proposition was predated by Henry Ford's insight: it is smart to pay employees enough to enable them to purchase the products they produce. A proxy for this function of good governance, which was not available for this study, would have been an index for the spread of development among the population or an index of social and political articulation (de Janvry, 1981).

Since good governance has not entered the empirical work in this chapter, the regression results can be interpreted as subject to the proviso that governments are neither inept nor corrupt. This is a strong presumption that will be examined in Part III of this book. The case studies serve as a qualitative proxy for the variable of good governance that cannot be pinned down empirically. Success in economic development is predicated on correct economic policies and good governance. Failure in development is more complicated. Development politics failure can doom the prospects for growth even though the economic policies were largely appropriate. Moreover, there are the hopeless cases that combine the wrong economic policies with clientilistic politics.

---

20 For a parallel argument for higher wage policies and overvaluation of the NER, but from the labor-demand side, see Rodrik (1995a).

Conclusion

The empirical examination of the trade–development nexus is at the core of this study. In the spirit of a fast-growing body of literature, the variance in rates of growth in real GDP per capita among countries was related to the variance in a number of "endogenous growth" variables. The novel element in this study is that the primary variable of interest is the *RER*. Relating it to growth amounts to testing directly what the conventional literature has tested only indirectly through trade-regime-orientation indexes.

The negative, strong, and robust relationship discovered might seem at first blush counterintuitive. But it is a strong confirmation of a testable hypothesis. High *NER*, which can lead directly to high values of *RER*, may cause suboptimal Pareto results by overallocating resources to tradables. The policy instrument for obtaining high rates of growth is setting the NER below its equilibrium value by quantity closure (rationing). This highly controversial result is perfectly consistent with a model of an incomplete foreign exchange market, in which setting the NER at its equilibrium value does not necessarily result in an equilibrium RER in an LDC. The cause of market incompleteness is nonseparation in tradables and nontradables, which is in turn related to the existence of "hard" and "soft" currencies. The market incompleteness is related systematically to the level of underdevelopment, so that the need for intervention abates as development progresses.

Government intervention opens the Pandora's box of rent-seeking. The rents created in incomplete markets and by government intervention can be captured and ploughed back into development. Or they can be squandered in capital flight or in wasteful import substitution for the benefit of ruling elites. The empirical result depends on whether the LDC benefits from good governance or not. The confirmation of the hypothesis that relates overriding incomplete markets to growth is remarkable since the good governance variable, which ideally should proxy both competence and integrity, is conspicuously missing from this analysis.

Appendix: Tables

Table A7.1. *Basic statistics of variables*

Variable Group/year	GRGDPC	RER	RER*RGDPC	OPEN	DIR	INV	GINFL	GOVCONS	SECENRL	GPOP
All countries/all years										
Mean	0.016	1.18	5808	0.46	0.37	0.23	0.16	0.19	0.58	0.016
Standard deviation	0.026	0.30	3934	0.27	0.15	0.06	0.19	0.07	0.30	0.022
Max	0.099	2.07	14158	1.72	0.70	0.40	1.41	0.44	1.05	0.149
Min	-0.073	0.69	216	0.05	0.11	0.08	0.01	0.09	0.03	-0.137
Low and middle countries/all years										
Mean	0.011	1.27		0.39	0.41	0.24	0.20	0.20	0.40	0.023
Standard deviation	0.030	0.34		0.19	0.14	0.07	0.21	0.07	0.23	0.009
Max	0.099	2.07		0.82	0.69	0.40	1.41	0.37	0.90	0.040
Min	-0.073	0.69		0.05	0.13	0.08	0.02	0.09	0.03	-0.001
All countries, 1980										
Mean	0.009	1.12		0.48	0.38	0.24	0.22	0.21	0.53	0.019
Standard deviation	0.028	0.24		0.29	0.14	0.06	0.25	0.08	0.30	0.031
Max	0.068	1.70		1.72	0.68	0.40	1.41	0.44	1.05	0.149
Min	-0.073	0.69		0.09	0.13	0.10	0.05	0.09	0.03	-0.137
All countries, 1985										
Mean	0.014	1.20		0.48	0.36	0.22	0.11	0.18	0.67	0.014
Standard deviation	0.021	0.33		0.28	0.15	0.06	0.13	0.06	0.32	0.012
Max	0.044	2.07		1.43	0.69	0.40	0.76	0.34	1.05	0.038
Min	-0.039	0.83		0.05	0.11	0.08	0.01	0.09	0.04	-0.002

Note:
For definition of variables see text.

Table A7.2. *Hausman's exogeneity tests of endogenous growth models*

Variable	Equations (7.12) (1)	Equations (7.12) (2)	Equations (7.13) (3)	(4)	(5)	(6)	(7)	(8)	(9)	(10)
Constant	0.749 (0.542)	0.474 (0.351)	−0.831 (−3.079)	−0.806 (−2.947)	−0.741 (−2.656)	−0.760 (−2.744)	−0.733 (−2.639)	−0.747 (−2.712)	−0.953 (−3.601)	−0.962 (−3.662)
DumL/M	0.008 (0.936)		−0.000 (−0.128)	−0.001 (−0.209)	0.004 (0.550)	0.005 (0.612)				
Dum80/85	−0.017 (−3.356)	−0.015 (−3.225)	−0.011 (−2.279)	−0.011 (−2.328)	−0.012 (−2.309)	−0.012 (−2.324)	−0.011 (−2.251)	−0.011 (−2.248)		
RER	−0.020 (−2.340)	−0.018 (−2.195)	−0.022 (−2.725)	−0.022 (−2.686)	−0.024 (−2.862)	−0.024 (−2.883)	−0.023 (−2.818)	−0.023 (−2.825)	−0.022 (−2.630)	−0.220 (−2.632)
OPEN	−0.018 (−1.838)	−0.017 (−1.699)	−0.013 (−1.537)	−0.013 (−1.464)	−0.016 (−1.704)	−0.017 (−1.740)	−0.016 (−1.643)	−0.016 (−1.669)	−0.016 (−1.704)	−0.017 (−1.736)
GINFL	−0.037 (−1.716)	−0.029 (−1.463)			−0.016 (−1.318)	−0.021 (−1.739)	−0.014 (−1.203)	−0.018 (−1.633)	−0.014 (−1.199)	−0.020 (−1.732)
INV	0.085 (2.123)	0.097 (2.559)	0.045 (1.130)	0.046 (1.131)	0.039 (0.915)	0.036 (0.850)	0.045 (1.083)	1.043 (1.039)	0.034 (0.810)	0.032 (0.769)
DIR	−0.020 (−1.195)	−0.018 (−1.073)	−0.019 (−1.165)	−0.019 (−1.179)	−0.019 (−1.157)	−0.019 (−1.152)	−0.017 (−1.089)	−0.017 (−1.075)	−0.019 (−1.176)	−0.019 (−1.158)
GOVCONS	0.000 (0.266)	0.000 (0.016)			−0.000 (−0.270)	−0.000 (−0.223)	−0.000 (−0.413)	−0.000 (−0.377)	−0.000 (−0.756)	−0.000 (−0.707)
SECENRL	0.005 (0.347)	−0.000 (−0.049)			0.011 (0.717)	0.011 (0.749)	0.008 (0.545)	0.008 (0.552)	0.005 (0.339)	0.005 (0.340)
GPOP	−0.024 (−0.223)	−0.042 (−0.398)			−0.013 (−0.128)	−0.012 (−0.119)	−0.024 (−0.229)	−0.024 (−0.233)	−0.028 (−0.272)	−0.029 (0.278)
FRER	−0.191 (−0.596)	−0.117 (−0.379)	0.184 (3.074)	0.180 (2.935)	0.171 (2.636)	0.174 (2.733)	0.174 (2.720)	0.177 (2.801)	0.221 (3.578)	0.223 (3.646)
FINV	−2.055 (−0.479)	−1.239 (−0.295)	2.840 (3.236)	2.756 (3.107)	2.533 (2.778)	2.597 (2.861)	2.484 (2.747)	2.531 (2.817)	3.184 (3.682)	3.217 (3.739)
Number of observations	123	123	123	123	123	123	123	123	123	123
Adjusted R^2	0.188	0.189	0.243	0.238	0.234	0.238	0.239	0.242	0.211	0.214
F-value	0.668	0.351	5.260	4.830	3.990	4.260	4.000	4.220	7.120	7.370

Notes:

T-statistics in parentheses. For specifications of models and definitions of variables see text. FRER and FINV are the fitted values of RER and INV respectively. F statistics for Hausman's exogeneity test: at the 5% level of significance the critical value for accepting the hypothesis that the coefficients of FRER and FINV are zero is, for Model I, approximately 3.08.

Table A7.3. *Estimation results of simultaneous equations system, alternative models*

Method	3SLS	3SLS	3SLS	3SLS	3SLS	GLS	FIML
	Equations (7.13a) to (7.13c)			Equations (7.13a) to (7.13b)			
Variable	(1)	(2)	(3)	(4)	(5)	(6)	(7)
	Growth equation						
Constant	−0.168	0.219	0.238	0.075	0.075	0.075	0.074
	(−0.616)	(0.602)	(0.960)	(2.082)	(2.084)	(1.812)	(1.621)
DumL/M	−0.029						
	(−0.361)						
Dum80/85	−0.006	−0.019	−0.019	−0.016	−0.016	−0.015	−0.015
	(−0.264)	(−2.181)	(−23.077)	(−3.343)	(−3.362)	(−3.365)	(−2.975)
RER	0.035	−0.063	−0.069	−0.042	−0.043	−0.044	−0.044
	(0.279)	(−1.822)	(−2.423)	(−2.066)	(−2.071)	(−1.460)	(−1.312)
OPEN	−0.012	−0.018	−0.021	−0.017	−0.017	−0.016	−0.016
	(−0.518)	(−0.840)	(−1.192)	(−1.770)	(−1.772)	(−1.741)	(−1.180)
GINFL	−0.012	−0.020	−0.022	−0.024	−0.023	−0.023	−0.023
	(−0.336)	(−0.856)	(−1.224)	(−2.155)	(−2.085)	(−2.085)	(−1.659)
INV	0.919	−0.440	−0.452	0.091	0.092	0.097	0.096
	(0.940)	(−0.235)	(−0.347)	(2.400)	(2.415)	(2.724)	(2.515)
DIR	−0.044	−0.007	−0.021	−0.019	−0.019	−0.018	−0.018
	(−1.034)	(−0.037)	(−0.169)	(−1.227)	(−1.235)	(−1.132)	(−1.120)
GOVCONS	0.000	−0.000	−0.000	−0.000	−0.600	−0.000	−0.000
	(0.099)	(−0.239)	(−0.257)	(−0.154)	(−0.168)	(−0.020)	(−0.044)
SECENRL	−0.043	0.012	0.007	0.000	0.000	−0.000	−0.000
	(−0.379)	(0.136)	(0.109)	(0.054)	(0.044)	(−0.055)	(−0.026)
GPOP	−0.196	−0.001	−0.030	−0.038	−0.038	−0.041	−0.041
	(−0.496)	(−0.003)	(−0.105)	(−0.377)	(−0.374)	(−0.409)	(−0.205)
R^2	0.072	0.006	0.006	0.226	0.226	0.226	0.225

(continued on facing page)

Table A7.3. (*continued*)

Method	Equations (7.13a) to (7.13c)			Equations (7.13a) to (7.13b)			
	3SLS	3SLS	3SLS	3SLS	3SLS	GLS	FIML
Variable	(1)	(2)	(3)	(4)	(5)	(6)	(7)
RER equation							
Constant	2.441	2.365	2.353	2.254	2.264	2.272	2.272
	(11.38)	(11.007)	(11.108)	(10.919)	(11.035)	(11.572)	(10.569)
RGDPC	−0.168	−0.152	−0.149	−0.129	−0.132	−0.133	−0.133
	(−5.794)	(−5.090)	(−5.179)	(−4.813)	(−4.971)	(−5.612)	(−4.631)
Lagged	4.813	2.641	2.307	−0.484	0.209		
GRGDPC	(2.188)	(1.046)	(0.983)	(−0.285)	(−0.128)		
NER	0.003	0.000		−0.005			
	(0.420)	(0.049)		(−0.587)			
R^2	0.174	0.213	0.217	0.193	0.199	0.203	0.204
INV equation							
Constant	0.154	0.154	0.154				
	(3.597)	(3.600)	(3.600)				
RGDPC	0.010	0.010	0.010				
	(1.878)	(1.878)	(1.878)				
R^2	0.029	0.028	0.028				

Notes:
Numbers in parentheses are *T*-statistics. For specifications of models and definition of variables see text.

CHAPTER 8

Are devaluations possibly contractionary? A quasi-Australian model with tradables and nontradables

The landscape of development is strewn with overvalued domestic currencies. This phenomenon flies in the face of conventional wisdom, which emphasizes the salubrious effects of devaluation: by "setting the prices right," devaluation restores competitiveness and through its effect on the balance of payments leads to an expansion in output and employment.[1] The leading explanation of this paradox considers overvaluation as one of the instruments that debauched politicians employ for capturing economic rents (Krueger, 1974; Bhagwati, 1982). Yet, again paradoxically, in the majority of the 24 cases of devaluation that Cooper (1971a) analyzed, the finance minister who had presided over the devaluation had been ousted from office within the next 18 months. This uncharitable verdict on hapless ministers is easier to understand if devaluations perchance turn out to be contractionary, thus imposing a real cost to the economy. Even then, the former paradox would still remain. If an overvalued nominal exchange rate rests on base motivations, why isn't the world replete with venal, rent-seeking bureaucrats?

This chapter first sets the stage by providing a short review of the literature on the effects of devaluations. Next, nominal exchange rate devaluation is introduced in a quasi-Australian model in real variables that includes tradables, nontradables, and their respective prices, which define the real exchange rate. The model is not dynamic. As a result, it cannot compare the real gross domestic product at time t with that at time 0 in terms of purchasing power parity in order to capture the output effects of devaluation. At best, it describes the necessary but not the sufficient conditions that could link nominal exchange rate devaluations with economy-wide contractionary effects. The impact of devaluation on employment is also studied separately, but its impact on income distribution is ignored.[2]

---

1 There is an economic policy counterpart of the conventional wisdom against overvalued domestic currencies. The World Bank list of most distorted countries considers overvaluation as the main contributor to overall domestic price distortions (World Bank, 1983, Chapter 6).

2 The income distributional effects of devaluation are incorporated implicitly in the model through the effect of a decrease in wages on output. For a fuller discussion of the distributional effects of nominal devaluation see also Binkert (1992) and Díaz-Alejandro (1963).

The quasi-Australian model in real variables in Chapter 4 suggested that real exchange rate devaluation is likely to lead to decreased levels of welfare. The model in this section illustrates the conditions under which nominal exchange rate devaluation may lead to contraction. What is still missing is the link between the nominal and the real exchange rate. It is provided in the last section of this chapter, which investigates empirically real exchange rates and studies the pass-through from the nominal exchange rate to the real. The finding on nominal exchange rate overshooting further strengthens the contractionary effects of devaluation that are discussed in this chapter.

The paradox of the merits of overvaluation in the face of the risks from rent-seeking activities remains unanswered. Doesn't the combination create a precariously unstable equilibrium? This issue is taken up in the concluding chapter, after the insights from the case studies of success and failure in economic development have been digested.

Review of the literature

The conventional analysis of the macroeconomic impacts of devaluation has rested on the income and substitution effects from an increase in the price of tradables relative to nontradables. As long as the substitution effect is sufficiently strong to offset the adverse income effect, the net outcome on output and employment is bound to be expansionary.[3] This is predicated on the existence of idle capacity. In the absence of idle capacity, a nominal devaluation will lead to an equiproportional increase in all prices that will leave the real exchange rate unchanged and output and employment constant. The balance-of-payments effect of devaluation is also positive as the supply of exports shifts to the right (since domestic exportables production becomes more profitable), the demand for imports shifts to the left (since world demand shifts to the home country), and the supply of import-competing domestic tradables increases. Johnson (1976) summarizes the traditional view on the macroeconomic effects of devaluations.

The exceptions to the traditional views taken in the literature were first based on the Marshall–Lerner condition. Hirschman (1949) introduced a modification of the Marshall–Lerner condition wherein a country starts from an initial deficit in the balance of payments that makes contraction a more likely result of devaluation. Cooper (1971b) confirmed this view in a general equilibrium model and Krugman and Taylor (1978, p. 446) adopted it in their influential article. They find that:

---

3 Meade's (1951) model of international trade ruled out by assumption that the Marshall–Lerner condition is not satisfied. It thus ruled out the possibility of nonexpansionary devaluations. The model was instrumental in shaping the mainstream literature on devaluations, until very recently.

> When devaluation takes place with an existing trade deficit, price increases of traded goods immediately reduce real income at home and increase it abroad, since foreign currency payment exceeds receipts. Within the home country the value of "foreign savings" goes up ex ante, aggregate demand goes down ex post, and imports fall along with it. The larger the initial deficit, the greater the contractionary outcome (Krugman and Taylor, 1978, p. 446).

The inflationary impact of devaluation has always been considered a downside risk. It is likely to induce a real balance effect, which under certain conditions can lead to contractionary activity. Other contractionary effects of devaluation were noticed quite early by Díaz-Alejandro (1965) who based his argument on changes in income distribution. By decreasing real wages in terms of tradables, devaluation reduces purchasing power and demand for home goods. The reasoning is that income effects dominate in the short-run, while the neoclassical substitution effects, on the other hand, take time to develop. Other demand-side effects that originate in the distribution of income were noticed by Lipschitz (1979) and were incorporated in the model of Krugman and Taylor (1978). Devaluation creates windfall profits in the tradable sector. Should wages follow the increase in prices with a lag, and should the marginal propensity to consume be lower for profit recipients than for wage earners, aggregate consumption decreases and contraction follows. Similarly, if there are ad valorem taxes on exports and imports, devaluation redistributes income from the private sector to the government. Contraction follows as long as the marginal propensity of the latter to save is greater than that of the private sector. The same chain of causality operates when foreign investment directs remittances of profits abroad. Demand for nontradables decreases as a result of this income redistribution and their relative prices may decrease (Barbone and Rivera-Batiz, 1987).

A comprehensive overview of the literature (Lizondo and Montiel, 1989) identifies the following demand-side effects of devaluation: The real income effect is negative if devaluation occurs under an initial trade-balance deficit, and/or demand for imported inputs is inelastic. The tax effects are negative, especially if the public sector is external debtor and relies on taxes to finance debt servicing. The wealth effects on consumption are also negative, except if the foreign sector holds foreign-exchange denominated assets. The intertemporal terms of trade for consumption and investment (interest rate) have a contractionary impact in the event of expected inflation. And the expectation of inflation depends on the extent to which the real exchange rate overshoots its long-run equilibrium level as a result of a nominal devaluation.

Besides the demand channels mentioned above, supply channels of contractionary devaluation have also been developed. They work through the increase in the cost of production of domestically produced goods, especially nontradables, that shifts domestic supply curves to the left. Along with a downward-sloping demand, this would lead to a higher price and a lower level of output, certainly of nontradables. The impulse coming from the Ricardo Principle extends this cost argument to tradables also, since devaluation expands the range of tradability to exportables that are produced in LDCs at high domestic resource cost, in comparison to nontradables. The mechanisms through which the supply effects are introduced are the change in the mix of tradables toward higher-cost exports, the increase in nominal wages, the increase in the cost of working capital, and the use of imported inputs. For instance, van Wijnbergen (1986), in a model that incorporates intermediate imports and informal credit, has devaluation shifting the supply curve to the left and leading to economic contraction.

More recently Edwards (1989) developed a model that incorporates both demand and supply-side effects to explore the recessionary effects of devaluation. His empirical analysis of 39 devaluation episodes ". . . strongly suggests that in many cases devaluations have been historically associated with declines in the level of economic activity around its trend" (Edwards, 1989, p. 324). The finding remains largely valid after other policy disturbances were introduced in the model, along with devaluation. Edwards also finds the income distribution effects of devaluation to be negative. While real wages normally increased in the year before the devaluation, they declined subsequently, with agricultural wage declines leading real manufacturing wages. Edwards' model incorporates some overly restrictive assumptions, which, if released, would make the contractionary effects even stronger. Still, the author treats his results merely as probationary evidence.

The discussion so far has not questioned the increased competitiveness and efficiency that results from nominal devaluations. However, increased competitiveness needs be separated from setting the prices right and the efficiency gains that follow automatically. Any devaluation – even a series of "competitive devaluations" – increases foreign competitiveness by definition. It does not necessarily also restore equilibrium in the real exchange rate, in the sense that it equalizes the opportunity cost of resources in producing one unit's worth of tradables and nontradables. In fact, the message of the discussion of incomplete markets in Chapter 3 and of the empirical work in Chapter 7 is that a free market regime instills in LDCs a tendency for spiral devaluations. These can introduce more trade bias in the structure of the economy and real efficiency losses are likely to occur as a country shifts away from comparative-advantage trade to competitive-devaluation trade.

Devaluations, whether they are contractionary or not, are need-induced. The initial conditions of devaluation are disequilibrium positions in the goods market (imports and exports) and the asset market (reserves), or of output and interest rates. A balance of payments deficit indicates that an economy is running down a finite stock of international reserves by buying more tradable goods and services than it can pay for through exports or through borrowing. This makes the stock of foreign exchange reserves inadequate to defend the nominal exchange rate at a certain level. The fact that both a tight monetary policy to solve the problem (Chapter 4) and a devaluation (Chapter 7) are contractionary, does not make the initial external disequilibrium any more sustainable. Rather, the appropriate solution for LDCs is to increase the efficiency in the production of tradables. Increased profitability because of decreased costs in the production of tradables is Pareto-improving; increased profitability because of a price support of output – the effect of devaluation – is not. Failing this supply-side alternative, the usual prescription for incomplete markets applies: rationing. This means that the nominal exchange rate is held below its market-clearing level through exchange controls, interventions in trade through licensing and tariffs (for imports), and input subsidies (for exports). Since the disequilibrium is systematically related to incomplete foreign exchange markets, it must be addressed at that level. This is the systematic component that relates the study of contractionary devaluations to the theme of this book. As the economy develops and productivity improvements tend to decrease the price of tradables (Balassa, 1964) while labor absorption tends to increase the price of nontradables (Bhagwati, 1984), the incompleteness of the market of the open economy tends to be removed and liberalization of the trade and the capital account can gradually take place.

A theoretical model

The real model in Chapter 4 treated the nontradable sector as the effective constraint on the expenditure side. The requirement that there be no excess demand in the nontradable sector implied that expenditures had to be depressed below the level of real income (Chapter 4, Figures 4.1b and 4.2). So a devaluation of the real exchange rate coupled with sectoral clearing in the nontradable market implies that expenditure by consumers has to fall. Hence a devaluation of the real exchange rate is always contractionary.

But central banks are able to change only nominal variables. So the question is: can a nominal devaluation lead to a real devaluation that results in overall contraction in the economy? If a devaluation of the nominal exchange rate leads to a real devaluation, i.e., to an increase in the price of tradables relative to nontradables, the real model showed that consumer expenditures may be constrained below the level of income. This result becomes even stronger if the nominal exchange rate becomes undervalued (for any of the reasons mentioned in Chapter 3) and there is overshooting of the real exchange rate. In order to show contractionary effects of devaluation it suffices to show that the mix of output changes, and in particular that a nominal devaluation lowers the equilibrium output of nontradables. We attempt to find sufficient conditions that generate this result.

The model is an adaptation of Edwards' (Edwards, 1989) with two production sectors for tradables and nontradables.[4] Capital stock is sector-specific and fixed during the relevant run underlying the model. Labor and imported intermediate inputs are the factors of production, with the latter used exclusively in the production of nontradables. This assumption builds on the insight of many structuralist macromodels in which the devaluation acts like a supply shock (Taylor, 1983). In any event, the supply effect of a nominal devaluation will be more pronounced with imported inputs in the nontradable sector, where there is no simultaneous increase in the output price to cushion the increase in the price of imports, as there is in the tradable sector. Real balances enter the demand for nontradables and labor markets are characterized by some form of wage indexation. Based on these assumptions Edwards finds that the output and employment effects of a nominal devaluation are ambiguous depending on the actual magnitudes of the parameters of the model. The reason is that while the supply curve of nontradables shifts to the left, the income and substitution effect of the devaluation tends to increase demand for nontradables. Hence, if the demand elasticities are big enough, production of nontradables need not fall.

The model

We extend the Edwards (1989) model in a way that allows us to work with more general functional relationships among the different variables of the model. The basic structural difference from Edwards' model is the flexible wage rate, which is an endogenous variable. The price of nontradables is the second endogenous variable. In this respect, and unlike Edwards', the model is an equilibrium model, with the labor market and the nontradable market clearing, and with income equal to expenditure. In this last respect the model is different from the real model of Chapter 4.

The model can be written as:

$$y = N^s + (e/P_N)(P_T T^s - P_I I_N - rD) \tag{8.1}$$

$$N^d = N^d\left(y, \frac{M}{P_N}, \frac{P_N}{eP_T}\right) \tag{8.2}$$

$$N^s = N^s\left(\frac{eP_I}{P_N}, \frac{w}{P_N}\right) \tag{8.3}$$

---

4 Although imports and exports are distinguished in Edwards' model, their prices are the same and the two effectively collapse into a composite tradable commodity.

$$T^s = T^s(w/eP_T) \tag{8.4}$$

The superscripts s and d indicate supply and demand and the subscripts T, N, and I indicate tradables, nontradables, and intermediate inputs, respectively; I_N is the amount of imported intermediate goods used in the nontradable sector; e and w are the exchange rate (defined as the domestic currency price of foreign exchange) and the nominal wage rate, respectively; P_T and P_I, the prices of tradables and intermediate inputs, are expressed in foreign currency and they are assumed fixed; P_N, the price of nontradables, is expressed in domestic currency. Equation (8.1) is the real national income in terms of nontradables. The formulation accounts directly for expenditure for servicing the foreign debt, which is the product of D, the dollar amount of foreign debt, and r, the exogenously given world rate of interest.

The demand function for nontradables, equation (8.2), besides income and prices also includes real balances (M/P_N). By introducing real balances, nominal devaluation becomes nonneutral, in the sense that devaluation cannot simply lead to an equiproportionate change in all domestic prices.[5] One of the conditions for equilibrium in this model is that the market for nontradables clears. An equiproportionate increase in all nominal prices will leave all relative prices unchanged but will reduce real balances. Hence, there will be excess supply in the market for nontradables.

The supply functions in equations (8.3) and (8.4) are derived from profit-maximizing behavior by firms under conditions of perfect competition. Firms in the nontradable sector freely choose the profit-maximizing quantities of intermediate inputs that they need and firms in both sectors choose the profit-maximizing quantities of labor that they need. More formally, we have the following optimization problems being solved in the two sectors:

$$\max_{I_N, L_N} \pi_N = F_N(L_N, I_N) - (w/P_N)L_N - (eP_I/P_N)I_N \tag{8.5}$$

$$\max_{L_T} \pi_T = F_T(L_T) - (w/eP_T)L_T \tag{8.6}$$

where L_N and L_T are the quantities of labor demanded by each sector. Here it is understood, of course, that the Fs are functions of sector-specific capital stocks.

The input demand functions are now given by:

---

5 Katseli (1983) and Branson (1989) have made the argument that devaluation, through its effect on the price level, will generate negative real balance effects; these will lead to lower aggregate demand and, under certain conditions, to lower output. Following Edwards (1989) in introducing real balances in this fashion, we greatly truncate the treatment of the monetary sector by ignoring it. The payoff is that the two endogenous variables are put in sharper focus.

$$I_N = I_N\left(\frac{eP_I}{P_N}, \frac{w}{P_N}\right) \tag{8.7}$$

$$L_N^d = L_N^d\left(\frac{eP_I}{P_N}, \frac{w}{P_N}\right) \tag{8.8}$$

$$L_T^d = L_T^d(w/eP_T) \tag{8.9}$$

We shall assume that the supply of intermediate inputs is infinitely elastic at the world price P_I. Furthermore, there is only a fixed amount of labor available in the economy equal to $\bar{L}$. The market-clearing condition in the labor market is given by:

$$L_N^d + L_T^d = \bar{L} \tag{8.10}$$

Our conditions for equilibrium then become market clearing in both the nontradable and labor markets.

Formal comparative statics

Our interest in analyzing the problem is to make explicit the set of parameters on which the output effect depends. The equilibrium conditions of the model are:

$$y = N^s\left(\frac{eP_I}{P_N}, \frac{w}{P_N}\right) + \frac{e}{P_N}\left[P_T T^s\left(\frac{w}{eP_T}\right) - P_N I_N\left(\frac{eP_I}{P_N}, \frac{w}{P_N}\right) - rD\right] \tag{8.11}$$

$$N^d\left(y, \frac{M}{P_N}, \frac{P_N}{eP_T}\right) = N^s\left(\frac{eP_I}{P_N}, \frac{w}{P_N}\right) \tag{8.12}$$

$$L_N^d\left(\frac{eP_I}{P_N}, \frac{w}{P_N}\right) + L_T^d\left(\frac{w}{eP_T}\right) = \bar{L} \tag{8.13}$$

Totally differentiating (8.12) and (8.13) we get:

$$dN^d = N_y^d\, dy + N_{P_N}^d\, dP_N + N_e^d\, de$$

$$dN^s = N_w^s\, dw + N_{P_N}^s\, dP_N + N_e^s\, de$$

$$L_{N,e}\, de + L_{N,P_N}\, dP_N + L_{N,w}\, dw + L_{T,w}\, dw + L_{T,e}\, de = 0$$

Since $dN^d = dN^s$ in equilibrium, we simply use the term dN to stand for the change in the output of the nontradable sector. Now we can substitute out the term dy by totally differentiating equation (8.12) and substituting the resulting expression in the total differential of (8.13). It turns out that:

$$dy = dN + f_1\, de + f_2\, dP_N + f_3\, dw$$

where we denote the partial derivatives of y with respect to e, P_N, and w, as:

$$f_1 = (e/P_N)(P_T T_e^s - P_T I_{N,e}) + (1/P_N)(P_T T^s - P_I I_N - rD)$$
$$f_2 = -(e/P_N^2)(P_T T^s - P_I I_N - rD) - e P_I I_{N,P_N}/P_N \qquad (8.14)$$
$$f_3 = (e/P_N)(P_T T_w^s - P_T I_{N,w})$$

We make the following assumptions about the signs of the partial derivatives:[6]

$$
\begin{array}{llll}
1 > N_y^d > 0 & N_{P_N}^d < 0 & 1 > N_e^d > 0 & \\
N_w^s < 0 & N_{P_N}^s > 0 & N_e^s < 0 & T_w^s < 0 \\
L_{N,P_N} > 0 & L_{N,w} > 0 & L_{N,e} > 0 & \qquad (8.15) \\
L_{T,w} < 0 & L_{T,e} > 0 & & \\
I_{N,e} < 0 & I_{N,P_N} > 0 & I_{N,w} > 0 &
\end{array}
$$

To say that $L_{N,e} > 0$ is to assume that labor and intermediate inputs are gross substitutes in production (hence it implies that $I_{N,w} > 0$ as well, since the Jacobian of the input demand functions must be symmetric). Hence an increase in the cost of intermediate inputs increases the demand for labor while an increase in the nominal wage increases the demand for intermediate inputs.

Consider the partial derivatives of y with respect to e, P_N, and w, given in equation (8.14). Referring to the wage rate, derivative f_3 is clearly negative. An increase in the nominal wage (holding everything else constant) tends to lower real income. With reference to the exchange rate, partial derivative f_1 is positive; whereas partial derivative f_2, with respect to the price of nontradables, is negative. The signs for partial derivatives f_1 and f_3 can be reversed only if the debt service rD/P_N is large so that the respective terms in parentheses become negative.

Here w, P_N, and N are the three endogenous variables of the system whereas e is the parameter that we shall exogenously alter. We can put the total differentials of (8.12) and (8.13) in matrix form. It is:

$$
\begin{bmatrix} a_{11} & a_{12} & a_{13} \\ 1 & a_{22} & a_{23} \\ 0 & a_{32} & a_{33} \end{bmatrix}
\begin{bmatrix} dN/de \\ dP_N/de \\ dw/de \end{bmatrix} =
\begin{bmatrix} c_1 \\ c_2 \\ c_3 \end{bmatrix}
$$

where,

$$a_{11} = 1 - N_y^d > 0$$

---

6 For proof see Appendix.

$$a_{12} = - (N^d_{P_N} + N^d_y f_2) > 0$$

$$a_{13} = - N^d_y f_3 > 0$$

$$a_{22} = - N^s_{P_N} < 0$$

$$a_{23} = - N^s_w > 0 \tag{8.16}$$

$$a_{32} = - L_{N,P_N} < 0$$

$$a_{33} = - (L_{N,w} + L_{T,w}) > 0$$

$$c_1 = N^d_e + N^d_y f_1 > 0$$

$$c_2 = N^s_e < 0$$

$$c_3 = (L_{N,e} + L_{T,e}) > 0$$

The parameter c_1 is the sum of N^d_e, which is the cross-price elasticity between nontradables and tradables, measuring the substitution effect on the demand for the former as a result of a rise in the price of the latter, and $N^d_y f_1$, which measures the income effect of a devaluation on the demand for nontradables. We have assumed that N^d_e is positive and so is $N^d_y f_1$ as long as f_1 in equation (8.14) is positive. The sign of c_1 is positive, although the parameter might be small, as the discussion below will indicate.

A sufficient condition for the determinant of the coefficient matrix to be negative is:

$$a_{22} a_{33} - a_{23} a_{32} < 0 \tag{8.17}$$

We can make the inequality more transparent by expressing it in terms of the underlying parameters of the model. It can be written as:

$$N^s_{P_N}(L_{N,w} + L_{T,w}) - N^s_w L_{N,P_N} < 0. \tag{8.18}$$

Using Cramer's rule we find that:

$$dw/de = [c_3(a_{22}a_{11} - a_{12})/\mathbf{D}] - [a_{32}(a_{11}c_2 - c_1)/\mathbf{D}] > 0 \tag{8.19}$$

$$dP_N/de = [a_{33}(a_{11}c_2 - c_1)/\mathbf{D}] - [c_3(a_{11}a_{23} - a_{13})/\mathbf{D}] > 0 \tag{8.20}$$

$$dN/de = [c_1(a_{22}a_{33} - a_{23}a_{32})/\mathbf{D}] - [c_2(a_{12}a_{33} - a_{32}a_{13})/\mathbf{D}]$$

$$+ [c_3(a_{12}a_{23} - a_{22}a_{13})/\mathbf{D}]^2 \lessgtr 0 \tag{8.21}$$

$$\frac{dy}{de} = f_1 + f_2 \frac{dP_N}{de} + f_3 \frac{dw}{de} + \frac{dN}{de}, \text{ indeterminate} \tag{8.22}$$

Wages go up unambiguously from equation (8.19). In equation (8.20) the effect of devaluation on the price of nontradables is likely to be positive as long as c_{13} is small (or N^d_y is small). Equation (8.20) describes the real pass-through from the nominal to the real exchange rate and is the object of the empirical research of the next section, where the value of that partial derivative turns out to be positive. If so, although nominal wages increase from (8.19), real wages, and incomes, may decrease as a result of devaluation.

The crucial relationship is equation (8.21). The second and third terms on the right-hand side of (8.21) are both negative. Given our assumptions in (8.15), the first term is positive. Hence the nontradable output effect of a devaluation hinges on the size of the first term. It is composed of the elasticity of supply of nontradables with respect to prices of nontradables and the wage rate, both within the parentheses and both accounting for a shift of the supply curve to the left; and the impact of the multiplicative factor c_1, which is related to the substitution and income effects of a devaluation on the demand for non-tradables. This is how the Marshall–Lerner condition that was identified as important in the review of the literature (and in Chapter 2) becomes formalized.

We can write $c_1 = [(\eta_y)(f_1/y) + \eta_e]N$, where η_y is the income elasticity of demand for nontradables; and η_e is the cross-price elasticity between non-tradables and tradables, measuring the substitution effect on the demand for the former as a result of a rise in the price of the latter. The devaluation leads consumers to switch towards the relatively cheaper nontradables, so this auto-matically shifts the demand for nontradables to the right. If the devaluation also increases real income, then the income effect will reinforce this positive shift. In general, the smaller the cross-price and income elasticities are, the more likely that a devaluation will be contractionary: the shift in the supply to the left will not be fully compensated by the shift of the demand to the right, and output of nontradables will decrease.

There are plausible reasons, however, to believe that c_1 will be small. In certain LDCs the demand for tradables is socioeconomic-class-specific, ema-nating mostly from the government and the upper and middle income classes. Hence there might be little room for substituting nontradables for tradables at the margin after a devaluation. Therefore it may not be implausible to assume that the substitution parameter η_e is small in magnitude. This supports the argument that c_1 could also be small.

Service on external debt, D, appears in all three equations (8.19)–(8.21) through the variables a_{12}, c_1, as well as through the value of the determinant, **D**. In the presence of large external debt, devaluation can amount to a decrease in disposable income that leads to contraction. The real value of interest payments that are expressed in foreign currency increases through devaluation. This represents a decrease in real income that can reverse the direction of the income effect by reducing the demand for nontradables. In this case, the partial derivative with respect to e in equation (8.14) becomes negative, as already noted above. This is the condition that Hirschman (1949) first identified and Krugman and Taylor (1978) reiterated, as we noticed in the review of the literature. The combination of the Marshall–Lerner condition and of the size of foreign indebtedness make it very likely for a nominal devaluation to lead to an output contraction in nontradables. This conclusion will be further strengthened in the next section.

So far the argument has established that contraction in the nontradable sector is likely. Is this unambiguously equivalent with a contraction in the economy? From equation (8.22) the effect of e on y is ambiguous as long as f_1 and f_2 switch signs.[7] The following are plausible outcomes of the derivations above:

$$f_1 < 0, f_2 > 0, c_1 > 0, a_{12} > 0, \frac{dw}{de} > 0, \frac{dP_N}{de} > 0, \frac{dN}{de} < 0$$

However, even then the argument on contraction can be valid as long as real balance effects are introduced.[8]

In conclusion, this model gives strong and unambiguous results with respect to the impact of devaluation for LDCs with a significant debt overhang and with high degree of income inequality. Devaluation increases the price of nontradables, but not proportionally to the increase in the price of tradables; the relative price of nontradables, therefore, decreases. This implies that the pass-through from the nominal to the real exchange rate is less than full: the impact of devaluation on the price of tradables (and the real exchange rate) decays early with the price of nontradables catching up. The proposition on the rate of decay of devaluation is tested in the next section. Devaluation also increases wages. The combined impact on the prices of nontradables and on wages suggests the possibility that causality between devaluation and inflation goes from the former to the latter. The equilibrium value of nontradables output decreases unambiguously and so does the real output in the economy. Further-

---

7 See Appendix for proof.
8 If f_2 and f_3 switch signs, a possibility mentioned earlier, one can still make a plausible argument that $(dy/de) < 0$.

One approach is using the marginal effect of real money balances on demand, introduced in equation (8.2). Define $M/P_N = m$ in the nontradable demand function. As already stated, in the absence of any real money balance effect, i.e., $N_m^d = 0$, the equilibrium is invariant to changes in the nominal exchange rate. This means that $(dw/de)(e/w) = (dP_N/de)(e/P_N) = 1$ and $(dN/de) = (dy/de) = 0$. In terms of equation (8.22) this means not only that its value is equal to zero, but that the sum of its first three terms on the right-hand side is also equal to zero as long as $(dN/de) = 0$.

Now let the real money balance effect, N_m^d, deviate positively from zero. Its effect is to increase a_{12}. But a_{12} only enters equation (8.21), which determines dN/de and its coefficient is $[1/\mathbf{D}(-c_2 a_{33} + c_3 a_{23}] < 0$. Therefore, the marginal contribution of including the real money balance effect is to make the last term in equation (8.22) negative. As long as the sum of the three previous terms is zero, this means $dy/de < 0$ of the margin.

This can also be derived by solving directly the equilibrium equations (8.20) to (8.22) for (dy/de), (dP_N/de), (dw/de).

more, the contractionary effects of devaluation become accentuated if there is substantial foreign debt overhang in the economy.

The contractionary effects of devaluation captured in this model are stronger than the ones emanating from its parent model. Edwards (1989, pp. 318–319) finds determinate effects of devaluation only on the quantity of imports, exports, and the price of nontradables, and indeterminate effects of devaluation on employment and output of the nontradable sector. He evaluates all these imponderables of the model as having "... clearly indicated that there is a (nontrivial) possibility for devaluations to reduce aggregate output."

An empirical model of the pass-through

The discussion in Chapter 4 was cast in terms of real exchange rates. The theoretical model that preceded in this chapter is cast in terms of nominal exchange rates. The nominal exchange rate is the policy control instrument that is designed to affect the real magnitudes in the economy through its impact on the real exchange rate. The question is how are the two related? This section will address empirically the issue of the pass-through, which is the mechanism of transmission from the nominal exchange rate to the relative prices of tradables.

The quasi-Australian model of Chapter 4 dealt with disequilibrium real exchange rates, in the sense that the market for nontradables did not clear. Such disequilibrium was associated with loss in welfare. The model that preceded argued the plausible case that devaluation of the nominal exchange rate could lead to contraction in output. Could "excessive" nominal devaluation lead to severe output contraction? The meaning of "excessive" will be based on the need for overshooting the nominal exchange rate in order to forestall the rapid decay of the impact of devaluation on relative prices of tradables and nontradables.

Diagrammatical definitions and measurement

In order to define terms, Figure 8.1 shows the quantity of tradables (exports and imports) and their local-currency price. To simplify the graph, assume that point a represents the intersection of demand and supply curves for both exports E and imports I before devaluation. Devaluation is equivalent to a shift in the demand for exports to the right, D_E' (since domestic producers become lower-cost producers) and a shift in the supply of imports to the left, S_I' (since world demand is shifted to the home country), thus increasing the quantity of exports to Q_E' and decreasing that of imports to Q_I'. The distances de and cb represent the effect of devaluation on exports and imports, respectively, while the effect on domestic prices of exports and imports, the *price-through*, is

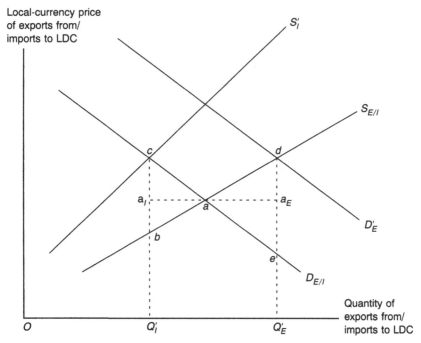

Figure 8.1. *Price-through and pass-through effects of devaluation*
Source: Bhagwati (1991).

captured by the distances da_E and ca_I, respectively. The *pass-through* on prices is represented by the respective elasticities, da_E/de and ca_I/cb.

Two conclusions arise from the diagram. The pass-through of a devaluation on prices of tradables (exports and imports) is positive, with a value of between zero and one.[9] With perfectly elastic supply and the law of one price holding fully, the limiting value of the pass-through on tradable prices, P_T, is one, as shown in Figure 8.2.

The diagrammatic exposition of the pass-through focuses on prices of exports and imports in the home market. The theoretical modeling of the phenomenon more often than not relates devaluation to the pricing of exports in the foreign country, and the empirical studies refer mostly to DCs. For example, the pass-through from devaluation to dollar prices of U.S. imports was 50–80%,

---

9 There are a few instances in the literature where the empirical value of the pass-through is greater than one, e.g., Dornbusch (1987, p. 98) and Liu (1993). The most likely origin of this anomaly is strategic trade, as will be discussed below.

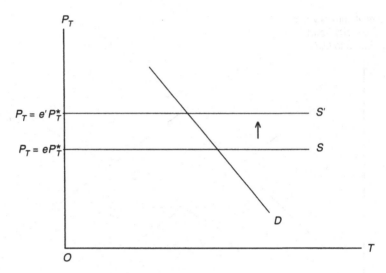

Figure 8.2. *Full pass-through*

whereas more recently its value has declined substantially (Hooper and Mann, 1989).[10] Two types of basic models seek to explain the actual value of the pass-through on export prices.

Static profit-maximization models originate from the considerations underlying Figure 8.1. Market conditions determine the shape of the demand and marginal cost (supply) curves an exporter is facing. In an oligopolistic model, marginal revenue will be equal to marginal cost at pass-through values less than one (complete pass-through) as long as the demand curve does not have constant (unitary) elasticity (Dornbusch, 1987, Knetter, 1989, Krugman, 1987a, Mann, 1986). This conclusion is modified by making unusual assumptions about the marginal cost curve, e.g., if it is decreasing. Then demand and cost curves jointly determine the pass-through coefficient, which can be greater than unity in certain cases (Feenstra, 1989, Marston, 1990).

Models that develop a "pricing-to-market" explanation of the phenomenon become more creative than the elasticity story in the diagram. Besides imper-

10 There is ample parallel empirical evidence that the pass-through from exchange rate variations to prices of tradables is, as a rule, less than full. See Dunn (1970), Isard (1977), Kravis and Lipsey (1977), Richardson (1978), Giovannini (1988), Knetter (1989), and Ohno (1989). Edwards (1989, p. 145) also provides empirical values for the pass-through for certain LDCs.

fect competition, they also involve dynamic supply-side or demand-side effects with some story about maintaining market share in the face of exchange rate fluctuations, and expectations about the behavior of the exchange rate. Under these conditions the pass-through becomes path-dependent and "hysteresis" occurs. Home monopoly tends to increase the pass-through to tradable prices (Dornbusch, 1987). Sunk entry costs on the supply side (such as setting up a distribution network) tend to decrease it, with exporters opting to absorb the costs of devaluation through reduced margins in order to stay in the market and protect their share (Baldwin, 1988; Baldwin and Krugman, 1989). Parallel to this is the case of exchange rate appreciation with sunk entry costs on the demand side, such as sticky consumer demand because of brand loyalty (Froot and Klemperer, 1989). Such considerations are especially pertinent if exchange rate fluctuations can be considered as stochastic, moving around an equilibrium trend with strong mean reversion (Baldwin and Krugman, 1989). In their model, movement of the exchange rate beyond the bounds of its equilibrium trend induces entry or exit of firms and alters the supply curve permanently. Dixit (1989), on the other hand, assumes the exchange rate to follow a random walk. This makes exchange rate fluctuations more pronounced and less fore-seeable.

The factors outlined in the literature become relevant in the analysis of LDCs that have in general a less competitive environment. The monopolistic structure of the economy is reinforced by the asset-value-dynamics considerations that lead to expectations of spiral devaluations of freely floating LDC currencies. Monopolies are commonly strong for the reason, among others, that supply side hysteresis with expectations of permanent (let alone continuing) devaluations makes foreign firms unwilling to enter the market for a wide band of exchange rates. Market share in small LDCs might not be that important for an exporter, who is even less interested in protecting it aggressively under expectations of spiral devaluations. The joint effect of these factors is likely to increase the value of the pass-through on prices of tradables in LDCs. But the story so far is incomplete. Nominal exchange rate devaluation affects real variables in the economy, such as quantities produced and traded, only to the extent that it changes relative prices. In a model that includes nontradables, the pass-through on their prices need also be considered. Devaluation is "neutral" if prices of nontradables reflect the effect of devaluation to the same extent as tradable prices do. Domestic producers, in that case, do not benefit from cost decreases and therefore world demand is not shifted to the home country. In Figure 8.1 above, the intersection of demand and supply curves remains at a – the result of a demand function that is homogeneous of degree zero in all its arguments – and inflation occurs.

The empirical test that follows generalizes the discussion by considering the impact of devaluation on all prices, and especially on prices of tradables versus those of nontradables.[11] In this respect, the test of the pass-through from the nominal to the real exchange rate is novel in this literature.[12]

Testable hypotheses and data

The relationship of interest for the empirical study of the pass-through is equation (8.20) above. As already mentioned, c_1 and a_{13} are the crucial coefficients in determining the sign of the relationship between the price of non-tradables and the nominal exchange rate. Should both coefficients be small (a fortiori, if they are approaching zero) we can anticipate that dP_N/de could be unambiguously positive. That is, the effect of a devaluation is to increase the price of nontradables, thereby beginning the process of undoing the initial relative price effect of the devaluation. The sign of this relationship will be put to further scrutiny in what follows.

The pass-through from the nominal to the real exchange rate is defined as the "real pass-through." Define the elasticities of the price of tradables and price of nontradables with respect to the nominal exchange rate, respectively, as:

$$\varepsilon_{P_T \cdot e} = (\partial P_T / \partial e)(e / P_T)$$

$$\varepsilon_{P_N \cdot e} = (\partial P_N / \partial e)(e / P_N)$$

Real pass-through, ε_v, is then defined as:

$$\varepsilon_v = \frac{d(P_T/P_N)/(P_T/P_N)}{de/e} = \varepsilon_{P_T \cdot e} - \varepsilon_{P_N \cdot e}$$

The real pass-through is thus defined as the elasticity of the real exchange rate with respect to the NER. If the real exchange rate remains unchanged, $d(P_T/P_N) = 0$, the real pass-through is zero. The real pass-through is one when the nominal devaluation is fully reflected into the real exchange rate, $d(P_T/P_N)/(P_T/P_N) = de/e$.

This implies that if a nominal devaluation ultimately leaves the real exchange rate unchanged, the real pass-through is zero; the maximum value that the elasticity can take is one when a nominal devaluation is fully reflected into a real devaluation.

---

11 Froot and Klemperer (1989) note one obvious reason why foreign exporters might be expected to sell their goods at higher prices in the U.S. than abroad when the dollar appreciates: some of their costs, like advertizing, selling, and distributing in the U.S. relate to nontradables and are denominated in dollars. Our argument generalizes this commonsensical observation by considering relative prices of tradables in terms of nontradables.

12 Edwards (1989, Chapter 7) performs a similar test for the pass-through. But his real exchange rate relates to relative PPP and it is estimated as an index of changes in relative prices of tradables to nontradables, proxied, respectively, by the changes in the WPI and the CPI.

Since the mechanism of transmission from the nominal devaluation to P_T and to P_N differs, one can formulate certain testable hypotheses on the relationship between nominal and real exchange rates. A nominal devaluation initially results in all tradable prices adjusting through the operation of the law of one price. The implication is that in the extreme case, when purchasing power parity holds fully, $e = P_T/P_T^*$, and the supply of tradables is perfectly elastic, (P_T^* is constant), a nominal devaluation has a price-through on tradables of one, $\varepsilon_{P_T \cdot e} = (dP_T/P_T)/(de/e) = 1$. If, additionally, the price of nontradables does not change, $\varepsilon_{P_N \cdot e} = 0$, the real pass-through is equal to 1. If, however, $\varepsilon_{P_N \cdot e} = d(P_N/P_N)/(de/e) > 0$, then $\varepsilon_v < 1$.

The first hypothesis to be tested relates to the value of the real pass-through in the year of the devaluation and how it evolves through time as the adjustment in the price of nontradables reverses the effects of the initial devaluation. The test of the hypothesis is formulated by regressing the real exchange rate at time t on current and past realizations of the nominal exchange rate over a period that is defined as a devaluation episode. The decay coefficient of devaluation determines how much of the initial nominal devaluation persists in the long run. A variation of this hypothesis would also consider the level of development of a specific country, as proxied by per capita income, and the level of external debt as percent of GDP.

The weight of the argument from the literature review suggests that the LDCs in the data sample would have a higher price-through to the price of tradables, and thus a higher real pass-through also, as compared to the values that would obtain for DCs. The trade monopoly effect for LDCs should account for a large part of the initial real pass-through value. In the extreme case of the DCs, pricing-to-market and competitive share considerations may leave the price of tradables largely unchanged, and thus limit the value of the real pass-through. Another factor that is reflected in the value of the real pass-through coefficient is the composition of output between tradables and non-tradables. It determines the weights that the prices of the two groups receive in forming the index of the real exchange rate. The greater the share of tradables in GDP, the more the overall price index (and thus the ratio of prices of tradables to nontradables) is likely to reflect the effects of devaluation. The converse is true for a low share of tradables in GDP. It is not clear, however, how the shares of tradables and nontradables may vary in the process of development. LDCs may be expected to have a lower share of traded (as opposed to tradable) commodities than DCs, for they have more foreign exchange constraints, less exposure to trade, and a higher share of commodities that become expensive to trade (import) systematically, such as subsistence food, or other labor-intensive goods. DCs, on the other hand, may approach the same result through the shift of the composition of output toward services, which are largely nontraded.

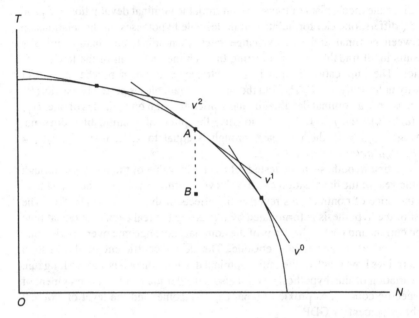

Figure 8.3. *Overshooting of the nominal exchange rate*

If one considers the dynamic effects of devaluation occurring in years after the event, there are good structural reasons to suggest that the final value of the real pass-through may be low in LDCs: they include bottlenecks and small values of the elasticity of substitution in production and consumption between tradables and nontradables. Thus, although the initial value of the real pass-through may be considerable in LDCs, its decay coefficient may also be high, with P_N increasing quickly in an otherwise inflationary environment in LDCs.

Overshooting of the nominal exchange rate may be related to the effectiveness with which a nominal devaluation is reflected on the real exchange rate. If so, one would expect to observe that, other things being equal, the smaller the final value of the real pass-through, the larger the initial devaluation required in order to achieve a targeted trade surplus. Figure 8.3 illustrates the implications of the above propositions. Suppose that policy makers want to target a trade surplus of size AB. The real exchange rate necessary to accomplish that is v^1. We shall assume that government is willing to contract expenditures by the amount of the surplus so that it can maintain v^1 as an equilibrium real exchange rate. Let v^0 be the current real exchange rate. The necessary real devaluation (d_r) to achieve the targeted trade surplus is $d_r = (v^1 - v^0)/v^0$. But if the real pass-through is less than one $(\varepsilon_v < 1)$ then achieving the targeted surplus requires that the nominal exchange rate be devalued by (d_r/ε_v) > d_r (which is more than the requisite devaluation of the real exchange rate).

Since a nominal devaluation affects prices of tradables instantaneously, with prices of nontradables adjusting with a lag, the initial effect would drive the real exchange rate to v^2 where it satisfies $v^2 = v^0(1 + d_r/\varepsilon_v)$. At v^2 there is over-shooting of the targeted real exchange rate, which finally settles down to v^1 only after a lag. So apart from the costs of contracting the economy (in terms of the shortage of nontradables represented in the move from v^0 to v^1) in order to preserve the targeted real exchange rate v^1, there is a further cost involved in the initial overshooting of the real exchange rate (to v^2). That initial cost involves the unnecessary reallocation of resources between tradables and non-tradables induced by the severe change in relative prices because of the initial devaluation.

The second hypothesis, therefore, specifies a relationship between the deviation of the real exchange rate from its equilibrium value and the adjustment in the lagged real exchange rate in the following period. The sign and the size of the coefficient of the relationship determines whether there is mean reversion in the real exchange rate.

Two data problems arise in the empirical model: measuring the real exchange rate and identifying the devaluation episodes.

Unlike the nominal exchange rate, the real exchange rate is not an observable price. Although its definition is unambiguous, its measurement and the determination of its equilibrium value is not. For the purpose of testing the second hypothesis (and despite the caveats raised in Chapter 6) we define the equilibrium real exchange rate as the ratio of prices of tradables to nontradables that yields the RER index value of one.

The ICP-based prices of tradables and nontradables and the RER index exist for the benchmark countries for the years 1970, 1975, 1980, and 1985. We derive estimates for the intervening years by using the formula suggested by Edwards (1989) in his study of devaluation episodes in the pre-1970 period. He defines the real exchange rate as $e(WPI^{US}/CPI^j)$, where e is the nominal exchange rate of country j's currency with respect to the U.S. dollar, and WPI and CPI are the respective wholesale and retail price indexes for the U.S. and country j. The implicit assumption is that the common basket of tradables can be proxied by the basket that makes up the U.S. WPI and that the basket of nontradables for the j country is similar to the basket of goods that is used to calculate that country's CPI. It is, of course, an imperfect measure but it does not seem an unreasonable first estimate. Hence, suppose we have an ICP-based estimate of the real exchange rate in 1970, v_{1970}. Then our estimate of the real exchange rate for 1971 is:

$$RER_{1971} = [e_{1971} WPI^{US}_{1971})/CPI^j_{1971}] \, [CPI^j_{1970}/(e_{1970} WPI^{US}_{1970})]RER_{1970}$$

where the anchor year RER_{1970} becomes the nearest year for which ICP-based real exchange rates exist for the country. The data on nominal exchange rates and prices indices are from International Monetary Fund (1990).

The problem of determining whether a change in the nominal exchange rate is indeed a devaluation is rather vexing in the post Bretton-Woods world. Most countries have adopted some form of managed float, resulting in greater variability in the nominal exchange rate on a year-to-year basis. A real devaluation is to be identified by its nontrivial magnitude, which is interpreted as a discrete alteration in policy intended to devalue the domestic currency. In a model that focuses on the real effects of a nominal devaluation, one would expect "the beachhead effect" to hold: large exchange rate shocks can have a real effect, while small shocks cannot (Baldwin, 1988). This is another reason for concentrating on nontrivial devaluations.

We choose to define a change in the nominal exchange rate as being a devaluation if it meets the following two criteria: (1) the change in the exchange rate exceeds 20%; and (2) it exceeds by at least 10% the rate of inflation as measured by the *CPI* index. Although the rule is ad hoc, it serves in getting around the uncertainty that was introduced after 1971.

Using this definition, we are able to identify 108 devaluation episodes in the 1970–1986 period for the set of countries for which we have ICP-based estimates of the real exchange rates. However, given our interest in tracing the time path of the real exchange rate several years after the nominal devaluation, the analysis becomes complicated if there are devaluations occurring one or two years after the initial one. For example, Brazil had successive devaluations in 1983 and 1984. Thus the value of the real exchange rate in 1984 is the result of the devaluation of the previous year and the current year's devaluation, and it would be difficult to untangle the effect of the one from the other. For this reason, we decided to study only the devaluations of those countries that did not experience another devaluation until three years had elapsed from the initial devaluation.[13] This reduces the sample to 42 distinct devaluation episodes, as identified in Table 8.1.

Empirical results

As a preliminary step in the analysis, we examine the average change in the real exchange rate for the first three years after the devaluation. The results are presented in Table 8.1. The average rate of the nominal devaluation is 63%, with the range being from a high of 419% for Chile in 1974 to a low of 21% for Malawi in 1982. The real devaluation in the year when the nominal ex-

---

13 The definition of mid-period devaluation is as the original definition above. If in any one year of the subsequent three-year period the exchange rate depreciated by over 20% (subject to exceeding the rate of inflation by 10% or more) the observation was dropped from the sample.

Table 8.1. *Devaluations and change in the RER*

Country	Year	Nominal devaluation (%)	$t-1$	t_0 (year of devaluation)	$t+1$	$t+2$	$t+3$
				Real exchange rate in:			
Ecuador	1970	38.89	0.80	1.09	1.05	1.01	1.01
Philippines	1970	63.74	1.15	1.69	1.66	1.62	1.59
Turkey	1970	65.15	0.45	0.71	0.60	0.56	0.53
Cameroon	1971	30.87	1.64	2.14	1.47	1.38	1.32
Yugoslavia	1971	36.00	1.00	1.21	1.09	0.94	1.00
Pakistan	1972	130.15	0.51	1.17	0.97	0.91	0.82
Uruguay	1972	97.84	1.06	1.28	0.96	1.12	1.13
Chile	1974	419.44	2.20	2.72	2.70	1.83	1.63
Italy	1976	28.00	1.29	1.26	1.23	1.20	1.16
Mexico	1976	59.60	2.01	1.88	1.74	1.61	1.48
Sri Lanka	1977	76.26	1.45	1.30	1.15	1.00	0.86
Jamaica	1978	86.45	0.47	0.70	0.64	0.58	0.56
Peru	1978	53.85	0.63	1.04	0.73	0.76	0.74
Brazil	1979	100.00	1.17	1.14	1.11	1.09	1.09
Japan	1979	23.18	1.15	1.18	1.21	1.26	1.31
Cameroon	1981	27.28	1.20	1.50	1.58	1.71	1.80
Costa Rica	1981	321.12	1.07	3.59	2.15	1.77	1.78
Denmark	1981	21.78	0.96	1.01	1.07	1.12	1.17
Kenya	1981	35.91	0.89	0.94	1.00	1.05	1.10
Tunisia	1981	23.17	0.82	1.02	1.09	1.20	1.35
Belgium	1982	22.00	1.02	1.07	1.12	1.18	0.96
Finland	1982	21.44	0.90	1.02	1.05	1.13	0.88
Malawi	1982	20.89	1.64	1.69	1.75	1.80	1.71
Norway	1982	21.46	1.05	1.11	1.16	1.21	1.20
Pakistan	1982	29.70	0.89	0.94	0.99	1.05	1.75
Sweden	1982	30.94	0.89	1.09	1.12	1.19	0.93
France	1983	24.13	1.08	1.13	1.19	1.24	1.09
Ivory Coast	1983	24.13	1.29	1.53	1.72	1.33	1.03
Morocco	1983	28.61	1.14	1.19	1.24	1.07	0.86
Philippines	1983	52.68	1.72	1.77	1.83	2.07	2.15
Portugal	1983	47.59	1.33	1.39	1.44	1.23	0.99
Spain	1983	24.76	1.06	1.11	1.17	1.09	0.84
Turkey	1983	51.43	0.88	1.03	1.12	1.00	0.95
Greece	1984	30.21	1.57	1.62	1.42	1.05	0.84
Jamaica	1984	50.41	0.89	1.08	0.95	0.80	0.77
Mauritius	1984	32.04	1.16	1.15	1.07	1.10	1.07
Uruguay	1984	71.68	2.10	2.38	2.32	1.85	1.80
Chile	1985	43.37	2.36	2.58	2.33	2.32	1.03
Colombia	1985	51.20	1.68	2.04	2.12	2.12	2.19
Ireland	1985	25.42	1.36	0.92	0.97	1.15	1.06
El Salvador	1986	100.00	0.80	1.18	0.97	0.84	0.75
Mexico	1986	148.45	2.31	2.99	3.17	1.58	1.60

(*continued on next page*)

Table 8.1 (continued)

Country	Year	Nominal devaluation (%)	$t - 1$	t_0 (year of devaluation)	$t + 1$	$t + 2$	$t + 3$
				Real exchange rate in:			
Average Annual % change of RER	63.15		1.21	1.43	1.36	1.25	1.17
				18.61	−5.12	−7.86	−6.30
Pass-through 1[a]				0.29	−0.08	−0.12	−0.10
% Change of RER from year $t - 1$[b]				18.61	12.41	3.57	−2.95
Pass-through 2				0.29	0.20	0.06	−0.05

Source: International Monetary Fund, International Financial Statistics, various issues.
Notes:
The data for the empirical analysis of pass-through consist of 43 "clean" devaluation episodes that occurred in the entire sample of benchmark countries and for the period 1969–1987.
[a]Pass-through 1 is defined as the percentage change in the real exchange rate (RER) divided by the nominal devaluation (%).
[b]Pass-through 2 is defined as the percentage change in RER from year $t - 1$ divided by the nominal devaluation (%).

change rate was devalued averaged 18.6%. Confirming our conjecture, we find that the effect of the nominal devaluation on the real exchange rate tends to wear off over time. The amount of the real devaluation falls off to 13% the first year, then to 6% the following year, and is totally wiped out in the third year.

This example, while suggestive, is still not very rigorous because the nominal exchange rate does not remain constant throughout the three-year span of our study. It will fluctuate over this time span (although its variation for any given year will not exceed 20%). Mid-period exchange rate variability might have muffled the effects of the nominal devaluation so that they cannot be discerned by just looking at averages.

One way to control for this would be to specify the percentage change in the real exchange rate as a distributed lag on previous changes in the nominal exchange rate (Hooper and Mann, 1989). Let Y_t be the percentage change in the real exchange rate at time t, and X_t be the percentage change in the nominal exchange rate at time t. Then we regress Y_t on current and past realizations of X_t:

$$Y_t = a_0 + a_1 X_t + a_2 X_{t-1} + a_3 X_{t-2} + a_4 X_{t-3} + u_t$$

Table 8.2. *Distributed lag results of test of real pass-through*

Variable	Coefficient				
	Test 1	Test 2	Test 3	Test 4	Test 5
Constant	-1.032	12.266	-0.799	40.378	45.014
	(-0.670)	(1.142)	(-0.403)	(2.019)	(2.237)
NER^a	0.220	0.220	0.216	0.227	0.222
	(3.192)	(3.202)	(3.048)	(3.089)	(2.979)
$NER(-1)^a$	-0.159	-0.159	-0.162	-0.157	-0.156
	(-5.059)	(-5.071)	(-5.099)	(-5.01)	(-4.956)
$NER(-2)^a$	-0.045	-0.045	-0.045	-0.041	-0.038
	(-2.469)	(-2.471)	(-2.367)	(-2.304)	(-2.176)
$NER(-3)^a$	-0.015	-0.016	-0.011	-0.004	-0.003
	(-0.742)	(-0.743)	(-0.544)	(-0.230)	(-0.179)
ln $RGDPC^b$		-1.640		-5.415	-5.452
		(-1.285)		(-2.038)	(-2.089)
D/GNP^c					-0.078
					(-2.259)
Adjusted R^2	0.395	0.414	0.404	0.425	0.436
F-statistic (zero slopes)	28.917	22.697	21.847	19.219	16.879
Number of observations^d	172	172	124	124	124

Source: RGDPC: Summers and Heston (1991); *D/GNP*: World Bank, *World Tables*.
Notes:
The dependent variable is percentage change in the real exchange rate. Numbers in parentheses are *T*-statistics.
^{a}NER is the nominal exchange rate for the year of devaluation and lagged for years one to three thereafter.
^{b}ln *RGDPC* is the log of the real per capita GDP.
^{c}D/GNP is the ratio of total long-term external debt to GNP. External debt figures are not available for DCs.
^{d}Tests 1 and 2 are for all countries in the sample. Tests 3, 4, and 5 are for LDCs only.

The coefficients $a_1, \ldots, a_4$ can then be interpreted as the real pass-through for each of those years. The sum of the coefficients $\Sigma_{i=1}^{4} a_i$ represents the long-run value of the real pass-through. Besides the NER, other exogenous variables that may determine the pass-through as measured by the change in the RER are per-capita income, ln *RGDPC*, and the ratio of debt to GNP, *D/GNP*. The former relates to the degree of market incompleteness that determines the relationship between NER and RER, and their changes. The latter has featured prominently in the discussion of contractionary devaluations that preceded. They are both included in the estimating equation.

The data for the econometric estimation are pooled time series of country observations. Each devaluation episode in Table 8.1 has been subjected to a different exogenous shock. The error terms, therefore, are unlikely to be independently distributed and problems of heteroscedasticity arise. We have used White's (1980) estimator in order to obtain a heteroscedasticity-consistent covariance matrix. The results of the estimation appear in Table 8.2.

The results are remarkably consistent, whether the estimation involves the entire sample or the LDCs alone, and consistency is maintained as the two auxiliary variables, real per-capita income and ratio of debt to GNP, are added seriatim. All coefficients are significant, with the exception of the third lag on *NER*, and *RGDPC*.

The real pass-through for the year of the devaluation is on the order of 0.22. But this real devaluation is fully reversed in the next three years: all the succeeding lagged variables have negative coefficients. The pass-through coefficient for the first year is −0.16. Hence more than two-thirds of the real devaluation is reversed after the first year. The sum of the coefficients a_i, $i = 1, \ldots, 4$, is close to zero, indicating that the long-run real pass-through is about zero. Hence we conclude that the effect of a nominal devaluation on the real exchange rate is almost fully reversed after about three years.

The NER variables in the regression are intended to control for the adjustment process of devaluation. Other factors that contribute to the early decay of a nominal devaluation are the level of development (weakly) and the level of debt, which is strongly significant. The intuition about the former variable is that in the extreme case of DCs, with separation between tradables and nontradables, a nominal devaluation will immediately affect prices in both the tradable and the nontradable sectors. An equilibrium nominal exchange rate (formed in the world of tradables) is also equivalent to an equilibrium real exchange rate. The sign and the significance of the debt variable confirms the expectation from the theoretical part of this chapter. The presence of a serious debt overhang, not only renders devaluations more contractionary in LDCs, but it also contributes to reversing the initial impact on the real exchange rate by price increases throughout the economy, especially in the nontradable sector.

The second hypothesis we examine is whether the deviation of the real exchange rate from its "equilibrium value" tells us anything about the future change in the real exchange rate. The conjecture is that a deviation of the real exchange rate from its equilibrium value will further contribute to reversing the effects of the nominal devaluation. To test this hypothesis we ran the following regression:

$$V_t - V_{t-1} = a + b(V_{t-1} - V_0) + u_t$$

Here V_t is the log of the real exchange rate and V_0 is the log of the equilibrium real exchange rate.

If we assume that the equilibrium real exchange rate is unity, $P_T/P_N = 1$, $V_0 = 0.$[14] Then we can rewrite the equation above as:

$$V_t - V_{t-1} = a + bV_{t-1} + u$$

$$V_t = a + (b + 1)V_{t-1} + u$$

This is an autoregressive model AR(1). If $b = 0$, then V_t is not a stationary process. In this formulation, V_t is a random walk process. If $b < 0$, then V_t is a stationary process.

Since all variables are in logs, the coefficient a has the interpretation of an elasticity. The larger the coefficient, the greater is the absolute change in the real exchange rate in the next period. Our hypothesis predicts that a should be negative, i.e., there should be mean-reversion of the real exchange rate. The results are presented below:

$$V_t - V_{t-1} = 0.037 - 0.200V_{t-1}$$
$$(1.945) \quad (-3.575)$$

Figures in parentheses are standard errors of estimate; $R^2 = 0.127$; $DF = 164$; F-statistic $= 23.579$. The coefficient has the correct sign and is statistically significant. We conclude that V_t is a stationary process and will converge to a finite value.[15]

Conclusion

The model in this chapter develops and expands the quasi-Australian model that was presented in Chapter 4 in real variables. The nominal exchange rate enters into the model, and its impact on output, wages, and the equilibrium prices and quantities of nontradables is examined in order to determine the exact conditions under which a nominal exchange rate devaluation can be contractionary. A broad range of such conditions exists, over and above the obvious case of contraction in the face of onerous obligations for servicing accumulated debt. A contractionary impact of devaluation appears more plausible than what an initial examination of the literature would have suggested.

The empirical test of the pass-through has been intended to link the nominal exchange rate, which is the policy control instrument, with the real exchange

14 This is a questionable assumption. See Chapter 4.
15 The characteristics of the stationary process are:

$$E(V_t) = \mu < \infty$$
$$\mathrm{Var}(V_t) = \gamma(0) < \infty$$
$$\mathrm{Cov}(Y_t, Y_{t-s}) = \gamma(s)$$

rate that is the allocation-decision variable in the real economy. The important finding is that the transmission mechanism from the nominal to the real exchange rate is incomplete. The impact of a nominal devaluation is only partly transmitted to prices of tradables in the year of the devaluation; thereafter it decays rapidly as prices of nontradables increase to fully offset the initial effects of devaluation within two years.

There are two implications of this finding. First, if the policy objective of devaluation is to achieve a certain target, such as export promotion or macroeconomic balance, it is likely that policy makers might attempt to overshoot, lest the rapid decay of devaluation foreclose the targeted objective. If nominal devaluation has contractionary effects, excessive devaluation is likely to impose additional costs of economic contraction.

Second, the relative ineffectiveness of the monetary instrument of devaluation may induce policy makers to engage in direct interventions instead, such as subsidies to exports, tariffs on imports, nonmarket allocations of foreign exchange, and so on. The more incomplete the link between nominal and real variables is, the more policy makers will tend to operate on the real plane.

Based on the theory and the empirical evidence in this chapter, one must conclude that devaluations are clumsy instruments for achieving real goals and "setting prices right." This strong conclusion is further emboldened if one moves beyond a comparative statics model that captures only impact coefficients. The thread that runs through this study is part of a dynamic argument that globalizes the effects of contractionary devaluations. On the strength of the Ricardo Principle, and its empirical verification, the regularity in the relative prices of tradables and nontradables across stages of development suggests that the poorer the country, the higher is its resource cost for a given quantity of traded goods. Left to free-market determination, its equilibrium exchange rate requires a poor country to pay a greater social opportunity cost for its traded goods than its more affluent neighbors. This penalty becomes greater as the income gap widens. Moreover, the penalty is not a one-time efficiency loss. The argument of an incomplete market in foreign exchange is grounded on reputation effects that tend to create a devaluation spiral and dynamic Pareto losses for the LDC that sets the nominal exchange at its market-clearing level. The finding of contractionary devaluations in this chapter has totally ignored these dynamic implications of the argument.

In the canonical case of incomplete markets, quantity closure (rationing) is Pareto-improving. But overvaluing the nominal exchange rate is incompatible with the free-market strategy. Overvaluation, however, is sustainable under the alternative approach of containing the excess import demand for tradables by direct rationing devices and allocating the resulting gains from trade to capital formation and to supporting export sectors that can ultimately achieve dynamic comparative advantage.

The important caveat that applies to government intervention and to rationing allocations must be emphasized at this point. The advantages of widespread intervention of the state in economic affairs, as well as the merits of state association with large corporate firms, are assumed never to be outweighed by their potential drawbacks: corruption, nepotism, rent-seeking behavior, and permanent protection of inefficiency. The condition of broadly based, pluralistic development reflects this basic assumption. The next three chapters will further illustrate this caveat, both in cases of success and failure in economic development.

Appendix: The signs of the partial derivatives

The assumptions under (8.15) relate to the maximization conditions (8.11), (8.12), and (8.13).

Let us define the argument in these equations as:

$$\frac{eP_T}{P_N} = q \qquad \frac{eP_I}{P_N} = i \qquad \frac{M}{P_N} = m$$

$$\frac{P_N}{eP_T} = q' \qquad \frac{w}{P_N} = u \qquad \frac{w}{eP_T} = v$$

The assumptions on the partial derivatives given in equation (8.15) can be rewritten as follows:

$$N_y^d > 0$$

$$N_{P_N}^d < 0 \Rightarrow N_m^d \frac{\partial m}{\partial P_N} + N_{q'}^d \cdot \frac{\partial q'}{\partial P_N} = -\frac{M}{P_N^2} N_m^d + \frac{1}{eP_T} N_{q'}^d < 0$$

It is relevant to assume $N_m^d > 0$ (positive real balance effect) $N_{q'}^d < 0$ (negative own price effect). Then

$$0 < N_e^d < 1 \Rightarrow 0 < \frac{P_N}{e^2 P_T} N_{q'}^d < 1$$

$$N_w^s < 0 \Rightarrow \frac{1}{P_N} N_u^s < 0$$

$$N_{P_N}^s > 0 \Rightarrow -\frac{eP_I}{P_N^2} N_i^s - \frac{w}{P_N^2} N_u^s > 0$$

It is also relevant to assume $N_q^s < 0$, $N_w^s < 0$. Then:

$$N_e^s < 0 \Rightarrow \frac{P_I}{P_N} N_i^s < 0$$

$$T_w^s < 0 \Rightarrow \frac{1}{eP_T} T_v^s < 0$$

$$L_{N,P_N} > 0 \Rightarrow -\frac{eP_I}{P_N^2} L_{N,i}^d - \frac{w}{P_N^2} L_{N,u}^d > 0$$

$$I_{N,w} > 0 \Rightarrow \frac{1}{P_N} I_{N,u} > 0$$

$$L_{N,e} > 0 \Rightarrow \frac{P_I}{P_N} L_{N,i} > 0$$

$$L_{T,w} < 0 \Rightarrow \frac{1}{eP_T} L_{T,v} < 0$$

$$L_{T,e} > 0 \Rightarrow -\frac{w}{e^2 P_T} L_{T,v} > 0$$

With these assumptions, it is obvious that $f_3 < 0$. However, both f_1 and f_2 cannot be negative because:

$$f_1 = \frac{e}{P_N} (P_T T_e^s - P_I I_{N,e}) + \frac{1}{P_N} (P_T T^s - P_I I_N - rD)$$

Defining the last term in the equation above as X, we have:

$$f_2 = -\frac{e}{P_N^2} (P_T T^s - P_I I_N - rD) - \frac{e}{P_N} \frac{P_I}{I_{N,P_N}} = -\frac{e}{P_N} X - \frac{e}{P_N} \frac{P_I}{I_{N,P_N}}$$

$$f_1 < 0 \Rightarrow X < -\frac{eP_T}{P_N} T_e^s + \frac{eP_I}{P_N} I_{N,e} = \frac{eP_T}{P_N} \frac{w}{e^2 P_T} T_v^s + \frac{eP_I}{P_N} \frac{P_I}{P_N} I_{N,i}$$

$$f_2 < 0 \Rightarrow X > P_I I_{N,P_N} = -P_I \frac{eP_I}{P_N^2} I_{N,i} - P_I \frac{w}{P_N^2} I_{N,u}$$

$f_1 < 0$ and $f_2 < 0$ implies:

$$-\frac{eP_I^2}{P_N^2} I_{N,i} - \frac{P_I w}{P_N^2} I_{N,u} < \frac{w}{eP_N} T_v^s + \frac{eP_I^2}{P_N^2} I_{N,i}$$

$$\therefore \frac{w}{eP_N} T_v^s + \frac{2eP_I^2}{P_N^2} I_{N,i} + \frac{P_I w}{P_N^2} I_{N,u} > 0$$

However, this cannot happen because

$$T_v^s < 0, \quad I_{N,i} < 0, \quad I_{N,u} < 0$$

If $f_1 < 0$ then $f_2 > 0$. If $f_2 < 0$ then $f_1 > 0$. If $f_1 > 0$ then $f_2 > 0$ is feasible.

PART III

Successes and failures in development: Good/bad economics and governance

CHAPTER 9

Japan: Overvaluation without rent-seeking

The preceding chapters were devoted to building a case for the existence of systematic incompleteness in certain markets in LDCs. One important implication of such a case is that the debate in development economics may have to change from "whether governments should intervene in the process of development" to "how can governments intervene appropriately for development success."

In what follows, the reinterpretation of the Japanese development success since World War II will focus on state intervention that resulted in systematically overriding certain crucial incomplete markets, especially the labor market and the foreign exchange/trade markets. The analysis will examine specific policy packages that allowed Japan to find shortcuts to the long road from underdevelopment to development.

The discussion of the new development economics in Chapter 3 emphasized the importance of leapfrogging the process of economic development. The empirical handle used in this book to make operational the concept of leapfrogging is the Ricardo Principle and the relative prices of tradables and nontradables at various stages of development. At the two extremes of the continuum of economic development that the Ricardo Principle maps, we can distinguish two stages. Stage I, underdevelopment, is characterized by cheap labor and expensive capital, and implies a comparative advantage for an open-economy LDC of specializing in labor-intensive, low-value added exports. Low wages, absence of significant technological rents, and low living standards follow. Stage II, development, is characterized by expensive labor and relatively cheap capital, and implies specialization in capital- and technology-intensive exports with high value added, and significant technological rents associated with products that have high income elasticity of demand and, conceivably, low price elasticity. High wages and high living standards follow. The challenge of economic development is how to *leapfrog* from Stage I to Stage II, lest a country be trapped in its static comparative advantage. The obverse side of the same issue is how a developing country can adapt early to its *dynamic comparative advantage*.

Leapfrogging from Stage I to Stage II requires, at a minimum, overriding two markets: the foreign exchange market and the labor market.

Leapfrogging into Stage II requires that labor-intensive exports, which are

191

"cheap" in (domestic) price, are discouraged and the composition of production be shifted instead towards commodities that can eventually be made "cheap" (in both domestic *and* foreign prices) in order to be exported. An overvalued domestic currency cum an appropriate industrial policy could do the trick. This is where the overriding of the foreign exchange market comes in.

But Stage I is linked with the classical unlimited supplies of labor that allow for increasing wages – and therefore increasing capital intensity – in a gradual and slow process as the "turning point" is being approached. Leapfrogging into Stage II means overriding the labor market by moving the turning point forward, whether by increasing the marginal product in the labor-intensive residual sector and/or increasing prices, and thus raising the value-marginal product alone. In either case, wages will increase, thus leading to a more capital-intensive process of production.

The case study of Japan is intended as a classic example of successful leapfrogging from Stage I to Stage II. Through the late 1950s, Japanese development policies fell into the stylized mold of developing countries in general, that emphasize labor-intensive production of low-value-added tradables. A new development strategy was adopted in the early 1960s that centered on capital- and technology-intensive exports. The data in Table 6.1 (see Chapter 6) indicate that from the beginning of the period (1970), Japan's real exchange rates (RER) ranked consistently among the lowest in the international cross-section of countries. This indicates that the Japanese nominal exchange rates (NER) were most likely overvalued. Overvaluation entails overriding of the incomplete foreign exchange and trade markets. In the meanwhile, the strategy of capital- and technology-intensive production would have been doomed to fail if the condition of excess labor supply that existed at the end of World War II had continued. This involved overriding the incomplete labor market by "artificially" shifting the Lewis "turning point" (the end of the unlimited labor supply) forward. Finally, a proactive industrial policy ensured that the sequencing of the industrialization process was consonant with the broad parameters of the domestic demand that boomed as a result of wage and income increases that followed the end of the unlimited supplies of labor. Thus pluralistic economic development became the foundation of the Japanese domestic-demand-led industrialization and nurtured the export drive.

The explanation of the "Japanese Miracle" has spawned a veritable cottage industry in the literature of comparative development. This chapter does not propose to attempt a systematic review, let alone to provide a complete historical explanation of Japan's economic development. It will draw, instead, on various strands of this literature to highlight the empirical implications of overvaluation and to provide the details on the institutional structure that played a prominent role in turning a necessary condition for long-term, self-sustained growth into a sufficient condition as well. Only in this limited sense does this chapter dwell on the economic miracle and its antecedent literature.

Within that literature, however, the interpretation put forward herewith can be labeled as "nonrevisionist." In this context the rest of this chapter can be viewed as providing the mortar around this scaffolding of a "nonrevisionist" interpretation of the Japanese Miracle.

The aftermath of World War II

The self-inflicted disaster of World War II took a heavy toll on Japan. Between Japan's invasion of China in 1937 and the final desperate surrender in August 1945, 3.1 million Japanese were killed, or 4% of the population. Virtually every city was left in ashen rubble, and the awesome war-time industrial structure lay ravished. Although the economic growth rate of the reconstruction period was respectable (between 8 and 9%), the characteristics of the economy through the 1950s were typical for the stage of underdevelopment: high rate of inflation (44% from 1946–1950, declining thereafter), serious unemployment,[1] and deficits in the balance of payments (Kosai, 1988, p. 4). The bright spot in the disheartening inventory of resources for development was the educated and skilled labor force. Labor discipline, however, was lax and industrial strife and strikes became rampant after the Labor Union Law was introduced at the initiative of the Occupation Administration in 1945 (Kosai, 1988, pp. 27–29).[2]

Early Japanese exports concentrated on labor intensity and cheapness: textiles, light industry products, inexpensive cameras, and so on. Those achieved notoriety with the "dollar-blouse" trade war with the United States in the late 1950s. The complete reversal of development strategy in the 1960s was long in coming. But it was certainly precipitated by the trade friction with the U.S. that was bred by the Japanese success in the classical Stage I of labor-intensive exports. The three legs of Japanese leapfrogging to Stage II were the overriding of the foreign exchange and trade markets, the early absorption of surplus labor that established a domestic-demand-led model of industrialization, and the appropriate industrial policies that focused on the country's dynamic comparative advantage and marshalled domestic demand in reaching it.

Overriding the foreign exchange and trade markets

Overvaluation of nominal exchange rate

The RER index in Table 6.1 (Chapter 6) provides evidence for the likely overvaluation of the Japanese NER. While the index implies nothing about the

---

1 The rate of unemployment in the period 1956–1960 was over 2%. Strange as it sounds, this was considered high by the international standards of the time and it was historically high for Japan until the 1990s.
2 By 1949 almost 35,000 unions had been launched, with the proportion of workforce organized exceeding 50%. At their peak in 1948 there were 913 strikes, with 2.6 million workers participating, or 40% of the organized labor force (Kosai, 1988, Table 1-7).

equilibrium value of the real exchange rate, it certainly suggests that countries that lie at the bottom of the rankings in Table 6.1 are most likely to have an overvalued NER. A high NER is a sure way of inducing high prices of tradables and land a country near the head of the RER list; and vice versa for a low NER. The case for the overvaluation of the Japanese NER is made on comparative grounds. How credible is it, based on the Japanese experience alone?

There has been a lively controversy on the equilibrium exchange rate in Japan and whether the yen has been overvalued or undervalued. Komiya has inferred overvaluation, especially in the period 1955–1967, using as criterion "... the exchange rate that would have brought the balance of payments into equilibrium without import restrictions and export promotion measures" (Komiya and Itoh, 1988, p. 176). This inference had been early coupled with the call for liberalization of the Japanese economy. Shinohara, on the other hand, has maintained that the yen was undervalued at 360 yen to the dollar, and has considered as vindication the revaluation that took place since 1973 under the floating-rate system (Shinohara, 1982, p. 12). Shinohara has been more sympathetic to the economic management of Japan.

More recently Hamada and Patrick (1988, p. 122) assumed that the nominal exchange rate was at equilibrium in 1975 and estimated real exchange rates for the period 1970–1987 based on CPI, WPI, and unit-labor-cost indexes. They came to the conclusion that the yen was overvalued both before and after the base year, with the exception of 1975. On the other side, undervaluation of the yen has been assumed by various observers, including the U.S. policy makers who, until very recently (and not before exchange rates dipped below 120 yen per U.S. dollar in early 1989), have always pressured Japan into revaluation in the belief that it would remedy the U.S. deficit in the trade account.[3]

Operating at "nominal exchange rate disequilibrium," i.e., with overvalued domestic currency, requires a mechanism for foreign exchange control and an active policy for restraining imports and promoting exports, through taxes and subsidies, respectively. The review of the Japanese experience with trade and exchange rate policies can only add some hues of subtlety to the common knowledge among policy makers of "how to do it."

Foreign exchange control and import policies

The control and husbanding of foreign exchange becomes a crucial component in a regime of nominal exchange rate overvaluation. Japan had a long history of public expertise in managing scarce foreign exchange resources. In view of the fact that the country had been deprived (until 1911) of tariff autonomy, the

---

3 For a detailed account of the international monetary exchange regime as it relates to Japan see Hamada and Patrick (1988).

Meiji government required all of its agencies to prepare a foreign exchange budget along with their yen budget. Such a requirement lasted in one form or another until 1964, when it was abolished in the early round of trade liberalization (Johnson, 1982, p. 25). In an era of high growth with increasing demand for imported raw materials, control of the foreign exchange budget meant control of the economy. This became an important industrial-policy control instrument in the hands of MITI (Ministry of International Trade and Industry).

The foreign exchange budget facilitated total control of foreign currency for the purpose of coping with the chronic deficits in the current account that persisted until 1968, with the objective of targeting the scarce exchange proceeds on imports of raw materials and machinery essential for domestic production while severely restricting imports of final products and especially of consumer goods. The whole arsenal of tools for import restrictions was used very effectively: discriminatory tariffs, quotas and nontariff barriers, variable levies, and minimum price systems. The list of commodities under import restrictions was large (1,443, four-digit classification) and in combination with low or no tariffs for the preferential imports of raw materials, the system yielded in 1961 as low a ratio of tariff revenues to imports as that of the U.S., Germany, France, or Italy (Komiya and Itoh, 1988, p. 193). The difference is that in Japan low tariff revenues were the outcome of total limitation of imports; in the other countries they were due to reasonably free trade at low tariff rates.

The barriers to trade erected by the Japanese started coming down rapidly in the mid-1960s, after the Kennedy Round was completed. Tariffs were decreased and only 161 commodities were under import restrictions in 1965, further decreasing to 79 in 1981. "Residual" import restrictions, i.e., restrictions that are illegal under the various articles of GATT, remained on 27 items in 1981, mostly in agriculture and fisheries (Komiya and Itoh, 1988, p. 192; Saxonhouse, 1988, pp. 231–232; Hayami, 1988, p. 53).

The distribution system in Japan has always served to hitch imports and exports to the wagon of industrial policy. The importance of the distribution system as a nontransparent barrier to imports much increased after the liberalization of the 1960s. The wholesale distribution system was dominated by few well-established trading companies and it was designed to provide industry with the raw materials and components it needed and to secure domestic outlets for industry's output. Few imports of consumer goods would trickle through that system, and where they did they were effectively blocked by the retail distribution system, which, based on mom-and-pop stores,[4] was too fragmented and unsophisticated for handling foreign merchandise.

---

4 In 1988, mom-and-pop-type retail distribution outlets accounted for 80% of total outlets, as opposed to 3% in the U.S. See below.

Export policies

The reversal of the Stage I export policies that indiscriminately favored trad-ables was gradual. In the early 1950s, while unemployment was still high, Japan had already made the decision to extricate itself from labor-intensive, low-value-added exports in favor of an industrial structure that would later nurture dynamic comparative advantage: capital-intensive, high-technology, high-value-added industries, which were facing high income elasticity of de-mand for their products (and possibly low price elasticity) and had the potential of accruing high economic rents. Such were the criteria set out by the Minister Okano of MITI, who saw "heavy and chemical industrialization" as the means of delivering Japan from recurring balance-of-payments constraints. The Oka-no Plan was formally adopted in 1954; the empirical evidence on the elasticity of demand of Japanese exports and imports, as compared to those of other industrialized countries appears in Table 9.1.

Although eschewing cheap labor, cheapness and comparative advantage were at the heart of the Japanese industrial strategy. Given the poor resource base of the country and the technological backwardness that came from the destruction of the war, industry relied heavily on imported raw materials and components. The overvalued yen made them available at low domestic prices. A battery of other policy instruments were also intended to decrease the cost and increase the profitability of exports, and more generally of priority in-dustrial production.

The tax system provided special incentives to exports through tax deductions on export earnings (1953–1963) and on income from foreign transactions relating, e.g., to technology (1959–present), as well as through accelerated depreciation allowance for exports and incentives for reserves for the develop-ment of foreign markets (1964–1972). Still, the impact of the tax incentives on exports is judged as rather small, estimated at only 1% of the total value of exports (Itoh and Kiyono, 1988, p. 171).[5]

In many countries the financing of export trade takes place through the rediscounting of the letter of credit, which, at the same time, serves as collateral for the bank. The Bank of Japan engaged in such export financing at interest rates that were 1–2% lower than those applied to other commercial drafts. Moreover, and in contrast to the experience of other countries, the Bank of Japan also financed (1946–1972), on the same terms, the production and processing of exportable commodities starting from the signing of an export contract clear through the bill-of-lading stage (Itoh and Kiyono, 1988, p. 169). Since export production involved as subcontractors a large number of medium and small firms, the benefits of formal and low-cost credit were spread broadly

5 In comparison, the tax subsidies on exports in Korea rose from 2.3% of the value of exports in 1958 to 27.8% in 1970.

Table 9.1. *An international comparison of growth rates in GNP, exports, and imports, and income elasticity of exports, 1956/1957–1964/1965*

	Rate of growth			Income elasticity		
	Real GNP	Exports	Imports	Exports	Imports	(4–5)
Country	(1)	(2)	(3)	(4)	(5)	(6)
Japan	9.8	14.2	11.5	3.55	1.23	2.32
West Germany	6.2	7.0	10.7	2.08	1.80	0.28
Italy	5.5	14.7	12.8	2.95	2.19	0.76
Denmark	5.2	7.7	9.6	1.69	1.31	0.38
France	5.1	7.9	6.3	1.53	1.66	−0.13
Netherlands	4.7	8.4	8.5	1.88	1.89	−0.01
Sweden	4.4	6.8	7.1	1.76	1.42	0.34
Norway	4.2	7.6	7.2	1.59	1.40	0.19
Belgium[a]	3.9	7.2	7.2	1.83	1.94	−0.11
United States	3.6	4.9	5.2	0.99	1.51	−0.52
United Kingdom	3.3	3.3	4.2	0.86	1.66	−0.80

Source: Itoh and Kiyono (1988), p. 157; Houthakker and Magee (1969).
Notes:
Column (2) is exports of goods and services; column (3) is imports of goods and services. Income in columns (4) and (5) refers to world income.
[a]Belgium is Belgium plus Luxembourg.

throughout the economy. Finally, the export insurance system (1950–present) operated to cover export transactions against risks not normally insurable by the private sector.

In sum, Japan's export policy can be considered rather unremarkable, and none too different from export regimes that apply in other countries.

Overriding the labor market and the role of domestic demand

Domestic demand

Domestic demand has not become a full-fledged component of the (English-language) "Japanese-Miracle literature," although it has been noticed in many respects. Kindleberger (1973, p. 17) posits the riddle of how Japan "produced Keynesian policies as early as 1932 without Keynes." The reference is to how Japan pulled itself through the depression by means of deficit spending on armaments, which started in 1932 (Johnson, 1982, pp. 6, 103, 119). More significantly, The Economist (September 1 and 8, 1962), which is credited with having introduced the "miracle" terminology and for having established its

Table 9.2. *Exports as percentage of GNP, selected countries, 1966 and 1986*

Country	1966	1986
Japan	10.5	13.5
Canada	19.2	24.9
France	13.8	21.0
Germany	18.1	33.1
Italy	16.1	20.0
United Kingdom	19.6	21.3
United States	5.1	5.1

Source: World Bank, *World Tables*, various issues.

chronological coordinates at 1962, pointed to expansion of demand, along with high productivity, comparatively serene labor relations, and a very high rate of savings, as the reasons behind the "miracle" in its two-part article, "Consider Japan."

Emphasis on domestic demand flies in the face of the conventional "economic-miracle" literature, which emphasizes export growth.[6] This interpretation of the Japanese experience often disregards the facts. The share of exports in GNP was 10.5% in 1966 and rose to 13.5% in 1986, which in either case is much lower than that of the other six industrialized countries in Table 9.2, with the exception of the U.S., which has a share of 5.1%. In comparison, the share of exports in GNP was one-third in prewar Japan (Johnson, 1982, p. 16).

The role of domestic demand first received full recognition in the early 1950s, when the Okano Plan saw "heavy and chemical industrialization" as the means of extricating Japan from recurring balance-of-payments constraints. The intent was to have MITI promote both exports and domestic sales so that:

> [W]hen problems in the international balance of payments arose, the government could curtail domestic demand and promote exports; when the problems of paying for imported raw materials eased, the focus should be on enlarging sales at home. If this could be achieved Japan's factories could keep operating throughout all phases of the business cycle. . . . [This] combined export promotion and high-speed growth into a coherent theory (Johnson, 1982, p. 229; reprinted by permission of the publisher, Stanford University Press).

An effect of learning-by-using (Rosenberg, 1982) can be hypothesized to explain how the development of domestic demand could provide a testing

---

6 Among the exceptions to the general trend one should mention Felix (1989), Wade (1990, pp. 50–51), and Eswaren and Kotwal (1993). See also Chapter 11.

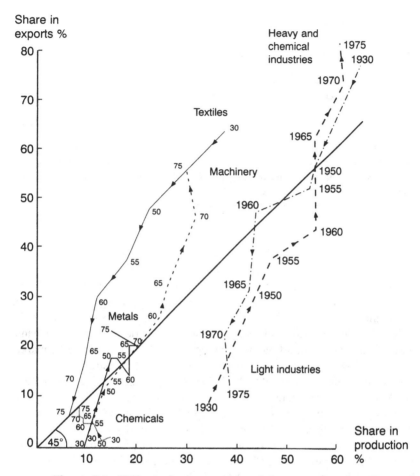

Figure 9.1. *Shifts in Japanese industrial structure and patterns of trade, 1930–1975*

Source: Itoh and Kiyono (1988), p. 156; by permission of the publisher, Academic Press.

ground for Japanese manufactures before they were launched into export markets. This seems to be consistent with the Japanese experience, where the growth of such industries as automobiles, household electric appliances, pianos, and integrated circuits (e.g., calculators) was heavily leveraged on domestic demand, and the products that developed in the process reflected the tastes of Japanese consumers. However, for lack of a better formal test of the hypothesis, Figure 9.1 provides some corroborating circumstantial evidence at

Table 9.3. *Household ownership of consumer durables in Japan, 1957–1980 (percentage)*

	1957	1960	1965	1970	1975	1980
Electric washing machine	20.0	45.4	68.5	88.3	97.6	98.8
Electric refrigerator	2.8	15.7	51.4	84.6	96.7	99.1
Black and white TV	7.8	54.5	90.0	90.2	48.7	22.8
Color TV				26.3	90.3	98.2
Automobile		1.2		22.1	41.2	57.2

Source: Yasuba (1991); by permission of the publisher, Oxford University Press.
Note:
Missing entries denote negligible or data unavailable.

a level of high aggregation. If one considers observations above the 45° line as export-driven, and those below as domestic-demand-induced, the entire phase of textile manufacturing (including the period before the war) belongs to the former, and so does the early phase of light industries (among others, transistor radios and cameras), which, however, became domestic-demand-driven in the 1960s. The heavy, chemical, and machinery industries, on the other hand, started with a high proportion of their output absorbed by the domestic market in order to mature in the 1960s into important export industries.

Industrial policy played a direct role in ushering in the consumer revolution. The Ministry of Finance, in particular, adjusted excise taxes on domestic goods at the opportune times,[7] thus inducing the particularly Japanese phenomenon of synchronous purchases of the same good by the majority of households: "the three sacred treasures"[8] (television, washing machine, and refrigerator) in the early 1960s, or the "three c's" (car, cooler, and color TV) in the late 1960s (Johnson, 1982, p. 236). Table 9.3 (Yasuba, 1991) dramatically brings this point home. It shows, as an example, that ownership of electric washing machines by Japanese households jumped by about 20% increments from 1957 to 1960, 1965, and 1970; and ownership of black and white TV went from 55% in 1960 to 90% in 1965.

The government also played an indirect role in stoking development by

7 "The Ministry of Finance credits itself with nurturing the Sony Corporation through its formative years because it lifted commodity taxes on transistor radios for the first two years after their appearance in the market and because it levied taxes on television receivers only in two-year stages as mass production brought down their prices: taxes went up as prices, calculated in terms of the price per inch in picture tubes, went down" (Johnson, 1982, p. 236).
8 The analogy refers to the three sacred treasures possessed by the Emperor that confirm his divine origins according to the Shinto religion.

fanning domestic demand through wage and income policies. Not unlike all other developing countries, Japan faced the problem of keeping surplus and subqualified labor from driving wages down (which would drive the prices of tradables up in relation to nontradables) and lowering incomes to levels that limit effective domestic demand and trigger pressures for setting up a welfare state. Agricultural protection is one conventional mechanism for this goal. The second and unconventional Japanese solution was the retail trade.

The unlimited supplies of labor and incomplete markets

A stylized fact about the early stages of development is the existence of huge reservoirs of labor in the agricultural sector. As development occurs, labor shifts to manufacturing and the share of agriculture, both in GDP and in employment, decreases. Such was also the case in Japan, where the share of agriculture in employment was 39% in 1950 and 10% in 1980 (see Table 9.4). The challenge of development is to effect this transfer in an orderly fashion, without increasing in the process the pool of the urban unemployed. Therein lies the incompleteness of the labor market and the need for overriding the free market mechanisms.[9] The dilemma can be illustrated with a diagrammatic reference to the classical Lewis argument on unlimited supplies of labor.

Figure 9.2 presents the familiar Lewis-type story of labor and wage disequilibrium between the agricultural/rural (*A*) and the manufacturing/urban (*M*) sectors. The marginal productivity curve of labor in each sector slopes downward from the left axis, *AA'* for agriculture, and from the right axis, *MM'* for manufacturing. The marginal productivity curve is the derived demand for labor. Ruling out unemployment, *L'* represents the equilibrium position, with agricultural employment to the left and manufacturing employment to the right, and with equilibrium wage rate at w^*. The initial position, however, is characterized by disequilibrium, with manufacturing wage w_M and agricultural w_A and the respective labor allocations at *L*. The disequilibrium is reflected in the wage differential between agriculture and manufacturing, and in the suboptimal labor allocation that produces the welfare losses described by the shaded triangle. It also produces the incentive for rural people to vote with their feet in pursuing the immediate payoff of a higher urban wage through a cityward migratory movement. The ultimate solution of the Lewis model is the "turning

---

9 An alternative interpretation of incomplete markets in LDCs rests on the efficiency-wage hypothesis, which posits a positive relationship between the wage received by laborers in low-income economies and their productivity (Leibenstein, 1957, 1958; Yotopoulos, 1965). This is sufficient to explain the existence of open unemployment, and under certain special conditions, of disguised unemployment also, i.e., the option of removing part of the labor force without causing a decline in the aggregate level of output. See Bliss and Stern (1978), Dasgupta and Ray (1986, 1991), Stiglitz (1974, 1976), and Basu (1992). Yet another interpretation rests on the transaction costs of labor supervision (Eswaren and Kotwal, 1985).

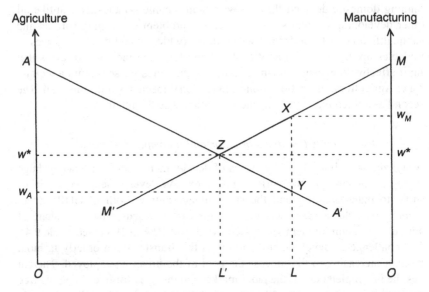

Figure 9.2. *Marginal productivities: Agriculture and manufacturing, plotted against labor force*

point" of agriculture, with an end to the unlimited supplies of labor. It represents an up-by-the-bootstraps, optimistic outcome of economic development.

The process of transferring labor out of agriculture takes place in time and is fraught with uncertainty. In uncertainty lies the incompleteness of the market that warrants intervention for the early exhaustion of the unlimited supplies of labor. It can be illustrated by a simple extension of the Lewis model (Todaro, 1969; Harris and Todaro, 1970).

Not unlike the classical model, Todaro's is a gravity-type model in which migration is activated by earnings differentials. It is distinguished by three important features: (1) it is expected, rather than actual, wages that are capitalized into the earnings differentials; (2) the expectation on wages is formulated based on the probability of finding a job in the urban sector, which in turn is inversely related to the urban unemployment rate; (3) unemployment is thus explicitly introduced, as is the possibility that migration rates will exceed the growth rates of urban job opportunities.

Corden and Findlay (1975) have provided an attractive diagrammatic formulation of the model by extending Figure 9.2. In Figure 9.3 the market-clearing equilibrium wage rate is w^* and point E corresponds to the market-clearing labor allocation at L'. Unlike in Figure 9.2, however, an agricultural wage rate w_A' is also determined, corresponding to employment $O_A L_A$. Since the manufac-

Agriculture   Manufacturing

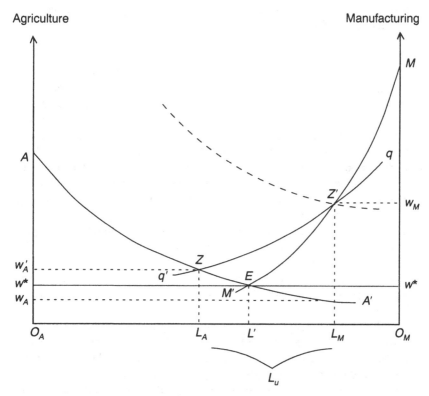

Figure 9.3. *Marginal productivities: Agriculture and manufacturing, and the equilibrium wage in the Todaro Model*

turing-sector employment is at $O_M L_M$, the modification introduced in Figure 9.3 determines the the level of unemployment at $L_A L_M$.

How are the agricultural-sector wage and the unemployment level determined? If unemployment exists at all, the potential rural migrant has to consider the probability that while aiming for w_M he or she may instead end up in urban unemployment at zero wages. More precisely, assume that the risk-neutral migrant perceives urban jobs as allocated by lottery, and compares the expected value of the lottery ticket to the certain employment in the A sector. Migration takes place up to the point of equating the expected urban wage to the rural wage. Given the urban wage w_M, what is the w_A that satisfies that condition? The simplest way of forming expectations, given the lottery specification of the search process, is to consider the probability of getting a favored urban job directly related to the ratio of employment in manufacturing, L_M, to the total urban labor pool of the unemployed, L_U:

$$w_A = (L_M/L_U)w_M$$

where L_M and w_M are given. With L_M fixed, as one shifts leftward on the axis $O_A O_M$, L_U increases. The lower wage is therefore the expected wage for the potential migrant. Then solving the equation for any value of w_M gives a pair of values for w_A and L_U that indicate the agricultural wage for which the potential migrant is indifferent about employment locations. The locus of these solutions is given by the line qq' in Figure 9.3 (the expected urban wage), which is by definition a rectangular hyperbola. It represents the expected urban wage, given the wage and the employment level in the manufacturing sector. Point Z on that solution line also lies on the demand curve for labor in A, thus setting the equilibrium agricultural wage at w_A' and employment in agriculture at $O_A L_A$. At that point, with expected urban wage equal to the agricultural wage, migration of labor stops. The implication is that the Lewis equilibrium cannot be reached and a certain equilibrium level of urban unemployment, L_U, becomes a permanent feature of the economy. This is just another case where price closure cannot clear the market – which is a characteristic of market incompleteness (see Chapter 3).

A shift of the marginal productivity curve of agriculture upwards solves the problem in that the sector (as well as any other designated "informal" sector) becomes a holding ground for the urban unemployment. This is shown by equilibrium point Z'. Starting from that position, manufacturing employment can increase from L_M only at the expense of agricultural employment, and both agricultural and manufacturing wages increase in tandem. There are two ways of increasing marginal productivity in agriculture. The first, and obvious, way is through modernization and technological change. This was practiced in Japan until the country ran into the conventional "farm problem" of excess agricultural supplies. Once technological possibilities are exhausted, the marginal productivity can still be increased by shifting the "value of marginal product" curve outward, through providing agricultural subsidies. That was also done in Japan, as in most other countries as well. The subsidies were paid either by the state (and ultimately the taxpayers) in the form of subsidized inputs, or were paid by the consumers in the form of high prices of output. The specific Japanese solution, however, lies in having the retail manufacturing network also serve as the residual sector and the holding ground of the potential urban unemployed, along with agriculture. This solution also involved higher prices, and its cost was borne by consumers.

Agriculture. Japan emerged from the war with a food crisis. It went briefly through a "food problem" period and has now graduated to the era of the "farm problem," the endemic problem of agricultural adjustment that plagues the developed mature economies.

The food crisis broke out in 1937 when supplies of fertilizers and agricultural materials from China became unreliable, and it worsened during the war years. The wartime strict control and rationing of all food items continued well into the period of reconstruction, with the measures being lifted sequentially until the last controls – on rice purchases – were lifted in the mid-1950s. It is not surprising under the circumstances that agriculture received priority; but it was farsighted that agricultural development was considered a precondition for industrial reconstruction:

> In the program for the rehabilitation of industry, called Differential Production Scheme that began in 1946, the government fund was first allocated to coal mining. Increased deliveries of coal were allocated to fertilizer, iron and steel industries; increased deliveries of food from fertilizers together with those of iron and steel were returned to coal mining to expand the cycle of reproduction (Hayami, 1988, p. 44; by permission of the publisher, St. Martin's Press).

The combination of low incomes and "high food drain" leads to the "food problem," as described by Schultz (1953). At low levels of development, high rates of population growth and high demand for subsistence food, which is price-inelastic and fairly income-elastic, combine to increase food requirements. Low productivity in agriculture, on the other hand, makes the supply curve fairly inelastic. The result is high and rising food prices. Given low income levels and a high Engel coefficient of demand (which describes the share of the family budget devoted to food, Table 9.4), real incomes decrease drastically as a result of rising food prices. Figure 9.4 shows a relatively (price-) inelastic supply and demand schedule for food. Following a given increase in income, the shift of the demand curve to the right is great as a result of the high Engel coefficient; this can be further accentuated by high rates of population growth. A substantial price increase ensues. Thus, and for the purpose of safeguarding a minimum threshold of subsistence income, food price increases are strongly resisted – lest they lead to increasing wages.

The two available mechanisms for containing food prices are food subsidies at the consumption level, often targeted as wage supplements, and price controls at the production level. Japan went through a brief "food-problem" period during reconstruction and opted for the latter mechanism, instituting a guaranteed "parity price," which actually amounted to compulsory delivery of rice by producers at prices below the market equilibrium level (Hayami, 1988, p. 43).

Japan's graduation into the "farm problem," faced by high-income, low-food-drain economies, was swift. At higher levels of income the Engel coeffi-

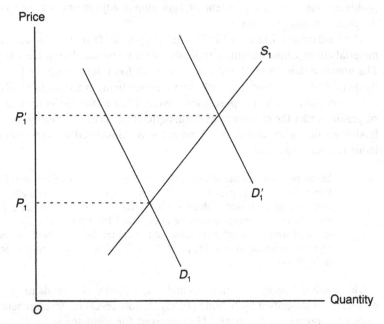

Figure 9.4. *The food problem*

cient decreases (Table 9.4). Moreover, with a low population growth rate, the demand for the subsistence commodity is fairly fixed and the mix of the food-consumption basket becomes heavily weighted towards commodities that improve the quality of diet, especially feedgrains (coarse grains) for the production of animal protein.[10] Moreover, agricultural productivity, which has been historically increasing, at least in the developed countries, accounts for an elastic supply of food. The combination is shown in Figure 9.5, where both demand and supply curves are elastic (as compared to Figure 9.4) and an

10 Feedgrains are likely to have a high income elasticity of demand, at least initially; and, being an ever-decreasing share of the budget, they are likely to have a relatively low price elasticity of demand. While the improvement of diets for those who can afford it is under way, agricultural price increases may occur and food crises may be precipitated. Once diets have been improved, however, feedgrain price increases could lead to downgrading the consumption of the well-off and releasing grains for direct consumption by the hungry. This could alleviate food crises. The 1974 food crisis, as an example, was only in part due to the drought. The improvement in diets in the USSR led to converting grains into feed and thus decreased the supply of foodgrains. The temporary downgrading of U.S. diets, on the other hand, released some grains which, however, ended up primarily feeding animals, and only at the margin providing for some famine relief (Yotopoulos, 1985).

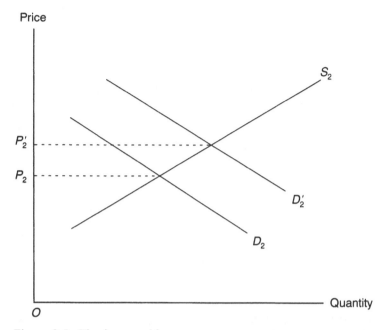

Figure 9.5. *The farm problem*

increase in income leads to a relatively small price increase in P_2'. Moreover, the canonical example is that productivity growth in manufacturing is even greater than that in agriculture, while competition is more imperfect and prices more rigid. The internal terms of trade shift against agriculture. The disparity between agricultural and nonagricultural incomes that results sets in motion the process for a huge transfer of resources out of agriculture. A common response to the "farm problem" is to resort to protectionist increases in food prices, which are now easily countenanced owing to the low Engel coefficients and the small share of food in the budget at higher income levels.

Table 9.4 presents the data on the transformation of Japanese agriculture and on productivity gaps with nonagriculture. The shrinkage of agriculture is pronounced since 1960, when the share in labor force dropped to 32% and declined rapidly thereafter. The sector's share in GDP went from 21% in 1955 to 13% in 1960. Between 1960 and 1970, Japanese agriculture seems to have encountered the farm problem, with a decrease in the Engel coefficient from 43 to 34% as a result of an increase in real per-capita GDP from $2690 to $6920 (1980 prices). At the same time, labor productivity was growing fast in Japanese agriculture (5.3% per year on a 1960–1980 basis), although not as fast as labor productivity in manufacturing (6.7% per year) (Hayami, 1988, p. 11).

Table 9.4. *Agriculture in Japan's economic development, 1935–1980*

| | Real GDP per capita (US $, 1980) | Share of agriculture | | Engel coefficient[b] (%) | Labor productivity,[c] agriculture/ industry (ratio) | Terms of trade,[d] agriculture/ manufacturing (1885 = 100) |
		In labor force[a] (%)	In GDP[a] (%)			
	(1)	(2)	(3)	(4)	(5)	(6)
1935	1620	47	18	50	24	136
⋮	⋮	⋮	⋮	⋮	⋮	⋮
1955	1850	39	21	52	55	163
1960	2690	32	13	43	39	169
1970	6920	17	7	34	25	304
1980	9890	10	4	31	17	347

Source: Hayami (1988), p. 20, adapted.
Notes:
[a]Agriculture includes forestry and fisheries.
[b]The share of food-consumption expenditure in total private-consumption expenditure in current prices.
[c]The ratio of real GDP per worker in agriculture, forestry, and fisheries to real GDP per worker in mining and manufacturing.
[d]The ratio of the price index of agricultural products to the price index of manufacturing products.

Starting in 1955, as a result, the ratio of agricultural to industrial labor productivity was declining. These trends are consistent with the stylized facts of the shrinkage of agriculture in the process of development.

The issue of "agricultural adjustment" refers to policy interventions that propose to smooth and lengthen the process of agricultural shrinkage. It addresses the questions of how fast and how far the transfer of resources out of agriculture should proceed, and whether a country can afford to pay the price of protection – which is the retardant antidote to the farm problem. Table 9.4 provides inferential evidence of active government intervention for agricultural adjustment. With the onset of the farm problem, one would have expected the agriculture/manufacturing terms of trade to decline, reflecting lower agricultural prices. Instead they were relatively stable (and in favor of agriculture) in 1955 and 1960 and they improved by another 75% by 1970. The analysis of these trends provides a useful insight into the role that agriculture played in fomenting the Japanese Miracle.

Tables 9.5 and 9.6, which draw from the excellent review of Japanese agriculture under protection by Hayami (1988), constitute the basis for our analysis. The self-sufficiency rates in Table 9.5, although crude analytical

Table 9.5. *Comparison of food self-sufficiency rates between Japan and other industrial countries (percentage)*

	Japan			1982					
	1960	1975	1985	U.S.	U.K.	France	Germany	Italy	Netherlands
Grains	83	43	34	183	111	179	95	89	31
Food grains	91	76	74	312	109	208	104	99	59
Rice	102	110	107						
Wheat	39	4	14	320	111	216	109	94	62
Coarse grains	66	2	2	161	114	156	90	79	14
Pulses	44	9	8	147	51	119	16	98	9
Vegetables	100	99	95	102	66	92	36	122	255
Fruits	100	84	76	90	18	69	51	117	28
Dairy products	89	82	89	99	96	116	127	67	183
Eggs	101	97	98	103	99	105	71	95	298
Meat	91	77	81	98	78	100	89	75	213
Total final food consumption	91	76	73						

Source: Hayami (1988), p. 3.

devices, can indicate some basic tendencies. A time trend of increasing self-sufficiency rates may mean increasing comparative advantage in agriculture and/or increasing protectionism. Declining self-sufficiency rates, on the other hand, may indicate increasing "food drain," relative to gains in agricultural productivity, which cannot be the case in Japan, or increasing liberalization. The latter hypothesis is reflected in the data after 1960, given the trade policies already discussed. A self-sufficiency rate over 100 indicates heavy protection, which is the case of rice in Japan, and in any event may signal the existence of stockpiles available for export as a result of a combination of protection and efficiency, which is the case of the U.S. and the European Economic Community countries. The shift in the food consumption basket towards animal protein is also evidenced in Japan by the dramatic decline in self-sufficiency rates of coarse grains and pulses.

We have already indicated that agricultural protection is not politically feasible as long as incomes are low and food, rice in particular, is a (subsistence) wage good; and/or as long as manufacturing relies on cheap labor and labor-intensive technologies.[11] These conditions probably existed before 1960,

11 Hayami (1988, pp. 47–50; Appendix A) provides an excellent analysis of the political economy of protection.

Table 9.6. *Comparisons of income levels between farm households and urban worker households for Japan*

| | Farm household income (000 yen)[a] | | | | Urban worker household income (000 yen) | | Relative income | |
| | Per household[b] | | | Per household member | Per household | Per household member | Per household | Per household member |
Year	Agriculture (1)	Off-farm (2)	Total (3)	(4)	(5)	(6)	(3/5) (7)	(4/6) (8)
1955	256	102	358	57	350	74	102	77
1960	225	224	449	78	502	115	89	68
1965	365	470	835	157	797	194	105	81
1970	508	1084	1592	326	1390	358	115	91
1975	1146	2815	3961	867	2897	760	137	114
1980	952	4651	5603	1273	4254	1111	132	115
1985	1065	5860	6926	1596	5388	1422	128	112
1985								
Full-time	2520 (56)	1969 (44)	4489 (100)	1207	5388	1422	83	85
Part-time I[c]	4124 (56)	3275 (44)	7399 (100)	1465	5388	1422	137	103
Part-time II[d]	495 (7)	6971 (93)	7466 (100)	1682	5388	1422	139	118

Source: Hayami (1988), pp. 92–93.
Notes:
[a]Off-farm income includes private grants and government transfer payments.
[b]Percentage shares are shown in parentheses.
[c]Farms with farm income larger than off-farm income.
[d]Farms with farm income less than off-farm income.

when incomes were low and industrialization relied on cheap labor. The latter was no longer the case after industrial policy shifted to capital- and technology-intensive heavy and chemical industries; and besides, the low Engel coefficients meant that the high incomes could handily support increased food costs. An increase in agricultural prices would not be strongly resisted by employers, employees, and the political constituency.

Careful examination of Table 9.6 shows the results of agricultural protection in terms of relative incomes, and reveals indirectly an additional rationale for income policies favoring agriculture: providing employment for subqualified labor so that rural–urban migration is stemmed and the urban wage level is protected. Comparison of columns (3) and (5) of the table – their ratio in column (7) – shows that farm household income was roughly equal to urban workers' household income in the period 1955–1965. Farm households, however, substantially lagged behind urban worker households on an income-per-member basis. By 1970 the situation was changing drastically. In 1985 farm-household income from agriculture was four times that of 1955. The increase reflects, at least in part, the substantial price supports for agriculture. At the same time, the off-farm component of farm household income was more than five-fold the income-from-agriculture component, rising from 28% of farm household income in 1955 to 85% in 1985. Considering both agricultural and off-farm income, income parity with the urban worker household, on a per-member basis, was achieved some time after 1970 and the ratio has favored agriculture since then.

The comparison of the two components of farm household income at the bottom panel of Table 9.6 is instructive on the political economy of agricultural price supports. Based on the source-of-income criterion, the table shows that full-time farm households, defined as farms with farm income larger than off-farm income, have lower agricultural income than part-time I households. This seeming paradox is explained by the high proportion of full-time agricultural households that have no member below 65 years old – 38% of the total number of full-time farms. Full-time agriculture thus serves the purpose of keeping off the welfare rolls subqualified workers who are too old to work hard on the farm, let alone to accept off-farm employment. Among agricultural commodities, rice is the crop that is ideally suited for "old-age farming":

> Part-time and elderly farmers tend to concentrate on rice farming because it is a very stable crop offering a high return on only intermittent labor without much managerial effort. Because rice marketing is carried out exclusively by the government, rice farmers are guaranteed a high price and can easily sell their harvest through agricultural cooperatives, the sole agent of government rice marketing. In addition, agricultural research and extension services have traditionally concentrated on the rice crop to the extent that rice cultivation has become highly standardized and there is little difference in productivity

between part-time and full-time farmers, and between young and elderly farmers (Hayami, 1988, p. 90).

The pivotal position that rice plays in deflecting the pressures for establishing a welfare state in Japan was established in 1960, when price supports were introduced, through the "production cost and income compensation formula." The formula established the price of rice based on the cost of production of the paddy field with yields of one standard deviation below the national average. Since the below-average-yield producer is also above-average-cost producer (given the linear and inverse relationship between yield per hectare and cost per unit), the price support for rice is set so as to support the subqualified labor force and to reward generously the efficient producers. The level of the support for the marginal producer (the one with yields of one standard deviation below the national average) is set at the daily wage rate of nonfarm workers, which is assumed as the opportunity cost of the family labor off the farm (Hayami, 1988, p. 48).

The instruments of agricultural protectionism, besides the price supports already mentioned, include quantitative restrictions, state trading, and a modest level of border protection through tariffs and levies.[12] Of the 27 restricted commodities that are still subject to import quotas that violate the GATT provisions, 22 are agricultural commodities. They consist of dairy products (3 commodities, including fresh and evaporated milk and cream, processed cheese, etc.), meats (2 commodities, including beef and processed meat products), processed grain products (2 commodities, including flour and flour meal), fresh and processed fruit (6 commodities, which include the celebrated case of oranges), starches and sugars (2 commodities, including dextrose), local agricultural products and seaweed (3 commodities, including the well-known peanut case), fish and shellfish (3 commodities), others (1 commodity), and coal (1 commodity, briquettes).

A more effective and less transparent instrument of protection is state trading. Trade monopolies and governmental or parastatal agencies that control imports of several agricultural commodities (such as rice, wheat, barley, beef, butter, silk, and leaf tobacco) can see to it that imported quantities are kept within orderly levels. Moreover, the advantage of this type of control instrument is that it does not violate GATT rules.

The distribution network. The distribution network has been singled out as a barrier to entry into the Japanese market by the U.S. Trade Administration;[13] it has been judged grossly inefficient by the Japanese Economic Planning

---

12 For a detailed discussion see Hayami (1988).
13 The successive rounds of bilateral negotiations under the Structural Impediments Initiative have focused on the distribution network, among other barriers to U.S.–Japanese trade.

Table 9.7. *Number of establishments and persons employed for "small" category and total wholesale and retail trade for Japan, 1951–1985 (thousand)*

	Wholesale and retail trade				Retail trade			
	Establishments		Persons		Establishments		Persons	
Year/Category	No.	%	No.	%	No.	%	No.	%
1951:								
Small	1,294	89.9	2,426	59.1				
Total	1,439	100	4,106	100				
1960:								
Small	1,546	81.6	3,115	45.9				
Total	1,895	100	6,802	100				
1968:								
Small	1,355	81			1,248	87.1		
Total	1,672	100	7,343	100	1,432	100	4,646	100
1976:								
Small	1,538	77.6	3,287	36.1	1,382	84.2	2,871	51.5
Total	1,981	100	9,093	100	1,641	100	5,580	100
1985:								
Small	1,546	75.7	3,422	33.1	1,348	82.8	2,895	45.7
Total	2,042	100	10,327	100	1,629	100	6,329	100

Source: Prime Minister's Office, Statistics Bureau, *Japan Statistical Yearbook*, various years.
Notes:
The "small" store category is defined as 4 or less persons employed ("mom-and-pop" stores).
Missing entries are due to unavailability of data.

Agency (EPA).[14] The inefficiency of the system is attributed to the size mix of its establishments, which can be traced to government regulations that condoned an extremely labor-intensive mode of operation.[15]

Almost all (99.5%) of the distribution establishments in Japan are categorized as small and medium (less than 300 employees). Table 9.7 shows that the small establishments, with four workers or less, constituted 76% of the total

14 The high cost of living in Tokyo, almost twice that of New York in 1988, is attributed by the EPA at least partly to the distribution network. The same agency estimated that 40% of the retail price of domestic goods and 59% of imported goods were allocated to distribution costs. See Upham (1993).
15 In overall comparisons, the Japanese distribution system appears to be the least efficient of OECD countries, although in terms of value added per employee the United Kingdom trails the

distribution outlets in wholesale and retail trade in 1985. They employed 33% of the total labor force in the distribution network – 3.4 million workers. The number of small establishments in wholesale and retail trade has consistently increased in absolute terms since 1951, the beginning of the period. It has shrunk in relative terms from 90% of the total to 76%. In terms of the total employment picture, small establishments provided 9% of the total nonagricultural sector employment in 1960, which has decreased to 6.4% in 1985.

The picture becomes more clear if one examines the retail trade component of the distribution network. The number of small establishments has varied little – between 1.2 and 1.4 million – and in 1985 they represented 83% of the total, down from 87% in 1968. They had 31% of the total annual sales of the retail trade, and they provided 46% of the employment in the sector. In contrast, only 3% of the establishments in the U.S. are "mom-and-pop" stores (Yokokura 1988, pp. 516, 519–520). It is true that the Japanese distribution network, especially the retail trade, is characterized by many stores of extremely small scale, densely packed into small shopping areas.

Historically, Japanese manufacturers have been involved at all stages of distribution by establishing exclusive long-term relationships with the agents, in which the distributors' margins were guaranteed in return for price stability. The system operated in a *keiretsu* fashion and resulted in keeping non-*keiretsu* consumers' goods, including imports, out of the market and in erecting an effective barrier of entry into the industry. The system was built on legal foundations that existed before the war, were repealed subsequently, were reinstituted in 1956, and culminated in the codification of the Large-Scale Retail Stores Law of 1973.[16] The legislation required a permit for opening single stores that contained more than 1500 m^2 of floor space ("department stores"). The permit could be issued by MITI only after the binding recommendation of a board consisting of the neighborhood merchants, consumers, and representatives of the public interest. The permit process effectively amounted to requiring that a large retailer, before going into business, purchase the right to locate stores from the local merchants, in the same way as purchasing rights to land and other factors of production. As a result, the paperwork and the other transaction costs involved in entering the market with a large store often involved delays of as long as ten years (Yokokura, 1988; Upham, 1993).

The benefits of "orderly retailing" that the system provided were certainly

---

list, and in terms of size distribution both Italy and France are more dominated by small stores than Japan. See OECD (1988), Table 27.

16 The Large-Scale Retail Stores Law of 1973 was amended in 1991 as a result of pressure from the Structural Impediments Initiative. For a fascinating account of the legal aspects of the regulation of retail stores see Upham (1993).

bought at the cost of transferring wealth away from consumers. The latter's gains transcended strict economic accounting: in a country where storage space is limited and taste for freshness is strong (in fish, tofu, vegetables, even rice), requiring frequent trips to the neighborhood store, it makes good sense to have many small retail outlets. There are also convenience reasons for Japanese consumers, who are fastidious and expect a pleasant attitude and plenty of service when they shop. There may also exist social benefits from small and family owned retail stores, such as social stability, neighborhood cohesion, retirement security, and the effect on the family structure (Patrick and Rohlen, 1987). However, by far the most convincing rationale for the proliferation of small retail outlets in the Japanese cities and countryside is the employment they provide to 6.3 million people, almost 17% of the total nonprimary sector employment. Moreover, being the residual sector, the extensive distribution network also keeps the marginal and the subqualified workers at work, among others the elderly and the infirm, thus weakening the pressures for establishing a welfare state.

In this appraisal, in conclusion, the regulation of the retail distribution network shares with the regulation of agriculture the same policy imperative: how to provide employment to large, and often marginal, segments of the population (and thus avoid welfarism) without unleashing pressures for decreasing wages. Maintaining a high-wage economy was an essential component of the Japanese development strategy.

Appropriate industrial policies

In discussing Japanese industrial policy it is helpful to distinguish three broad groups of industries.

First, industrial policy mildly but successfully discouraged tourist development, supermarkets, shopping centers, and fast-food restaurants. One can think of ex post ratiocinations for such disfavor, including the high leakage through imports those industries have and their negative impact on the marginal propensity to save. Although the initial rationale for such policy is unclear, the effect is still visible to the casual observer.

The second group includes some industries that came into prominence in the 1950s, before the industrial policy was fully articulated: sewing machines, cameras, bicycles, motorcycles, pianos, zippers, and transistor radios.[17] These industries were treated with benign neglect on the grounds that they were no longer infant industries and could continue to rely on the strong domestic

---

17 The classification of industries, although not the rationale behind it, follows Komiya and Itoh (1988).

demand to prosper. Another group was added in the mid-1960s, presumably also on the grounds that the domestic demand created from the overall industrial policy was a sufficient inducement: color televisions, tape recorders, magnetic recording tape, audio equipment, fishing gear, watches and clocks, calculators, electric wire, machine tools, digitally controlled machine tools, textile machinery, agricultural machinery, insulators, communications equipment, ceramics, and robots.

Finally the group that squarely belonged to the "heavy and chemical industries" classification and became by commission the main beneficiary of the industrial policy was electricity, iron and steel, shipbuilding, merchant marine, machine industries in general, heavy electrical equipment, and chemicals; to which later was added: automotives, petrochemicals, nuclear power, computers, and semiconductors and related industries. The famed "shifting band of protection" fully applied to these industries, focusing on one at a time, bringing it up to the level of world competition, and moving on to the next (Krugman, 1987b).

Both general policies and specifically targeted policies were used to achieve cost reduction in the heavy and chemical industries, the priority industrial group. The fiscal measures included accelerated depreciation and tariff exemptions for "important" machinery, exemptions from import and other taxes for important raw materials, and property tax exemptions for facilities that were "modernized." These exemptions were substantial, totalling 5.7% of corporate tax receipts in fiscal 1955 (Kosai, 1988, p. 35).

Government financing of priority industries came to 28.3% of the total credit to industry extended in the period 1952–1955, excluding loans from the World Bank and foreign currency lending by the Bank of Japan. Government credit was extended at preferential rates, although the extent of the subsidy involved was not always clear. Shipbuilding was probably the exception; here important interest subsidies were involved, amounting to 10.3 billion yen in the period 1953–1957 (Kosai, 1988, p. 36).

The major part of credit for Japanese industry came from indirect financing by bank *keiretsu* (bank conglomerate groups), at least until the development of the capital market in the 1970s (Johnson, 1988, p. 204; Aoki, 1988, p. 138; Aoki, 1994). Unlike the U.S., and more akin to the European system, "main banks" are allowed to take equity participation in industrial and trading companies which, in turn, meet their capital needs by borrowing from the bank of the conglomerate.[18] Banks also compete in lending to their *keiretsu*, and the constituent firms are thereby induced to invest more. In a vicious circle, one can

---

18 For more detail on the Japanese banking system see Patrick (1972, 1984), Horiuchi (1984), Teranishi (1986, 1990), Aoki and Patrick (1994).

imagine situations in which strong interdependence (and mutually reinforcing risk) is created between the banks and industrial firms through overloaning, and excess capacity is built, fostering excessive ("more than appropriate") competition.

Industrial policy focused on "industrial rationalization," which has as major components guarding against insufficient scale and preventing excessive competition. In industries with many suppliers and low market concentration, industrial policy attempted to coordinate the division of products among firms, to foster a system of specialized producers, and to develop cooperation in production. The intervention to establish specialized machine tool producers provides an example of such a case (Tsuruta, 1988, p. 61). Through its authority to approve the creation of cartels, MITI also effectively acquired the power to supervise competition. The case of petrochemicals provides a textbook example and illustrates as well the industry-by-industry rationalization programs that extended from supplying government funds for the industry to drawing up of industry standards for the purpose of modernization:[19]

> In its fully elaborated form, the late 1950s MITI system of nurturing (*ikusei*) a new industry (for example, petrochemicals) included the following types of measures: First, an investigation was made and a basic policy statement was drafted within the ministry on the need for the industry and on its prospects – an example is the Petrochemical Industry Nurturing Policy adopted by a MITI ministerial conference on July 11, 1955. Second, foreign currency allocations were authorized by MITI and funding was provided for the industry by the Development Bank. Third, licenses were granted for the import of foreign technology (every item of petrochemical technology was obtained on license from abroad). Fourth, the nascent industry was designated as "strategic" in order to give it special and accelerated depreciation on its investment. Fifth, it was provided with improved land on which to build its installations, either free of charge or at nominal cost. Sixth, the industry was given key tax breaks – in the case of petrochemicals, exemption from customs duties on imported catalytic agents and special machinery, the refund of duties collected on refined petroleum products used as raw materials for petrochemicals, and special laws exempting certain users from gasoline taxes. Seventh, MITI created an "administrative guidance cartel" to regulate competition and coordinate investments among firms in the industry – in this case the "Petrochemicals Cooperation Discussion Group" established on December 19, 1964 (Johnson, 1982, pp. 236–237).

19 Kosai (1988, p. 37) provides a table with the specific industry standards that were introduced in certain cases as a result of rationalization and shows cost reductions that ranged from 4% in pig iron (preprocessing of raw materials) and 10% in steel (oxygen-process steel production and mass-production-sized open-hearth furnaces), to 25% in rayon fibers (continuous process compared to prior method), and 30% in steel pipe (Flettsmunn process compared to old seamless-pipe facilities).

Control of imports was a most important component in preventing excessive competition. Given an environment of restricted imports, licensing of foreign capital (including foreign borrowing), purchases of foreign technology, and imports of foreign machinery became control instruments of industrial policy. The policy of permitting initial but not subsequent items to be imported was beneficial to the development of domestic industry by encouraging imitation (Kosai, 1988, p. 43).

The locus of industrial policy was the *genkyoku*, the ministerial bureau or division that had oversight responsibility for a specific industry. The MITI was principally responsible for formulating industrial policy and accumulated the greatest number of *genkyoku*: the Heavy Industries Bureau (which included the sections for iron and steel, industrial machinery, electronics and electrical machinery, automobiles, aircraft, and rolling stock), the Chemical Industries Bureau, the Textile and Light Industries Bureau, the Coal and Mining Bureau, and the Public Utilities Bureau. Among other ministries, the Ministry of Agriculture, Forestry, and Fisheries had responsibility for the various food and processing industries, the Ministry of Health and Welfare for pharmaceuticals, the Ministry of Transport for shipbuilding, and the Ministry of Finance for banking, insurance, securities, and alcoholic beverages.

The role of the state

State-led capitalism

Although the literature on the Japanese Miracle is not monolithic, the role played by the Government is consistently mentioned. In its most benign formulation, the Government is credited for doing well what all governments are supposed to do (administer justice, guarantee law and order, provide education and some basic infrastructure, while in this specific case also enjoying the special dispensation from providing for defense) plus some more, in the form of trade restrictions for protecting and nurturing infant industry, and, especially, in providing mechanisms for collecting, processing, and transmitting information valuable for the activities of private enterprises. Beyond that, and in particular in the 1950s and the 1960s, ". . . the initiative and vitality of the private sector . . . [u]ndermined the plans of government authorities to try to utilize direct interventions in the nature of 'controls' " (Komiya, Okuno, and Suzumura, 1988, p. 553).

Other scholars have seen the state casting the long shadow of "Japan, Inc." and evaluated it for better or worse.[20] Our approach on this issue is analytical and focuses on explaining the economic anatomy of the successful outcomes of developmental interventions.

[20]Okimoto, 1989; Prestowitz, 1988; Tyson, 1992, among others.

Johnson (1982), not unlike other researchers, sees a direct line of developmental orientation and organization running from the Meiji restoration of 1868 to the present of "Japan, Inc." The heritage of state enterprises of the Tokugawa era had yielded its share of corruption, bureaucratism, and inefficient monopolies. The solution of the Meiji era was the collaborative relationship between government and the *zaibatsu* (privately owned industrial empires) on a selective basis and to the extent that the latter were committed to the national goals of economic development and military strength and they were able and willing to adopt new technologies. Deep are the historical roots of the "development imperative" that has been shared broadly by government, business, and the citizenry.

The dominant relationship between government and business developed after the war and is the result of the formal abolition of the *zaibatsu* and of increasing the number of privately controlled industrial enterprises that were freed from their earlier family domination. The most apposite description of this relationship is "responsive dependence":

> The government did not normally give direct orders to businesses, but those businesses that listened to the signals coming from the government and then responded were favored with easy access to capital, tax breaks and approval of their plans to import foreign technology or establish joint ventures. But a firm did not have to respond to the government. The business literature of Japan is filled with descriptions of the very interesting cases of big firms that succeeded without strong governmental ties (for example, Sony and Honda), but there are not many to describe (Johnson, 1982, p. 24).

This is a familiar pattern of interaction in a society that is nonconfrontational and where communication takes place indirectly by contextual reference and by conjectural variations ("body language") as much as it is conveyed by the direct word. Japan is the country where operating on the same frequency is a prerequisite for communication and where long antennas to pick up the "vibes" emitted certainly help. It is no wonder that business firms were induced to operate on the "developmental imperative" frequency.

Besides providing the "ambience" for development, the state also engaged in direct interventions. In my view these were enabling interventions that became necessary by the condition of operating with overvalued currency.

Administrative guidance

In the early 1960s, the combination of excess capacity in light manufacturing in Japan (the export flood of "dollar blouses"), the world recession, and the Kennedy Round of the GATT agreements built up the pressure for the (first) opening of the Japanese economy. The trade liberalization[21] and the exchange liberalization that led to the abolition of foreign exchange budgets meant that MITI lost two effective policy control instruments for implementing industrial policy. The "administrative guidance" system developed to fill the gap. It is a system that has been much misunderstood abroad and quite underplayed in Japan for fear that it would lend credence to the "Japan, Inc." stereotype.

> There is nothing very mysterious about administrative guidance. It refers to the authority of the government, contained in the laws establishing the various ministries, to issue directives (*shiji*), requests (*yōbō*), warnings (*keikoku*), suggestions (*kankoku*), and encouragements (*kanshō*) to the enterprises or clients within a particular ministry's jurisdiction. Administrative guidance is constrained only by the requirement that the "guidees" must come under a given government organ's jurisdiction, and although it is not based on any explicit law, it cannot violate the law (Johnson, 1982, p. 265).

Lacking an explicit legal foundation, administrative guidance is not legally enforceable. Instead, ". . . [i]ts power comes from government–business relationships established since the 1930's, respect for the bureaucracy, the ministries' claim that they speak for the national interest, and various informal pressures that the ministries can bring to bear" (Johnson, 1982, p. 266). The set of mechanisms that makes administrative guidance operational is broad: it ranges from cooptation (e.g., investment coordination done in "cooperative discussion groups"), to midwifery (e.g., inducing mergers by bringing the parties together and endorsing their union in front of the Fair Trade Commission), to "getting even" with the miscreants (through "taking revenge on Edo by striking at Nagasaki," as the old Japanese proverb goes).[22]

Administrative guidance, of course, is not without parallels in other countries ("jawboning" in the U.S. is an example), only in Japan it becomes a form of "body language" that is well suited to the general ambience of doing business. Johnson quotes the special commission of Japanese and American "wisemen" that had been appointed in 1979 to examine the long-term economic relationship between the two countries:

> One of the most difficult aspects of the Japanese economic system for non-Japanese to understand is the nature of the government–business relationship. The more embracing set of consultations between the private and public sectors and less of an adversary relationship than in the United States lend substance in some American eyes to the concept of "Japan, Inc." This image

---

21 Trade liberalization was defined in terms of the percent of the commodities listed in the Brussels Customs Schedule that would be exempted from quantitative barriers to trade. All that time the figure of 80 to 90% was being negotiated between the IMF and Japan. See Johnson (1982, p. 251), Komiya and Itoh (1988, pp. 182, 192–193).
22 For specific examples see Johnson (1982, pp. 265–274).

presents a very false and misleading impression of the Japanese economy. It is also very harmful to United States–Japan economic relations because it creates the false impression that Japan can manipulate exports and imports at will. Business does not meekly respond to government fiat nor is government the creature of business. Most Japanese, however, do acknowledge the existence of government reliance on administrative guidance, usually describing the informal means by which government attempts to influence business without resorting to legislative or regulatory measures as would be the case in the United States (Johnson, 1982, pp. 272–273).

The Japanese system, not unlike the Anglo–American and the Continental European, certainly rests on a legal foundation. How far the law prescribes, and to what extent it is a matter of interpretation and improvisation and by whom is a question of degree. The European system of the codified law (Napoleonic law, and Roman and Byzantine law before that) is more specific and leaves less room for creative interpretation than the Anglo–American case-law system allows, which in turn is more constrained than the Japanese system of short and very general laws that leave the actual details to the interpretation of bureaucrats so that the effects of legislation can be narrowly targeted. There is no gainsaying that the Japanese system is effective and efficient: it enhances the ability of officials to respond to new situations rapidly and with flexibility; it is economical, having eliminated the legal middlemen; and it is nurturing by avoiding the adversarial relationship in private–public dealings. There is no denying either that the system is open to abuse and that the cultural and ethnic homogeneity of the Japanese society has so far effectively limited the costs of potential excesses of administrative guidance.

Conclusion: a nonrevisionist interpretation

To many Western observers, Japanese industrialization seemed counterintuitive in the period before World War II. As an example, the noted American demographer Warren S. Thompson (1929) posed the question whether Japan could ever become a great manufacturing nation and answered it with a resounding No! After the devastation of the war a Japanese Miracle seemed even more improbable. Again Thompson (1950), as an example, repeated his earlier prediction based on pessimism about labor relations, industrial prospects, and trade opportunities. Ex post, the same episodic approach and special traits have been used to rationalize the emergence of Japan into top economic prominence in the world.

> The national-character explanation argues that the economic miracle occurred because the Japanese possess a unique, culturally derived capacity to cooperate with each other. This capacity to cooperate reveals itself in many ways: lower crime rates than in other less homogeneous societies; subordina-

222   *Successes and failures in development*

tion of the individual to the group; intense group loyalties and patriotism; and last, but not least, economic performance. The most important contribution to economic life is said to be Japan's famous "consensus," meaning virtual agreement among government, ruling political party, leaders of industry and people, on the primacy of economic objectives. Some of the terms invented to refer to this cultural capability of the Japanese are "rolling consensus," "private collectivism," "inbred collectivism," "spiderless cobweb," and "Japan, Inc." (Johnson, 1982, p. 8).

Parallel economic explanations abound. They all seem to emphasize one or another aspect of Japanese economic "perversity."

The sympathetic interpretation in this chapter suggests that the Japanese Miracle was indeed impressive, especially because its traditional ingredients were unremarkable. The initial conditions of Japan after the war were none too dissimilar from those other developing countries faced; the initial constraints were often more binding. Export policies, in comparison with other countries, were tame; exports did not drive development in the early period, contrary to the conventional wisdom.

The novel component of the Japanese development success is systematically overriding incomplete markets, especially in employment, foreign exchange, and trade. In our analytical framework, "trade bias" arises as a result of a systematic relationship in the prices of tradables and nontradables in the process of development; it reflects the existence of an inherent asymmetry in the international economic order that binds the DCs and LDCs. The need for an industrial policy was fostered upon Japan – as it befalls all other LDCs that try to avoid "trade bias." Industrial policies, as such, are not new in the development experience. The remarkable feature of Japanese industrial policy was that it picked the winners – the industries that had dynamic comparative advantage down the road. This is due less to an uncanny instinct possessed by Japanese bureaucrats (although competence in government helps, as discussed in Chapter 3) than to the paramount role that domestic demand played in Japanese economic development. The sequence of industrialization went *in tandem* with the increasing levels of consumption enjoyed by the majority of the population, through an economic strategy that spread broadly the rents of economic development. Put another way, this means that the economic rents created through state intervention in overriding incomplete markets, whether captured by businessmen or by an honest bureaucracy, were ploughed back into economic development. This was probably the linchpin of the Japanese Miracle. The process of development in Japan was as successful as it was articulated (Chapter 2).

The institutional analysis of Japanese state-led capitalism in this chapter centers on the formative period of Japan's industrial policy, roughly through the mid-1980s. With some lags considered, this period provided the foundation for Japan's economic structure and was the fountainhead of the phenomenal Japanese economic growth that ensued. Japan was on its way to becoming an economic superpower. Once a country reaches the level of development of its main trading partners – of the U.S. in the case of Japan – external and internal equilibrium tend to converge and market liberalization needs to be promoted, as opposed to being controlled and constrained. There is a stage of economic development when overvaluation, if it exists, has other purposes than fulfilling the condition of internal macroequilibrium in the face of diverging external macroequilibrium. At this stage, the role of regulatory bodies changes accordingly and their extra functions slowly become obsolete. MITI did not avoid this fate. Its functions since the early 1980s focused more on managing the mature economy (e.g., smoothing the ground for – and often frustrating – the process of capital liberalization) and on self-denial of its obsolescence than on controlling the process of development of an LDC. State-led capitalism is not necessary when market capitalism can do the job.[23]

---

23 The story of MITI for yet another decade from where we have left it is continued in Johnson (1982, Chapter 7). It is lively, and also peppered with incidents of abuse that were rather rare in the previous historical stretch. It may be just another example of a bureaucracy having outlived its function.

CHAPTER 10

The Philippines: Failure in policy and politics

By the time of its independence and for at least the next 10 years the Philippines had a high growth rate of GDP and one of the highest per-capita incomes in Asia. The 9% aggregate annual growth rate of the 1950s declined to 5% in the 1960s, briefly increased 6.8% in 1973–1979, hovered around zero till the end of the Marcos era in 1985, peaked briefly at 5.8% in the early Aquino period, and has stagnated since 1990 (Table 10.1). Considering the sizeable rate of population growth of 2.7%, this aggregate growth record produced an annual growth rate of 1.3% on a per-capita basis for the period 1965–1990. Incomes are only the tip of the iceberg. In fact, the economy has unravelled so rapidly since the 1960s that today the Philippines is considered a distinct development failure.

The development play of the Philippines was enacted on a stage of some enduring institutional features and in the shifting setting of various policy regimes. The stage and the setting are discussed in the next section. They are followed by a more detailed analysis of various policy initiatives and of the development outcomes.

The stage and the setting

Land concentration and land reform

The Spanish colonial period bequeathed the Philippines the legacy of large agricultural estates run by landlord elites. The U.S., which succeeded Spain as colonial master at the beginning of the 20th century, was primarily interested in the Philippine cash-crop exports and in placing American consumer goods in the local market. This led to a long period of a dualistic economic and agrarian structure and to the neglect of subsistence agriculture (Ranis and Stewart, 1993).

A number of hesitant moves toward land reform took place in the period 1930–1971. Their main components were: (1) regulation of tenancy relations, which provided for a 50–50 sharing of the crop, limitation of usurious interest rates, and providing safeguards against arbitrary dismissal of tenants by landlords; (2) organizing settlement in Mindanao for the landless from other islands; (3) issuing free titles to homesteaders on cultivable public land; and (4)

224

Table 10.1. *Key macroeconomic and financial indicators for the Philippines, 1950–1990*

	1950–1959	1960–1969	1970–1979	1980–1984	1985–1989	1990
Growth rates						
Real GDP	9.0	5.0	5.8	1.3	2.6	2.1
Key rates						
Exchange rate[a]	2.0	3.5	6.9	10.4	20.5	24.3
Interest rate, deposits	2.2	4.2	7.3	14.9	12.8	18.5
Interest rate, treasury bills			11.3	18.2	18.2	20.7
Ratios to GDP						
Gross investment	15.4	19.5	26.0	26.7	15.8	18.2
Gross domestic savings	12.2	15.9	23.3	22.5	17.3	16.1
Current account balance		0.4	−2.1	−6.0	−0.6	−6.1
Domestic liquidity (M_3)	19.3	24.7	24.9	26.6	23.3	18.8
Domestic public debt	11.6	14.9	17.2	16.0	22.9	22.4
Total external debt			34.5	63.0	77.7	70.8

Source: Central Bank of the Philippines, *Annual Report*, various years; Central Bank of the Philippines, *Selected Economic Indicators*, 1989; National Statistical Council, *Philippine Statistical Yearbook*, various years.
Note:
[a]Yearly average, pesos per U.S. dollar.

setting a policy on "landed estates" that provided funds for the negotiated purchase of large holdings and resale to tenants.

These half-hearted measures failed to address the basic issue of land redistribution. The effective beginning of land reform in the Philippines had to wait for the proclamation of martial law in 1972 and for "operation land transfer" and the "leasehold operation." The emphasis was on the latter, providing that some tenants could be "deemed owners" of the lands they were cultivating in 1972 and could proceed with purchase.[1] The proviso, however, was that the program was applicable only to rice and corn lands, thus excluding coconut, sugar, and other cash crop lands and the tenants and landless workers who cultivated them. Finally, the program instituted a ceiling of 25% of "normal" output, net of the costs of agricultural inputs, for the landlord's share in tenancy contracts.

1 It is reported that both measures called for the transfer of a total of 731,000 hectares of land to 396,000 peasants.

As Hayami, Quisumbing, and Adriano (1987) observe, this type of land reform worked against both equity and efficiency in Philippine agriculture. The limitation to tenanted land provided a strong incentive to landlords to evict tenants and administer directly the cultivation of their land. This flies in the face of efficiency, since the higher productivity of the family, small-size farm in LDC agriculture is well documented (Lau and Yotopoulos, 1971; Berry and Cline, 1979). Moreover, by reducing labor input per hectare below an optimal level, the program reduced the labor absorption capacity of agriculture and the income of the laboring population.

The prohibition of sharecropping in favor of tenancy rests on another misunderstanding of the recent empirical evidence. It is also widely agreed that the share contract can achieve the same degree of efficiency as the owner-operation or fixed-rent contract, and furthermore, it is beneficial to tenants because of risk-sharing and because of the interlinkage of the contractual relationships on land and on credit from the landlord (Otsuka, Chuma, and Hayami, 1992; Floro and Yotopoulos, 1991).

The provision favoring large-scale agriculture for cash crops is consistent with the export-led growth strategy that had been adopted earlier in the Philippines. Specifically, presidential decrees allowed 100% foreign equity in agribusiness corporations; provided numerous incentives to national and foreign investors in export-oriented agribusiness enterprises, ranging from various tax credits, deductions, and exemptions, to preferential credit from private and public banking institutions; and lifted the previous safe haven that small farmers and peasants had in staple grain production by allowing both domestic and foreign corporations to enter production and trade of grains (Hayami et al., 1987, p. 44). As a result of these measures significant foreign investment in agribusiness poured into the country between 1972 and 1985. A large portion of it went into plantation agriculture, which grew so rapidly that by 1984 it occupied one-quarter of the total land area of the Philippines (Table 10.2).

The most recent attempt at land reform was undertaken by the Aquino administration in the form of the Comprehensive Agrarian Reform Program of 1988. The program is framed within the constitutional provision that Congress will prescribe reasonable retention limits for landlords, considering specific circumstances, and that just compensation is paid. With the confiscatory element that is inevitable in all land reforms missing in this case, and with a Congress controlled by landed interests, the current action on all accounts is on legislating blanket exceptions from land reform rather than on redistributing land (Putzel, 1988).[2]

The persistent land concentration problem and the absence of any genuine

---

2 "Farm News and Views" (May 1993) of the Philippine Peasant Institute reports examples of legislated dilatory measures of the Program: increasing the basic 5 hectare retention limit by

Table 10.2. *Status of land use for the Philippines, 1970–1984*
(million hectares)

	1970		1977		1984	
	Hectares	Percent of total	Hectares	Percent of total	Hectares	Percent of total
Total Philippines	30.00	100.00	30.00	100.00	30.00	100.00
Forest	15.90	53.00	13.00	43.67	11.50	38.33
Productive	14.10	47.00	11.30	37.67	9.30	31.00
Unproductive	1.00	6.00	1.80	6.00	2.30	7.67
Nonforest	14.10	47.00	16.90	56.33	18.40	61.33
Open land	2.60	8.67	1.00	3.33	0.80	2.67
Managed pasture	0.80	2.67	1.00	3.33	0.70	2.33
Marsh and small bodies of water	0.20	0.67	0.10	0.33	0.10	0.33
Plantation			6.80	22.67	7.50	25.00
Cultivated cropland	9.8[a]	32.67[a]	7.20	24.00	8.20	27.33
Urban and others	0.60	2.00	0.80	2.67	1.10	3.67

Source: Hayami et al. (1987), p. 47.
Note:
[a]The figure combines plantation and cultivated croplands.

land reform became an enduring part of the stage for Philippine economic development.

Inadequate infrastructure

The Philippines was not as fortunate as some other former colonies, India and Taiwan for instance, that were endowed with adequate infrastructure on independence. Part of the reason is the geography of the country, with its multiplicity of heterogeneous islands; another part is that no elaborate rural road network or inland transport system is necessary for the export of plantation cash crops that were the trade link of the Philippines with the rest of the world.

This tradition continued after independence. The decision-making process on the location and the type of infrastructural investment was thoroughly centralized and left no initiative to the local bodies at the barrio level. The result

adding another 3 hectares for each child; substituting for land reform a stock distribution option for corporate farms; and providing for international corporations for 50-year land leases (renewable for another 25 years) that are exempted from land reform.

was that Manila was heavily favored by infrastructural investment, which led to the concentration of 80% of all industry there. The same concentration favoring Metro-Manila is apparent in electricity production, distribution, and rate structure (Ranis, 1978). A belated government effort in the 1970s to stimulate infrastructural investment proved counterproductive. It was urban-biased and had long gestation periods and questionable economic justification. Among the most notorious examples are the Chico River Basin Dam and the Bataan Nuclear Power Plant.[3] Even where transport infrastructure extended to the countryside it mainly served extractive as opposed to linkage purposes. The official name of "penetration highways" describes well this situation.

One type of infrastructural investment that was favored during the colonial period was education. The U.S. sought to achieve broad primary education coverage. Moreover, with participation of the Catholic Church and missionaries, secondary and higher education spread considerably. The legacy for investment in human capital still persists in the Philippines. The education industry is also heavily located in the capital city, as are the other infrastructural investments.

The basic policy regime

Not unlike other LDCs, the Philippines began development with import substitution industrialization. The stage was set in the 1940s, when the government enacted foreign exchange controls accompanied by quantitative restrictions and discriminatory tariffs on imports. The first phase of import substitution, primary import substitution of consumer goods, was quite successful in filling the demand for light consumer manufactures: processed foods, shoes, and garments, which were then becoming increasingly expensive as imports. The strategy was also successful in creating a small national entrepreneurial class.

Import substitution possibilities were exhausted by the late 1960s, due to the stall in broadly based income growth. By then, two alternative policy reactions were available. One approach was to widen the scope of import substitution to imported durable consumer goods, capital goods, and the raw materials for processing industries. This strategy was foreclosed by limited effective domestic demand (Ranis, 1978; Ranis and Mahmood, 1992). Unlike Japan, the Philippines did not have a broad income base to support a domestic durable goods industry. The requisite economies of scale would not be achieved to propel the industries into the international market. Low incomes made inappropriate any industrial sequencing based on effective domestic demand.

The other strategy, which was followed, was export-led industrialization that

---

3 The latter, although discontinued, still costs the government $300,000 daily for maintenance and servicing (Lamberte et al., 1992, p. 311).

focused on labor-intensive exports with the participation of foreign capital. This involved opening up the economy to a greater extent, abolishing protective tariffs and partially lifting foreign exchange restrictions (Bello, 1987, pp. 25–26). The liberalization and promotion of exports had already started in the 1970s with a drastic reduction in tariffs, the establishment of free-trade zones and bonded warehouses, and with fiscal and administrative incentives provided by the Board of Investments. The tempo of liberalization picked up in 1981 under the auspices of the IMF and continued unabated.

Table 10.3 summarizes the play of Philippine economic development that was enacted in the setting of export-led growth. Following Lamberte, Lim, Vos, Yap, Tan, and Zingapan, (1992), four main policy regimes are distinguished, with the fifth still being enacted.

> The first phase covers the years 1970–1974 and could be termed the "Consolidation" phase, which witnessed a period of stabilization and recovery, and [the] establishment of an authoritarian state with a clear economic program. The next phase could be labelled "Debt-led Growth," which began in 1975 in the aftermath of the first oil shock and ended in 1979, [with] the advent of the second oil shock and the rise of the international interest rates. This period was characterized by expansionary investments and export promotion programs. A "Pre-Crisis Stage" followed, covering the period 1980–1982, which featured a failed attempt to adjust to an adverse international environment, including an extremely deep recession and a fall in the net financial transfer from abroad. The reduced [net] foreign financing came . . . from the increased debt service burden caused by the debt accumulated in the previous period, and the sudden and steep rise in world interest rates following a shift in macroeconomic policies in industrialized countries. The period also experienced the World Bank imposition of a structural adjustment program, which directly clashed with the government's attempt to bail out distressed but favored firms, and to continue protecting privileged firms and monopolies. The "Crisis Stage" in 1983–1985 saw the deepest post-war recessionary period. . . . [F]inally, the most recent period is labelled a "Difficult Recovery" (since foreign financing was minimal and, in fact, a net resource outflow occurred due to the debt overhang) and witnessed the beginning of a new economic crisis (Lamberte et al., 1992, p. 308).

These regimes correspond to the endogenous policy interventions and the exogenous policy shocks described with considerable detail in Table 10.3.

The policy tools

Persistent undervaluation of the exchange rate

The Philippines has placed consistently very high in the ranking of countries based on RER: at the very top in 1970, 1980, and 1985, and in the top quartile in 1975 (Table 6.1). The history of NER devaluations, which appears in Tables

Table 10.3. *Major economic shocks and policy responses in the Philippines*

Shock	Responses				
	1970–1974	1975–1979	1980–1982	1983–1985	1986–1990
External shock	Foreign debt crisis	Cheap foreign credit inflow	Oil price shock	Stoppage of foreign debt inflow	Negotiated debt rescheduling
	Commodity price boom	Increased foreign investment	Recession abroad		Resumed multilateral and bilateral loan inflows
	Oil price shock	Deteriorating terms of trade	High world interest rates		Net resource outflow due to debt payment
			Restricted foreign credit		
Domestic shock	Rise of strong nationalist movement/Martial law declaration		Dewey Dee financial crisis	Assassination of Aquino	Takeover of Aquino government
Monetary Policy	Tight due to inflationary pressures from devaluation; more expansionary in 1973 and 1974	Expansionary, subsidized credit to priority areas	Highly expansionary and countercyclical, financial liberalization	Restrictive and deflationary; high interest rates	Expansionary in initial years; tight with high interest rates in later years
Fiscal policy	Tight due to inflationary pressures from devaluation; more expansionary in 1973 and 1974	Expansionary, particularly on government investment	Countercyclical	Contractionary, concentrated on debt service and bailout of government corporations	Initially expansionary; tight in later years with concentration on domestic borrowings and tax reforms

Trade and industry policy	Devaluation; export promotion	Export promotion; continued protection of import substitute sector; failed plan for heavy industrialization	Beginning of removal of quantitative restrictions	Suspension of trade liberalization; taxation of tradables; rationing of foreign exchange; devaluation	Trade liberalization; slowly depreciating peso in 1990
Combined effects	High growth; high inflation	High growth; shift to nontraditional exports	Slow growth; inflation	Deep economic recession; high inflation	Economic recovery up to 1989; increasing current account deficits; slow growth in 1990
Private response	Favorable; high investments	Favorable; high savings and investments	Unfavorable; reduced savings, capital flight but continued investments spurred by government pump-priming	Collapse of business confidence	Renewed confidence initially, erratic behavior in later years
Foreign investors' response	Caution in 1970 to 1972; favorable and high investments starting 1973	Favorable; high investments, especially in nontraditional export sector	Caution and lower growth rate of foreign investments	Reduced investments; higher withdrawals	Caution in the beginning; stepped up inflows in 1988 to 1989; reduced investments in 1990
Bilateral and multilateral response	Substantial increase in aid and loans	Continued increase in inflow of loans and aid, particularly in support of energy and infrastructure	Imposition of structural adjustment programs, particularly trade liberalization and financial liberalization	Imposition of IMF stabilization program	Resumption of loans and aid; stringent conditions in 1989 and 1990 on monetary and fiscal targets
Foreign commercial banks' response	Commercial bank lending begins to increase in 1974	Rapid and massive inflow of commercial loans	High variable-interest rates for short-term commercial loans; move from medium- and long-term loans to short-term loans	Stoppage of medium- and long-term loans due to debt moratorium	Rescheduling of principal payments of loans in 1987; new money ($700 million) and buy-back scheme in January 1990

Source: Lamberte et al. (1992), p. 77.

Table 10.4. *Exchange rates, nominal and inflation-adjusted, for the Philippines, 1960–1986*

Year	Nominal exchange rate (1)	Inflation-differential adjusted rate[a] (2)	Ratio (1/2)
1960–1969	3.50	4.63	0.76
1970–1974	6.51	5.53	1.18
1975–1979	7.37	4.57	1.61
1980–1984	10.40	4.60	2.26
1985–1989	20.51	5.24	3.91
1990	24.32	5.39	4.51

Source: Central Bank of the Philippines, *Annual Report*, various years.
Notes:
Exchange rate is pesos per U.S. dollar.
[a]The Inflation-differential adjusted rate is defined as the nominal rate multiplied by the ratio of the world price index to the Philippine price index.

10.1 and 10.4, corroborates the hypothesis of RER undervaluation, with high prices of tradables, in the four benchmark years 1970, 1975, 1980, and 1985. Moreover, the inflation-rate-differential adjusted method of approximating real exchange rates confirms that a period of NER undervaluation probably started in 1970, following a 60% devaluation of the peso that came on the heels of the 1969 reelection of Ferdinand Marcos.[4] The trend of persistent undervaluation of the peso was emboldened with the advent of the stabilization and structural adjustment programs that came rather early in the Philippines.[5]

The sequence of discrete devaluations reflected in the NER in Table 10.1 shows a break in 1985. The NER went from an average 10.4 pesos in 1980–1984 to 20.5 pesos in 1985–1989 and 24.3 pesos in 1990. This break coincides with the adoption of a trade liberalization regime and the lifting of restrictions on foreign exchange transactions (Table 10.3). The era of propping up the exchange rate by command and by quantitative restrictions had closed and the period of the full operation of the asset-value dynamics mechanism that can lead to spiral devaluations had started. The evolution of the exchange rate in the Philippines after 1985 illustrates the mechanics of supporting the exchange

4 For a different reading on the NER, judged against the "free trade equilibrium rate," see Intal and Power (1991), who consider the peso undervalued only in the period 1970–1974.
5 Stabilization started as early as 1972 with the conditionalities imposed by IMF for standby arrangements in support of the balance of payments. The programs of structural adjustment started formally in 1982.

rate in the present international environment (Krugman, Alm, Collins, and Remolona, 1992, p. 40).

In a free-market regime with an open foreign account, the options that a government has for stabilizing the NER dwindle to only two: selling (or buying) foreign exchange reserves, and monetary policy. Countries with high debt burden have normally low foreign exchange reserves and high foreign exchange liabilities for servicing the debt and for forward cover of necessary imports such as oil. This leaves the lever of monetary policy which drives interest rates up. The resulting contraction operates on the side of aggregate demand, thus alleviating the pressure on the NER. High interest rates also have a direct effect on the quantity of foreign reserves as long as the interest rate differential makes the sale of debt instruments by the Central Bank attractive to holders of foreign exchange. Private investors then buy peso debt, which "flushes out dollars" for the Central Bank, without even increasing the price of the foreign exchange. The "premium," instead, is paid in terms of higher interest rates – high enough to compensate for the risk of future depreciation of the peso – and of the ensuing contraction in the economy.[6]

Figure 10.1 plots the short-term interest rate for the Philippines and the U.S. (Treasury Bills) for the period since 1980. Disregarding the period of political instability, 1983–1985, there is no visible trend in the deviation of the two rates until 1986, when a systematic divergence started and lasted until 1990. The figure has to be interpreted against the backdrop of the information in Tables 10.3 and 10.4 about exchange rate policies. In a trade liberalization regime, with free currency markets and no restrictions on holding foreign exchange, local peso asset holders are inclined to hedge their currency risk by shifting into dollars. This is the corollary of the asymmetric reputation between the hard currency (dollar) and the soft (peso). This precautionary demand for dollars tends to increase the peso price of foreign exchange – to depreciate the local currency. In such circumstances the choice for the government is either to allow devaluation to occur or to engage in monetary policy that attracts short-term foreign capital. The tight monetary policy that started in the 1986–1990 period (Table 10.3) and the increase in interest rates shown in the systematic divergence in the Philippine and U.S. short-term rates in Figure 10.1 are driven by the attempt of the Central Bank to support the peso. Short-term capital inflow allows the bank to sell dollar-denominated assets to peso asset holders while the NER remains stable and the inflationary effects of devaluation are avoided. In the process, the increase in external debt (Table 10.1) and the mounting short-term foreign currency obligations of the Central Bank reinforce the expectation that devaluation will eventually become inevitable. Short-term speculative capital can depart, and the hot-money inflow can exit as abruptly as it was

6 For a more detailed discussion of these issues see Chapter 11.

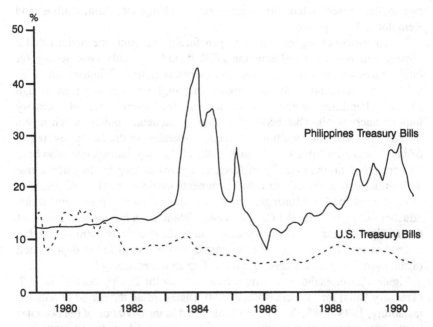

Figure 10.1. *Treasury Bills rates, Philippines and U.S., 1980–1990 (percent)*

Source: World Bank (1992b), p. 16.

attracted, thus making the expectation of devaluation a self-fulfilling prophecy. Foreign equity capital, on the other hand, and direct foreign investment are not foot-loose. They are adversely affected by devaluation and they are hesitant to come in when foreign exchange risk lurks. In the meantime, the goverment has paid in foreign-currency-denominated obligations to buy time and an expensive instrument for exercising monetary policy to control the NER. The inevitable devaluation acts to increase the peso value of external debt obligations and affects the fiscal deficit in particular. Since 1990, on the other hand, efforts to support the peso have waned, its depreciation has accelerated, and the pressure on interest rates has been released.

The increasing divergence between Philippine and world short-term interest rates implies nothing directly about the relative prices of tradables and the RER. It underscores, however, the familiar paradox. In a world of free markets and capital flows, a net inflow of capital is predicated on stable NER and competitive RER. But the soft currency tends to devalue in free currency markets and, for lack of a broad menu of government interventions (rationing of foreign exchange and controlling imports, among others) achieving a stable NER becomes an expensive proposition. As a result, less exchange rate stability is likely to be achieved. The implication is that the exchange rate is more unstable, and the peso more undervalued, than the case would have been without free currency markets and with selective controls on capital movements. High NER can lead to high RER, which is not tantamount to a competitive RER. It can lead, instead, to misallocation of resources (toward tradables) and to competitive-devaluation trade.

Intervention policies for (or despite) undervaluation

The canonical argument goes that equilibrium exchange rates, let alone undervalued NER, dispense with the need for intervention for balance of payments reasons or for growth-promoting reasons.[7] The Philippines by the 1960s had largely reversed the protection regime that was set up during the primary import substitution period, had liberalized to a significant degree, and had embarked on an export-led growth strategy. The study of interventions during the period that followed will illustrate the perils of undervaluation and premature liberalization, and the opportunities that such an economic regime can offer to self-serving elites in a setting like the Philippines of the Marcos period.

Interventions for export-led industrialization

In most LDCs, and specifically in the Philippines, labor is the most abundant natural resource. The strategies of development and industrialization have to rely on labor. The most common approach to surplus labor is to enlist it as a cheap factor in the process of production in order to produce savings to finance industrialization (Lewis, 1954). The experience of Japan, as detailed in the previous chapter, illustrated an alternative strategy of prematurely exhausting the unlimited supplies of labor and then turning effective domestic demand, spurred by increasing labor incomes, into the engine for industrialization and growth. This is an almost Keynesian policy, plausibly originating with Henry Ford, who believed that it is smart to pay employees enough to enable them to buy the products they produce.

Export-led industrialization is focused on the former approach of cheap labor. The undervalued exchange rate that complements this strategy puts the spotlight on vigorous growth in tradables, in the form of exports and import substitutes, and on the inflows of foreign capital and foreign investment as enabling factors for industrialization.

The Philippines is today one of the overindebted countries, with a ratio of

---

7 The equilibrium exchange rate is defined in this context as the one that would have obtained if a country abandoned tariffs and quantitative restrictions while incurring a sustainable current account deficit – that is, a deficit small enough to be financed through foreign aid and long-term capital inflows. See Krueger, Schiff, and Valdés (1991).

foreign borrowing to GNP of 70% (1990). External indebtedness rose steadily over a period of 20 years as a means of covering current account deficits. The 1970s saw the largest increases as a result of incremental requirements of foreign lending for financing imports during the period of the oil shock and for covering gaping public sector deficits. Whether the origins of the debt were endogenous (imprudent fiscal policy) or exogenous (the world economic conjuncture) the conclusion is that Philippine economic development did not run against the foreign exchange constraint until the mid-1980s (Vos and Yap, 1994).

Since 1970, the record of the Philippines on foreign capital inflows has been jagged and its record on direct foreign investment has been irregular. The low share of investment in capital inflow (less than 20%) lasted until the late 1970s and was due to a combination of inconsistent government policies, the power of local monopolies, and the political risk. The net inflow of capital, on the other hand, was substantial in the period 1973–1978; it was negligible or turned negative from 1979–1984; and it has been positive and sizeable since 1985 (Lamberte et al., 1992, Chapter 3). The capital inflow in the 1970s was attracted by the commodity boom and it was fueled by migrant workers' remittances from the booming economies of the Middle East. The period of capital outflow also had a national-origin stamp. Capital flight in the period 1971–1988 is estimated at U.S. $13 billion, nearly one-half the outstanding foreign debt (Lamberte et al., 1992, Chapter 5; Vos and Yap 1994, Chapter 3). It is ironic that the same national-origin stamp marks the more recent period of net capital inflow that started in 1985. The "Aquino revolution" aroused admiration about the Philippines and contributed to the positive capital inflow trend; so did the liberalization of Taiwanese and Japanese regulations on investment abroad. But the most important factor was perhaps the operation of the debt conversion schemes that started during the period. While it is difficult to judge the "additionality" of debt conversions, it is telling that Philippinos accounted for 47.2% of the transactions. "In this regard, debt conversion schemes were simply a more profitable mechanism to revert capital flight back into the country which, given the conditions at that time (high real interest rates, expectations of stable exchange rates, prospects for economic recovery), would have occurred anyway" (Lamberte et al., 1992, p. 103). In this sense, capital flight and external capital inflows can be seen as a "revolving door" wherein external debt is mainly used to finance private accumulation of assets (Boyce and Zarsky, 1988).

The industrial development of the Philippines was designed to capitalize on foreign investment attracted by the availability of cheap labor. The massive inflow of loans in the 1970s was at least partly used to that effect, although in a misguided fashion that the country came to regret. Lamberte et al. (1992, pp. 310–311), in describing the investment strategy of the second half of the 1970s, remark:

Multilateral agencies gave the go signal to the Marcos government to pursue an ambitious infrastructural investment program that will support a manufactured export strategy and, following the first oil price shock, to develop domestic energy sources which will reduce dependence on oil imports. Promoting foreign investments included tourist activities such as the Philippine hosting of the Miss Universe Beauty Pageant in 1974 and the IMF-World Bank Conference in 1976. These international promotion activities also led to a massive use of (external finance) resources for the construction of four-star and five-star hotels, convention centers, cultural centers, and the like. The injections into construction and infrastructure coincided with and, to some extent, led to a "crowding in" of private investment, that was further stimulated by overall income growth and the lifting of financial constraints with the influx of foreign loans. As more foreign investors were attracted, direct foreign investment inflows increased significantly from 1975 to 1977. Much of these investments were channeled to the production of garments and semi-conductors, spurring strong growth in the non-traditional export sector.

The dilemma lies precisely in explaining how the infrastructural investment and export diversification in favor of nontraditional commodities, which is reminiscent of the pattern of structural transformation of the other successfully industrialized Southeast Asian countries, failed to produce self-sustained growth in the Philippines.

Table 10.5 shows that until the late 1970s the country relied mostly on primary commodity exports. "Other" exports became significant for the first time in 1980 with the dramatic transformation of the industrial structure in favor of nontraditional exports, mostly garments and electronic components. Nevertheless, the growth of exports since 1980 has been rather sluggish and erratic.

On the import side, Table 10.5 shows a high share of producer goods in total imports for the entire period. Even prior to the country's diversification into manufacturing exports, imports of semiprocessed raw materials accounted for one-half of the total import bill. Table 10.6 complements the picture of a very narrow export base that consisted of export processing of imported materials by low-wage Philippino labor. Imports of unprocessed and semiprocessed raw materials included a wide array of machinery and component parts for the light export industry, but also cartons for banana exports and cans for exporting processed foods. High effective rates of protection on importables (Lamberte et al., 1992, Table 3.12) tended to offset the effect of exchange rate under-valuation that makes imported materials expensive. Protection also thwarted domestic sourcing for the nontraditional export sector. Thus the high share of imports in total supply of manufactures was also increasing for most industries throughout the period. It remained so at the end of the period – Philippine manufacturing contributed a thin slice of value added to imported components and reexported them (Krugman et al., 1992, p. 11; Broad, 1988, pp. 190 ff).

Table 10.5. *Structure of imports and exports for the Philippines, 1950–1983 (percentage)*

	1955	1960	1965	1970	1974	1975	1980	1983
Exports								
Coconut products	36	33	34	19	22	20	14	14
Sugar and products	27	25	19	17	28	27	11	6
Forest products	11	18	25	26	12	11	8	7
Mineral products	7	7	9	20	19	15	18	9
Fruits and vegetables	1	5	2	3	3	5	6	4
Abaca and tobacco	8	9	5	3	3	3	2	2
Other[a]	10	4	7	12	12	19	44	56
Total	100	100	100	100	100	100	100	100
Imports								
Producer goods								
Machinery and equipment	11[b]	25	19	19	15	20	16	11
Unprocessed raw materials	5[b]	10	14	15	24	26	29	27
Semiprocessed raw materials	52[b]	42	44	55	47	43	43	50
Supplies	15[b]	10	5	5	6	4	8	7
Subtotal	83[b]	86	82	94	92	93	96	95
Consumer goods	17[b]	14	18	6	8	7	4	5
Total	100	100	100	100	100	100	100	100

Source: Shepherd and Alburo (1991), p. 152; by permission of the publisher, the World Bank.
Notes:
[a]Mainly manufactures.
[b]For 1957.

Table 10.6. *Shares of imports in total supply of manufactures for the Philippines, 1980–1983 (percentage)*

Industry	1980	1981	1982	1983
Food manufactures	15.6	15.8	16.8	16.0
Beverages and tobacco	6.5	6.9	8.5	10.3
Petroleum and coal products	63.9	64.2	60.9	62.6
Chemicals and chemical products	48.4	50.1	50.8	54.8
Paper and paper products	35.2	32.4	38.3	37.6
Textile manufactures	19.0	19.3	19.4	26.6
Nonmetallic mineral products	24.8	15.6	14.5	12.6
Metal products	47.6	48.2	50.6	50.5
Machinery except electrical	84.0	81.3	81.2	82.0
Electrical machinery	57.6	55.2	52.3	52.3
Transport equipment	72.3	61.0	57.7	65.6
Miscellaneous manufactures	63.7	59.7	55.6	57.3

Source: Shepherd and Alburo (1991), p. 253.
Note:
Imports at c.i.f. values (in pesos) are divided by the nominal exchange rate.

Under these circumstances, Philippine manufacturing remained an enclave sector with few linkages to the rest of the economy.

Interventions for export-led agricultural growth

Agriculture has been the lagging sector in Philippine economic development; its growth has been at best modest. Agricultural output (gross value added) grew at the rate of 3–4% in 1953–1973 (as opposed to 5.6% in Taiwan). It grew by 4.2%, 5.3%, 1.8%, and 0.8% in the periods between 1970, 1975, 1980, 1985, and 1990. The growth of subsistence agriculture (mostly palay and corn) lagged a little behind the growth of agricultural production, while the growth of export crops (sugar, coconut, pineapple, bananas, and timber) was erratic. Export crops increased by 13.6% and 7.8%, respectively, in 1971–1975 and 1976–1980, and declined by 12.7% in 1981–1985. Agricultural employment remained stagnant at 6.4 million between 1963 and 1971, and changed little thereafter. Even more significant was the inability of agriculture to meet the country's growing food needs: in 1960 the Philippines imported U.S. $2 million worth of rice, the staple commodity for the population; in 1972 it imported $34 million.

There is a bimodal distribution in the Philippine agriculture. It relates to farm size: about 85% of the total of about 3.5 million crop and livestock farms were less than 5 hectares in size and accounted for 50% of the total farm area (1980). The remaining 15% accounted for 50% of the total cultivated area. The bimodal distribution extends to ownership also. Only about 60% of all farms and farm area are owned by the farmers. Bimodality also covers technology and productivity. Rice and corn farms that produce the staple commodities are the most numerous. It is usually large estates that produce the cash crops for export: sugar and copra (coconut), the primary traditional export crops, and bananas, pineapples, mangos, and timber, the nontraditional recent export entries. This bimodalism overlaps to a large extent with the distribution of technology and yields. The smallholder sector is engaged in food production, and it is characterized by backward technology and low productivity. The cash crops that are part of the strategy of the export-led growth are grown in the estate mode of production, or by "contract smallholder growers" (mainly for bananas). They are often run by international conglomerates with high capital intensity and high productivity per unit of labor.

Rice and white corn are staple commodities in the Philippines, with the latter consumed directly by 10% of the population. Moreover, with the increase in the size of the middle classes and the graduation of significant population groups to "chicken twice a week" (Yotopoulos, 1985), yellow corn, used previously only for animal feed, became a staple subsistence commodity also.[8] All three com-

8 The use of corn and wheat for animal feed grew at 10% per year between 1980 and 1989. The feed-use of these commodities that represented 59% of their total production in 1980 grew to 65% by 1989.

modities – rice, white corn, and yellow corn – were tradable importable commodities, since growth in food production did not meet the demands of population growth and of improvement in diets. Few LDCs can afford the foreign exchange requirements for sizeable imports of the subsistence commodity of the majority of the population; and even fewer can risk the food entitlement of large segments of the population that can result from the combination of nominal exchange rate instability with the instability in world food prices for grain products. It is not surprising, therefore, that some intervention was targeted at stabilizing prices of rice and corn, relative to the border prices (Intal and Power, 1991, pp. 154, 173). It took various forms. The occasion for intervention in 1971–1973 was a 17% drop in rice production (which paralleled generally smaller declines in other countries during the period of the "world food crisis") and a sharp rise in the world prices of rice and corn. The government attempted to obtain a balance between producer and consumer interests. Thus it instituted price controls and rationing, in addressing the consumer demand side, and it planned for self-sufficiency in rice, on the supply side, by providing incentives for producers to adopt high-yielding varieties in the form of packages of credit and modern inputs (fertilizers, pesticides, and herbicides) along with extension services (Masagana-99 Program). By the late 1970s the program had met with some success and the Philippines became a marginal exporter of rice for the first time in a century. Pragmatic intervention in this case averted the dire problems that dogmatic liberalization could have foisted upon the country.

The reasons for intervention in the case of sugar and copra were less compelling. Both are tradables and exportables for which undervaluation was equivalent to a price subsidy, but without the imposition of a symmetric tax on the input side, since both products have minimum inputs from imported raw materials or intermediate products. The actual subsidy for sugar was even more substantial.

The world price of sugar was for a period effectively set by the international sugar agreement. For the Philippines, however, the export price of sugar was the one granted by the U.S. quota; it was higher than the world price in the period 1960–1986. There was, therefore, a premium to be captured in the form of the U.S. quota. That could have profited the producers if they were assigned pro-rata quota allocations; it could have materialized in higher government revenues if quota allocations were sold or auctioned off; it could have even benefitted the local consumers at present or overall economic development for the future, depending on the use made of the proceeds. Instead, rent-seeking took its toll. A commission (marketing board) was set up as the monopsonist buyer of Philippine sugar; it also had powers to restrict production by seizing the sugar mills that were "inefficient" or that did not honor their contractual obligations. The presidential crony who was assigned to head the commission and by extension was assigned the exclusive rights on the economic rents of sugar exports was rich even before martial law, owning vast sugar estates in Negros. For a time, he headed the Philippine National Bank, through which large sugar transactions were financed, and subsequently he also controlled two private banks, of which one was specifically set up for the sugar industry (Poole and Vanzi, 1984, pp. 254-255).

When the U.S. sugar quota expired in 1986 and the premium over the world sugar price disappeared, economic rents were captured by using the exclusive franchise to pay Philippine sugar producers a fixed price that was below the world price. Producers were normally paid one-fourth of the world price, even though for most of the period the world price of sugar was abysmally low. Producers tried to shift the tax by squeezing cane-workers' wages, which led to a measurable increase in poverty, especially on the main sugar-producing island of Negros.

Cronyism is also importantly related with intervention in coconut production. Compared to sugar, coconut production is decentralized, with 20% of the farmers growing coconuts (as opposed to 1% for sugar). The government's agenda was to export the commodity processed (as copra) and implicitly, perhaps, to shake off the reputed ethnic Chinese presence in the milling of coconuts. Conveniently, two of Marcos' cronies (one the defense minister and the other the "coconut plantation king") controlled singly or jointly (through interlocking arrangements) the United Coconut Mills (UNICOM), the association of big coconut planters (COCOFED), and the government regulatory board, the Philippine Coconut Authority (PCA). In the fall of 1979, a presidential decree was issued ordering all coconut processing mills to sell out or else to be affiliated with UNICOM. Moreover, an onerous levy of U.S. $10 per 100 kg of copra produced (equivalent to 20% of the export price), was imposed on millions of coconut smallholders, for the ostensible reason of promoting the vertical integration and restructuring of the industry and for paying for long-term schemes of replanting and improving the coconut varieties (Bello, 1982, p. 196). The end result of this type of intervention was to create a parastatal but legally private bureaucracy that worked outside the purview of government auditors and whose finances were totally inaccessible to public scrutiny (Intal and Power, 1991, p. 183).

Other public or private monopolies that were granted in agricultural commodities were both misplaced and rife with mismanagement. There was a public monopoly in international trade in rice and corn. This was extended in 1975 to wheat, and subsequently it was also expanded to cover domestic trade. The wheat monopoly not only generated economic rents, it appears to have also disrupted the domestic flour market considerably.[9]

9 There other are examples of rampant cronyism that set up almost farcical monopolies, for the sole purpose of private enrichment. Among them, as cited by Shepherd and Alburo (1991, p. 229), is the majority-government-owned PAGCOR, a corporation that was created to operate a

The overarching characteristic of Philippine agriculture is low productivity and low incomes. In comparison to other development success cases in Southeast Asia, the Philippines has little double cropping, few high-value crops, low labor intensity of land utilization, and a low ratio of agricultural research workers (Ranis, 1978, p. 404). These characteristics are at least in part the outcome of the land tenure system. The stagnation of incomes in the agricultural sector is further exacerbated through the lack of nonagricultural rural employment opportunities (Ranis and Stewart, 1993, pp. 80, 82). The result is that outmigration is mostly of the push-type, with workers "leaving the soil," rather than of the pull-type of Taiwan or Korea, where labor is intersectorally reallocated from low- to high-productivity occupations.

Governance

From independence in 1946 until 1972, constitutional democracy in the Philippines consisted of two main political parties that gingerly balanced the power of similar conglomerations of patrons (mostly originating from the landlord elites) and clients. The parties alternated in power and thus in opportunities of controlling the government machinery and doling out the spoils to their followers. The masses participated in the political system through traditional patron–client relationships, with occasional ethnic or ideological uprisings (the Muslims in Mindanao and the communist-led Huk rebellion in 1948) that the army could normally contain easily.

This unwritten rule of "elite constitutionalism" (Bello, 1987, p. 20) was broken by Ferdinand Marcos, who managed to get himself reelected in 1969 (an unprecedented first) in a corrupt and violent show of electoral force. Thus the regime of elite democracy became destabilized and was brought to an end by the declaration of martial law in September 1972.

The subsequent regime of "authoritarian modernization" needed to gain support for a rather comprehensive economic policy agenda as well as for Marcos' political ventures by keeping potential challengers off balance. On both counts the approach was to control the disaffection from below and to consolidate the support from the middle and upper classes. The regime of authoritarian modernization was erected on three (and one-half) pillars: the military (and the paramilitary that constituted the one-half), the President's cronies, and the technocrats (Bello, 1987).

The scope of the military was much expanded beyond its professional and

---

public monopoly in gaming and of which the government is the majority owner. In another case the government-owned Experimental Cinema of the Philippines was exempted from censorship (under executive order) for the purpose of fostering artistic creativity. This enabled it to acquire a de facto monopoly for showing pornographic movies.

counter-insurgency duties to include building political support for the regime, preventing surprises, in part running the economy, and profiting from these activities in the process. Military commanders became integral parts of the power structure, especially in the provincial administrations. They also became part of the economic order through wide-ranging appointments to head government parastatal organizations, planning agencies, and fully one-half of the Presidential Regional Offices for Development. Their efforts were well rewarded financially, on an individual and collective basis, both legally and often illicitly.

A network of local, provincial and regional kingpins who ran private armies and wielded influential patron–client relationships became an adjunct of the military elite. They were co-opted in the support of the regime with economic rewards and in some instances with paramilitary power, being designated as "Civilian Home Defense Forces."

Marcos' cronies were either the beneficiaries of parochial Illocos nepotism or else economic magnates and kingpins whose hallmark was to use state power in order to absorb their competitors and build huge empires in key economic sectors – sugar, coconut, energy, communications, construction, banking, beer, large department stores, and so on. They also shared with the military in the management of public enterprises.

Finally, the technocrats were the guardians of the economic regime of export-led industrialization. They were more cohesive than the cronies and frequently in competition with them in the attempt to decentralize the economy. They lacked a political base and they drew their strength from their professional convictions and from the tacit support of their counterparts in the international bureaucracy.

In previous chapters (Chapters 3 and 7) the components of good governance were described as competence and integrity. The cases of agricultural interventions in the previous section and the discussion of the role of the elites that immediately preceded are intended as operational discriminants for good governance.

All governments intervene. In LDCs in particular, the scope of intervention increases both because of underdeveloped market infrastructure that leads to market failure and because of systematic factors that lead to incomplete markets. It is especially important, then, to have a government graced with the competence to tell when intervention is appropriate and when it is not. It is one thing to intervene in the credit market and to regulate banking, and it is entirely another proposition to intervene in domestic or foreign trade in wheat by creating a marketing board. It is unlikely that intervention is indeed needed in the market for wheat, since private trading companies would improve both competition and efficiency. While competence in government always helps, it is less important in a regime of economic liberalization and privatization, which tends to err on the side of the market. The remarkable feature in the case of the Philippines is that competence became a limiting factor of development policy despite the underlying neoliberal economic regime.

In the early stages of development, bounteous economic rents exist to be captured, both because of intervention and because of the underdeveloped market structure. Any country that is undertaking a radical transformation runs the risk of the rise of large conglomerates, monopolies, and sundry elites that claim these economic rents. Rents can be suborned in illicit ways and thus give rise to corruption. The way integrity is used as an operational discriminant of good governance relates not to the means by which economic rents were captured but rather to the ends to which they were put. Dedicating the economic rents to solidifying the support of the middle and upper classes for the regime was bad only because it was likely to abort the process of economic development – as it did. The alternative of investing the economic rents in improving the earning power of the broad population base could have made domestic demand the engine of growth. The resulting sequence of industrialization could have augured better for self-sustained development, as will be illustrated in the next chapter.[10] In the end, it was not the disaffection of the low-income classes that aborted economic development in the Philippines and brought the downfall of the Marcos regime. It was, instead, the stagnation of the incomes of the broad population base and the lack of broadly based domestic effective demand. The outcomes of Philippine economic development are thus causally connected with the operational discriminants of good governance.

The outcomes

Low productivity

It is not surprising that a country that is labor-abundant and has a high rate of population growth has low productivity under conditions of unlimited supplies of labor. Nor is it surprising to find a significant differential between productivity in agriculture and that in manufacturing, in favor of the latter. The surprise is that productivity has not been increasing and not that the surplus labor has not been exhausted. Figure 10.2 in fact shows productivity being stagnant in the early 1980s and declining since 1983. This feature of the Philippine economy rules out the productivity avenue for underpinning growth and inducing a broadly based increase in incomes.

10 Felix (1989) approaches the same issue in analyzing the different sequences of industrialization in the Asian miracles and the Latin American debacles. He considers the impact of culture and history on consumer preference formation, and through this on the survival and modernization of the craft industry, as the operational tool for linking ex ante the process of industrialization with the success of its outcome.

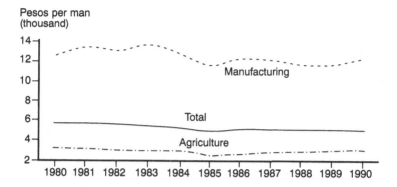

Figure 10.2. *Productivity trends for the Philippines (at 1972 prices; thousand pesos per man)*
Source: Krugman et al. (1992), p. 5; by permission of the publisher, the United Nations Development Fund.

Low labor-absorptive capacity

An alternative road to growth is reallocation of labor from low- to high-productivity sectors. This has not happened in the Philippines either. The share of manufacturing in total employment declined between 1970 and 1990 from 12.3% to 10.1%, while that of agriculture declined from 52.3% to 45.2%. Services account for the increasing balance in employment. This conclusion is also roughly correct if absolute employment figures are considered. Between 1970 and 1989 12.6 million workers were added to the labor force. Slightly less than a million found jobs in manufacturing (Krugman et al., 1992, p. 5; Ranis and Stewart, 1993, pp. 80, 82; Ranis, 1978, p. 404).

Low incomes

With no significant productivity gains across sectors, and no visible sectoral reallocation toward higher productivity industries, one would have expected constant or slightly declining wages. Figure 10.3 shows instead that real wages have systematically declined for most of the period since the mid-1950s, and plummeted in the 1970s. Conscious government effort may well have contributed to this outcome. The strategy of export-led industrialization gave priority to the type of investment that relied on cheap labor, be it in manufacturing or in services. The implementation of this economic regime led to a policy of wage restraint that was pursued through the prohibition of strikes during martial law and through the "cheap food policies" that motivated the interventions for agricultural development.

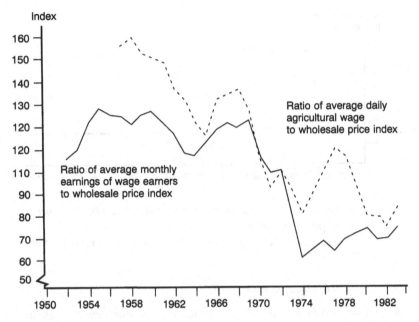

Figure 10.3. *Index of real wage costs, 1952–1983, for the Philippines (at 1972 prices; 1972 = 100)*
Source: Shepherd and Alburo (1991), p. 151.

Low incomes are the outcome of low productivity; but they also reinforce the causes that constrain productivity growth. Low incomes make for a small market. A large population with low effective demand can afford to spend little on the sophisticated manufactures that the country produces. The inappropriate sequencing of industrialization and the lack of significant demand linkages further account for the low productivity in the industrial sector, especially where economies of scale become important.[11] The emphasis thus has shifted to light manufacturing and assembly activities that rely mostly on cheap labor and do not count on technology-based decreases in costs or on learning-by-doing (and learning-by-using) increases in efficiency that create export growth while increasing labor productivity at home. An alternative sequencing of development that prioritizes agriculture and small-scale unincorporated rural and urban enterprises has been found to have strong linkage effects that could

11 Krugman et al. (1992) cite the example of the automobile industry, which consisted of five producers in 1980, manufacturing 26,000 cars. By 1988 only two had survived, with an output of 18,800 units.

have induced high income growth broadly in the economy (Vos and Yap, 1994). Domestic demand could thus have become the engine of growth and development might have been sustained.

Conclusion

The starting point of this chapter is that the Philippines has had consistently high RER in comparison with the other countries in the sample. It is most likely that it also had undervalued NER for most of the period examined. Moreover, the Philippines was an early proponent and practitioner of liberalization policies, from at least the late 1960s, in connection with the strategy of export-led industrialization that the country has unfailingly followed. Both the premises of undervalued NER and of outward-oriented strategies can be contested, especially when it comes to degree, as opposed to the direction of the policies.[12]

The outcomes of economic development in the Philippines are low productivity, low labor-absorptive capacity, and low incomes. This chapter has attempted to weave together a story of systematic policy interventions, or lack thereof, that led to these outcomes, and which, in turn, consigned the development effort to a narrowly circumscribed slow-growth path. The thesis of this chapter is not that undervaluation of NER, let alone liberalization, are solely responsible for the failure of development in the Philippines. They contributed, however, to an economic structure in which the leading sector, whether it was traditional export agriculture or nontraditional agricultural and light-manufacturing exports, was responsible for only a thin sliver of value added to total output and to GDP. Huge leakages to imports for producer goods, intermediate products, and raw materials severely limited the backward and forward inter-industry linkages of the leading sector. In terms of the typology of Chapter 2 (Figure 2.3) the leading sector in the Philippines fits closely the stylized case of sectoral disarticulation.

Low productivity, low labor-absorptive capacity, and low incomes severely limited domestic effective demand. The economic rents that were created by incomplete markets and by inappropriate government interventions were captured by individuals who had high propensity to import (including capital flight) and little effective demand for the domestic output. The domestic demand emanating from low incomes could not be ratcheted up to the prevailing sequence of industrialization. The broad domestic demand patterns, as a result,

12 For a good account of the liberalization episodes in the Philippines see Shepherd and Alburo (1991). Although a large number of liberalization policies are documented, both at the micro and the macro level, the general conclusion is that the practice did not measure up to the purity of the model. The quantitative index of liberalization that the authors developed, on a scale from zero (least) to 20 (most liberalized) have the Philippines going from 5 in 1960 to 14 in 1968, and thereafter hovering around 10 to 12 until 1983.

were not concordant with the structure of the output produced by the leading
sectors: processing of nontraditional agricultural commodities, processing apparel on a subcontracting basis (where cloth was imported and clothing exported), assembling electronic components, and manufacturing wood or rattan
furniture. As a result only a small proportion of domestic value added was spent
on buying domestic goods. Again in terms of Chapter 2 (Figure 2.3) the case
fits closely the stylized characteristics of social disarticulation.

Growth in the Philippines has not been domestic-demand driven, and it has
not been self-sustained. The growth episodes that were observed were due to
one-shot exogenous factors: the impact of the Green Revolution in rice cultivation in the early 1970s; the massive capital expenditures that led to the accumulation of the current debt burden in the late 1970s; the idle capacity that had
been built in industry during the severe contraction and led to the growth in the
late 1980s (Krugman et al., 1992, p. 20; Vos and Yap, 1994). The conclusion
can be stated even more boldly. Economies like the Philippines that have
severely constrained domestic effective demand also have a low potential
growth path. This is especially troublesome for the Philippines, which des-
perately needs vigorous self-sustained growth in order to ease the burden of
servicing its external debt, let alone to alleviate poverty.

Competence and integrity have become the two operational discriminants of
good governance in the Philippines. Incompetent interventions, as illustrated by
the case of the agricultural sector, precluded broadly based increases in productivity and incomes in the farm sector and in small-scale enterprises. The
lack of integrity in governance is evidenced by the utilization of economic rents
for the increase in earning opportunities and incomes for the upper middle
classes and the elites. The dysfunctional relationship between domestic effective demand and the sequence of industrialization was the cardinal failing of the
Philippine strategy of development. Failure in development can occur because
of the wrong economic policies or because of the wrong government. The
Philippines has failed on both scores: failure in economic policies and failure
in good governance.

CHAPTER 11

Financial integration and the refractory role of intervention: Uruguay and Taiwan

Uruguay is an anomaly for the maintained hypothesis of this book. In 1975 and 1980, the two years for which micro-ICP data are available, Uruguay ranked close to the bottom of the LDC distribution of the RER index (Table 6.1). The expectation of the rate of growth in real GDP per capita that one might have associated with the apparent severe overvaluation of the peso has never been matched by meritorious development performance. Uruguay has certainly not helped the goodness of fit of the endogenous growth regressions (Chapter 7). This is what makes it a good candidate for demonstrating that overvaluation may be a necessary but certainly not a sufficient condition for success in development. The refractory characteristics of good governance have an important role to play in generating development policy outcomes. The ex-post operational definition of good governance is pluralistic economic development. There is general agreement that Uruguay has failed this test (Table 11.1). But defining good governance teleologically, in terms of achieving egalitarian development outcomes, is circular. The crucial question arises: To what extent can one predict ex ante that specific types of intervention are likely not to lead to pluralistic economic development? This is a more difficult task. The issue can best be explored by comparing two sets of interventions and using the good governance case as a control to judge the deviations of the alternative. The control case for this discussion is Taiwan.

The comparison of Uruguay and Taiwan may strike one as unfelicitous. The analytical difficulty arises because the micro-ICP data that are scant for Uruguay are totally nonexistent for Taiwan.[1] There is consensus, however, that the NT dollar has been consistently overvalued (see below). Besides that, the two countries were roughly comparable in the 1960s – from the point of view of population, of per-capita income, of resource base, and of the importance of agriculture – with the edge going definitely to Uruguay, which had per-capita GNP in 1962 of $550 as compared to Taiwan's $170. By 1991 the economic structure of the two countries had substantially diverged as Uruguay grew in the

1 The author has in fact produced micro-ICP data for Taiwan for 1985 that were collected locally and processed according to the ICP methodology and guidelines (Yotopoulos and Lin, 1993). The computed RER index for 1985 is 1.29. But these data are not strictly comparable with the public micro-ICP information, since the link country is Japan, and they are expressed in terms of NT dollars per Japanese yen, instead of per international dollar.

249

Table 11.1. *Household income distribution for Uruguay, 1961–1962 and 1984*

Percentage of households	1961–1962		1984	
	Percentage of income	Cumulative	Percentage of income	Cumulative
10	2.5	2.5	2.2	2.2
20	4.0	6.5	3.5	5.7
30	5.0	11.5	4.4	10.1
40	5.6	17.1	5.5	15.6
50	7.0	24.1	6.7	22.3
60	8.3	32.4	8.3	30.6
70	9.9	42.3	10.1	40.7
80	11.8	54.1	12.9	53.6
90	15.2	69.3	17.3	70.9
95	10.0	79.3	11.7	82.6
100	20.7	100.0	17.4	100.0
Gini Index	0.3661		0.4837	

Source: Adapted from Favaro and Bensión (1993), p. 198; by permission of the publisher, Oxford University Press.
Note:
All results were obtained using the methodology of Kakwani (1980).

interim at an average rate of 1% per year in comparison to Taiwan's annual per-capita growth of 7% (Tables 11.2 and 11.3). The real per-capita income of Taiwan in 1991 was somewhere close to that of Spain and double the real per-capita income of Uruguay (Yotopoulos and Lin, 1993; World Bank, 1993c).

The juxtaposition of the two cases is illuminating. In comparing the real sectors of the two countries insights can be drawn about the need for governing the market at early stages of development and about the orderly sequence of liberalization. The contrast between the two countries becomes especially stark in comparing the ultimate step in the process of liberalization – financial integration.

Agriculture

In both Taiwan and Uruguay, agriculture was the foundation of development whereas trade became the engine of growth. The development paths of the two countries diverged as Uruguay's agricultural foundation proved weak to support a broadly based increase in incomes. Despite some vigorous intersectoral linkages agriculture ultimately offered only limited possibilities for the diver-

Table 11.2. *Rate of growth of GNP and financial statistics for Uruguay, 1945–1992*

Averages	Growth rate of real GNP (percent)	Inflation rate (percent)	Interest rate (percent per annum)	Exchange rate (pesos per US $)
1945–1950	5.4	8.00		
1951–1955	4.2	8.00		
1956–1959	−0.9	19.60		
1960–1961	3.2	30.40		
1962–1968	0.3	55.70		
1969–1970	5.4	18.60		
1971–1973	−0.6	62.60		
1974–1978	4.1	40.80		
1979–1981	4.7	46.20		
1982–1985	−4.3	46.80		
1985	1.5	100.00		68
1986	8.9	76.00	166.18	181
1987	7.9	64.20	55.25	281
1988	0.4	61.94	60.50	451
1989	1.3	80.34	78.49	805
1990	0.9	102.01	98.01	1,594
1991	2.9	102.01	56.15	2,489
1992	7.4	68.46	39.82	3,480

Source: Favaro and Bensiôn (1993), p. 190; World Bank (1993d), Table A1.3; International Monetary Fund, *International Financial Statistics, Annual 1993*, and various years.
Note:
The annual GNP growth rates for 1985–1992 are at market prices.

sification of the industrial production base. Eventually, the trade-driven engine of growth became stalled. The opposite happened in Taiwan, where the early leading sector (agriculture) emitted strong interindustry and final-demand linkages to nurture subsidiary sectors into an economic key-sector relay wherein growth leadership was efficiently geared to the dynamic characteristics of domestic and export demand.

Taiwanese agriculture: The foundation of pluralistic development[2]

The legacy of agricultural development in Taiwan has deep roots in its colonial past under Japanese occupation (Christensen, 1968; Ho, 1968; Lee, 1971; Thorbecke, 1979, 1992). Taiwan was occupied in late 19th century to serve as

2 This section draws on Yotopoulos and Fafchamps (1994); by permission of the publisher, Organization for Economic Cooperation and Development.

Table 11.3. *Rate of growth of GNP and financial statistics for Taiwan, 1953–1992*

Averages	Growth rate of real GNP (percent)	Inflation rate (percent)	Growth in money supply (percent)	Interest rate (percent per annum)[a]	Exchange rate (NT $ per US $)
1953–1956	7.7				
1957–1963	7.5				
1964–1968	10.0				
1969–1974	10.2				
1975–1979	10.1				
1980–1989	8.0				
1970	11.4	3.6		9.25	40.00
1971	12.9	2.8	27.20	8.50	40.00
1972	13.3	3.0	33.50	10.75	40.00
1973	12.8	8.2	45.40	12.00	37.90
1974	1.2	47.5	11.80	10.75	37.95
1975	4.9	5.2	24.70	9.50	37.95
1976	13.9	2.5	21.90	8.25	37.95
1977	10.2	7.0	34.40	8.25	37.95
1978	13.6	5.8	35.30	11.00	35.95
1979	8.2	9.7	10.20	11.00	35.98
1980	7.3	19.0	19.10	11.75	35.96
1981	6.2	16.3	13.80	7.75	37.79
1982	3.6	3.0	14.60	7.25	39.86
1983	8.4	1.4	18.40	6.75	40.22
1984	10.6	0.0	9.30	5.25	39.42
1985	5.0	-0.2	12.20	4.50	39.80
1986	11.6	0.7	51.40	4.50	35.45
1987	12.3	0.5	37.80	4.50	28.50
1988	7.3	1.3	24.40	7.75	28.12
1989	7.4	4.4	6.10	7.75	26.12
1990			-6.60	6.45	
1991			12.10		

Source: The Central Bank of China, *Financial Statistics*, Monthly and Annual issues; Council for Economic Planning and Development, Republic of China, *Taiwan Statistical Data Book 1990*.
Note:
[a] Interest rate is the rediscount rate of the Central Bank of China.

Japan's rice granary. The Japanese colonial government put into effect an energetic development program that tried to export Japan's own experience of "agricultural revolution from above."

The Japanese administration undertook a major cadastral survey and land reform similar to the Meiji reform in Japan during the 1870s. Land rights were removed from a class of absentee landlords and transferred to local landlords who had been managing the lands – who then became supporters of the Japanese regime. A good communications infrastructure was laid down, designed not with the narrow purpose of extracting some primary raw material but with the aim of increasing production of smallholder rice and sugar, both wanted in Japan. Under these policies, expansion of irrigation and drainage, dissemination of improved or better seeds, and spread in the use of fertilizers and manures were all energetically attempted, sometimes even with the aid of the police force (Wade, 1990, p. 73).

Ishikawa (1967), in his study of the colonial period, found a continuously rising trend in Taiwanese agricultural production stretching to the outbreak of World War II. Until 1923, agricultural output was increased by bringing traditional factors into production: more land was brought into cultivation and more working days per year went to agriculture. Technology remained traditional and fertilizers farm-produced. As a result, total production increased by 2.7% per year between 1913 and 1923. During the period 1923–1937, total agricultural production increased even faster – by 4.0% per year – as a result of the introduction of new technology based on modern inputs: a new rice variety (ponlai), chemical fertilizers, and irrigation.[3] Output growth was interrupted after 1937, at which time Taiwanese agriculture suffered the consequences of the depression and the war.

The pivotal position of agriculture in Taiwan was restored after the war. In the first years of Taiwanese economic development (until the mid-1960s) agriculture provided the foundation for pluralistic, self-sustained growth in the economy. Growth of agricultural output was extremely high during the rehabilitation period 1947–1953. By early 1950, the sector had gotten back to its prewar output levels. The quick recovery was essentially achieved by restoring full-capacity utilization of agricultural resources. However, during that same period, a number of important institutional reforms also established the basis for continuing agricultural growth during subsequent periods (Mao and Schive, 1991).

First of all, land reform was gradually introduced in three distinct stages over the period 1949–1953 (Klein, 1958). In 1949, farm rents were capped at 37.5% of the annual yield of the major crop. This step substantially improved the lot of tenants, who at that time still constituted the majority of the rural population. The second initiative consisted of selling to farm families small lots of public lands that had been acquired from Japanese nationals after the war. In all 20% of the farm families benefitted from this measure, which extended to 8% of the total cultivated area. Finally, and most importantly, the Land-to-the-Tiller

---

3 The proportion of total cultivated area using ponlai rice increased from 5% in 1924 to 21% in 1930 and 50% in 1940. The consumption of fertilizers (chemical and vegetable, in the form of soybean oil cakes) approximately tripled during the period. Land under irrigation grew from 311,000 hectares in 1921 to 532,000 hectares in 1938 (62% of the total). See Thorbecke (1979).

program was instituted in 1953. It expropriated all lands exceeding 2.9 hectares from landlords, in return for two types of commodity bonds (linked to the prices of rice and sweet potatoes, respectively) that yielded 4% in interest and matured in 10 years, and shares of stock in four government enterprises. The reformed land amounted to 16.4% of the total cultivated area, and was distributed in small plots to 195,000 landless tiller households, i.e., 28% of the total farm families. This bold measure not only set the stage for the famed "unimodal" agricultural development of Taiwan, but if one compares the situation of tenants with and without land reform and rent reduction, it also increased directly the income of the average tenant by as much as six times between 1948 and 1959 (Thorbecke, 1979, p. 176). The land reform initiatives fueled a broadly spread domestic demand, thus laying early on the foundation for pluralistic economic development (Lee, 1974; Yotopoulos and Nugent, 1976, p. 279; Mao and Schive, 1991).

Second, the Chinese–American Joint Commission of Rural Reconstruction (JCRR), established in 1948, was more than a ministerial-type bureaucratic institution responsible for planning Taiwan's agricultural development. It developed strong presence in the field and served as the nerves and sinews that would connect, through intermediary institutions, the country's leadership with the farm population. The Farmer's Associations, inherited from the colonial period, evolved into a crucial link in this network. They were well led and enlisted broad-based support in transmitting to the center the signals needed for agricultural planning, while delivering to the countryside modern inputs, credit, and marketing facilities. The coordination between JCRR and farmer's associations gave a new impetus to crop and livestock improvement, water resource development, soil conservation, agricultural organization and extension, agricultural financing, rural health improvement, and agricultural research (Thorbecke, 1979, p. 182). Moreover, the substantial U.S. foreign aid, initiated in 1951, was directed preponderantly towards agriculture and channeled through JCRR along with technical assistance.

A "hidden tax" on agriculture served to create a massive investment fund for industrialization. The specific instruments of taxation were the setting of the government procurement price of rice at below its market price at the farm, and the rice-fertilizer barter program. The government had control and supervision of the distribution and marketing of rice but had no monopoly in it. The government was also the ultimate lender to the farm sector that had to make tax payments, land-rent payments, and loan repayments. All payments were due in kind (in rice), which was evaluated at the government procurement price. This was set anywhere from one-half to three-quarters of the farm-gate price of rice. Purchases of fertilizers were even more effective in yielding tax revenues, since chemical fertilizers were a government monopoly. The rice-fertilizer barter program established the internal terms of trade of various types of fertilizer for the rice paddy. The barter ratios were set at levels that initially made chemical fertilizers quite expensive in terms of rice but declined subsequently until they were abolished in 1972. From 1952 to 1963 the fiscal revenue from the hidden tax on agriculture was estimated to exceed the revenues from all income taxes in the economy. The two components, the procurement price and the rice-fertilizer barter program, yielded equal parts to the tax (Kuo, 1983, Chapter 3).

The advantage of the hidden tax on agriculture was that it was levied on the one sector that was in a position to finance the early stages of industrialization; it was also evasion- and avoidance-proof. The government-controlled price of rice helped stabilize the price of the subsistence commodity and contributed to price stability throughout the economy. The rice-fertilizer barter program also had its advantages. It effectively rationed a scarce commodity, which was also the modern input in production, in a way that made it accessible to all farmers; it provided a source of cultivation credit that was an alternative to rural moneylenders; and it reduced the price risk to farmers. The small size of the island and the good transportation network – which are not readily replicated in all LDCs – were instrumental in the success of the barter program.

The second phase of agricultural development (1954–1965) bears the signs of a mature agriculture within a successfully growing economy. After the rehabilitation period, agricultural growth rates declined to an average 4.4% as they were based on increased intensity of cultivation and increased yields, rather than increasing the extensive margin by bringing into production un-utilized inputs. Multiple cropping was expanded and modern inputs were broadly adopted, especially chemical fertilizers.

By late 1960s, Taiwanese agriculture was approaching Lewis' "turning point" and exhausting its unlimited supplies of labor (Schive, 1987).[4] This led to the substitution of animal labor for human labor and the first phase of mechanization (adoption of power tillers) that advanced rapidly towards the end of the decade. The decentralized industrial development that penetrated the countryside broadly provided further work opportunities for farmers and led to part-time farming (and usually more than full-time employment). The famed Taiwanese equality in income distribution was the result of the labor scarcity that developed early, as much as it was the effect of supplemental nonfarm incomes for agricultural workers.

The 1960s were the golden years of Taiwanese crop agriculture. New heights were reached in production of rice and other crops, area under cultivation, index of multiple cropping, agricultural exports, and so on. Towards the end of the decade, the transformation of agriculture to meet the needs of a newly industrializing country was already taking place. Livestock production (particularly hogs) increased rapidly to reflect the shift in consumption towards

4 Lewis' turning point is placed in 1968–1970 (Fei and Ranis, 1975; Fei, Ranis, and Kuo, 1979).

improved diets. This led to a virtually total dependence on imported feed by the end of the 1980s. Rice output stagnated in the 1970s and fell in the 1980s. The output mix changed from rice to high-value-added specialty crops, such as mushrooms, vegetables, and fruits. Large investments in off-shore fishing boats during this period dramatically increased the output of that industry. Both specialty crops and fishing found their place among Taiwan's exports, replacing the more traditional commodities, and especially timber.

The policy matrix that elicited the smooth structural change in Taiwan's agriculture was in constant evolution. Policies that did not work were quickly abandoned and so were the policies that had outlived their usefulness. As agriculture yielded its key-sector function to industrial sectors, the rationale for the hidden tax on agriculture disappeared. The importance of rice as the staple food commodity for the majority of the population decreased as higher incomes led to the improvement of diets. The rice-fertilizer barter program became obsolete and was abandoned in 1972. In the meantime, specific programs supported the replacement of rice by more remunerative crops. As the unemployment problem was solved, an agricultural mechanization campaign was started in the early 1970s. Taiwan also fell into the usual agricultural success trap in that it ended up with a "farm problem": with high yields on the supply side, and with low Engel's coefficients on the demand side agriculture reaches a point when it fails to provide remunerative family incomes at par with the other sectors in the economy (see Chapter 9). In answer to this challenge, Taiwan promulgated the "second land reform" in 1981, this time designed to ease out of agriculture manpower needed elsewhere. A series of measures were adopted to promote joint cultivation and contract farming and to enlarge the family farm size through consolidation. The success of the program in the face of skyrocketing land values is still uncertain.

Uruguay: Agricultural stagnation

In Uruguay, as was also the case in neighboring Argentina, grazing cattle and raising sheep in open range was the predominant agricultural activity in the 19th century. The cattle were traditionally raised for their hides, and only later for meat and meat products; the sheep were raised for their wool and after the turn of the century for the export of mutton. By 1880 the political process was able to impose central authority over factional interests for the first time, with the result that property rights no longer depended on the ability of landlords to protect them with local *caudillos*. This led to the modernization of the livestock sector by the investment in fences. This innovation decreased the labor required directly in production and indirectly in policing and protecting the herd. It was thus responsible for creating the first reservoir of surplus labor in Uruguay. Social and demographic change followed by reducing the share of labor in agricultural output and by driving migration streams not only to Montevideo, but also to Argentina and Brazil.[5]

The modernization of the livestock sector produced both private profits and public revenues, especially after shipping of chilled and frozen meat became commercially feasible. Exports of chilled beef and frozen lamb, almost exclusively to the United Kingdom, doubled before World War I; they continued strong until World War II, with a dip in the early 1930s during the depression.

The dominance of the livestock sector, and the constraints it imposes upon transforming agriculture, is largely due to the topography of the country. Although 16.5 million hectares, 90% of the total land area of the country, is agriculturally productive, only 10% is arable. The balance consists of natural grasses, which can be improved, but due to the thin soil (and unlike the huge pampas of Argentina) cannot readily be replaced by non-native plants like alfalfa.

The size distribution of land is highly skewed. *Minifundia* account for 60% of rural enterprises and occupy less than 12% of the total agricultural area. Less than 3% of rural enterprises occupy 44% of the total area. Both tails of the land distribution are considered to be of inappropriate size. In between lie the majority of livestock farms, which range in lot sizes from 500 to 2500 hectares. This size is also associated with the absence of economies of scale (Favaro and Spiller, 1991). The livestock sector represents 25% of the roughly 200,000 rural enterprises in the country. The balance of the farms (75%) engage in crop production and share the remaining 10% of the agricultural land (Favaro and Bensión 1993). Wheat had been the major cereal crop, but its land share has been decreasing with the increase in industrial crops (linseed and sunflower), and in rice, which was introduced as an export crop in the 1970s.

The dominant form of land tenancy ranges from ownership and self-management to leasing and share tenancy. There is no legislative definition of the rights of land owners and tenants with respect to farm investments and land improvements. This deters the modernization of agriculture and the introduction of capital-intensive technology, especially in the livestock sector. The value of the unimproved land is low, which further encourages its extensive use. Land

---

5 The social instability in the livestock sector and the growth of the urban sector that resulted from the modernization of the livestock economy led to violent struggles for power in the 19th century, sometimes approaching civil war. This friction led eventually to the development of Uruguay's autochthonous form of socialism, the *batllismo* (named after President José Batlle y Ordóñez, 1903–1907, 1911–1915; he had personal influence until his death in 1929, and an ideological following through the 1950s). It represented a liberal, humanitarian, bourgeois way of defusing social frictions. The policy instruments included high taxes on land, inheritance, and absentee ownership, minimum wage legislation, colonization schemes, and so on (Finch 1981, Chapter 1). In a way, *batllismo* was Uruguay's answer to the peasant uprisings and land reforms that occurred during the same period in other Latin American countries.

value, as a result, represents about 60% of all capital in livestock production, and the stock of cattle and sheep accounts for the remainder. Dairy production is largely independent of livestock enterprises. It is carried out in smallholdings close to the urban centers. Not unlike the livestock sector, the productivity of the crop sector has also stagnated, with the possible exception of rice.

The livestock sector in Uruguay was responsible for emitting strong inter-industry linkages. Meat and wool production supplied the raw materials for a large industrial sector that included slaughterhouses, textiles, and leather manufacturing. Livestock production along with its derivative industries accounted for 30% of GDP. It also produced almost 90% of the country's exports. In terms of interindustry linkages, agriculture must have played as important a role in Uruguay as in Taiwan, where agricultural processing was the beginning of industrialization. But the situation is reversed if one considers the employment and income-generation linkages. While agriculture ranked on top in Taiwan, it must have lagged in Uruguay because of the unequal income distribution that constrained domestic demand for commodities at the high end of the food chain.

Misguided development interventions have also contributed to making the agricultural supply more inelastic. The *batllista* ideology favored progressive land taxes and inheritance taxes as a means for intensifying the use of land, either by increasing its productivity, or by forcing its subdivision. The latter is more likely in an urban environment and under heavy population pressure. A land tax is not the most appropriate instrument for land reform of range lands, especially if the industry is characterized by economies of scale. Land taxes have been used elsewhere as productivity-enhancing instruments (in Meiji Japan and Maoist China, among others). But they work best when productivity has been increasing, as opposed to being stagnant, and then they are staggered in order to provide a clear profit motive for further agricultural intensification.

The tax on exports was the other agricultural policy instrument. It was imposed initially through the system of multiple exchange rates that discriminated against certain types of exports, including meat. After a unified exchange rate was introduced in 1959, the burden on agriculture was maintained through the export retention tax that captured some part of the local currency proceeds of exports. In the case of meat and wool production, specifically, the tax was considered as a complement to the land tax. But again, in an environment of stagnant productivity, it was placed on production rather than on the ownership of land.

The structure of taxation provided a disincentive for intensive land utilization and for increasing carrying capacity. In the absence of pasture improvement or seeding, livestock grazed on natural ranges lose weight in the winter season, are more prone to disease, have lower calving ratios, and take longer to reach slaughter weight. The limitation on carrying capacity is not only on head per unit of land but also on yield per animal unit, which in Uruguay is well below that of other countries.

The regulatory environment that hampered growth in the agricultural sector was liberalized in 1978. Controls on domestic prices for agricultural commodities were abolished, beef and wool exports were liberalized, and so were imports of agricultural goods, which became subject only to a moderate tariff. Liberalization has had so far only minimal impact on the livestock sector. But in the crop sector it has intensified the process of shifting away from wheat and favoring alternative crops, especially industrial products and rice.

In summary, the notable characteristic of agricultural production in Uruguay has been its slow growth in the first part of this century and its stagnation in the last 40 years. The share of agriculture, which was 16% of GDP in the early postwar years, has declined to 11%. Nevertheless, the sector accounted for 90% of total exports in 1955, and it still accounts for two-thirds today.

Industrialization

In both countries industrialization started from modest beginnings, building on the legacy of the agricultural sector. The difference in final outcomes is partly due to the strength or weakness of the agricultural foundation and partly to the configuration of domestic demand as it relates to the sequence of industrialization.

Uruguay: The change in track and the spurts of growth

The urban orientation of the *batllista* ideology favored the industrial sector. Import-substitution industrialization was pursued with renewed determination in the 1930s for offsetting the impact of the world depression on export earnings from agriculture and as a means of employment creation. Although the rates of growth of industrial production immediately before and during the war are contested, thoughtful evaluation of the evidence (Finch, 1981, pp. 171–172) suggests that the dominant thesis on the impact of the depression and the war on Latin America also holds for Uruguay: the disruption in the relations between the center countries and the periphery provided a stimulus to industrialization (Griffin, 1969, p. 270). In any event, the postwar decade saw a remarkable growth of industrial production in Uruguay of 7.7% per year (Finch, 1981, pp. 171, 220).

The import-competing nature of industrialization was validated by strictly targeted allocations of foreign exchange and by according specific priority to imports of some consumer goods considered necessary: drugs, and raw materials, intermediate products, and machinery for agricultural and industrial production. In the composition of imports, the ratio of consumer goods was less

Table 11.4. *Composition of imports for Uruguay, selected periods, 1909–1956 (percentage)*

Period	Consumer goods	Raw materials	Capital goods	Total
1908–1910	40.7	52.4	6.9	100.0
1924–1926	29.5	60.4	10.1	100.0
1939–1940	22.6	68.1	9.3	100.0
1948–1950	16.6	61.5	21.9	100.0
1954–1956	11.1	66.2	22.7	100.0

Source: Favaro and Bensión (1993), p. 223.

than 10% and the ratio of final goods (excluding oil) less than 50% until the 1960s (Finch 1981, p. 157; Favaro and Spiller, 1991, p. 350).

The protectionist policies of the 1930s brought about a remarkable trans-formation in the structure of the economy (Favaro and Bensión, 1993, p. 220). The period 1930–1955 recorded an annual growth rate of GDP of 2.5%. Manufacturing was the growth sector, increasing by 4.9% per year, while the livestock sector grew by an annual 1.2%. As a result, by the end of the period, the agricultural sector had shrunk from 14.9% of GDP to 12.5%; while the manufacturing sector grew from 10.7% to 22%. Within manufacturing, the dynamic sectors were those oriented towards the domestic market. The share of import-substitution activities – rubber, chemicals, and oil refining – in-creased, while that of food, the export-oriented sector, declined. As a result, the share of consumer goods in total imports decreased between 1940 and 1956 from 23% to 11%, while that of capital goods increased from 9% to 23%; the balance accounted for raw materials (Table 11.4).

There was another spurt of industrial growth in the mid-1970s. In the wake of the oil shock a serious liberalization attempt took place in 1974. It freed the economy of administrative controls and lifted most restrictions imposed on foreign trade. The main objective was to change the industrial structure by promoting and diversifying nontraditional exports. The focus was on export-oriented industrial activities and the key sectors were clothing, leather, shoes, and fishing. In contrast, the sectors that had led the recovery in the previous period contracted (Favaro and Spiller, 1991). Competing imports in sectors like metallic products, electrical machinery and equipment, and transport machin-ery and equipment faced a dramatic increase. In the process, the share of final goods to total imports (excluding oil) rose from 31% in 1974 to over 50% in the 1980s (Favaro and Spiller 1991, p. 350).

Table 11.5. *Composition of exports and imports for Taiwan and their shares, selected years, 1952–1988 (percentage)*

	Exports			Imports		
	Agricultural products	Processed agricultural products	Industrial products	Capital goods	Raw materials	Consumer goods
1952	22.1	69.8	8.1	14.2	65.9	19.9
1960	12.0	55.7	32.3	27.9	64.0	8.1
1964	15.0	42.5	42.5	22.1	71.8	6.1
1970	8.6	12.8	78.6	32.3	62.8	4.9
1974	4.8	10.7	84.5	30.7	62.4	6.9
1980	3.6	5.6	90.8	23.4	70.8	5.8
1984	1.7	4.3	94.0	13.6	78.6	7.8
1989	0.7	3.9	95.4	16.4	72.1	11.5

Source: Council for Economic Planning and Development, Republic of China, *Taiwan Statistical Data Book, 1990*.

Taiwan: The train of industrialization and the locomotive of trade[6]

Agriculture was the early key sector in Taiwan and it provided the foundation for self-sustained growth. With that in place, trade became the locomotive of growth while the rolling stock was an orderly and strictly sequenced industrialization. The two tracks of the roadbed were factor endowments and the characteristics of domestic demand. The distance from LDC to middle-income country was traveled in less than 50 years. The journey of Taiwanese economic development can best be divided into three periods: 1949–1964, 1965–1974, and after 1975.

Table 11.5 chronicles Taiwan's industrialization in terms of the composition of imports and exports. The first period, 1949–1964, provided the link between the transformation of agriculture and the birth pangs of industrialization. In the 1950's the key sector was agriculture and export trade was land-based. The share of agricultural products (including timber and partly processed agricultural commodities) amounted to three-quarters of total exports. The major earners of foreign exchange were processed agricultural exports, followed by timber. The light industrialization bore the stylized features of primary (con-

6 This section draws on Yotopoulos and Fafchamps (1994).

sumer goods) import substitution that is common to many LDCs. Domestic and imported raw materials were channeled to the consumer goods industry, which consisted primarily of textiles, apparel, wood and leather products, bicycles, and other labor-intensive commodities. The bulk of imports was in capital goods (machinery and transport equipment) and in raw materials (fibers, chemical materials, and oil).

The primary import substitution period ran out of steam in the late 1950s as the domestic market became saturated. The rate of industrial growth had ebbed and export of processed agricultural products had peaked (Table 11.5). The share of consumption goods in imports decreased gradually, from 20% in the beginning of the period to 7% in early 1960s. The change in the trade patterns was related to expanding domestic production of consumer durables and of previously imported intermediate and capital goods. Certain secondary import substituting industries were set up, such as chemicals, fertilizer, rayon fibers, and so on. At the same time, and leading domestic demand, the role of the industrial sector was changing into favoring manufacturing of nondurable consumer goods for export markets (Ranis, 1979; Ranis and Mahmood, 1992). Industries like wood products, processed food, fabrics, garments, nonmetallic minerals, artificial fibers and plastic products, and miscellaneous products, were exporting from 9% to 35% of their output by the mid-1960s.

The second phase of economic development lasted from the early 1960s to the mid-1970s, and represents a distinct change in the industrial structure of Taiwan by accelerating the growth of heavy industry. The Third (1961–1964) and Fourth Plan (1965–1968) are explicit about the goals of policy makers:

> For further development, stress must be laid on basic heavy industries (such as chemical, wood pulp, petrochemical intermediates, and large-scale integrated steel production) instead of end-product manufacturing and processing. Industrial development in the long-run must be centered on export products that have high income elasticity and low transportation cost. And around these products there should be development of both forward and backward industries, so that both specialization and complementarity may be achieved in the interest of Taiwan's economy (Wade 1990, p. 87).

Besides the capital-intensive industries, skill-intensive ones were also targeted for promotion in this period by planning authorities: electrical appliances and electronics, including transistor radios, electronic components, watches, and clocks. These industries were also primarily intended to feed domestic demand, in particular the investment and intermediate input demand generated by export industries. In so doing, however, they further solidified the foundation for the next phase of Taiwanese economic development, that is, the secondary import substitution period.

While the restructuring of Taiwan's manufacturing was under way, existing industries, especially light manufacturing, dominated exports. Consumer-goods sectors that had achieved considerable weight in GDP during the previous period, such as textiles and food, came to predominate in exports as well. Other consumer-oriented industries that were trivially small in 1954 gained in importance both in GDP and in exports: household electrical appliances, household electronics, plastics, and miscellaneous products (Table 11.6).

Taiwan's third industrialization phase started in 1975 and can best be characterized as intensive secondary import substitution. It was ushered in with the progressive exhaustion of surplus labor in the previous period and the ensuing rise in real wages. As a result of the change in factor proportions, economic development shifted its focus toward relatively capital-intensive industries producing intermediate inputs for domestic use, as well as capital goods industries (e.g., machinery, transport equipment, etc.). The growth of consumer durables was also rapid (Schive, 1987).

In this period, light manufactures were replaced by machinery as the dominant export sector (Table 11.6). Furthermore, over the period, the electrical machinery industry grew faster than the less capital intensive nonelectrical machinery sector, and the electronics industry expanded both backward and forward by increasing the domestic component of its processing activities. The speed of change in this period was astounding: in 1978 electrical and electronic products made up 15.8% of exports, whereas textiles still accounted for 25.1%. By 1983, their shares were about equal at 19.3% and 19.6%, respectively. In 1984, textiles finally lost their dominant position: electronic and electrical products jumped to 21.6% of total exports, whereas textiles' share dropped to 18.6%. More recently, the sectors that have a high ratio of exports to domestic production include machinery, electronics, miscellaneous products, metals, and chemicals.

The preceding chronology describes the transformation of Taiwanese industrialization from the stage of primary import substitution, to export substitution, and on to secondary import substitution. The same chronology corresponds to the sequencing from land-based, unskilled-labor-intensive manufacturing, to skill-intensive, capital-based industries; it is roughly concordant with the sequencing from nondurables, to durables, and to intermediate goods. A ranking of industries in that order, which also matches their capital–labor ratios, correlates with the rate of growth of their respective outputs for distinct subperiods since 1954. Table 11.7 reproduces and extends Ranis' (1979, p. 235) calculations. They generally suggest that the labor-intensive industries grew faster in the early days of Taiwan's development than later on, while the opposite is true for capital-intensive industries. The patterns present in the table would probably emerge even more clearly if it were not for excessive sectoral aggregation.

Table 11.6. *Participation in imports and exports by industry classification in Taiwan, 1952–1989 (U.S. $ million and percentage)*

Period	#1 Imports	#1 Exports	#2 Imports	#2 Exports	#3 Imports	#3 Exports	#4 Imports	#4 Exports
1952	13.37	8.62	0.53	2.59	6.95	83.62	19.25	0.86
1960	15.49	9.76	7.41	2.44	3.37	58.54	12.46	14.02
1964	18.71	10.85	6.93	0.92	2.54	46.65	15.01	24.71
1970	17.65	8.67	4.53	0.14	2.03	13.49	8.60	43.68
1974	15.55	2.96	4.49	0.07	2.76	11.31	4.74	35.59
1980	12.69	2.48	23.70	0.04	2.72	6.73	3.33	31.06
1984	11.62	1.87	20.70	0.02	4.04	4.27	5.21	27.79
1989	6.08	0.95	7.96	0.04	3.76	3.62	6.52	22.27

Period	#5 Imports	#5 Exports	#6 Imports	#6 Exports	#7 Imports	#7 Exports	#8 Imports	#8 Exports
1952	5.88	0.00	25.13	3.45	6.42	0.86	3.21	0.00
1960	1.35	1.83	16.84	4.88	10.77	3.66	1.68	0.61
1964	1.15	4.39	17.32	4.16	12.01	3.23	1.15	0.92
1970	1.51	3.56	12.34	2.52	9.84	4.54	1.38	1.96
1974	0.30	1.19	5.46	1.42	13.54	2.41	1.28	2.57
1980	0.52	1.93	6.31	2.25	12.08	2.00	0.69	4.35
1984	0.68	2.32	14.59	4.08	9.28	2.42	0.72	5.71
1989	0.97	1.81	14.65	4.17	15.58	2.26	1.05	5.99

Period	#9 Imports	#9 Exports	#10 Imports	#10 Exports	#11 Imports	#11 Exports	#12 Imports	#12 Exports
1952	5.88	0.00	3.74	0.00	3.21	0.00	3.74	0.00
1960	15.15	0.00	5.39	0.61	6.40	0.00	3.37	0.61
1964	9.47	1.15	4.85	1.15	6.93	0.23	2.54	1.62
1970	13.25	3.35	11.75	10.62	10.70	0.91	3.15	7.97
1974	15.96	4.13	10.85	17.73	3.90	2.34	14.00	18.27
1980	12.14	3.76	9.79	18.17	3.72	3.25	12.31	23.98
1984	9.87	3.76	14.35	21.60	2.91	3.97	6.02	22.18
1989	10.06	5.81	16.48	27.32	7.50	4.56	9.40	21.21

Period	Total Imports	Total Exports
1952	187	116
1960	297	164
1964	433	433
1970	1,524	1,431
1974	6,966	5,639
1980	19,733	19,811
1984	21,959	30,456
1989	52,249	66,201

Industry classification

#1 Agriculture, forestry, hunting and fishery products
#2 Minerals
#3 Food, beverage and tobacco preparations
#4 Textile, leather, wood, paper, and related products
#5 Nonmetallic mineral products
#6 Chemicals and pharmaceutical products
#7 Base metals
#8 Metal products
#9 Machinery
#10 Electrical machinery and apparatus
#11 Transportation equipment
#12 Other

Source: Council for Economic Planning and Development, Republic of China, *Taiwan Statistical Data Book, 1984*, and *1990*.
Notes:
The columns under industry classification are percentages. The columns under total are U.S. dollars in millions.

Table 11.7. *Annual growth of gross product of industries for Taiwan ranked by decreasing labor intensity, 1954–1980*

Industry	Industry ranking 1954–1971[a]	1954–1961	1961–1966	1966–1971	1954–1971	1972–1980
Furniture and fixtures	35.64	13.7	13.1	17.7	14.7	—[b]
Miscellaneous manufacturing industries	42.99	0.9	23.2	18.9	11.5	15.2
Metal products	49.89	21.8	14.5	8.5	15.6	11.7
Printing, publishing, and allied industries	54.14	13.8	3.3	12.1	10.1	7.1
Machinery (except electrical)	56.26	19.4	21.1	12.4	17.8	6.7
Leather and leather products, except footwear	63.83	8.5	10.1	15.5	4.9	21.6
Rubber products	75.69	13.3	8.9	19.9	13.9	6.2
Chemical and chemical products	87.06	0.6	18.2	10.4	10.8	10.2
Electric machinery, apparatus, appliances, and supplies	94.18	16.8	37.8	31.0	26.8	14.4
Beverages	98.42	15.1	19.8	18.3	17.4	12.9
Wood and cork products, except furniture	98.68	14.1	8.0	10.4	10.5	—[b]
Textiles, footwear, and wearing apparel	105.28	1.4	14.7	22.5	11.2	—[b]
Nonmetallic mineral products	109.12	13.8	11.3	7.4	11.2	8.6
Food	119.68	8.6	4.9	7.4	7.1	7.9
Trasport equipment	121.09	16.8	25.4	16.1	19.0	19.8
Paper and paper products	132.87	14.1	11.7	15.6	13.8	—[b]
Basic metal industries	201.23	21.4	1.6	15.6	13.5	13.3
Tobacco	408.41	3.0	15.4	16.4	7.7	4.6
Products of petroleum and coal	504.04	17.1	19.8	18.8	18.4	3.9

Source: Ranis (1979), p. 235; by permission of the publisher, Cornell University Press; Ministry of Economic Affairs, Department of Statistics, Republic of China, *Taiwan Industrial Production Statistics Monthly* (various issues).
Notes:
[a]Average total assets to labor ratio (N.T. $1,000).
[b]Dash indicates negligible.

Comparative evaluation of the growth in the real sector: The role of domestic demand

The brief discussion that preceded is sufficient to compose a picture of a dynamic Taiwanese agriculture that is constantly transforming itself, and a stagnant sector in Uruguay that introduced its last significant innovation in the 19th century. Sectoral dynamism is measured by improvements in productivity and by the elasticity of supply response, both crop-specific and especially sector-wide. Accurately targeted interventions in Taiwan produced specific productivity gains. Broad interventions in Uruguay seemed to pursue fiscal objectives more than productivity improvements. It is incontestable that agricultural productivity has failed to increase in Uruguay. Various well-trodden hypotheses exist in the literature to explain agricultural stagnation, in general, and in Latin America in particular. The juxtaposition of Uruguay with Taiwan is intended to highlight one particular, and unorthodox aspect of the *latifundio* mode of agricultural production:[7] The concentration of land ownership among a small number of families, over a long period of time, may have prevented the intensification of agricultural production on the supply side;[8] by preventing the broadly based increase in incomes among the population, it may well have stifled the domestic demand side that becomes an important stimulus in industrial diversification and in pluralistic economic development.

Agriculture becomes an early beneficiary of broadly based increases in incomes because of the inevitability of Engel's law – the high share of expenditure on food at low levels of income that decreases as development occurs. It also becomes its victim as development proceeds. The sector can escape the claws of Engel's law by fine-tuning its output mix in accordance with the requirements of improving diets. This has been a continuous process in Taiwan. Such dynamism was never evident in Uruguay's agriculture, partly because the broadly based increase in incomes never occurred. Only since 1974 has the mix of agricultural output changed slightly, by including industrial crops and rice. And even then, the success of the sectoral diversification is predicated on increasing world demand for these crops and for meat, and on improving terms of trade.

The same demand constraints may have impinged on industrial growth also. There have been various spurts of industrial growth in Uruguay but in the end they proved as unsustainable as agricultural growth was. Whether under artificial protection or in a free-market regime, as import-substituting or export-promoting, industry never became the leading sector in Uruguay's economic development. Not unlike the case of agriculture, lacking broadly based effective demand for its output, industrial growth became artificial, relying exces-

7 The traditional structuralist hypothesis on *latifundismo* is nonprofit-maximizing motivation. Casual empiricism suggests that private wealth, which is at least partly the result of entrepreneurial drive, and *latifundismo* are correlates. This strains the credulity in the hypothesis. For alternative hypotheses relating to Uruguay see Finch (1981, Chapter 4). The hypothesis suggested here is a descendant of de Janvry's (1981) disarticulation hypothesis.
8 Conversion of pasture to crop land is one way of increasing the intensity of land cultivation. It is estimated that crop land can be readily doubled to 20% of the total agricultural area. Within the livestock sector, the shift to non-native or improved natural pasture has been very small, despite various development plans and international support in extending cheap credit and subsidizing fertilizer use (Finch, 1981, p. 117).

Table 11.8. *Production and imports of consumer goods for Uruguay, 1974–1978 (1974 = 100)*

	Production			Imports		
Year	Beverages	Tobacco	Lottery expenditure	Electrical applicances	Radios	Refrigerators
1974	100.0	100.0	100.0	100.0	100.0	100.0
1975	99.0	106.7	109.5	105.9	137.0	
1976	86.5	112.2	115.5	125.0	200.0	137.0
1977	96.9	110.0	117.9	150.0	904.0	147.0
1978	104.2	111.1	123.8	147.1	514.0	109.0

Source: Favaro and Bensión (1993), p. 277.
Note:
Blank indicates not available.

sively on exogenous shocks. The growth in the 1950s was based on the increase in incomes that followed the liquidation of the war-blocked sterling reserves in London and the windfall of strong primary commodity prices that followed the Korean War; it was foreign-demand induced. The growth episode in the 1970s was the result of once-and-for-all increase in efficiency by eliminating the interventions that had repressed the industrial sector; it was liberalization- and devaluation-induced.

In the meanwhile, the distribution of income had become even more skewed (Table 11.1). The real wage decreased in the 1970s by about 30%, and the minimum wage index by 25% (Favaro and Bensión, 1993, p. 276). There is probative evidence that on the low side of the distribution, inequality restricted the domestic market for industrial output, such as textiles and leather. More than 90% of the output of the processing industries was exported. At the same time, the imports of upscale middle-class domestic appliances, like radios and refrigerators, increased dramatically (Table 11.8). This is certainly the result of pent-up demand; but it also illustrates the dysfunctional relationship between income growth and domestic demand. Domestic effective demand stalled and the engine of growth sputtered, not for lack of high incomes, but for dearth of broadly based increases in incomes. In LDCs in general, where over 50% of the population is in agriculture, incomes cannot increase broadly unless agricultural, incomes do so first. This in turn cannot be done unless the surplus labor that the residual sector shelters is absorbed. This is where intensification of agriculture, whether through land reform or other means, becomes an important precondition for pluralistic economic development. Uruguay missed this opportunity in the late 19th century with the enclosure of livestock, and it has yet to create an environment for absorbing agricultural surplus labor.

Taiwan, on the other hand, illustrates how broadly based increases in income are harmoniously geared to the evolution of the industrial structure. The conventional interpretation of Taiwan's development success rests on land reform that led to productivity increases, which in turn promoted equal income distribution. The inverse relationship between farm size and productivity is now a stylized fact of agricultural development (Berry and Cline, 1979; Singh, 1990, pp. 102–107). Controlling for the type of agricultural activity, the superior productivity of small farms is probably related to the inverse relationship between farm size and economic efficiency (Lau and Yotopoulos, 1971, 1989; Yotopoulos and Lau, 1973). However, as already pointed out, agricultural productivity had been increasing in Taiwan since the turn of the century and whatever contribution to that trend land reform might have made is probably small. The salient contribution of land reform, instead, was that it increased dramatically the incomes of more than one-half of farm households in three stages – of tenants, first; of the recipients of the distributed public land next; and finally, of the beneficiaries of the redistribution of private lands. This represented a broadly based increase in incomes which, through strong demand linkages, became the foundation for vigorous agricultural and overall economic development.

Yotopoulos and Lin (1975) have addressed the issue of domestic demand linkages for that period in Taiwan with the 1966 input–output table. Table 11.9 ranks 12 sectors from the point of view of interindustry, employment, and income generation linkages (direct and indirect), all expressed as multipliers in terms of per unit of expenditure.[9] Sector 2, agricultural production for raw materials, has the highest income and employment multiplier, and sector 1, agricultural production for food, the third highest (with sector 5, mining, coming in between). This is because of the combination of high interindustry demands for these sectors, high share of wages and salaries in value added, and a high marginal propensity to consume these sectoral outputs by households as a whole, given the level of household income. This income-boosting effect of a thriving agricultural sector becomes even more dramatic once the per-unit multipliers are weighed by the high share of each sector (and of agriculture in general) in GDP in the early stages of development (Yotopoulos and Nugent, 1976, pp. 269–270). Generalizing the approach within a computable general

---

9 The calculation of linkage effects traces an autonomous increase in one unit of final demand for a sector's output. An initial increase in demand increases the level of production within each sector through the interindustry linkage effect, and the level of employment through the employment linkage effect. The increases in output and employment arising from these linkages are also reflected in increased incomes which, through the income-generation linkage, lead to increased demand for final goods, inducing, in turn, more output and employment.

Table 11.9. *The importance of broadly-based demand: rankings of industry sectors by linkage coefficients for Taiwan, 1966*

Groups	Industry	Total interindustry linkage	Employment linkage	Income-generation linkage
Agriculture	1. Agricultural production for food	1.898 (7)	0.852 (3)	1.637 (3)
	2. Agricultural production for raw material	1.497 (10)	0.908 (1)	1.804 (1)
Industry	3. Working capital for agriculture	2.455 (3)	0.725 (10)	1.140 (8)
	4. Food processing	2.158 (6)	0.673 (12)	1.089 (11)
	5. Mining	1.580 (11)	0.863 (2)	1.673 (2)
	6. Textiles and rubber	2.623 (2)	0.819 (6)	1.100 (10)
	7. Nonmetal products	2.172 (5)	0.764 (9)	1.110 (9)
	8. Metal products	2.793 (1)	0.825 (5)	1.067 (12)
Services	9. Utilities	1.883 (8)	0.713 (11)	1.355 (6)
	10. Construction	2.417 (4)	0.839 (4)	1.416 (5)
	11. Transportation and communications	1.858 (9)	0.787 (7)	1.329 (7)
	12. Other services	1.286 (12)	0.768 (8)	1.517 (4)

Source: Yotopoulos and Nugent (1976), p. 267.
Note:
Numbers in parentheses are rankings.

equilibrium model confirms these intuitively plausible results (Yotopoulos and Fafchamps, 1994).[10] The conventional description of the Taiwanese development experience as the result of an open-economy, free-trade strategy has emphasized the reliance on imports for building up the industrial infrastructure. Taiwan's successful import substitution policies, and especially the secondary import substitution, have received less attention.[11] Import substitution is usually induced by protection of the domestic market from competitive imports. Taiwan was no exception to this rule. But the sequencing of import substitution and indus-

10 See also Ranis (1979, p. 227) who decomposes the demand for the output of various sectors into domestic-demand-driven, export-driven, and import-substitution-driven. The evolution of the three components over various periods confirms the importance of domestic demand in laying the foundation for growth.
11 A welcome exception is Schive and Kao (1986) who extend the Morley–Smith (1970) measure of import substitution and emphasize the important role it played in Taiwan's structural transformation. Wade (1990) emphasizes the interplay between state and the market in promoting Taiwan's economic development.

Table 11.10. *Rates of growth of industrial gross product for Taiwan at periods corresponding to the product cycle (percentage)*

Primary import substitution

Export substitution

Secondary import substitution

	1953–1958	1958–1963	1963–1968	1968–1972	1972–1976	1976–1983	1983–1988
Fertilizer	9.6	15.9	12.9	0.4	1.5	−1.9	
Cotton fabrics	0.2	8.7	11.2	16.4	2.8	−1.9	
Electric fans	—	9.6	15.9	16.0	−5.4		
Steel bars	—	8.6	16.4	17.9	14.9	14.4	
Radios	—		89.6	22.8	−13.9	1.2	
Television sets	—			41.1	−2.8	2.2	
Motorcycles	—			7.0	15.7	8.2	
Telephone sets	—		29.9	23.0	23.5	51.8	
Tape recorders	—			37.0	20.5	23.4	−2.1
Integrated circuits	—				13.9	18.2	15.8
Electronic watches						23.0	5.8
Electronic calculators						35.1	18.0
Microcomputers							128.5
Monitors							35.6
VCRs							32.7

Source: Directorate General of Budget, Accounting and Statistics, Republic of China, *Industrial Production Statistics Monthly*.
Note:
Dash indicates negligible.

trialization is remarkable in gearing into the patterns of domestic demand that emerged from Taiwan's legendary equality in income distribution. Table 11.10 gives the rates of growth of selected industrial sectors during the various phases of Taiwan's economic development: import substitution in 1953–1958 and 1958–1963; export substitution in 1963–1968, 1968–1972, and 1972–1976; and secondary import substitution from 1976 on. Industrial sectors are ranked according to their growth performance in the various periods. The ranking, especially in the earlier periods, reflects the progression of the elasticities of demand in an environment where development increases incomes broadly across all population groups. Products that were introduced early on, like fertilizer, cotton fabrics, and electric fans, see their rates of growth increase as broad masses of consumers graduate into higher incomes. As those products peak, the same pattern is reproduced, with a lag, for products introduced in the next period, like radios, TV sets, tape recorders, watches, and calculators; and so on into the latest period with products like microcomputers, monitors, and VCR's.

Not unlike in the case of Japan (see Chapter 9), import substitution industrialization that is nurtured by strong domestic effective demand may account for another remarkable feature of Taiwanese economic development. In contrast to other developing countries where import-substituting industries never became viable at world prices, in Taiwan, most sectors have successfully passed the world trade test. In a twelve-sector classification (Table 11.6), imports exceeded exports in 10 cases in the 1950s, the exception being the food–beverage–tobacco sector. In recent years, imports exceed exports in only five sectors. Three of those, i.e., agricultural, mineral, and basic metal products, reflect the country's small land base and lack of mineral resources. The other two trade-deficit sectors are pharmaceuticals and machinery (not to be mistaken for electrical machinery, for which Taiwan is a net exporter). Out of ten net importing sectors in the 1950s, the remaining five have gradually become net exporters. The value of exports exceeded the value of imports for the first time (and forever thereafter): in 1961 for nonmetallic mineral products; in 1962 for textiles; in 1970 for metal products, and electrical machinery and apparatus; and in 1981 for transportation equipment. Perhaps the most impressive feature of Taiwanese economic development is that the initial import-substitution phase did not create stunted infant industries. It produced vigorous, strapping industrial sectors that graduated to the world market and thrived in the international competitive arena.

The tradable financial sector

Uruguay: The costs of asymmetric financial integration

The service sector in Uruguay represents 55% of GDP. Such a high share is atypical for a country of Uruguay's level of income. It is partly explained by the institutional inability of agriculture to absorb the surplus labor, which makes services the residual sector. But more importantly, it is related to the proximity of Argentina and Brazil, and the demand from their sizeable middle-income classes for tourist, residential, and especially financial services in Uruguay.

The financial sector became largely tradable as a result of the financial liberalization of the mid-1970s. In a bid to make Uruguay a regional financial center, the financial sector underwent a comprehensive deregulation that abolished restrictions on capital movements and exchange transactions, eliminated

Table 11.11. *Deposits by private sector for Uruguay, in local currency and in dollars, 1984–1991 (end of period, perentage of GDP)*

	State banks			Private banks		
	Total deposits	Local currency	Dollars	Local currency	Dollars, nationals	Dollars, foreigners
1984	54.5	7.8	9.7	8.9	15.2	12.9
1985	58.1	7.8	13.9	8.0	15.1	12.3
1986	54.7	7.9	12.6	6.7	15.8	11.7
1987	49.1	7.3	12.6	4.8	13.6	10.8
1988	51.5	7.1	14.8	4.3	14.4	15.2
1989	68.1	4.0	19.6	3.5	17.6	23.4
1990	79.1	6.6	22.3	2.7	19.0	28.5
1991	69.6	4.1	21.1	2.3	17.6	24.5

Source: World Bank (1993d), p. 31.

controls on interest rates, credit and deposits, and freed the entry into the field, especially the establishment of foreign banks. Subsequent rulings authorized tax-free offshore banking with strong secrecy laws for foreign depositors and tax-exempt status. In the wake of these policies, the economy is currently essentially dollarized: 70% of financial assets are held in dollars, of which about one-half are thought to be foreign owned (Table 11.11).

What are the implications of financial deregulation, and how do they relate to the exchange rate theme of this book?

One important motivation for opening the foreign account and removing restrictions in foreign exchange transactions was acknowledging a situation that preexisted in Uruguay and trying to use it to advantage. The rate of inflation was moderate in the 1960s, while the foreign exchange rate was controlled at a stable level (Table 11.2). In the 1970s, both exchange rate instability and political instability turned a reputation deficit into a collapse of confidence that fanned the capital flight into deposits in Miami.[12] Opening and liberalizing the foreign account stops the capital outflow and lures some dollars back into the country. The anticipated inflow of capital was a basic motive for making finance into a tradable service. Additionally, stabilization of the economy and improvement in its fundamentals were expected to follow as by-products of the monetary and exchange rate policies of liberalization. In this respect, the comparison of Taiwan and Uruguay in sequencing the liberaliza-

12 The experience was repeated after the Mexican debt crisis of February 1982. The estimated capital outflow for this event was US $2.0 billion (Favaro and Bensión, 1993, p. 280).

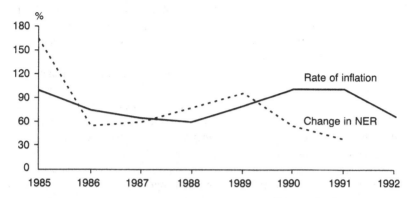

Figure 11.1. *Rate of inflation and percentage change in nominal exchange rate for Uruguay, 1985–1992*
Source: Table 11.2.

tion of the capital market is instructive on the chicken-or-egg question of the stabilization of the financial and real sectors.

The asset–value dynamics theorem (see Chapters 3 and 7) predicts for LDCs that once restrictions on capital movements and exchange transactions are abolished, the portfolio demand for holding foreign exchange increases – and in the worst cases the transaction demand also. This puts pressure for depreciation of the home currency (devaluation of the nominal exchange rate). Devaluation in turn feeds inflationary pressures and leads to further depreciation of the domestic currency. The process can thus create a spiral for devaluation and for inflation. In fact, integration in an environment of inflationary finance is a special case of financial integration under asymmetric reputation. In an unstable inflationary environment residents anticipate future inflation by engaging in massive substitution of foreign exchange for their domestic money balances.

Two policy responses are available in an environment of asymmetric reputation. One is to give up on the foreign exchange rate as a policy control instrument and to surrender to the process of currency substitution; the other is to engage monetary policy in defending the exchange rate and use it as an anchor to stabilize the economy. Either policy involves heavy costs for an LDC.

In conforming to the general Latin American tradition, Uruguay found it difficult to control the rate of inflation, which averaged over 50% per year in the period 1965–1980 (Table 11.2; World Bank, 1992a). In using foreign exchange as an anchor for inflation the pegged rate had to crawl behind the rate of inflation. Figure 11.1 plots the annual rate of inflation (change in CPI) and the change in the foreign exchange rate. In 1986 the change in the latter led the rate of inflation. The two were tracking closely in 1987–1989. Since then, and for the years 1990–1992, the two diverged markedly, with the annual rate of inflation being around 100% while the nominal exchange rate increased annually by about 50%. Under these circumstances of inflationary finance residents discounted or anticipated future inflation by engaging in massively substituting foreign exchange for their domestic money balances. Such monetary substitution leads to a depreciation of the domestic currency, which makes the exchange rate even more ineffective in anchoring inflation. Thus more currency substitution is needed to curtail inflation.

In the extreme case of complete "dollarization," a currency board is established that holds interest-earning foreign exchange reserves against the domestic currency. As the practice has devolved, e.g., in Argentina, it amounts to fixing the exchange rate and also fixing the rate of inflation at its international level. As gradual dollarization of the economy sets in, the balance of payments deteriorates. Loss of seigniorage revenues leads to deterioration of the fiscal deficit and to reducing the base of the inflation tax. Moreover, inequality in income distribution is likely to increase as those in the higher income brackets are better able to substitute dollars for pesos, making the inflation tax even more regressive.

Of these various costs of dollarization, the seigniorage component is more readily measurable. In contrast to bank deposits and securities, notes and coins do not yield interest. They represent an interest-free loan extended by the public to the issuer – the central bank. The total interest earned on the amount of fiat money in circulation, minus the cost of minting and printing it, is the yield of the loan (seigniorage). This yield increases as currency is destroyed or goes out of circulation, and also as its value is eaten away by inflation. Currency decay and inflation favor the borrower at the expense of the lender: The central bank's net worth increases, because its liabilities are reduced and its assets are not. The amount of revenue that is lost to the state by accepting the dollar in financing transactions and in denominating accounts can only be accurately known if the total stock of dollars in the country is known. In a wide range of cases, however, the seigniorage cost has been estimated at a one-time stock of 8–10% of GNP plus an annual flow of 1% of GNP. These are indeed large numbers relative to other sources of state revenues (Fischer, 1982, 1992; Melvin, 1988).[13]

Currency substitution is costly. So are the available measures for containing it. Barring foreign exchange restrictions, one alternative is to promote foreign currency deposits in the domestic financial system. This has the advantage of

13 The corresponding gain that dollarization represents for hard-currency countries is estimated at 0.5–1% of GNP.

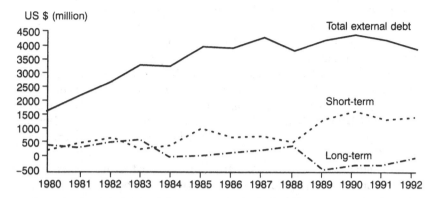

Figure 11.2. *Long- and short-term capital inflows for Uruguay and total external debt, 1980–1992 (millions of US $)*
Source: International Monetary Fund, *International Financial Statistics*, various issues.

reducing the pressure on international reserves and on the exchange rate, along with improving the central bank's balance sheet in foreign assets if reserve requirements are imposed.[14] The process is reflected in the figures for external debt (Figure 11.2). In 1981 Uruguay's debt was US$2.1 billion, which is equivalent to the value of exports for two years. By 1986 the debt reached US$4.0 billion, corresponding to 4.1 years of export value. Only a small part of the increment in foreign capital was used for investment purposes. The largest part was incurred by the Central Bank (the Banco de la Republica) and the central government to cover the loss of reserves induced by the foreign exchange policy (Favaro and Bensión, 1993).

Attracting foreign currency deposits requires a contractionary monetary policy that drives interest rates up so they appeal to foreign depositors. The contraction on the side of aggregate demand is a real cost to the economy but it helps alleviate the pressure on the exchange rate. Differential interest rate policies that make domestic currency deposits more attractive to foreign investors can also help stem the dollarization of the economy and thus reduce the pressure on reserves. The interest rate differential can make the sale of debt instruments by the Central Bank attractive to holders of foreign exchange. Private investors then buy peso debt, which "flushes out dollars" for the central

---

14 This improvement, however, can prove illusory. As long as the foreign exchange holdings of the central bank represent foreign currency liabilities to commercial banks, they should not be treated as net foreign assets, but they are. See Ramírez-Rojas (1985, p. 661).

bank to use in defending the exchange rate. The "premium" in this scenario is paid in terms of higher interest rates that compensate for the risk of future depreciation of the currency, but which also lead to a more protracted contraction in the economy. This scenario of engaging the interest rate in a futile battle to prop up the exchange rate and to stabilize the rate of inflation is borne out in Table 11.2 and Figure 11.2. Real interest rates on loans both in domestic and foreign currency increased steadily in the 1980s and remained above 20% (Favaro and Bensión 1993, p. 279). In the meantime, the external debt increased steadily, with increases in private debt and short-term indebtedness leading the way.

The contractionary effect of dollarization discussed so far relates to aggregate demand. But demand consists of tradables and nontradables. It is only natural to impose contraction in the tradable sector as a result of the foreign exchange constraint. It is an entirely different story to impose the same contraction in dealing with the nontradable sector, where transactions do not (or should not) involve foreign exchange. This amounts to countenancing a higher rate of optimal inflation for LDCs, in proportion to the importance of their nontradable sector. Otherwise, the excessive and unwarranted contraction in the nontradable sector exacerbates the impact of contractionary devaluations that has been discussed earlier (see Chapters 4 and 8).

One might conclude from the discussion above that the policy mistake in Uruguay was in overriding the exchange market and using the foreign exchange rate as an inflation anchor. The policy outcomes would have probably been the same, only more gradual, if the exchange rate were instead freed to provide the appropriate signals to the economy. In fact, the policy failure lies in the premature attempt of asymmetric financial integration in an inflationary environment. It becomes a special case of the basic scenario that builds on the asset–value dynamics theorem. Once restrictions on capital movements and exchange transactions are abolished, the portfolio demand for holding foreign exchange increases in an LDC, and in worst cases so does the transactions demand. This puts pressure for depreciation on the domestic currency. A stable exchange rate can be achieved only at the cost of having more and more reserves at the ready to defend it. This is premised on improving the current account or on net inflow on the capital account. Improving the current account implies improving productivity in tradables and increasing exports. In many cases this is easier said than done. There are no quick fixes for the destabilized real economy, including liberalization. So in many instances the pressure for adjustment is placed on the employment and wage side. This has social and economic costs. Still worse, it can provide only temporary relief. Even considering the possibility of overbloated industrial sectors, there is only a slim margin of safety before an LDC faces recriminations from DC trading partners about violating labor standards and workers' rights through low real-wage policies.[15]

Substantial inflow of capital could have provided a neat solution, but capital inflows dried up in the aftermath of the Mexican debt moratorium in the early 1980s, increased modestly from 1984 to 1988, and have turned negative since then (Figure 11.2). Moreover, the parallel experience in other countries indicates that (save for exceptional circumstances again) most of the capital inflow is either swaps (repatriated capital flight) or short-term capital. Both come in at onerous terms: at 50 cents on the dollar for the swaps, and at real short interest rates for the loans that are substantially higher than the international interest rates. What is even worse, the short-term hot money is as quick to leave as it was fast in coming in. This means that both the exchange rate risk and the political risk are higher in LDCs, given observationally equivalent events. In Uruguay's case, the failed attempt to build reputation on the dollarization of the economy and on the anchor of a pegged exchange rate has led to reverse financial integration: the net capital flows are from poor Uruguay to its rich financial partners. Under these circumstances, it becomes only a question of time before the foreign deposits are confiscated and the feeble attempts to build reputation from scratch collapse.[16]

Taiwan: Financial integration with exceptional circumstances

The exception of special circumstances qualified this skeptical analysis of the prospects for asymmetric financial integration. The case of Taiwan provides an apposite example of these special circumstances.

Stung by the experience of hyperinflation in the 1950s, the authorities have resorted to draconian measures since 1960 to combat inflation and secure price stability. The policy instruments used were fiscal, monetary, and an exchange rate that was pegged and stable through the 1970s (Table 11.3).[17] The NT$ was considered generally overvalued for most of the period (Kuo, 1983, Chapters

15 For a graphic presentation of this dilemma see *The Economist* (of London), April 9, 1994.
16 One can anchor this scenario in various countries from the worldwide experience. A few will suffice. In Bolivia foreign currency deposits were first allowed in 1973 and were confiscated in 1982. In Peru they were first allowed in 1978 and forcefully converted to domestic currency in 1984. In Mexico foreign currency deposits existed between 1977–1982 and became especially important toward the end of the period, just before they were confiscated. In these cases, and in Mexico in particular, the recurrence in the process is impressive. Although people are forced to convert their deposits back at the official rate at a huge capital loss, with a change in government enough credibility is perceived and people deposit their currency into these kinds of instruments again (Edwards, 1992).
17 There was a small appreciation of the NT$ in 1973, and a general appreciating trend after the introduction of the float in 1978.

10 and 14). The fiscal policy was premised on curtailing government consumption expenditure while favoring savings and capital formation in the private and in the public sector.[18] On the revenue side, income taxes were moderate, except for agriculture, which was also assessed the "hidden tax" incorporated in the rice-fertilizer barter program and in the compulsory government purchase of rice at prices below the market. The fiscal side produced a consistent surplus in the operating budget averaging over the period at above 1% of GNP.

The three components of monetary policy that will be examined here are interest rates, money supply, and the intersection of the two as it relates to the balance of payments and net foreign assets.[19] The criterion for evaluating the outcomes of monetary policy is the extent to which the growth of real GDP was accommodated and the rate of inflation was controlled.

The interest rate policy became the foundation of the monetary policy early on. The "preferential interest rate deposit scheme" that has been in existence for more than 40 years intended to lure out of the private sector a continuous increase in monetary savings. The incentive was interest rates that were consistently positive, turning to high when inflationary risks lurched (Table 11.3). The rate of personal savings rose from 3% of disposable income in 1952 to 21% in 1980 and has remained at that high level since then (Scitovsky, 1985). Real interest rates averaging 6% through the mid-1970s are very high in comparison to the negative real interest rates that are stylized facts in comparable growth histories. Still, the average productivity of capital was high enough so that the high-interest-rate policy did not choke off investment and growth.[20]

The second component of monetary policy was based on the stable growth of the money supply to finance the vertiginous growth in real GDP, bordering on an average of 8% per year (Table 11.3). The annual increase in the transactions demand for money for accommodating the rate of growth alone was 16% per year.[21] In addition, the requirements of financing foreign trade transactions, and those imposed by a significant increase in net foreign assets, resulted in a vigorous growth in the money supply throughout the period.[22] Nevertheless, with the combination of interest-rate policies and fiscal policies, along with the overvalued exchange rate that accounted for cheap imports of

---

18 The sizeable military expenditure of about 30% of the central government budget was partly underwritten by the U.S. in the period 1951–1964.
19 For a detailed account of the monetary policy of Taiwan see Chiu (1992) and Liu (1992).
20 It is estimated that the net productivity of capital was 25% in the 1960s, 20% in the 1970s, and 15% in the 1980s (Fry, 1990).
21 The estimated long-run GNP elasticity of the real demand for money is 1.7 (Chiu 1992).
22 The ratio of M_2 (money and deposits) to GNP was 9% in 1955, 56% in 1975, and 136% in 1990. The ratio of broad money to GNP approached that of Japan in just two decades (Lundberg, 1979).

raw materials and intermediate products, inflation was tamed. With the exception of an interlude of double-digit rates around the years of the oil crisis, inflation stabilized below 5% for most of the period (Table 11.3).

Interest rates in Taiwan were higher than in the U.S. In an open economy, the inflow of capital would have driven interest rates down. Similarly, in the textbook case, the overvalued currency would have contributed to capital outflow. The corollary of overvalued domestic currency and high-interest-rate policies in Taiwan was the strict control of both the outflow and the inflow of capital (Wade, 1990). Exchange and capital controls insulated the high interest rates from external influences both during the period of the current account deficits, prior to 1976, and afterwards, when the inflow of foreign assets was allowed to increase. But there were also specific policies that mitigated the effect of high interest rates on investment activity. Exporters enjoyed offsetting subsidies and they were always granted unrestricted access to foreign capital at interest rates that were lower than domestic interest rates. More recently, in the period of persistent current account surpluses, interest rates were nudged downwards, and some capital outflows were countenanced, but both remained strictly controlled.

In the meantime, the institutional structure of the financial market was becoming more diversified. Besides a security market that already existed, a bond market was established in 1974 and a money market in 1976. Both markets were exempted from interest ceiling regulations and they were intended to pave the way for interest rate deregulation and to contribute to capital deepening by channeling financial savings from the informal market to capital formation. The success of the policies is best gauged by the doubling of the value of money market instruments outstanding to the total banking loans (from 8.6% to 15.6%) in a period of only 18 months in late 1970's (Kuo, 1983, p. 321).[23]

With the preconditions met and the institutional structure established, a managed floating exchange rate was introduced in 1978 and the liberalization of the capital market followed in 1983.[24] Foreign capital transactions, however, continued to be closely monitored,[25] and strict oversight of the foreign exchange rate was maintained at least until 1989, when a "liberalized" floating

---

23 With the exception of treasury bills, all other money market instruments, including bankers' acceptances, certificates of deposits, and commercial paper, increased by multiple factors for a few years in a row, in comparison to total loans, which were increasing at the rate of 20% (Kuo, 1983, Chapter 15).

24 For a detailed chronology of the policy intervention in the Taiwan economy see Li (1988).

25 As example, there still remains an overall limit in foreign investment in Taiwan's stock exchange (effectively at about 7% of the market's capitalization); no more than one-tenth of a company's stock can be owned by foreigners; and the Central Bank drags its feet in processing investment applications from foreigners (US $4 billion worth were still pending in mid-1994).

exchange rate system was introduced. At the same time, interest rates were liberalized but remained closely monitored.

Conclusion

The comparison of Taiwan and Uruguay underscores the differences in the evolution of the real sector in the two economies and in the importance that the monetary sector achieves as a handmaiden of the real economy.

Agriculture was initially the leading sector in both countries. It produced vigorous interindustry linkages. But Uruguayan agriculture failed to generate significant employment gains, partly as a result of the technology of production of the livestock sector. With the preconditions for a broadly based increase in incomes missing, the demand both for agricultural commodities at the higher levels of the food chain and for industrial commodities was constrained. While at an early stage development in Taiwan was domestic-demand-driven, it always remained export-driven in Uruguay.

Starting in the 1970s, the monetary sector of Uruguay was delegated the function that the real sector did not meet – increasing productivity. Devaluation is most often advocated as an instrument for increasing productivity in the tradable sector, as well as for improving the current account balance. If there are no quick fixes for the real economy, devaluation may not work. It can lead instead to increasing inflationary pressures and to imposing undue contraction on the economy. In such cases, the role of the exchange rate becomes reversed: instead of serving as a variable (a signal for setting domestic prices right), it is used as a (semi-) fixed anchor to control inflation and to stabilize the economy. This is the Latin American solution, and it was adopted by Uruguay beginning in 1989. Then the interest rate becomes the policy control instrument that is relied upon to attract foreign capital for stabilizing the exchange rate, and ultimately for increasing productivity in the tradable sector through foreign investment. The downside of this approach is prolonging the contraction and choking off recovery. The ultimate risk is that the attempt at stabilizing the real economy through monetary policies alone will be judged by the markets as "creative finance" and then it is doomed to fail. In this scenario, Uruguay has ended up with high interest rates, high short-term debt, and sizeable net capital outflow.

In 1949 Taiwan underwent its monetary reform, which was largely similar to the most recent one for Uruguay. Amid the din of hyperinflation, the Taiwan currency was devalued at the rate of 40,000 to 1, was linked to the U.S. dollar, and was protected by the full backing of reserves in foreign exchange, gold, and silver and by a strict institutional limitation on the issue of money by the Central Bank. That was merely the beginning of the arduous process of eliminating inflationary psychology. The effects did not start showing results until the 1960s, when the government budget was habitually in balance and the money supply was soaked up into savings through the adept manipulation of interest rates.

The monetary sector was tightly controlled, and especially the external account, while the preconditions for symmetric financial integration were being established. The liberalization had to wait until there was a well-managed real sector: a largely balanced government budget, no foreign exchange constraints, no external debt, and a vigorous record in productivity and income growth.

The comparative analysis of the real and the financial sectors in the two countries helps underscore the importance of proper sequencing in the process of development. In the real sector, agricultural development lays the foundation for economic growth. As productivity increases in agriculture, incomes grow broadly among the population, which is largely agricultural in the early stages of development. Increased domestic demand is geared to the appropriate industrial sequencing and thus becomes the engine of growth. Eventually a vigorous export sector is phased in to provide strong industrial linkages with industrial trading partners and the wherewithal to pay for technology transfers. The process of the liberalization of the real economy is gradual and it quickens as development occurs.

The financial sector is truly the handmaiden of the real sector. It is tightly controlled and it is monitored so that it strictly adheres to its function of providing liquidity for the real sector to grow within a stable environment.

The growth of the real sector, with fiscal balance, external balance, and monetary stability, works slowly to create a reserve of reputation. Only then, and at the very last when the economy has been thoroughly derepressed, is the exchange rate freed, the capital account opened, and the capital controls on the movement of funds lifted.[26]

The juxtaposition helps to demystify the success of Taiwan and to explain the failure of Uruguay. The two crucial policy mistakes in Uruguay were the failure of domestic demand and the attempt, through premature liberalization, to use the financial sector as the engine of growth. The latter mistake was especially grievous.[27] Financial liberalization under conditions of a reputation deficit leads to depreciation of the currency. Then the smartest move is to substitute for it. Moreover, with prices lower tomorrow, only a fool buys today. So investment falls and people forego entrepreneurship to become inactive rentiers. Dollars in the mattress – or in Miami – become the only smart investment. Premature financial liberalization amounts to reverse financial integration, with the benefits flowing from the LDC to the DCs.

---

26 For the sequence and the timing of liberalization see Balassa (1982) and Krueger (1984). The sequence prescribed here for the financial sector is closer to McKinnon (1991).
27 For examples of the steps in the sequence described see Krugman (1979) on speculative attacks on the foreign exchange peg; or Lessard and Williamson (1987) on capital flight in case of macroeconomic imbalances and a serious debt overhang.

CHAPTER 12

Summary, conclusions, and policy recommendations

This book builds on the theme that distortions inherent in free currency markets lead LDCs systematically to misallocate resources. The intuition behind this theme is straightforward. Consider an equilibrium situation in the real world, where a bundle of resources produces tradables or nontradables, measured such that one unit of each is worth $1. Entrepreneurs should be indifferent between producing one unit of tradables or one of nontradables. Now introduce a slight complication that is ubiquitous in the real world of LDCs: tradables trade in dollars, a hard currency, whereas nontradables trade, say, in pesos, which is a soft currency. The soft currency may be devalued. Then it becomes risky for the Mexican entrepreneur to produce (or hold) one unit of nontradables that could not be converted into $1 for later spending. Expressed in another way, entrepreneurs are attracted to producing tradables because that is the only way they can acquire $1 they wish to hold for asset purposes. Thus, relative to productivities measured at "normal" prices, nontradables become undervalued and resources are drawn away towards tradables. This is manifest in a relative price of nontradables that is too low compared with productivities, or too high an RER.

This dilemma does not exist for the DC producer. In hard currency, $1 of tradables will always be worth $1 of nontradables, as opposed to the soft currency, where the expectation of devaluation becomes a self-fulfilling prophecy. In the process of converting soft currency into hard for asset-holding purposes the market-clearing NER becomes too high. This is manifest in a relative price of tradables that is too high compared with productivities – again too high an RER.

This intuition is so clear that one wonders why it has not been advanced before. The answer is simple. It is not easy to measure marginal productivities in producing tradables and nontradables. It is equally hard to normalize the prices of tradables and nontradables and to get their ratio, the RER. The direction in which the RER moves can be determined, but not its level – whether it is high or low. The micro-ICP data that are used in this book for the first time for analytical purposes have solved the problem of consistently expressing prices of tradables in terms of nontradables. The empirical research reported in an endogenous growth framework resoundingly confirms that LDCs are likely to have undervalued real exchange rates (relatively high prices of tradables in domestic currency). And it finds that undervaluation is detrimental to growth.

While the intuition and the findings so far may not sound controversial, their policy implications are provocative. They certainly challenge conventional wisdom. Some of the salient policy implications are being explored below using the Socratic dialectic method.

The foreign exchange rate is the link between the prices of tradables and nontradables. Liberalizing the market and freeing the foreign exchange rate should help set the prices right and thus eliminate the bias toward the tradable sector.

On the contrary, a free exchange rate would further exacerbate the situation. In the real-world-LDC parable that preceded, the only way for the producer of nontradables to lay claim to $1 is to shift resources into tradables. In a regime of floating rates with unrestricted access to foreign exchange, anybody can claim assets of $1 by offering the equivalent amount in pesos. The increased demand drives the price of foreign exchange up. The depreciation of the domestic currency leads to flight of domestic asset-holders to hard-currency-denominated assets in order to preempt further anticipated depreciation. Because the soft currency is expected to devalue, this expectation becomes a self-fulfilling prophecy. This sets the stage for spiral devaluations.

Devaluation of the NER increases the price of tradables, even though in the parable there was equilibrium in the real world and the marginal productivities were equalized across outputs. Thus RER becomes undervalued even though, or precisely because, the NER was allowed to find its market-clearing value within a free market and free trade regime, where foreign exchange restrictions have been removed. Setting the NER at its equilibrium market-clearing value does not produce an equilibrium RER. Instead, it produces an undervalued RER and trade bias. Stating this in another way, the allocation of resources that results from setting the NER at its equilibrium value is not the same as the one emanating from an equilibrium RER. The foreign exchange market in LDCs is incomplete. The source of market incompleteness lies in a reputation deficit, which is systematically related to the level of underdevelopment. As in the more familiar case of asymmetric information, asymmetries in reputation require nonprice closure through intervention and rationing. Barring that, the RER in LDCs is likely to be undervalued as opposed to overvalued, which is the general presumption in the literature.

If the origins of an incomplete market lie in free foreign exchange rates, would not dollarization of the economy, which in effect fixes the exchange rate, solve the problem?

Two policy responses are available in an environment of asymmetric reputation with free markets and unrestricted foreign exchange transactions. One is to give up on the foreign exchange rate as a policy control instrument and to surrender to the process of currency substitution as devaluation, whether creeping or spiral, occurs. The other is to engage fiscal and especially monetary policy in defending the exchange rate and using it as an anchor to stabilize the economy. The difference between the two is in degree only. The analysis of the benefits and the costs is the same for the two cases.

The benefits of currency substitution derive from removing uncertainty, reducing exchange rate risk, and cutting inflation, which translates to lower interest rates. Its costs, however, often have been overlooked. First, an LDC can currency-substitute only if it is successful in attracting the requisite foreign exchange. In the process, higher interest rates, not lower, may become necessary to lure foreign deposits. Second, holding foreign exchange as reserves in a currency-board system or as a store of value for asset-holders, instead of using it productively, has a definite opportunity cost. Both these factors can lead to deterioration in the balance of payments. Third, the seigniorage cost is another drawback of currency substitution. In contrast to bank deposits and securities, currency does not yield interest. Issuing it represents an interest-free loan extended by the public to the central bank. The revenue from seigniorage is the total interest earned on the amount of currency in circulation, minus the cost of minting and printing it. This yield increases as currency is destroyed or goes out of circulation and as its value is eaten away by inflation. The seigniorage revenue foregone to dollarization in poor countries has been estimated at a one-time stock of 10% of GNP plus an annual flow of 1% of GNP. These are large numbers for poor countries.

The contractionary costs of currency substitution enumerated so far may well offset the expansionary benefits of reduced uncertainty and foreign exchange risk. There is one additional downside to policies that target a fixed exchange rate through currency substitution. The contraction in aggregate demand is induced by the foreign exchange constraint. But aggregate demand consists of both tradables and nontradables. Whereas it is reasonable to impose contraction in the former because of lack of foreign exchange, it is unnecessary to impose it on goods and services that do not (or need not) trade in foreign exchange. Hence, the optimal rate of inflation for an LDC may not be the same for the tradable and nontradable sectors. In the former, containing inflation at its world level protects the nominal exchange rate. The same is not true for the nontradable sector, where imposing undue contraction on account of a foreign exchange constraint is gratuitous. This fourth and final cost of currency substitution would have been a sufficient reason alone to nail the coffin of the gold standard.

Dollarization of the economy may be a bad idea. Wouldn't a market-friendly approach to stabilizing the exchange rate, say a crawling peg, make more sense in comparison to interventionist alternatives?

The ultimate objective in defending the exchange rate is to prevent monetary factors from distorting the real balance between tradables and nontradables by increasing the prices of the former. One can accomplish this in an open economy by absorbing domestic-currency liquidity in a fashion neutral with regard to prices. Increasing domestic savings rates by selling government bonds, for example, would achieve that purpose, but for the fact that lack of reputation and the risk that the currency will depreciate stand in the way. Selling dollar-denominated bonds does not serve the same end, since the variance in their yield is directly translated into pressure for increasing the exchange rate. But selling bonds denominated in an index of currencies, as opposed to one currency, such as SDR (special drawing rights) or ECU (European currency unit) puts yet another filter between the nominal and the real exchange rate and may cushion the impact on the prices of tradables.

The alternative approach is to depend on foreign savings for defending the exchange rate. The current account deficit represents foreign savings. The prevailing policy response considers current account deficits tolerable as long as they can be financed. This is done by resorting to the interbank market or borrowing short-term funds when pressure builds in the currency market. As intervention is needed, the foreign exchange is dumped in the market to flush out local currency and achieve currency substitution without driving the foreign exchange rate up. The costs of dollarization that were accounted for earlier still exist. Moreover, if the operation of defending the exchange rate is successful, the country is left with a stiff interest bill in converting the short-term funds into long-term loans. Interest and principal, of course, have to be paid in dollars, i.e., by producing more tradables. If the operation fails, the country has to give up not only the tradables to service the loan but also more nontradables, since the government will have to purchase the foreign exchange at a higher rate, in local prices.

The problem has been identified as asymmetric reputation, which leads to depreciation of the domestic currency and to high prices of tradables. Are there conventional, orthodox macropolicies that focus on the fundamentals – as opposed to intervention – that would increase productivity, lead to development, and thus gradually solve the problem of reputation?

Responsible macroeconomic management is a cornerstone for building reputation. In particular, fiscal deficits need be limited to levels that can be prudently financed without increasing inflationary pressures. An external-sector deficit that does not exceed readily manageable levels is important for exchange rate stability. A vigorous growth of exports not only serves to support the exchange rate, but can also finance the transfer of foreign technology by paying for licenses, capital-goods imports, and foreign training.

Responsible macroeconomic management consists of a set of fundamental policies that promote growth. Prudent monetary policy leads to low interest rates. With fiscal balance, reflationary stimuli can be activated that rely on budgetary levers to boost output and jobs. External balance activates the most important developmental lever of an open economy – technology transfer.

There is no argument that responsible macroeconomic management is a cornerstone for building reputation and for maintaining it. But so is restoring growth. The disagreement with the neoliberal view is on the timing and sequencing of the various components in the fundamentals package. The issue is whether liberalization of the foreign exchange market and opening of the capital account should come early on or at the very last. The mainstream view holds that liberalization will restore confidence and produce growth by setting the prices right. The differentiation within this view exists as to the speed (big bang or gradual) and the sequence of (current and capital account) financial liberalization (McKinnon, 1991). The thesis of this book is that market-clearing prices are the wrong prices in incomplete markets. The premature opening of the capital account, in particular, will further inhibit growth. This creates a vicious circle in which the reputation deficit further distorts the currency market, misallocates real resources in favor of tradables, inhibits growth, and in the end increases the reputation asymmetry. The final outcome is a bias for trade, to the point that comparative-advantage trade turns into competitive-devaluation trade. The issue is not whether financial liberalization should precede or follow stabilization; it is rather that financial liberalization is perniciously premature if self-sustained development has not happened first.

One set of policies that would work consists of intervention in the foreign exchange market to fix the nominal exchange rate at a price below its market-clearing, equilibrium value.

The argument in favor of fixed exchange rates is not new. It represented the mainstream view after World War II. Fixed exchange rates were abandoned with the collapse of the Bretton Woods system. Defending fixed exchange rates became unfashionable when the development paradigm was reversed in the 1980s. More recently, fixed exchange rates have found new advocates among economists and policy makers, including Michel Camdessus, the Managing

Director of the International Monetary Fund. The main issue, however, is not fixing the exchange rate per se. The real challenge for policy makers lies in stabilizing the exchange rate without incurring the cost of induced contraction in the economy – whether it comes through higher interest rates for attracting a defense fund of foreign exchange or through excessive stimulation of tradables with undue contraction in the nontradable sector. A market-friendly approach for fixing the exchange rate could enlist a new lending facility to help countries that face unexpected foreign exchange emergencies, as proposed by Camdessus. The special feature of the proposal is that the facility would operate not with hard currencies, but with a new allocation of SDRs that the Fund's shareholders would be asked to approve. As long as the exchange rate of a country were "fairly valued," the facility would support it against unjustified market speculation.[1] The infusion of liquidity through SDRs makes the defense of the exchange rate virtually costless.

The true and tried way for supporting the exchange rate in LDCs is overriding the foreign exchange market. Rationing is used to absorb the excess demand that exists at any price below the market-clearing equilibrium NER.

Doesn't intervention in the foreign exchange market open Pandora's box by spilling into other markets as well? Appreciation of the exchange rate favors imports, whereas depreciation favors exports. Excess demand for imports and disequilibrium in the balance of payments would lead to controls on trade.

Controls on trade are inevitable. But the advantages of devaluation and the disadvantages of overvalued currencies have been greatly exaggerated. Cheap (in domestic currency) prices of imports are not necessarily bad for an economy, nor do they invariably lead to a flood of imported goods. Cheap imports can become an important instrument for industrial policy in the hands of competent bureaucrats. Imports that consist, e.g., of raw materials and intermediate products, can be targeted to priority export sectors, thus conveying an implicit subsidy for offsetting the toll that overvaluation takes on exports. Control of imports, of course, will promote import substitution activities. Again, import substitution can be good or bad, depending on the type of goods that are being import-substituted.

High prices of exports (again in domestic currency) are not necessarily good either, nor do they automatically promote exports. High prices, achieved through devaluation, convey a subsidy on all exportables, not only on those at the margin for entering the export market. They may shift the supply of exportables, depending on elasticities, and they will certainly increase profits.

1 For details see *The Economist* (of London), July 23, 1994.

High prices for exports do not automatically improve competitiveness in world markets. There is nothing inherently good about exports either; it all depends on what is being exported. Exports can be based on comparative advantage; but more often than not in LDCs they are based on competitive devaluation. Competitive-devaluation trade does not promote self-sustained growth. It deters development.

The main impact of devaluation is in favoring the prices of tradables, which shifts resources away from nontradables. Appreciation, on the other hand, favors the prices of nontradables and shifts resources away from tradables. Such relative price considerations should be the proper basis for making development policy, as opposed to blanket statements about import substitution or export-led growth.

Foreign exchange controls amount to trade controls. The volume of trade will be lower at controlled exchange rates compared to what it would have been under free exchange rates. What happens to the link between trade and growth?

The conjecture that trade promotes growth is primeval in economics, but the evidence to support it is scant. The reason, it has been assumed, is that trade is either too narrow a concept or too broad to support the empirical validation of the hypothesis. The tests of the relationship between trade and growth have been specified accordingly. In a broad definition of trade, the link is sought between liberalization of the "trade regime" and growth (Krueger, 1978). In a narrow definition, on the other hand, the relationship between export push and growth is studied (World Bank, 1993a). In either case, the empirical results still remain ambiguous (Rodrik, 1995b; Edwards, 1993).

The empirical analysis in this book focuses instead on the channels through which trade affects growth, along with accounting for other potential determinants of growth. In a global environment with imperfect technology markets, both exports and imports can provide a powerful mechanism for technological upgrading. Imports provide access to advanced intermediate inputs and exports provide the incentive to compete in the world market and the wherewithal to pay for the adoption of the new technology. The direction of trade then becomes the decisive variable. Trading with DC partners determines whether LDCs can absorb at a faster rate the technology developed in advanced countries and thus can grow, in equilibrium, more rapidly than without trade. After one accounts for the diffusion of technology and the technological spillovers, there is no general presumption that more trade is better than less. Resources should be allocated to tradables or nontradables according to their opportunity cost. If trade has pushed the limits of comparative advantage and a country engages in competitive-devaluation export trade, growth is bound to suffer. The empirical results give grounds to believe that many countries have exceedingly biased their production structures toward the tradable sector, to their serious detriment. To the extent that the RER index can provide evidence of such distortions, it can become a reliable measure of trade policy.

If growth is not export-led, what is the engine of growth?

In contrast to the export-push approach, the analysis in the case studies has focused on domestic demand as the engine of growth in the early stages of development. Successful development has been associated with the initial distribution of assets, in the form of education or of land reform, and with the initial distribution of income (World Bank, 1993a; Rodrik, 1994). The approach here, instead, makes a broadly based increase in domestic demand one of the initial conditions of growth.

The case studies in this book, of both successes and failures in development, draw a causal link between the broadly based increase in incomes (or failure thereof) and growth (or aborted development). The mechanisms that transmit broad income growth into self-sustained development are the Leontief–Rasmussen linkages in interindustry transactions and in final demand (Yotopoulos and Nugent, 1976, Chapter 15). Domestic demand is more likely to activate strong linkages for self-sustained growth at an early stage in development because it is in full concordance with domestic factor endowments. The production of commodities for subsistence and basic maintenance, such as staple food and traditional textiles, better dovetails with the abundance of labor and scarcity of capital and skill at the early stages of development than does, for instance, the production of sophisticated exports. As development occurs and incomes increase, both demand and supply requirements are ratcheted up to superior combinations of endowments and skills. The job of the policy maker, therefore, is to smoothly sequence the evolution of demand, both domestic and foreign, with that of domestic supplies and imported intermediate inputs, with an eye to the opportunity cost of resources in their alternative uses. The market alone cannot accomplish that in LDCs as long as the opportunity cost of foreign exchange is not determined in the process of production alone, but also in the consumption of luxuries for the middle classes and the elites and in the speculative hoarding of hard currencies for preempting the risk of devaluation. Say's law that supply creates its own demand does not hold automatically in LDCs. There are countries, like India, with large numbers of undernourished and ill-clad people and yet with vast grain surpluses and with languishing textile industries (Krishna, 1980). Average incomes might be increasing and some growth might have occurred, but self-sustained development will not be possible unless the broadly based increase in incomes is satisfied as an initial condition of growth.

The broadly based increase in incomes as a predicate for self-sustained growth is a less exacting condition than equality in income distribution or the broad distribution of educational attainment (Ahluwalia and Chenery, 1974). But they are correlates. On the other hand, policy makers are endowed with more degrees of freedom in achieving a broadly based increase in incomes than in attaining equality in income distribution. Japan achieved that through agricultural protectionism and discrimination against large-scale retailers, Taiwan achieved it through offering opportunities for ample overtime and moonlighting employment, and Malaysia achieved it through compensatory discrimination in favor of the "bumiputra," the indigenous Malay population.

Does not the argument for intervention in incomplete markets place an undue strain on the capacity of governments? Could it hold operational validity, especially in the aftermath of the collapse of the control economies?

The dominant policy implication of this book is that the nominal exchange rate needs to be held below its market-clearing level in the early stages of development. Although exchange controls and trade interventions are necessary for overvaluation to be viable, success crucially depends on the implementation of an appropriate development strategy. By allowing the local producers to become skilled at producing for the domestic market, this strategy can lead ultimately to the economy becoming internationally competitive at a high wage. In parallel, the early stage of the overvaluation of the foreign exchange rate is remedied as appropriate policy interventions lead to productivity increases in the tradable sector. Exports become competitive again through comparative advantage, as opposed to competitive devaluation.

In the aftermath of the collapse of the planned economies, the thesis of this book seems to be swimming against the tide. Therefore, the political economy of government intervention in incomplete markets was analyzed in a number of case studies of success and failure in economic development. Specific growth-policy packages were gleaned from the examination of success cases, such as Japan and Taiwan, and they were juxtaposed with wanton intervention in the failures in economic development, such as Uruguay and the Philippines.

Various examples of successful growth-policy interventions in incomplete markets were chronicled in the case studies. The existence of unlimited supplies of labor accounts for a market failure in LDCs. Setting the wage rate at its free-market level will not clear the market initially, and it is unlikely to lead to gradual wage and income increases down the road. Growth interventions, then, focus on raising incomes through productivity increases and, having exhausted these, through protection of the wage level by price supports (as with agriculture in Japan) or by employment enhancement (as with protection of the "mom-and-pop" stores in Japan and the easy access to overtime work in Taiwan). Similarly, modest financial repression in incomplete credit markets can contribute to higher rates of investment by holding interest rates below their market-clearing level. Finally, the incomplete market in foreign exchange has origins that are symmetrical to the unlimited supplies of labor: unlimited demand for hard currency. Unless it is overridden, it will lead to high nominal (and undervalued real) exchange rates that entail "trade bias" and Pareto-inferior outcomes when the production of both tradables and nontradables is considered. Foreign trade is controlled in tandem with the intervention in the foreign exchange market. The objective is to have tradability (of exports and imports) defined on the basis of the opportunity cost of domestic resources in producing the nontradable subsistence-staple commodity (commonly agricultural goods).

Growth-policy interventions in incomplete markets can lead to early increases in incomes broadly among the population. Then the package of growth policies can be fully specified by sequencing the industrial structure so that sectors are selectively and sequentially promoted based on their characteristics of economies of scale and their concordance with domestic demand. The purpose of growth policies is to account for the characteristics of the structure of production, while making the broadly based domestic demand the engine of growth and the foundation of pluralistic economic development. In a policy mix that makes domestic demand the leading sector, the participation of all groups in society in the benefits of growth is not an output of development; it is an input to growth (Rodrik, 1995a).

The thought of intervention opens the Pandora's box of the political economy of development. What are the appropriate types of intervention, and what happens to rent-seeking activities? Good governance becomes the political-economy precondition for successful intervention in development. The two components of good governance, competence and integrity, delimit both the extent of intervention and the issue of who captures the economic rents that arise in the process of development – and for whom. The operational criterion of good governance is the spread of development outcomes broadly among the population, i.e., pluralistic economic development. Lest this sound like a teleological definition of good governance, by the outcomes, the injection of growth-policy packages serves as an ex ante operational determinant. The microeconomic analysis of specific intervention instruments can determine whether they are targeted on incomplete markets or are gratuitous; it can also reveal whether the results of intervention are destined to increase the incomes of the few or of the many. Thus the identification of growth-policy packages along with the components of competence and integrity render good governance an operational concept in development.

The political-economy insight from this book is to place government intervention in development on a theoretically and empirically stable foundation. The thesis of the book is that appropriate interventions accelerate growth. But are such policy approaches feasible in today's increasingly global economic environment? Trade interventions that are based on increasing tariffs or placing quantitative restrictions on imports will certainly be viewed as unfair in major industrial-economy markets. They thus will run afoul of the conditions for market access under the General Agreement on Tariffs and Trade (GATT), the World Trade Organization (WTO), and other trading arrangements. Contemplating restrictions on a previously free foreign exchange regime will lead to anticipatory capital flight. In an environment where governments are liberalizing restrictions on capital flows, the scope for repressing interest rates without provoking capital flight is limited.

The new economic architecture of the post-cold-war era has probably decreased, but certainly has not foreclosed, the options LDCs have in adopting certain national growth policies.

Intervention breeds more intervention. Is there an end in sight?

The thesis of this book is that market incompleteness is systematically related to the level of underdevelopment. As development progresses, more market institutions come into place and other market defects are remedied. The distortion in the currency markets that leads LDCs to systematically misallocate resources is gradually redressed as development occurs and reputation accumulates. There is thus a virtuous circle in growth-policy interventions: successful interventions that bring about the desired development outcomes contain the seeds of their own extinction. Development success makes the gradual liberalization of the economy desirable and feasible. But there is also a vicious circle: failure in development interventions makes premature liberalization inevitable and its substantial costs foredoomed. This is the common link in a spate of recent liberalizations of the economies in transition, whether they are located in the Southern Cone or in the former Soviet-Bloc countries.

Epilogue

The book has raised a number of questions that often remain unspoken in economics.

- Do tradables provide the anchor for setting prices right in the economy?
- Does trade become the tail that wags the development dog?
- Does open interaction with the global economy short-circuit the proper sequence of development? Or does it ratchet up an LDC to rapid growth?
- Do you need a hegemon to run a system that imposes rationing on markets that cannot clear by price?

At the present state of the debate, the answers may still be tentative. But the questions were well worth raising.

Bibliography

Abramovitz, Moses (1956), "Resource and Output Trends in the United States Since 1870," *American Economic Review, 46* (May): 5–23.

Agènor, Pierre-Richard (1994), "Credibility and Exchange Rate Management in Developing Countries," *Journal of Development Economics, 45* (October): 1–16.

Ahluwalia, Montek S., and Hollis B. Chenery (1974), "A Model of Distribution and Growth." In H. B. Chenery et al., Redistribution with Growth. London: Oxford University Press. Pp. 209–235.

Ahmad, Sultan (1995), "Regression Estimates of per Capita GDP Based on Purchasing Power Parities." In D. S. Pasada Rao and J. Salazar-Carrillo, eds., *Intercountry Comparisons of Output and Productivity*. Amsterdam: North Holland (forthcoming).

Akerlof, George (1970), "The Market for Lemons: Qualitative Uncertainty and the Market Mechanism," *Quarterly Journal of Economics, 84* (August): 288–300.

Alesina, Alberto and Roberto Perotti (1993), "Income Distribution, Political Instability and Investment," *NBER Working Papers,* No. 4486. Cambridge, MA: National Bureau of Economic Research (October).

Althusser, L. and E. Balibar (1979), *Reading Capital*. London: Verso Editions.

Aoki, Masahiko (1988), *Information, Incentives and Bargaining in the Japanese Economy*. New York: Cambridge University Press.

Aoki, Masahiko (1994), "Monitoring Characteristics of the Main Bank System: An Analytical and Historical View." In Masahiko Aoki and Hugh T. Patrick, eds., *Japanese Main Bank System: Its Relevance for Developing and Transforming Economies*. New York: Oxford University Press. Pp. 109–141.

Aoki, Masahiko and Hugh T. Patrick, eds., (1994), *Japanese Main Bank Systems: Its Relevance for Developing and Transforming Economies*. New York: Oxford University Press.

Arrow, Kenneth J. (1962), "The Economic Implications of Learning by Doing," *Review of Economic Studies, 29* (June): 155–73.

Arrow, Kenneth J. (1974), "Limited Knowledge and Economic Analysis," *American Economic Review, 64* (March): 1–10.

Arrow, Kenneth J. and Gerard Debreu (1954), "Existence of an Equilibrium for a Competitive Economy," *Econometrica, 32* (July): 265–290.

Baland, Jean-Marie (1989), "Social Disarticulation Models: An Analytical Critique and a Re-exposition," *Journal of Development Studies, 25* (July): 521–537.

Balassa, Bela (1964), "The Purchasing Power Parity Doctrine: A Reappraisal," *Journal of Political Economy, 72* (December): 584–596.

Balassa, Bela (1978), "Exports and Economic Growth: Further Evidence," *Journal of Development Economics, 5* (June): 181–189.

Balassa, Bela (1982), "Structural Adjustment Policies in Developing Economies," *World Development, 10* (January): 23–28.

Baldwin, Richard (1988), "Hysteresis in Import Prices: The Beachhead Effect," *American Economic Review, 78* (September): 773–785.

Baldwin, Richard and Paul Krugman (1989), "Persistent Trade Effects of Large Exchange Rate Shocks," *Quarterly Journal of Economics, 104* (November): 635–654.

Barbone, Luca and Francisco Rivera-Batiz (1987), "Foreign Capital and Contractionary Impact of Currency Devaluation, with an Application to Jamaica," *Journal of Development Economics, 26* (June): 1–15.

Bardhan, Pranab K. (1982), "Unequal Exchange in a Lewis-Type World." In Mark Gersovitz, Carlos F. Díaz-Alejandro, Gustav Ranis, and Mark R. Rozenzweig, eds., *The Theory and Experience of Economic Development.* London: Allen and Unwin. Pp. 157–172.

Barro, Robert J. (1990), "Government Spending in a Simple Model of Endogenous Growth," *Journal of Political Economy, 98* (October, Part 2): 103–125.

Barro, Robert J. (1991), "Economic Growth in a Cross Section of Countries," *Quarterly Journal of Economics, 106* (May): 407–444.

Basu, Kaushik (1992), "The Broth and the Cooks: A Theory of Surplus Labor," *World Development, 20* (January): 109–117.

Baumol, William J. (1986), "Productivity Growth, Convergence and Welfare: What the Long Run Data Show," *American Economic Review, 76* (December): 1072–1085.

Behrman, Jere R. and Mark R. Rosenzweig (1994), "Caveat Emptor: Cross-country Data on Education and the Labor Force," *Journal of Development Economics, 44* (June): 147–171.

Bello, Walden (1987), *U.S. Sponsored Low-Intensity Conflict in the Philippines.* San Francisco, CA: The Institute for Food and Development Policy.

Berry, Albert and William Cline (1979), *Agrarian Structure and Productivity in Developing Countries.* Baltimore, MD: Johns Hopkins University Press.

Bettelheim, C. (1972), "Theoretical Comments." Appendix to *Unequal Exchange,* by Arghiri Emmanuel. New York: Monthly Review Press, 1972.

Bhagwati, Jagdish N. (1979), "International Factor Movements and National Advantage," *Indian Economic Review, 14* (October): 73–100.

Bhagwati, Jagdish N. (1982), "Directly Unproductive Profit-seeking (DUP) Activities," *Journal of Political Economy, 90* (October): 988–1002.

Bhagwati, Jagdish N. (1984), "Why Are Services Cheaper in the Poor Countries?" *Economic Journal, 94* (June): 279–286.

Bhagwati, Jagdish N. (1991), "The Pass-Through Puzzle: The Missing Prince from Hamlet." In Douglas Irwin, ed., *Political Economy and International Trade.* Cambridge, MA: MIT Press. Pp. 116–125.

Binkert, Gregor (1992), "Restructuring the Brazilian Economy, 1979–85: A 'Quasi-Australian Model'." Ph.D. Dissertation, Food Research Institute, Stanford University.

Bliss, Christopher and Nicholas Stern (1978), "Productivity Wages and Nutrition," *Journal of Development Economics, 5* (December): 331–398.

Bourgignon, François (1990), "Growth and Inequality in the Dual Model of Development: The Role of Demand Factors," *The Review of Economic Studies, 57* (No. 2): 215–228.

Boyce, J. and L. Zarsky (1988), "Capital Flight from the Philippines, 1962–1986," *Journal of Philippine Development, 15* (June): 191–222.

Branson, William (1989), "Exchange Rate Pass-Through in the 1980's: The Case of U. S. Imports of Manufactures: Comments," *Brookings Papers on Economic Activity, 1*: 330–333.

Broad, Robin (1988), *Unequal Alliance: The World Bank, the International Monetary Fund, and the Philippines.* Berkeley, CA: The University of California Press.

Buchanan, James M. (1986), *Liberty, Market and the State: Political Economy of the 1980's.* Brighton: Wheatsheaf.

Cain, Mead (1981), "Risk and Insurance: Perspectives on Fertility and Agrarian Change in India and Bangladesh," *Population and Development Review, 7* (September): 435–474.

Calvo, Guillermo A. and C. A. Rodríguez (1977), "A Model of Exchange Rate Determination under Currency Substitution and Rational Expectations," *Journal of Political Economy, 85* (June): 617–625.

Carvalho, José Luiz and Cláudio L. S. Haddad (1980), *Estratégias Comerciais e Absorção de Moa-de-Obra no Brasil.* Rio de Janeiro: Editora da Fundação Getúlio Vargas.

Cassel, Gustav (1921), *The World's Monetary Problems.* New York: E. P. Dutton.

Chenery, Hollis B. (1960), "Patterns of Industrial Growth," *American Economic Review, 50* (September): 624–654.

Chenery, Hollis B. (1979), *Structural Change and Development Policy.* New York: Oxford University Press.

Chenery, Hollis B., Sherman Robinson, and Moshe Syrquin (1986), *Industrialization and Growth.* New York: Oxford University Press.

Chenery, Hollis B. and Alan M. Strout (1966), "Foreign Assistance and Economic Development," *American Economic Review, 56* (September): 679–733.

Chiu, Paul C. H. (1992), "Money and Financial Markets: The Domestic Perspective." In Gustav Ranis, ed., *Taiwan: From Developing to Mature Economy.* Boulder, CO: Westview Press. Pp. 121–193.

Christensen, Raymond P. (1968), *Taiwan's Agricultural Development: Its Relevance for Developing Countries Today.* Washington, D.C.: U.S. Department of Agriculture, Economic Research Service.

Cooper, Richard N. (1971a), "Currency Devaluation in Developing Countries." In Gustav Ranis, ed., *Government and Economic Development.* New Haven, CT: Yale University Press.

Cooper, Richard N. (1971b), "Devaluation and Aggregate Demand in Aid-Receiving Countries." In Jagdish N. Bhagwati et al., eds., *Trade, Balance of Payments and Growth.* Amsterdam: North Holland. Pp. 355–376.

Corden, Warner M. (1977), *Inflation, Exchange Rates, and the World Economy.* Chicago, IL: The University of Chicago Press.

Corden, Warner M. and R. Findlay (1975), "Urban Unemployment, Intersectoral Capital Mobility and Development Policy," *Economica, 42* (February): 59–78.

Corden, Warner M. and J. Peter Neary (1982), "Booming Sector and De-industrialization in a Small Open Economy," *Economic Journal, 92* (December): 825–848.

Cuddington, John T. (1983), "Currency Substitution, Capital Mobility and Money Demand," *Journal of International Money and Finance, 2* (August): 111–133.

Dasgupta, Partha and Debraj Ray (1986), "Inequality as a Determinant of Malnutrition and Unemployment: Theory," *Economic Journal, 96* (December): 1011–1034.

Dasgupta, Partha and Debraj Ray (1991), "Adapting to Under-nourishment: The Biological Evidence and its Implications." In Jean Drèze and Amartya Sen, eds., *The Political Economy of Hunger*. Oxford: Oxford University Press. Pp. 191–246.

de Janvry, Alain (1981), *The Agrarian Question and Reformism in Latin America*. Baltimore, MD: Johns Hopkins University Press.

de Long, J. Bradford and Lawrence H. Summers (1991), "Equipment Investment and Economic Growth," *Quarterly Journal of Economics, 106* (May): 445–502.

Denison, Edward F. (1967), *Why Growth Rates Differ: Post-War Experience in Nine Western Countries*. Washington D.C.: Brookings Institution.

Dervis, Kemal, Jaime de Melo, and Sherman Robinson (1982), *General Equilibrium Models for Development Policy*. New York: Cambridge University Press.

Diamond, Peter and James A. Mirrlees (1971), "Optimal Taxation and Public Production," *American Economic Review, 61* (June): 261–278.

Diamond, Peter and James A. Mirrlees (1976), "Private Constant Returns and Public Shadow Prices," *Review of Economic Studies, 43* (No. 133): 41–48.

Díaz-Alejandro, Carlos (1963), "A Note on the Impact of Devaluation and the Redistributive Effect," *Journal of Political Economy, 71* (December): 577–580.

Díaz-Alejandro, Carlos (1965), *Exchange Rate Devaluation in a Semi-industrialized Economy: The Experience of Argentina 1955–1961*. Cambridge, MA: MIT Press.

Dixit, Avinash (1989), "Hysteresis, Import Penetration, and Exchange Rate Pass-Through," *Quarterly Journal of Economics, 104* (May): 205–228.

Dollar, David (1992), "Outward-Oriented Developing Economies Really Do Grow More Rapidly: Evidence from 95 LDC's, 1976–1985," *Economic Development and Cultural Change, 40* (April): 523–544.

Dorfman, Robert (1991), "Development from the Beginning to Rostow," *Journal of Economic Literature, 24* (June): 573–591.

Dornbusch, Rudinger (1975), "Exchange Rates and Fiscal Policy in a Popular Model of International Trade," *American Economic Review, 65* (December): 859–871.

Dornbusch, Rudinger (1980), *Open Economy Macroeconomics*. New York: Basic Books.

Dornbusch, Rudinger (1987), "Exchange Rates and Prices," *American Economic Review, 77* (March): 93–106.

Dornbusch, Rudinger and Stanley Fischer (1984), *Macroeconomics*. New York: McGraw-Hill (third edition).

Dunn, Robert M. (1970), "Flexible Exchange Rates and Oligopoly Pricing: A Study of Canadian Markets," *Journal of Political Economy, 78* (January): 140–151.

Edwards, Sebastian (1988), *Exchange Rate Misalignment in Developing Countries*. Baltimore, MD: Johns Hopkins University Press.

Edwards, Sebastian (1989), *Real Exchange Rates, Devaluation and Adjustment: Exchange Rate Policy in Developing Countries*. Cambridge, MA.: MIT Press.

Edwards, Sebastian (1992a), "Trade Orientation, Distortions, and Growth in Developing Countries," *Journal of Development Economics, 39* (July): 31–57.

Edwards, Sebastian (1992b), "Dollarization in Latin America." In Nissan Liviatan ed., "Proceedings of a Conference on Currency Substitution and Currency Boards." *World Bank Discussion Papers,* No. 207. Washington, D.C.: Pp. 1–3.

Edwards, Sebastian (1993), "Openness, Trade Liberalization, and Growth in Developing Countries," *Journal of Economic Literature, 31* (September): 1358–1393.

Eswaren, Mukesh and Ashok Kotwal (1985), "A Theory of Contractual Structure in Agriculture," *American Economic Review, 75* (June): 352–367.

Eswaren, Mukesh and Ashok Kotwal (1993), "A Theory of Real Wage Growth in LDC's," *Journal of Development Economics, 42* (December): 243–269.

Favaro, Edgardo and Pablo T. Spiller (1991), "Uruguay." In Demetris Papageorgiou, Michael Michaeli, and Armeane M. Choski, eds., *Liberalizing Foreign Trade: The Experience of Argentina, Chile and Uruguay*. Cambridge, MA: Basil Blackwell. Pp. 321–408.

Favaro, Edgardo and Alberto Bensión (1993), "Uruguay." In Simon Rottenberg, ed., *The Political Economy of Poverty, Equity, and Growth: Costa Rica and Uruguay*. New York: Oxford University Press. Pp. 187–362.

Feder, Gershon (1983), "On Exports and Economic Growth," *Journal of Development Economics, 12* (February): 59–74.

Feenstra, Robert (1989), "Symmetric Pass-through of Tariffs and Exchange Rates under Imperfect Competition: An Empirical Test," *Journal of International Economics, 27* (August): 25–45.

Fei, John H. C. and Gustav Ranis (1975), "A Model of Growth and Employment in the Open Dualistic Economy: The Case of Korea and Taiwan," *Journal of Development Studies, 11* (January): 32–63.

Fei, John H. C., Gustav Ranis, and Shirley W. Y. Kuo (1979), *Growth with Equity: The Taiwan Case*. New York: Oxford University Press.

Felix, David (1989), "Import Substitution and Late Industrialization: Latin America and Asia Compared," *World Development, 17* (September): 1455–1469.

Finch, M. H. J. (1981), *A Political Economy of Uruguay Since 1870*. New York: St. Martin's Press.

Fischer, Stanley (1982), "Seigniorage and the Case for a National Money," *Journal of Political Economy, 90* (April): 295–313.

Fischer, Stanley (1992), "Seigniorage and Official Dollarization." In Nissan Liviatan, ed., "Proceedings of a Conference on Currency Substitution and Currency Boards." *World Bank Discussion Papers,* No. 207. Washington, D.C.: World Bank. Pp. 6–10.

Floro, Sagrario L. and Pan A. Yotopoulos (1991), *Informal Credit Markets and the New Institutional Economics: The Case of Philippine Agriculture*. Boulder, CO: Westview Press.

Frenkel, Jacob A. and Harry G. Johnson (1976), *The Monetary Approach to the Balance of Payments*. Toronto: University of Toronto Press.

Frenkel, Jacob A. and Michael Moussa (1984), "Asset Markets, Exchange Rates, and the Balance of Payments." In Peter B. Kenen and Ronald W. Jones, eds., *Hand-*

book of International Economics. Vol. 2. Amsterdam: North Holland. Pp. 680–747.

Froot, Kenneth A. and Paul Klemperer (1989), "Exchange Rate Pass-Through When Market Share Matters," *American Economic Review, 79* (September): 637–654.

Fry, Maxwell J. (1990), "The Rate of Return to Taiwan's Capital Stock, 1961–1987," *Hong Kong Economic Papers, 20*: 17–30.

Fuchs, Victor R. (1968), *The Service Economy.* New York: National Bureau of Economic Research and Columbia University Press.

Giovannini, Alberto (1988), "Exchange Rates and Traded Goods Prices," *Journal of International Economics, 24:* (February): 45–68.

Greenaway, David, and Chong Hyun Nam (1988), "Industrialization and Macroeconomic Performance in Developing Countries under Alternative Trade Strategies," *Kyklos, 41* (3): 419–435.

Greenwald, Bruce C. and Joseph E. Stiglitz (1986), "Externalities in Economies with Imperfect Information and Incomplete Markets," *Quarterly Journal of Economics, 101* (May): 229–64.

Griffin, Keith B. (1969), *Underdevelopment in Spanish America.* London: Allen and Unwin.

Grossman, Gene M. and Elhanan Helpman (1991), "Trade, Knowledge Spillovers, and Growth," *European Economic Review, 35* (April): 517–526.

Grossman, Gene M. and Elhanan Helpman (1992), *Innovation and Growth in the Global Economy.* Cambridge, MA: MIT Press.

Grossman, Gene M. and Elhanan Helpman (1994), "Endogenous Innovation in the Theory of Growth," *Journal of Economic Perspectives, 8* (Winter): 23–44.

Haberler, Gottfried (1936), *The Theory of International Trade.* London: William Hodge and Co.

Hamada, Koichi and Hugh T. Patrick (1988), "Japan and the International Monetary Regime." In Takashi Inoguchi and Daniel I. Okimoto, eds., *The Political Economy of Japan.* Vol. 2. Stanford, CA: Stanford University Press. Pp. 108–137.

Harberger, Arnold (1986), "Economic Adjustment and the Real Exchange Rate." In Sebastian Edwards and Liaquat Ahmed, eds., *Economic Adjustment and Real Exchange Rates in Developing Countries.* Chicago, IL: University of Chicago Press. Pp. 371–414.

Hardin, Garrett (1968), "The Tragedy of the Commons," *Science, 162* (December): 106–112.

Harris, John R. and Michael P. Todaro (1970), "Migration, Unemployment and Development: A Two-Sector Analysis." *American Economic Review, 70* (March): 126–142.

Harrod, Roy F. (1939), "An Essay in Dynamic Theory," *Economic Journal, 49* (March): 14–33.

Hayami, Yujiro (1988), *Japanese Agriculture under Siege: The Political Economy of Agricultural Policies.* London: Macmillan Press.

Hayami, Yujiro, Ma. Agnes R. Quisumbing, and Lourdes S. Adriano (1987), *In Search of a Land Reform Design for the Philippines.* Los Baños, Philippines: The University of the Philippines at Los Baños Agricultural Policy Research Program.

Heston, Alan, Daniel A. Nuxoll, and Robert Summers (1994), "The Differential Productivity Hypothesis and Purchasing Power Parities: Some New Evidence," *Review of International Economics, 2* (October): 227–243.

Hill, T. P. (1977), "On Goods and Services," *Review of Income and Wealth, 23* (December): 315–338.

Hirschman, Albert O. (1949), "Devaluation and the Trade Balance: A Note," *Review of Economics and Statistics, 31* (March): 50–53.

Hirschman, Albert O. (1982), "The Rise and Decline of Development Economics." In Mark Gersovitz, Carlos F. Díaz-Alejandro, Gustav Ranis, and Mark R. Rozenzweig, eds., *The Theory and Experience of Economic Development*. London: Allen and Unwin. Pp. 372–390.

Ho, Samuel P. S. (1968), "Agricultural Transformation under Colonialism: The Case of Taiwan," *Journal of Economic History, 28* (September): 313–340.

Hooper, Peter and Catherine L. Mann (1989), "Exchange Rate Pass-through in the 1980s: The Case of U.S. Imports of Manufactures," *Brookings Papers on Economic Activity, 1*: 297–337.

Horiuchi, Akiyoshi (1984), "The 'Low Interest Rate Policy' and Economic Growth in Post War Japan," *Brookings Discussion Papers in International Economics*, No. 18. Washington, D.C.: Brookings Institution.

Houthakker, Hendrik S. and Stephen P. Magee (1969), "Income and Price Elasticities in World Trade," *Review of Economics and Statistics, 51* (May): 111–125.

Intal, Ponciano Jr. and John H. Power (1991), "The Philippines." In Anne O. Krueger, Maurice Schiff, and Alberto Valdés, eds., *The Political Economy of Agricultural Pricing Policy*. Baltimore, MD: Johns Hopkins University Press. Pp. 149–194.

International Monetary Fund (1990), *International Financial Statistics*. Washington, D.C.: International Monetary Fund.

Isard, Peter (1977), "How Far Can We Push the 'Law of One Price?' *American Economic Review, 67* (May): 942–948.

Isenman, Paul (1980), "Inter-Country Comparisons of 'Real' (PPP) Incomes: Revised Estimates and Unresolved Questions," *World Development, 8* (January): 61–72.

Ishikawa, Shigeru (1967), *Economic Development in Asian Perspective*. Tokyo: Hitotsubashi University, Institute of Economic Research.

Itoh, Motoshige and Kazuharu Kiyono (1988), "Foreign Trade and Direct Investment." In Ryutaro Komiya, Masahiro Okuno and Kotaro Suzumura, eds., *Industrial Policy of Japan*. New York: Academic Press. Pp. 155–181.

Jaffe, Dwight M. and Thomas Russell (1976), "Imperfect Information and Credit Rationing," *Quarterly Journal of Economics, 90,* (November): 651–666.

Johnson, Chalmers (1982), *MITI and the Japanese Miracle: The Growth of Industrial Policy, 1925–1975*. Stanford, CA: Stanford University Press.

Johnson, Harry G. (1976), "Elasticity, Absorption, Keynesian Multiplier, Keynesian Policy and Monetary Approaches to Devaluation Theory: A Simple Geometric Exposition," *American Economic Review, 66* (June): 448–452.

Jung, Woo S. and Reyton J. Marshall (1985), "Exports, Growth and Causality in Developing Countries," *Journal of Development Economics, 18* (May-June): 1–12.

Kakwani, Nanak (1980), *Income Inequality and Poverty: Methods of Estimation and Policy Applications*. New York: Oxford University Press.

300   Bibliography

Kaldor, Nicholas (1961), "Capital Accumulation and Economic Growth." In F. Lutz, ed., *The Theory of Capital*. London: Macmillan.

Katseli, Louka (1983), "Devaluation: A Critical Appraisal of IMF's Policy Prescriptions," *American Economic Review, 73* (May): 259–263.

Keynes, John Maynard (1923), *A Tract for Monetary Reform*. New York: Macmillan.

Khan, Moshin S. and J. Saul Lizondo (1987), "Devaluation, Fiscal Deficits, and the Real Exchange Rate," *World Bank Economic Review, 1* (January): 357–374.

Khan, Moshin S. and Peter J. Montiel (1987), "Real Exchange Rate Dynamics in a Small, Primary-Exporting Country," *International Monetary Fund Staff Papers, 34* (December): 681–710.

Khan, Moshin S., Peter Montiel, and Nadeem U. Haque (1990), "Adjustment with Growth; Relating the Analytical Approaches of the IMF and the World Bank," *Journal of Development Economics, 32* (April): 155–179.

Kindleberger, Charles P. (1973), *The World Depression, 1929–1939*. Berkeley, CA: University of California Press.

Klein, Sidney (1958), *The Pattern of Land Tenure Reform in East Asia after World War II*. New York: Bookman Associates.

Knetter, Michael M. (1989), "Price Discrimination by U.S. and German Exporters," *American Economic Review, 79* (March): 198–210.

Komiya, Ryutaro and Motoshige Itoh (1988), "Japan's International Trade and Trade Policy, 1955–1984." In Takashi Inoguchi and Daniel I. Okimoto, eds., *The Political Economy of Japan*. Vol. 2. Stanford, CA: Stanford University Press. Pp. 173–224.

Komiya, Ryutaro, Masahiro Okuno, and Kotaro Suzumura, eds. (1988), *Industrial Policy of Japan*. New York: Academic Press.

Kosai, Yutaka (1988), "The Reconstruction Period." In Ryutaro Komiya, Masahiro Okuno, and Kotaro Suzumura, eds., *Industrial Policy of Japan*. New York: Academic Press. Pp. 25–48.

Kravis, Irving B. (1984), "Comparative Studies of National Incomes and Prices," *Journal of Economic Literature, 22* (March): 1–39.

Kravis, Irving B., Alan Heston, and Robert Summers (1978a), *International Comparisons of Real Product and Purchasing Power*. Baltimore, MD: Johns Hopkins.

Kravis, Irving B., Alan Heston, and Robert Summers (1978b), "Real GDP Per Capita for More Than One Hundred Countries," *Economic Journal, 88* (June): 215–242.

Kravis, Irving B., Alan Heston, and Robert Summers (1982), *World Product and Income: International Comparisons of Real Gross Product*. Baltimore, MD: Johns Hopkins University Press.

Kravis, Irving B., Zoltan Kenessey, Alan Heston, and Robert Summers (1975), *A System of International Comparison of Gross Product and Purchasing Power*. Baltimore, MD: Johns Hopkins University Press.

Kravis, Irving B. and Robert E. Lipsey (1977), "Export Prices and the Transmission of Inflation," *American Economic Review, 67* (February): 155–163.

Kreps, David M. (1990), *Game Theory and Economic Modelling*, New York: Oxford University Press.

Krishna, Raj (1980), "Economic Development of India," *Scientific American, 243* (September): 166–178.

Krueger, Anne O. (1974), "The Political Economy of the Rent-Seeking Society," *American Economic Review, 64* (June): 291–303.

Krueger, Anne O. (1978), *Foreign Trade Regimes and Economic Development: Liberalization Attempts and Consequences.* Cambridge, MA: Ballinger.

Krueger, Anne O. (1980), "Trade Policy as an Input to Development," *American Economic Review, 70* (May 1980): 288–292.

Krueger, Anne O. (1984), "Problems of Liberalization." In Arnold C. Harberger, ed., *World Economic Growth.* San Francisco, CA: ICS Press. Pp. 403–423.

Krueger, Anne O., Maurice Schiff, and Alberto Valdés, eds., (1991), *The Political Economy of Agricultural Pricing Policy.* Baltimore, MD: Johns Hopkins University Press.

Krugman, Paul R. (1979), "A Model of Balance-of-Payments Crises," *Journal of Money, Credit, and Banking, 11* (August): 311–325.

Krugman, Paul R. (1987a), "Pricing to Market When the Exchange Rate Changes." In Sven W. Arndt and John D. Richardson, eds., *Real Financial Linkages Among Open Economies.* Cambridge, MA: MIT Press. Pp. 49–70.

Krugman, Paul R. (1987b), "The Narrow Moving Band, the Dutch Disease, and the Competitive Consequences of Mrs. Thatcher: Notes on Trade in the Presence of Dynamic Economies of Scale," *Journal of Development Economics, 27* (October): 41–55. .

Krugman, Paul R., James Alm, Susan M. Collins, and Eli M. Remolona (1992), *Transforming the Philippine Economy.* Manilla: United Nations Development Programme.

Krugman, Paul R. and Lance Taylor (1978), "Contractionary Effects of Devaluation," *Journal of International Economics, 8* (August): 445–456.

Kuo, Shirley W. Y. (1983), *The Taiwan Economy in Transition.* Boulder, CO: Westview Press.

Kuznets, Simon (1966), *Modern Economic Growth: Rate, Structure, and Spread.* New Haven, CT: Yale University Press.

Lamberte, Mario B., Joseph Y. Lim, Rob Vos, Josef T. Yap, Elizabeth S. Tan, and Socorro V. Zingapan (1992), *Philippine External Finance, Domestic Resource Mobilization and Development in the 1970s and 1980s.* The Hague: Institute for Social Studies; and Manila: Philippine Institute for Development Studies.

Lau, Lawrence J. and Pan A. Yotopoulos (1971), "A Test for Relative Efficiency and an Application to Indian Agriculture," *American Economic Review, 61* (March): 94–109.

Lau, Lawrence J., Wuu-Long Lin, and Pan A. Yotopoulos (1978), "The Linear Logarithmic Expenditure System: An Application to Consumption-Leisure Choice," *Econometrica, 46* (July): 843–868.

Lau, Lawrence J. and Pan A. Yotopoulos (1989), "The Meta-Production Function Approach to Technological Change in World Agriculture," *Journal of Development Economics, 31* (October): 241–269.

Leamer, Edward F. (1983), "Let's Take the Con Out of Econometrics," *American Economic Review, 73* (March): 31–43.

Leamer, Edward F. (1985), "Sensitivity Analyses Would Help," *American Economic Review, 75* (June): 308–313.

Leamer, Edward F. (1988), "Measures of Openness." In Robert E. Baldwin, ed., *Trade*

Policy Issues and Empirical Analysis. Chicago, IL: University of Chicago Press. Pp. 147–200.

Leclau, Ernesto (1979), *Politics and Ideology in Marxist Theory*. London: Verso Editions.

Lee, Teng-hui (1971), *Intersectoral Capital Flows in the Economic Development of Taiwan, 1895–1960*. Ithaca, NY: Cornell University Press.

Lee, Teng-hui (1974), "Agriculture: Dynamic Force for Industrialization." In T. H. Shen, ed., *Agriculture's Place in the Strategy of Development: The Taiwan Experience*. Taipei: Joint Commission on Rural Reconstruction. Pp. 66–70.

Leibenstein, Harvey (1957), "The Theory of Underemployment in Backward Economies," *Journal of Political Economy*, 65 (April): 91–103.

Leibenstein, Harvey (1958), "Underemployment in Backward Economies: Some Additional Notes," *Journal of Political Economy*, 66 (June): 256–258.

Lessard, D. and J. John Williamson (1987), *Capital Flight and the Third World Debt*. Washington, D.C.: Institute for International Economics.

Levine, Ross, and David Renelt (1992), "A Sensitivity Analysis of Cross-Country Growth Regressions," *American Economic Review*, 82 (September): 942–963.

Lewis, W. Arthur (1954), "Economic Development with Unlimited Supplies of Labour," *Manchester School*, 22: 139–191.

Lewis, W. Arthur (1958), "Unlimited Labour: Further Notes," *Manchester School*, 26: 1–32.

Lewis, W. Arthur (1978a), *The Evolution of the International Economic Order*. Princeton, NJ: Princeton University Press.

Lewis, W. Arthur (1978b), *Growth and Fluctuations, 1870–1913*. London: Allen and Unwin.

Li K. T. (1988), *The Evolution of Policy behind Taiwan's Development Success*. New Haven, CT: Yale University Press.

Lipschitz, Leslie (1979), "Exchange Rate Policy for a Small Developing Country, and the Selection of an Appropriate Standard," *International Monetary Fund Staff Papers*, 26 (September): 423–449.

Little, Ian M. D. and James A. Mirrlees (1974), *Project Appraisal and Planning for Developing Countries*. London: Heinemann.

Little, Ian M. D., Tibor Scitovsky, and Maurice Scott (1970), *Industry and Trade in Some Developing Countries*. London: Oxford University Press.

Liu, Bih-Jane (1993), "Cost-Externalities and Exchange Rate Pass-Through: Some Evidence from Taiwan." In Takatoshi Ito and Anne O. Krueger, eds., *Macroeconomic Linkage*. Chicago, IL: University of Chicago Press: Pp. 247–272.

Liu, Christina Y. (1992), "Money and Financial Markets: The International Perspective." In Gustav Ranis, ed., *Taiwan: From Developing to Mature Economy*. Boulder, CO: Westview Press. Pp. 195–221.

Lizondo, J. Saul and Peter J. Montiel (1989), "Contractionary Devaluation in Developing Countries: An Analytical Overview," *International Monetary Fund Staff Papers*, 36 (March): 182–227.

Lucas, Robert E. (1988), "On the Mechanics of Economic Development," *Journal of Monetary Economics*, 22 (July): 3–42.

Lundberg, Erik (1979), "Fiscal and Monetary Policies." In Walter Galenson, ed., *Eco-*

nomic Growth and Structural Change in Taiwan. Ithaca, NY: Cornell University Press. Pp. 263–307.

Maddala, G. S. (1988), *Introduction to Econometrics.* New York: Macmillan.

Malthus, Thomas R. (1798, reprint 1976), *An Essay on the Principle of Population.* New York: Norton.

Malthus, Thomas R. (1803, reprint 1960), *An Essay on the Principle of Population.* Second edition. Homewood, IL: Richard Irwin.

Malthus, Thomas R. (1815), *An Inquiry into the Nature and Progress of Rent, and the Principle by which it is Regulated.* London: John Murray.

Malthus, Thomas R. (1824), "Essay on Political Economy," *The Quarterly Review, 30*: 297–334.

Mann, Catherine L. (1986), "Prices, Profit Margins and Exchange Rates," *Federal Reserve Bulletin, 72* (June): 366–379.

Mao, Yu-kang and Chi Schive (1991), *Agricultural and Industrial Development in the Economic Transformation of the Republic of China on Taiwan.* Republic of China: The Council of Agriculture, Executive Yuan.

Marris, Robin (1984), "Comparing the Income of Nations: A Critique of the International Comparisons Project," *Journal of Economic Literature, 22* (March): 40–57.

Marston, Richard C. (1990), "Pricing to Market in Japanese Manufacturing," *Journal of International Economics, 29* (November): 217–236.

Marx, Karl (1867, reprint 1967), *Capital: A Critique of Political Economy. Vol. I, The Process of Capitalist Production.* New York: International Publishers.

McKinnon, Ronald I. (1964), "Foreign Exchange Constraints in Economic Development and Efficient Aid Allocation," *Economic Journal, 74* (June): 388–409.

McKinnon, Ronald I. (1973), *Money and Capital in Economic Development.* Washington, D.C.: Brookings Institution.

McKinnon, Ronald I. (1979), *Money in International Exchange.* New York: Oxford University Press.

McKinnon, Ronald I. (1991), *The Order of Economic Liberalization: Financial Control in the Transition to a Market Economy.* Baltimore, MD: Johns Hopkins University Press.

Meade, James E. (1951), *The Theory of International Economic Policy. Vol. I, The Balance of Payments.* Oxford: Oxford University Press.

Melvin, Michael (1988), "The Dollarization of Latin America as a Market-enforced Monetary Reform," *Economic Development and Cultural Change," 36* (April): 543–558.

Miles, Marc (1978), "Currency Substitution, Flexible Exchange Rates, and Monetary Independence," *American Economic Review, 68* (June): 428–436.

Monke, Eric A. and Scott R. Pearson (1989), *The Policy Analysis Matrix for Agricultural Development.* Ithaca, N.Y.: Cornell University Press.

Morley, Samuel A. and Gordon W. Smith (1970), "On the Measurement of Import Substitution," *American Economic Review, 60* (September): 728–735.

Murphy, Kevin M., Andrei Shleifer, and Robert W. Vishny, (1989a), "Industrialization and the Big Push," *Journal of Political Economy, 97* (October): 1003–1026

Murphy, Kevin M., Andrei Shleifer, and Robert W. Vishny, (1989b), "Income Distribution, Market Size, and Industrialization," *Quarterly Journal of Economics, 104* (August): 537–564.

Nabli, Mustapha K. and Jeffrey B. Nugent (1989), "Collective Action, Institutions and Development." In Mustapha K. Nabli and Jeffrey B. Nugent, eds., *The New Institutional Economics and Development: Theory and Applications to Tunisia*. Amsterdam: North Holland. Pp. 80–137.

Neary, J. Peter and Sweder van Wijnbergen (1986) "Natural Resources and the Macroeconomy: A Theoretical Framework." In J. Peter Neary and Sweder van Wijnbergen, eds., *Natural Resources and the Macroeconomy*. Cambridge, MA: MIT Press. Pp. 13–45.

Nugent, Jeffrey B. (1985), "The Old-Age Security Motive for Fertility," *Population and Development Review, 11* (March): 75–97.

Nugent, Jeffrey B. and Pan A. Yotopoulos (1979), "What Has Orthodox Economics Learned from Recent Experience?" *World Development, 7* (June): 541–554.

Ocampo, José Antonio. (1986), "New Developments in Trade Theory and LDCs," *Journal of Development Economics, 22* (June): 129–170.

Officer, Lawrence A. (1976), "The Purchasing-Power-Parity Theory of Exchange Rates: A Review Article," *International Monetary Fund Staff Papers, 23* (March): 1–60.

Ohno, Kenichi (1989), "Export Pricing Behavior of Manufacturing: A U.S.–Japan Comparison," *International Monetary Fund Staff Papers, 36* (September): 550–579.

Okimoto, Daniel I. (1989), *Between MITI and the Market: Japanese Industrial Policy for High Technology*. Stanford, CA: Stanford University Press.

Organization for Economic Cooperation and Development (1988), *OECD Economic Surveys, Japan, 1987/88*. Paris: OECD.

Otsuka, Keijiro, Hiroyuki Chuma, and Yujiro Hayami (1992), "Land and Labour Contracts in Agrarian Economies: Theories and Facts," *Journal of Economic Literature, 30* (December): 1965–2018.

Pack, Howard (1994), "Endogenous Growth Theory: Intellectual Appeal and Empirical Shortcomings," *Journal of Economic Perspectives, 5,* (Winter): 55–72.

Pagano, Marco (1993), "Financial Markets and Growth: An Overview," *European Economic Review, 37* (April): 613–622.

Patrick, Hugh T. (1972), "Finance, Capital Markets and Economic Growth in Japan." In Arnold Sametz, ed., *Financial Development and Economic Growth*. New York: New York University Press. Pp. 109–138.

Patrick, Hugh T. (1984), "Japanese Financial Development in Historical Perspective, 1868–1980." In Gustav Ranis, Robert L. West, Mark W. Leiserson, and Cynthia Taft Morris, eds., *Comparative Development Perspectives*. Boulder, CO: Westview Press. Pp. 302–327.

Patrick, Hugh T. and Thomas P. Rohlen (1987), "Small-Scale Family Enterprises." In Kozo Yamamura and Yasukichi Yasuba, eds., *The Political Economy of Japan*. Vol. 1. Stanford, CA: Stanford University Press. Pp. 331–384.

Platteau, Jean-Philippe, Jose Murickan, and Etienne Delbar (1985), *Technology, Credit and Indebtedness in Marine Fishing: A Case Study of Three Fishing Villages in South Kerala*. Delhi: Hindustan Publishing.

Platteau, Jean-Philippe (1991), "Traditional Systems of Social Security and Hunger Insurance: Past Achievements and Modern Challenges." In Ehtisham Ahmad, Jean Dréze, John Hills, and Amartya Sen, eds., *Social Security in Developing Countries*. Oxford: Clarendon Press. Pp. 112–170.

Poole, Fred and Max Vanzi (1984), *Revolution in the Philippines: The United States in a Hall of Cracked Mirrors*. New York: McGraw-Hill.

Prebisch, Raul (1959), "Commercial Policy in the Underdeveloped Countries," *American Economic Review, 49* (May): 251–273.

Prestowitz, Clyde V., Jr. (1988), *Trading Places: How We are Giving Our Future to Japan and How to Reclaim It*. New York: Basic Books.

Pritchett, Lant (1995), "Measuring Outward Orientation in LDC's: Can it Be Done?" *Journal of Development Economics* (forthcoming).

Putzel, James (1988), "Prospects for Agrarian Reform Under the Aquino Government." In Mamerto Canlas et al., Land, Poverty and Politics in the Philippines. Quezon City, Philippines: Claretian Publications.

Ramírez-Rojas, C. L. (1985), "Currency Substitution in Argentina, Mexico and Uruguay," *International Monetary Fund Staff Papers, 32* (December): 627–667.

Ranis, Gustav (1978), "Equity with Growth in Taiwan: How 'Special' is the 'Special Case'," *World Development, 6* (March): 397–409.

Ranis, Gustav (1979), "Industrial Development." In Walter Galenson, ed., *Economic Growth and Structural Change in Taiwan*. Ithaca, NY: Cornell University Press. Pp. 206–262.

Ranis, Gustav and Syed Akhtar Mahmood (1992), *The Political Economy of Development Policy Change*. Cambridge, MA: Blackwell.

Ranis, Gustav and Frances Stewart (1993), "Rural Nonagricultural Activities in Development: Theory and Application," *Journal of Development Economics, 40* (February): 76–101.

Rasmussen, Bo Sandermann (1989), "Stabilization Policies in Open Economies with Imperfect Current Information," *Journal of International Money and Finance, 7* (June): 151–166.

Rebelo, Sergio (1991), "Long Run Policy Analysis and Long Run Growth," *Journal of Political Economy, 99* (June): 500–521.

Rey, Pierre-Philippe (1973), *Les Alliances de Classes*. Paris: Maspero.

Reynolds, Lloyd G. (1985), *Economic Growth in the Third World, 1850–1980*. New Haven, CT: Yale University Press.

Ricardo, David (1817, reprint 1963), *The Principles of Political Economy and Taxation*. Homewood, IL: Irwin.

Richardson, J. David (1978), "Some Empirical Evidence on Commodity Arbitrage and the Law of One Price," *Journal of International Economics, 8* (May): 341–351.

Rivera-Batiz, Louis and Paul M. Romer (1991), "Economic Integration and Endogenous Growth," *Quarterly Journal of Economics, 106* (May): 531–556.

Rodrik, Dani (1994), "King Kong Meets Godzilla: The World Bank and the East Asian Miracle." In Robert Wade, ed., *Miracle or Design? Lessons from the East Asian Experience*. Washington, D.C.: Overseas Development Council. Pp. 13–53.

Rodrik, Dani (1995a), "Coordination Failures and Government Policy: A Model with Applications to East Asia and Eastern Europe," *Journal of International Economics* (forthcoming).

Rodrik, Dani (1995b), "Trade and Industrial Policy Reform in Developing Countries: A Review of Recent Theory and Evidence." In Jere Behrman and T. N. Srinivasan, eds., *Handbook of Development Economics*. Vol. 3. Amsterdam: North Holland (forthcoming).

Romer, Paul M. (1986), "Increasing Returns and Long-Run Growth," *Journal of Political Economy, 94* (October): 1002–1037.

Romer, Paul M. (1990), "Endogenous Technological Change," *Journal of Political Economy, 98* (October): S71–S102.

Romer, Paul M. (1994), "The Origins of Endogenous Growth," *Journal of Economic Perspectives, 8* (Winter): 3–22.

Rosenberg, Nathan (1982), *Inside the Black Box.* New York: Cambridge University Press.

Rosenstein-Rodan, Paul (1943), "Problems of Industrialization in Eastern and Southeastern Europe," *Economic Journal, 53* (June): 202–212.

Rosenzweig, Mark R. (1988), "Risk, Private Information, and the Family," *American Economic Review, 78* (May): 245–250.

Roubini, Nouriel and Xavier Sala-i-Martin (1992), "Financial Development, the Trade Regime, and Economic Growth," *NBER Working Papers,* No. 3876. Cambridge, MA: National Bureau of Economic Research.

Rowley, R. K., R. D. Tollison, and G. Tullock, eds., (1998), *The Political Economy of Rent-Seeking.* Boston, MA: Kluwer Academic.

Sah, Raj K. and Joseph E. Stiglitz (1986), "The Architecture of Economic Systems: Hierarchies and Polyarchies," *American Economic Review, 76* (September): 716–727

Salter, W. E. G. (1959), "Internal and External Balance: The Role of Price and Expenditure Effects," *Economic Record, 35* (August): 226–238.

Samuelson, Paul A. (1964), "Theoretical Notes on Trade Problems," *Review of Economics and Statistics, 46* (May): 145–154.

Saxonhouse, Gary R. (1988), "Comparative Advantage, Structural Adaptation, and Japanese Performance." In Takashi Inoguchi and Daniel I. Okimoto, eds., *The Political Economy of Japan.* Vol. 2. Stanford, CA: Stanford University Press. Pp. 225–248.

Schive, Chi (1987), "Trade Patterns and Trends of Taiwan." In Charles I. Bradford and William H. Branson, eds., *Trade and Structural Change in Pacific Asia.* Chicago: University of Chicago Press. Pp. 307–330.

Schive, Chi and Tze-Zer Kao (1986), "A Measure of Secondary Import Substitution in Taiwan," *Economic Essays, 14:* 159–175.

Schultz, Theodore W. (1953), *The Economic Organization of Agriculture.* New York: McGraw Hill.

Schumpeter, Joseph A. (1934), *The Theory of Economic Development.* Cambridge, MA: Harvard University Press.

Scitovsky, Tibor (1985), "Economic Development in Taiwan and South Korea: 1965–1981," *Food Research Institute Studies, 19* (No. 2): 215–264.

Shepherd, Geoffrey and Florian Alburo (1991), "The Philippines." In Demetris Papageorgiou, Michael Michaely and Armeane Choksi, eds., *Liberalizing Foreign Trade: The Experience of Korea, the Philippines, and Singapore.* London: Basil Blackwell. Pp. 133–308.

Shinohara, Miyohei (1982), *Industrial Growth, Trade and Dynamic Patterns in the Japanese Economy.* Tokyo: University of Tokyo Press.

Singh, Inderjit (1990), *The Great Ascent: The Rural Poor in South Asia.* Baltimore, MD: Johns Hopkins University Press.

Smith, Adam (1776, reprint 1937), *Inquiry into the Nature and Causes of the Wealth of Nations.* New York: Modern Library.

Solow, Robert M. (1957), "Technical Change and the Aggregate Production Function," *Review of Economics and Statistics, 39* (August): 312–320.

Solow, Robert M. (1962), "Technical Progress, Capital Formation, and Economic Growth," *American Economic Review, 52* (May): 76–86.

Solow, Robert M. (1994), "Perspectives on Growth Theory," *Journal of Economic Perspectives, 8* (Winter): 45–54.

Srinivasan, T. N. (1982), "General Equilibrium Theory, Project Evaluation and Economic Development." In Mark Gersovitz, Carlos F. Díaz-Alejandro, Gustav Ranis, and Mark R. Rosenzweig, eds., *The Theory and Experience of Economic Development.* London: Allen and Unwin. Pp. 229–251.

Srinivasan, T. N. (1988), "Introduction." In Hollis B. Chenery and T. N. Srinivasan, eds., *Handbook of Development Economics.* Vol. 1. Amsterdam: North Holland. Pp. 3–8.

Stern, Nicholas (1989), "The Economics of Development: A Survey," *Economic Journal, 99* (September): 598–685.

Stiglitz, Joseph E. (1974), "Alternative Theories of Wage Determination and Unemployment in LDCs: The Labor Turnover Model," *Quarterly Journal of Economics, 88* (May): 194–227.

Stiglitz, Joseph E. (1976), "The Efficiency Wage Hypothesis, Surplus Labour and the Distribution of Labour in LDCs," *Oxford Economic Papers, 28* (July): 185–207.

Stiglitz, Joseph E. and Andrew Weiss (1981), "Credit Rationing in Markets with Imperfect Information," *American Economic Review, 71* (June): 393–410.

Stockman, Alan C. (1983), "Real Exchange Rates under Alternative Nominal Exchange Rate Systems," *Journal of International Money and Finance, 2* (August): 147–166.

Streeten, Paul (1979), "Development Ideas in Historical Perspective." In Albert O. Hirschman, et al., eds., *Toward a New Strategy for Development.* New York: Pergamon Press. Pp. 21–52.

Summers, Robert and Alan Heston (1984), "Improved International Comparisons of Real Product and its Composition: 1950–1980," *Review of Income and Wealth, 30* (June): 207–262.

Summers, Robert and Alan Heston (1988), "A New Set of International Comparisons of Real Product and Price Levels Estimates for 130 Countries, 1950–1980," *Review of Income and Wealth, 34* (March): 1–25.

Summers, Robert and Alan Heston (1991), "The Penn World Table (Mark 5): An Expanded Set of International Comparisons, 1950–1988," *Quarterly Journal of Economics, 106* (May): 327–368.

Taussig, Frank William (1928), "The Theory of Economic Dynamics as Related to Industrial Instability," *American Economic Review, 18* (March): 30–39.

Taylor, Lance (1983), *Structuralist Macroeconomics.* New York: Basic Books.

Taylor, Lance (1991), "Economic Openness: Problems to the Century's End." In Tariq Banuri, ed., *Economic Liberalization – No Panacea: The Experience of Latin America and Asia.* Oxford: Clarendon Press.

Teranishi, Juro (1986), "Economic Growth and Relation of Financial Markets: Japanese Experience During Postwar High Growth Period," *Hitotsubashi Journal of Economics, 27* (December): 145–165.

Teranishi, Juro (1990), "Financial System and the Industrialization of Japan 1900–1970," *Banca Nazionale del Lavoro Quarterly Review, 174* (September): 309–341.

Terray, E. (1972), *Marxism and 'Primitive' Societies*. New York: Monthly Review Press.

Thompson, Warren S. (1929), *Danger Spots in World Population*. New York: Knopf.

Thompson, Warren S. (1950), "Future Adjustments of Population to Resources in Japan," *Modernization Programs in Relation to Human Resources and Population Problems*. Milbank Memorial Fund, New York. Pp. 142–153; reprinted in *Population and Development Review, 7* (March 1981): 111–117.

Thorbecke, Eric (1979), "Agricultural Development." In Walter Galenson, ed., *Economic Growth and Structural Change in Taiwan*. Ithaca: Cornell University Press. Pp. 132–205.

Thorbecke, Eric (1992), "The Process of Agricultural Development in Taiwan." In Gustav Ranis, ed., *Taiwan: From Developing to Mature Economy*. Boulder, CO: Westview Press. Pp. 15–72.

Todaro, Michael (1969), "A Model of Labor Migration and Urban Unemployment in Less Developed Countries," *American Economic Review, 59* (March): 138–148.

Tsuruta, Toshimasa (1988), "The Rapid Growth Era." In Ryutaro Komiya, Masahiro Okuno, and Kotaro Suzumura, eds., *Industrial Policy of Japan*. New York: Academic Press. Pp. 49–87.

Tyson, Laura d'Andrea (1992), *Who's Bashing Whom? Trade Conflict in High Technology Industries*. Washington D.C.: Institute for International Economics.

United Nations (1974 and subsequent), *Yearbook of International Trade Statistics*. Vol. 1. New York: United Nations.

Upham, Frank K. (1993), "Privatizing Regulation: The Implementation of the Large Scale Retail Stores Law." In Gary D. Allinson and Yasunori Sone, eds., *Political Dynamics in Contemporary Japan*. Ithaca, NY: Cornell University Press. Pp. 264–294.

Usher, Dan (1963), "The Transport Bias in Comparisons of National Income," *Economica, 30,* (May): 140–158.

van Wijnbergen, Sweder (1986), "Exchange Rate Management and Stabilization Policies in Developing Countries." In Sebastian Edwards and Liaquat Ahmed, eds., *Economic Adjustment and Exchange Rates in Developing Countries*. Chicago, IL: University of Chicago Press. Pp. 17–38.

Venieris, Yiannis P. and Dipak K. Gupta (1983), "Sociopolitical and Economic Dimensions of Development: A Cross-Section Model," *Economic Development and Cultural Change, 31* (July): 727–756.

Venieris, Yiannis P. and Dipak K. Gupta (1986), "Income Distribution and Sociopolitical Instability as Determinants of Savings: A Cross-Sectional Model," *Journal of Political Economy, 94* (August): 873–883.

Vos, Rob and Josef T. Yap (1994), *East Asia's Stray Cat: Finance and Development in the Philippines 1970–1992*. The Hague: Institute for Social Studies; and Manila: Philippine Institute for Development Studies.

Wade, Robert (1990), *Governing the Market: Economic Theory and the Role of the Government in East Asian Industrialization*. Princeton, NJ: Princeton University Press.

Wallace, Neil (1979), "Why Markets in Foreign Exchange Are Different from Other Markets," *Quarterly Review* (Federal Reserve Bank of Minneapolis), *3* (Fall): 1–7.

White, H. (1980), "A Heteroscedasticity-Consistent Covariance Matrix Estimator and a Direct Test for Heteroscedasticity," *Econometrica, 48* (May): 817–838.

World Bank (1983), *World Development Report 1983.* New York: Oxford University Press.

World Bank (1987), *World Development Report 1987.* New York: Oxford University Press.

World Bank (1992a), *World Development Report 1992.* New York: Oxford University Press.

World Bank (1992b), *Philippines Capital Market Study.* Report No. 10053–PH. Washington, D.C.: The World Bank.

World Bank (1993a), *The Asian Miracle: Economic Growth and Public Policy.* New York: Oxford University Press.

World Bank (1993b), *Social Indicators of Development 1993.* Baltimore, MD: Johns Hopkins University Press.

World Bank (1993c), *World Development Report 1993.* New York: Oxford University Press.

World Bank (1993d), *Uruguay: The Private Sector.* Washington, D.C: The World Bank.

Yasuba, Yasukichi (1991), "Japan's Post-war Growth in Historical Perspective," *Japan Forum, 3* (April): 57–70.

Yokokura, Takashi (1988), "Small and Medium Enterprises." In Ryutaro Komiya, Masahiro Okuno, and Kotaro Suzumura, eds., *Industrial Policy of Japan.* New York: Academic Press. Pp. 513–539.

Yotopoulos, Pan A. (1965), "The Wage-Productivity Theory of Underemployment: A Refinement," *The Review of Economic Studies, 32* (January): 59–66.

Yotopoulos, Pan A. (1980), "Population and Agricultural Development Models: The Promise of the Third Generation," *The Pakistan Development Review, 19* (Summer): 119–127.

Yotopoulos, Pan A. (1985), "Middle Income Classes and Food Crises: The 'New' Food-Feed Competition," *Economic Development and Cultural Change, 33* (April): 463–483.

Yotopoulos, Pan A. and Marcel Fafchamps (1994), "Structural Change in Taiwan: Emphasis on the Role of Agriculture." In Ian Goldin, Odin Knudsen, and Antonio S. Brandão, eds., *Modelling Economy-Wide Reforms.* Paris: OECD Development Centre Studies. Pp. 59–97.

Yotopoulos, Pan A. and Sagrario L. Floro (1992), "Income Distribution, Transaction Costs and Market Fragmentation in Informal Credit Markets," *Cambridge Journal of Economics, 16* (September): 303–326.

Yotopoulos, Pan A. and Lawrence J. Lau (1973), "A Test for Relative Economic Efficiency: Some Further Results," *American Economic Review, 63* (March): 214–223.

Yotopoulos, Pan A. and Jenn-Yih Lin (1993), "Purchasing Power Parities for Taiwan: The Basic Data for 1985 and International Comparisons," *Journal of Economic Development, 18* (June): 7–51.

Yotopoulos, Pan A. and Wuu-Long Lin (1975), "The Utilization of Linkage Analysis in Development Planning," *ADC Teaching Forum, 45* (April): 1–10.

Yotopoulos, Pan A. and Jeffrey B. Nugent (1976), *Economics of Development: Empirical Investigations.* New York: Harper and Row.

Index

Abramovitz, Moses, 17
"administrative guidance" system (Japan), 221–2
Adriano, Lourdes S., 226–7
adverse selection of risk
  in credit markets, 42
  in insurance markets, 43
Agènor, Pierre-Richard, 50n10
"agricultural adjustment," 207–8
agriculture
  food self-sufficiency rate comparisons, 209
  Japanese food crisis (1937), 205
  Japanese food/farm problem, 205–8
  Japan's economic development of, 208
  latifundio mode of, 266
  Philippine land reform, 224–7
  Philippines interventions for, 239–42
  Taiwan development of, 251–6
  transferring labor out of, 202–4
  Uruguay stagnation of, 256–9
Ahluwalia, Montek S., 289
Ahmad, Sultan, 129
Akerlof, George, 42
AK models, 121
Alburo, Florian, 238, 241n9, 246–7n12
Alesina, Alberto, 130
Alm, James, 245–6n11
Althusser, L., 28
Aoki, Masahiko, 216, 216n18
architecture systems, 106
Arrow, Kenneth J., 18, 34, 40, 56, 120–1
articulation/disarticulation model, 28–34
asset-value dynamics hypothesis, 51–2, 78, 273

asymmetric currency substitution, 50–1, 274–5, 284
asymmetric reputation, 8–9, 50–1, 144–5, 233–4, 272–7, 281 283–6
Australian model
  closed economy, 64–6, 68
  described, 4, 64
  Dutch disease illustrated by, 72–4
  growth-policy packages in, 76–7
  internal/external balance in, 70
  open economy, 66–8
  RER defined within, 92–3

balance of payments deficit, 162
Balassa, Bela, 46, 145n14, 162, 281n26
Balassa-Samuelson differential productivity model. *see* Ricardo Principle
Baldwin, Richard, 173, 178
Balibar, E., 28
Barbone, Luca, 160
Bardhan, Pranab K., 26n4
Barro, Robert J., 120, 123n2, 130
Basu, Robert J., 201n9
batllista ideology (Uruguay), 257–9
Baumol, William J., 120
Behrman, Jere R., 129n7
Bello, Walden, 229, 241–2
benchmark countries, 114–5, 177
Bension, Alberto, 250–1, 257, 260, 267, 272n12, 276
Berry, Albert, 226, 268
Bettelheim, C., 28
Bhagwati, Jagdish, 46, 53, 147, 158, 162, 171
"big push" theory, 28
Binkert, Gregor, 69n7, 113n9, 158n2

311

black markets, 151
Bliss, Christopher, 201n9
"body language" communication, 221
Bourguignon, François, 152
Boyce, J., 236
Branson, William, 164n5
Broad, Robin, 237
Buchanan, James M., 53
Bukharin, 19
"bumiputra" policy (Malaysia), 290

Calvo, Guillermo A., 50n10
Camdessus, Michel, 286
capital
  resources and accumulation of, 13–14
  Smithian model on, 13
  technology and formation of, 121
  wages as loss of, 30–2
capital goods markets, 40–1
Carvalho, José Luiz, 113n8
Cassel, Gustav, 89–90
causality tests, 139–41
Central Bank, 275–6
Chenery, Hollis B., 12, 19, 35, 130,
  141, 146–7, 289
Chinese-American Joint Commission of
  Rural Reconstruction (JCRR),
  254
Chiu, Paul C. H., 278n19
Christensen, Raymond P., 251
Chuma, Hiroyuki, 226
Cline, William, 226, 268
closed economy, 64–6, 68
collateral (credit market), 41–2
Collins, Susan M., 245–6n11
commodities
  cost-advantaged/disadvantaged, 109
  defining ERD for, 110
  shadow prices for, 118–19
  as tradable/nontradable, 106–8
commodity PPP, 90
competence (government), 55–6, 150–2,
  290–2
competitive equilibrium, 38
competitiveness, 161
Comprehensive Agrarian Reform Pro-

gram of 1988 (Philippine), 226
constrained-equilibrium expenditure
  curve, 81–4
Cooper, Richard N., 158–9
Corden, W. M., 64n1, 72n8, 202
corn laws, 16n2, 46n3
credit markets, 41–3
Cronyism (Philippines), 240–1, 243
cross-section/time-series regressions,
  132, 134–9
Cuddington, John T., 50n11
currency
  asymmetric substitution of, 50–1,
    274–5, 284
  hard vs. soft, 8–9, 50–2, 282–4
  high RER and distortion of, 8, 144–5,
    234–5, 276–7, 283, 287–8

Dasgupta, Partha, 201n9
DC (developed countries)
  currency value in, 51, 282
  food self-sufficiency rates of, 209
  LDC compared to, 8–9
deindustrialization, 72–4
de Janvry, A., 28, 30–3, 152, 266n7
Delbar, Etienne, 43
de Long, J. Bradford, 147
demographic variables, 129–30
Denison, Edward F., 17
dependent-economy model. *See* Australian model
devaluation
  benefits of, 158–9, 287–8
  empirical conclusions of, 183–5
  impact on LDCs of, 169–70
  literature review on, 159–62
  NER, 178
  policy recommendations on, 287–8
  price-through/pass-through effects of,
    170–83
  RER changes and, 179–80
  theoretical model of, 162–70
Diamond, Peter, 118
Díaz-Alejandro, Carlos, 158n2, 160
Differential Production Scheme (Japan,
  1946), 205